GLENN ROBINSON

Scholars, Saints, and Sufis

Published under the Auspices
of the Near Eastern Center
University of California
Los Angeles

Scholars, Saints, and Sufis

Muslim Religious Institutions in the Middle East since 1500

Edited by Nikki R. Keddie

University of California Press
Berkeley Los Angeles London

University of California Press
Berkeley and Los Angeles, California

University of California Press Ltd.
London, England

First Paperback Edition 1978
ISBN: 0-520-03644-1
Library of Congress Catalog Card Number: 77-153546

Designed by Wolfgang Lederer
Printed in the United States of America

2 3 4 5 6 7 8 9 0

IN MEMORIAM

Gustave Edmund von Grunebaum

1909–1972

SCHOLAR, TEACHER, FRIEND

Preface

The idea of a volume on Muslim religious institutions in the modern Middle East had its origins in a social history seminar given at the University of California, Los Angeles, in the academic year 1968–69. Because of the presence in California that year of several persons engaged in research on religious institutions, it seemed a good idea to try to enlist their services in a single graduate seminar. Those who kindly agreed to contribute papers for the seminar were: Aziz Ahmad, Hamid Algar, Amin Banani, Daniel Crecelius, Ernest Gellner, Michael Gilsenan, and Afaf Lutfi al-Sayyid Marsot. The quality of the papers was so high as to suggest the value of publication, and I undertook to solicit additional papers from persons known to be working on related topics. The response went beyond our original hopes, and although many persons may have been inadvertently overlooked, the number and range of papers is so large as to suggest parameters for future research and publication. Professors Banani and Gilsenan had already promised for publication elsewhere the papers discussed at the seminar and were unfortunately too occupied with other writing to be able to produce new papers in time for this volume. The volume has benefited not only from their original presentations, however, but also from their comments on several of the papers submitted. Also to be thanked for the comments offered on submitted papers are Professors Andreas Tietze and Stanford Shaw.

There was no attempt at complete coverage of the Middle East or at "equal time" for all areas; rather we went where the research on the volume's topic was being done. The number of papers on Morocco and Iran reflects no prior decision, but only the fact that relatively more research is being done in these countries than in others currently more difficult of access. The presence of several papers on these two areas suggests how varied can be the work on religious institutions even in a single country and time period, and what may be learned from a variety of approaches to a single topic. The book is essentially limited to the Middle East, although two areas whose affinity to the Middle East is disputed are also included—Pakistan and the Sudan.

Authors have been allowed to follow their own transliteration systems.

Thanks go to G. P. Maisonneuve-Larose for permission to reprint my paper from *Studia Islamica*, XXIX, 1969. Selections from *Guests of the Sheik* by Elizabeth Fernea (copyright © 1965 by Elizabeth Warnock Fernea) are reprinted by permission of Doubleday & Company, Inc. Thanks are due G. E. von Grunebaum and the personnel of the Near Eastern Center, University of California, Los Angeles, for providing material and spiritual aid and encouragement to the editor and authors, and to Mrs. Teresa Joseph for her intelligent and meticulous copy-editing.

NIKKI R. KEDDIE

Contents

PART II. Saints and Sufis: Popular Religious Institutions

Abbreviations

BSOAS	*Bulletin of the School of Oriental and African Studies*
EI[1], EI[2]	*Encyclopaedia of Islam,* first and second editions
JESHO	*Journal of Economic and Social History of the Orient*
JRAS	*Journal of the Royal Asiatic Society*
MIDEO	*Mélanges de l'Institut Dominicain des Études Orientales*
REI	*Revue des Études Islamiques*
ZDMG	*Zeitschrift der Deutschen Morgenländischen Gesellschaft*

Introduction

NIKKI R. KEDDIE

I

THE PAPERS IN THIS BOOK view different aspects of Muslim religious institutions of the Middle East as functional groups that have played a leading role in politics and society. The papers concentrate on the social role of these institutions, which the historically minded authors approach largely in terms of changes over time, while the anthropologists tell more about the functioning of an institution in a particular time or area. Even this limited number of studies, which is far from covering the modern Middle East, can give some idea of the immense complexity and variation in Muslim religious institutions.

The papers deal with two main types of institutions—the learned group of orthodox religious scholars and jurists whose Arabic name, *ulama*, has become familiar in Western languages, and the more popular and generally less learned religious groups often lumped together as Sufis, although, particularly in North Africa, the word Sufi is not always used and popular religious leaders possessing divine grace are known rather as saints. Although the papers in this volume alone should be caution enough against generalizing about the history of Muslim religious institutions, a few general words, however inadequate, may be useful particularly to orient the reader not familiar with the development of Islamic religious institutions before 1500, the starting date of this volume.[1]

Islam as revealed by the Prophet Muhammad did not provide for a priesthood or comparable religious institution, nor was any leader of the community after Muhammad deemed to have prophetic or infallible religious powers. The caliphs were "successors" of Muhammad as heads of the community, but they were never religious authorities or analogous to Popes, as some Westerners thought. Gradually, however, a body of men

[1] The early sixteenth century was chosen as the starting date of this volume in order to cover not only the period of major Western impact but also the preceding important late Middle Eastern dynasties—the Safavids in Iran, the Ottomans from the time of their conquest of Arab lands, and the formative period of premodern Morocco.

developed with specialized religious functions—chiefly readers or reciters of the Koran, and also experts in the Traditions (hadiths), recording the rules and sayings laid down by the Prophet as a guide for the behavior of believers. With the development of Muslim law as the pivot of Islam, these Traditionists more and more merged with legal scholars and jurists. The need for theology as, originally, a defense against heretical doctrines and against non-Muslim thinkers, gave rise to a small group of theological writers. While the first hereditary dynasty of caliphs, the Umayyads (661–749), often ignored the growing body of educated religious leaders, these men achieved a firmer status under the Abbasid dynasty (749–1258). The formation of an identifiable corps of ulama—scholars, jurists, and teachers learned in the Islamic sciences—is a product of the early Abbasid period. Building on the central role that law had played in Islam from the beginning, the leaders of the ulama concentrated on the development, exegesis, enforcement, and teaching of Islamic law, a law that embraced not only matters that Westerners would consider "religious," but most aspects of the life of a believer. The hallmark of an *alim* (singular of ulama) was his learning in Islamic law and the other Islamic sciences, and as Islamic learning came almost to monopolize the institutions of education, particularly from about the eleventh century A.D. on, it was often only the ulama who had experienced an extended education.

Although the role and power of the ulama must have differed as much according to time and place before 1500 as they did after, one may say that the ulama were a powerful and respected body of men with considerable sources of personal and corporate wealth and a large influence in the shaping of Muslim societies. Ulama who performed specific duties as teacher, preacher, or judge (*qadi*) were paid in various ways for their services. A source of both individual and corporate ulama wealth was the donation by individuals of inalienable property (*waqf*) for either charitable or religious purposes or to benefit the descendants of the donor. The former type of waqf brought direct income to institutions run by the ulama, such as mosques, schools, or hospitals; even in the latter type of personal or family waqf, members of the ulama class generally administered the waqf and received a fee for doing so. The ulama not only controlled considerable wealth, but they had further power as guardians of religious law, learning, and orthodoxy. In addition, they controlled and administered institutions that in modern times have come under the purview of the centralized state—the schools from the elementary through the highest levels, the courts, and hospitals and other charitable institutions. Except through the power of persuasion and alliance, however, the ulama lacked the ultimate sanction of military power; in most cases they also lacked a clear hierarchical organization and leadership. These factors meant that the secular government could often, though not always, ignore or ride roughshod over the wishes of the leading ulama. Secular governments were not unaware of the utility of religious orthodoxy to the state, however, and so, whatever the tensions in some periods between government and ulama, the two were generally allied in their desire to promote orthodoxy, acceptance of authority by the populace, and social peace. Whereas in late Umayyad times a key element in the effective movement that overthrew the dynasty was the so-called "pious opposition," as the centuries went on religious leaders in their deeds and writings became more and more reconciled to the acceptance of almost any nominally Muslim authority as a preferable alternative to discord or revolt. The well-organized Ottoman ulama, discussed in the papers by Richard Repp and Richard Chambers in this volume, were, however, sometimes able to find military allies and even help depose sultans.

The generalizations above have concentrated on the Sunni or "orthodox" ulama, and have not dealt with the various sectarian, popular, or mystical movements that began shortly after the rise of Islam and have continued until today. The most important group of sectarian movements was that associated with the "party" or Shi'a of Muhammad's cousin and son-in-law, 'Ali, and his descendants, whom the Shi'a regarded as the rightful leaders, or *imams,* of the Muslim community. Although the Shi'is, especially in the early centuries, comprised a bewildering variety of politico-religious sects, often of a revolutionary and messianic nature, over time it became possible to distinguish three main groups of Shi'is according to the line of imams they followed. Among the "conservative" "Fiver" or Zaidi Shi'is, the ulama played much the same role as in Sunni Islam, while among the "radical" "Seveners" or Isma'ilis the role of religious scholars and lawyers was strictly subordinate to that of the continuous line of living imams, who were presumed to be infallible and who had the right to rule the community both politically and religiously. The "moderate" Twelvers believed that the last imam was in occultation, and they came to believe that the most learned leaders of the ulama, the *mujtahids,* were the best interpreters of the will of this infallible hidden imam, in matters both religious and political. The only major Shi'i state of modern times is Iran, where, as indicated in the papers by Hamid Algar, Gustav Thaiss, and me, this theoretically superior position of the Twelver Shi'i ulama, as compared with that of Sunni states, came to have major political consequences. In the nineteenth and early twentieth centuries the leaders of the Iranian ulama became the chief spiritual guides and even organizers of a series of protests against an oppressive government and against foreign encroachments. Popular, but not Sufi, aspects of Twelver Shi'ism are discussed in the papers by Thaiss and Robert and Elizabeth Fernea.

As to the mystical and popular religious groups that did not usually identify with Shi'ism or with messianic revolts and rebellions, it has become common to group them together as "Sufi orders," but such nomenclature may assume that these groups share more in common than they really do. In the early centuries of Islam the word Sufi, from the Arabic *suf* (wool)—referring to their coarse woolen garments—was applied to ascetic mystics, men who rejected both the worldly ways of many of the ulama and the distant transcendental God of the orthodox, and who believed that they could attain direct knowledge of God, or even union with Him, by a variety of practices similar to those of mystics in every land. Although mystics too bold in proclaiming their achievement of identity with God were sometimes persecuted or even executed, mystical practices grew in popularity and provided a much shorter and easier path to knowledge of divinity than the lengthy and possibly expensive scholastic study of the ulama. Although the great Sunni theologian al-Ghazzali (d. 1111) is often said to have reconciled Sunni Islam with mystical ideas and practices, the relations between the ulama and Sufis continued to be ambivalent, ranging according to time and circumstance from complete hostility, as in seventeenth-century Iran, to a dual role of ulama as both part of the learned institutions of society and members or leaders of Sufi orders, as in parts of the Ottoman Empire or Morocco, noted in Edmund Burke's and Bradford Martin's papers.

The rise of large-scale religious orders or brotherhoods, often but not always with a mystical belief system, began only in the twelfth and thirteenth centuries A.D., but developed with amazing rapidity through these and later years. It is with the rise of these orders that the term "Sufi" becomes a bit misleading; for example, when one hears that nearly every urban adult male in the Ottoman Empire in the eighteenth century belonged to a Sufi order, one should not imagine that the entire population had become mystics. To call them as the French do, "religious brotherhoods," would perhaps be more satisfactory. For it is clear, as the papers by Ernest Gellner and Vincent Crapanzano bring out, that the functions of some popular religious orders might not even include an idea of the unification of man with God. The brotherhoods fulfilled a variety of functions for their members: social, "entertainment," charitable, intellectual, psychological, and sometimes political, as well as those that we might consider religious or mystical. The brotherhoods were also often missionary organizations on the borders of the Islamic world, a role that has continued in Africa into the twentieth century, and their nonscholastic and popular approach to religion has enabled them to win the allegiance of those to whom scholastic Islam might seem formidable, while the adaptability of the Islam of the brotherhoods to popular local custom has also helped their efforts at conversion. The brief history of one Sufi order given by Martin's paper suggests the variety of roles it has played in different societies, as well as the centuries-long vitality and growth of such a group. More detailed studies of particular orders in given times and places, such as are being done chiefly by anthropologists like Crapanzano and Michael Gilsenan, are providing a far more complete picture than was previously available of the actual role of orders in the lives of their adepts as well as in society as a whole.

II

The history of social and religious institutions in the modern Muslim World is a subject still in its infancy as a topic of serious research. The earlier concentration of scholars on political, literary, diplomatic, and more recently intellectual history is only now yielding to broader social and economic fields, resulting in studies that depict for the first time the totality of society, and do not concentrate simply on its elite or the ideal or literary version of reality. Until recently in the field of Muslim religion, most scholarship has focussed on doctrinal controversy and achievement, while for the modern period attention has been paid the intellectual modernists almost to the exclusion of traditional figures and institutions. Such concentration on the Islamic modernists is understandable and even, to a degree, justifiable. If historians are largely interested in change over time, it is not surprising that they should focus on those who advocate change and appear to be the pioneers of new social and intellectual movements, rather than on those who, at first sight at least, appear simply to be doing traditional things in traditional ways. Yet the emphasis on a few intellectual modernizers found in many recent studies of the Middle East has produced serious distortions: To take only one type of example of the distortion produced by concentration on the modernists, while most Islamic modernists rarely moved masses of people to action, again and again one finds religious movements with a largely traditional component in the forefront of nationalist or rebellious agitation. In many societies traditional religious leaders have achieved a popular and even political influence never matched by their better-known modernist counterparts. A close examination of nineteenth-century politico-religious mass movements—ranging from those tied to Sufi orders like Shamyl's resistance in the Caucasus, or the Sanusis of Cyrenaica, to the messianism of the Babis of Iran or of the Mahdists of the Sudan, to the orthodoxy of the Iranian ulama—indicates that a simplistic view that traditional religious forces simply underwent a gradual decline under the onslaught of Western ideas and realities must be profoundly modified. As will be seen in many of the papers in this volume, even such a simple generalization as that the ulama underwent a steady decline because of the introduction of Western ideas and the opening up of new professions must undergo considerable refinement.

At the two opposite ends of the Middle East, in Iran and Morocco—as the Hamid Algar, Keddie, Kenneth Brown, and Burke papers indicate—the interaction with the West of independent but rather weak and decentralized Muslim states served, temporarily at least, to strengthen rather than weaken the ulama. Yet even here, the nature of this strengthening was not identical in the Iranian and Moroccan cases. In both Morocco and Iran the ulama became, for a time, leaders of a national resistance to infidel foreigners, whose menace they understood on more than a purely religious level, but in Iran they were acting against the government largely on the basis of already recognized Shi'i theory and prior organization, while in Morocco they were actually strengthened by some of the early centralizing reforms of the government.

Concerning Islamic modernism, once again the difference of the impact of a single movement from one area to the other stands out. Whereas modernists or "purifiers" of religion like Jamal ad-Din al-Afghani and Muhammad 'Abduh were generally opposed by most of the ulama leadership of Ottoman Asia and Egypt (the Egyptian example is clarified in detail in the Daniel Crecelius paper), in much of North Africa the modernists, themselves a product of the interaction of the Middle East and the West, provided the twentieth-century ulama with ideological weapons both against the French and against the popular religious orders that were particularly strong in that area. Thus such forces as "Westernization" or even one of its offspring, modern "Islamic reformism," were far from having a uniform impact on the ulama of different countries.

Nevertheless, it can scarcely be doubted that interaction between the Middle East and the West has ultimately brought on a decline in the role of both ulama and the religious orders in every country of the Middle East where the Western impact has been profound and extensive. The ways in which interaction with the West, particularly after the Industrial Revolution, did serve to weaken the real and spiritual power of the ulama are almost too obvious to require mention, as, for example, in providing the new middle classes with new ideologies. Until recently, however, the intellectual challenge of the West may have been overstressed rather than the very real changes in power structure that helped undermine the control of the ulama over the key institutions in relatively decentralized societies. The organization of the ulama in two such societies before and on the eve of the Western impact is revealed in the papers by L. C. Brown on Tunisia and Richard Repp on the Ottoman Empire, both of whom provide clearer pictures of the nature of the learned institution than has hitherto been available. Details of a decline in ulama power under the Western impact emerge from the papers by Richard Chambers on Ottoman Turkey and Afaf Marsot and Daniel Crecelius on Egypt. These authors show that the process of decline was not a simple one. The French invasion of Egypt of 1798 and its immediate aftermath there actually enhanced the power of the ulama, the leading native Egyptian class, who profited from the disruption of other governing classes and from the weakening and final slaughter of the former non-Egyptian Mamluk rulers under the French and then Egypt's first great modern ruler, Muhammad 'Ali. This "Golden Age" of the ulama was short-lived, however, as the increasing governmental investment in secularized schools, translation bureaus, law courts, and other modern institutions decreased the demand and remuneration for ulama services, while the growth of the power of the central government and of secular ideas weakened the power of the ulama in society. The struggle of the ulama to retain their former position was, Crecelius shows, far less concerned with religion or ideology and more with jobs and income than a reading of most scholars would make us believe. Crecelius's study suggests that detailed studies of the issues over which the ulama fought the reformers and secularists in other parts of the Muslim world might similarly refocus attention away from ideological factors to the changing wealth and power position of the ulama in each Muslim area.

Richard Chambers's paper notes the importance the destruction of the Ottoman Janissary corps in 1826 had in weakening the ulama's power. Here the ending of a traditional military force had exactly the opposite effect to that of the destruction of the Mamluks in Egypt, for the Janissaries had not been the overlords of the ulama, but rather had often provided them with a military force to make their will effective. An earlier paper by the late Uriel Heyd, referred to by Chambers, detailed ways in which many of the Ottoman ulama were brought into governmental programs that ultimately limited the ulama's power and independence. Chambers shows that even later in the century individual ulama like Hoca Tahsin, head of the first Ottoman University, and especially Cevdet Paşa, were similarly brought into governmental programs for reform and centralization—programs that had the effect of weakening the power of the ulama as a whole. In the late nineteenth century, however, men like these did not represent the leadership of the organized corps of ulama, who are better typified by the famous late nineteenth-century Şeyhülislam, Hasan Fehmi, who effectively delayed reforms such as the establishment of a secular university and the codification of Muslim law. Although there was a temporary lull in secularizing reforms under Sultan Abdülhamid II, the Ottoman ulama were to suffer their most precipitous loss of power in any Muslim country after the creation of a secularized Turkey in the early 1920s.

As already indicated, the papers on the ulama of Morocco and Iran by K. Brown, Burke, Keddie, and Algar show quite a different pattern of changes in ulama power in the nineteenth and early twentieth centuries in those countries from that found in Egypt, Turkey, and possibly most Muslim countries. One reason for this important difference not mentioned above was the relative weakness of governmental reform and centralization in Morocco and Iran in this period as contrasted with the effective measures of centralization and secularization found in Egypt and Turkey. The governments of Iran and Morocco did not create a whole new network of governmental schools, courts, and bureaus in the nineteenth and early twentieth century, and the power base and employment opportunities for the ulama were not undermined as they were in Egypt and Turkey. Indeed, as Burke points out, nineteenth-century reforms in Morocco provided new areas of ulama employment. This continued power base and the relative self-confidence that accompanied it enabled the ulama of Morocco and Iran to be less on the defensive than they were in Egypt and Turkey, and to present a program to ward off the threat of the encroaching foreign imperialists. In the later twentieth century, however, the Moroccan and Iranian ulama also suffered an erosion of power arising from government-sponsored measures of centralization and secularization.

If the Moroccan and Iranian ulama were important political forces in the recent past, the role of the religious classes in national politics is still today a very live issue in several other Muslim countries, as indicated in the papers by John Voll on the Sudan and Aziz Ahmad on Pakistan. The "routinization" of charisma among the descendants of the self-proclaimed Mahdi of the Sudan, and the blurred lines between the different types of holy man, and between religion and politics, are points that come out for Sudan, a country where the forces of modernization and centralization have not penetrated as deeply as in the countries discussed above. In Pakistan, the period before the partition of India in 1947 is an interesting one for paradoxical contrasts; although one justification for the creation of Pakistan was the need for an Islamic state, the organized ulama had tended for decades before the partition of India to be partisans of national liberation for an undivided India, that is, all-Indian nationalism rather than Muslim nationalism. It was mostly men of secular training or inclination who led the movement for Pakistan. The role of the ulama in Pakistan since partition was achieved is complex and is unraveled in Aziz Ahmad's paper.

Popular religion is included in the papers by Voll, Burke, and L. C. Brown, all of whom point to the frequent identity of religious scholars, or ulama, and popular religious leaders; one may guess that this identity or lack of conflict is or was relatively stronger before modernization. Modernization was accompanied by movements among the religious establishment to define or purify the true religion—a definition or purification that often led to a denunciation of popular practices as superstitious. On the other hand, in some countries the learned institution remains intertwined with popular ones, both by role and by family and other ties.

One function of both popular and learned religious institutions, touched upon in several of the papers, was to provide an avenue of social mobility. Although we lack many quantified studies of the social origins of the ulama class and of the occupations of their sons in modern times—L. C. Brown's paper includes a pioneering example in that direction—enough is known of individual cases to be certain that religious study could provide an avenue for upward mobility for bright and studious sons of lower classes. Brown's figures suggest that in Husainid Tunisia mobility into the ulama class was small but significant. He states that the ulama class "appears as the institution . . . offering the greatest opportunity for both geographical and social mobility to the largest number of Tunisians." Interviews and case histories recorded by myself in Iran also indicate that, once having passed the barriers of study, a boy from the lower classes might enter more lucrative and far more prestigeful occupations than had been open to his father. In all countries, lack of money and of a family tradition of learning were in themselves barriers to the long course of study, but not always insurmountable ones; another barrier was the growth of nepotism and even sale of ulama offices in periods of decline and corruption as is documented by Repp for the Ottoman Empire of the eighteenth century. As modernization progressed, sons of the ulama have frequently gone into more modern professional training, leaving more places than ever in the religious schools to be filled by boys of the lower classes, but these boys have much less chance than ever before of achieving a lucrative, or even decently paying, position. The ease with which sons of prominent ulama families have entered modern professions, often after schooling abroad, underscores once more the role of the premodern ulama as a kind of professional learned class, many of whom were happy to see their sons enter the new but parallel modern professions, rather than opposing them on religious grounds.

Popular religion is dealt with as the main subject in the papers by Bradford Martin, Ernest Gellner, and Vincent Crapanzano. Martin gives a brief longitudinal history of a single Sufi order and its offshoots, suggesting the variety of roles it has played in different times and circumstances—political, social, missionary, medical, and magical, as well as "religious." In more detailed anthropological studies of particular popular religious groups, Gellner and Crapanzano suggest even more vividly the tremendous range of functions carried out by such groups. Neither the urban brotherhood studied by Crapanzano nor the saints living among the tribes of the Atlas studied by Gellner have as an important function the achievement of unity between man and God, the supposed main goal of mystics. The order studied by Crapanzano plays an important function of psychological and psychosomatic healing among members of the poorest urban classes. Gellner's saints, on the other hand, have a primarily political role in helping provide a political and arbitrational function among the "anarchic" Berber tribes of Morocco. Gellner subtly analyzes the dialectical relationship between the mountain saints and orthodox urban Islam. These papers and the longer studies by the same authors, as well as other studies now in progress, suggest a huge range in functions of popular religious groups and beliefs, and eventually it may be possible to construct a typology of Muslim religious groups more satisfactory than the lumping together of disparate groups as "Sufi orders." The functional approach of anthropologists like Gellner or Crapanzano should also be of value to historians of the Middle East in guarding them against, on the one hand, an idealized picture of Sufi orders in the past as being devoted almost entirely to otherworldly or spiritual goals, and, on the other hand, the opposite but related view that popular religious practices, insofar as they do not conform to purely spiritual aims or ideals, are nothing but a mass of superstitious hangovers from earlier beliefs whose living functions are of no particular interest.

The varying function of a single religious myth over time and among different segments of society is presented in the papers by Thaiss, Algar, and the Ferneas who, by unplanned coincidence, give examples from very different surroundings of the function of the central Shi'i story of the martydom of the Imam Husain. Thaiss notes that the repetition and popularity of this story over the centuries cannot be explained merely as an outcome of religious tradition, but that the story has a continuing function in enabling people to deal with what appear to be unjust sufferings in a world ruled by a just God. More specifically, however, the story has political significance in modern Iran, where Thaiss gives examples from the 1960s of the ulama implicitly comparing the government to the unjust Umayyads, and those who oppose the government to the martyred Husain and his followers. Examples of similar comparisons during earlier crises are given in Hamid Algar's book *Religion and State in Iran 1785–1906* (Berkeley and Los Angeles, 1969) and in Algar's paper in the present volume. The Ferneas, in discussing a Shi'i community in Iraq, note both the anti-Sunni function of the Husain story in a Shi'i community ruled by the Sunni Ottomans, and, especially the important social and emotional function of the story for women. One might guess that among Shi'i women there is an emphasis on the sufferings of women and children in the deaths of the followers of Husain, which would serve as a catharsis or a means of identification for mothers whose children often die for no comprehensible reason.

The Ferneas' paper is a pioneering and informative effort in the study of women in the Muslim world, a field that has been, as they suggest, neglected by serious scholars of Islam, women as well as men. The very existence in some Muslim societies of a body of learned women who perform functions for women similar to those performed by the ulama or other religious leaders for men has been unknown to most scholars. At least one scholar, the Ferneas note, denied the phenomenon even after the Ferneas had observed it. The religious life of women has been at least as closed as other aspects of their lives to Western scholars, who have often been contented, in this as in other spheres of women's activity, either to ignore the question or to generalize about the seclusion and isolation of women and their inferior religious and legal status. Much as the Islamic modernists have occupied the attention of intellectual historians, so have the feminists been almost the only women in the modern Muslim world to receive attention. As the Ferneas suggest, it is time for scholars (and in some cases this perforce means women scholars) to do far more intensive and extensive studies of the roles and social organization of women in the Muslim world. Such studies would increase our understanding not only of the present but also of the Muslim past, where the sources on the lives of women are scant, though far from nonexistent.

One subject treated only peripherally in this volume is the extent to which Islamic observance in many Muslim countries has become a class phenomenon, with the modernized upper and upper middle classes having discarded most of their traditional Muslim beliefs and practices while the bazaar petty bourgeoise and the lower classes in city and countryside retain most of their traditional ways and beliefs. The upper classes may still consider themselves Muslim in a general or cultural sense, but they often have little use for the mosque or the ulama, leaving the latter to minister to groups lower in the social scale. As the Ferneas point out, women are also more likely to adhere to traditional religious beliefs and practices than their more Westernized male relatives. The continued religiosity of the masses of the population helps explain the continued appeals to religious feelings made by political movements in recent years. Disturbed by social, economic, and cultural changes that may benefit the wealthier classes, but often disrupt the lives of the poorer ones, and may even make them worse, the Muslim masses may be open to appeals of groups like the Muslim Brethren, which call for a return to pure Islamic ways as a solution to current problems. The continuing political strength of the Iranian ulama is based partly on hostile mass reactions to government-induced changes, as Thaiss notes, as well as to the Iranian government's presumed complaisance to Western Christian or Zionist influences. This mass religiosity is also one reason why secular leaders like 'Abd al-Nasir of Egypt have continued to make appeals to Islamic ideas and symbols.

An important role of the ulama has been to justify the status quo and to guard both themselves and secular rulers from attacks by the dissatisfied or dispossessed. They formed an important part of the ideological underpinning of the rulers, needed to justify submission to existing landlords and government agents. They thus helped perpetuate the hierarchical and traditional order of things by teaching submission even to unjust rulers and maintaining that the hierarchical social order was both natural and good. With the rise of modern education for the upper classes and then for the new middle classes, Western influenced ideologies seemed more useful to them than traditional Islam in meeting newly felt needs. Although as Morroe Berger has shown (*Islam in Egypt Today* [Cambridge, 1970]), the middle classes are far from abandoning religious institutions, a specifically Islamic ideology is less influential as one goes up the economic scale. Tacitly, the ulama were increasingly left to deal with the bazaar petty bourgeoisie and the lower classes, whom they were presumed to influence in the direction of obedience, while the upper classes appropriated ideologies more attuned to their own needs. In practice, however, the religiosity of the masses has not proved a barrier to attacks on the upper classes, although these attacks have come more from army officers than from rebellious common people. Dissatisfied with their own position, the ulama have not always refrained from attacks on the upper and new middle classes, and the modern period has not seen the mutual reinforcement between the ulama and the ruling classes to anything like the degree of earlier periods. The political leaders of modern Egypt have been able to use and control the ulama, but the governments of Iran and Turkey have not always been so successful.

Fortunately, Western scholarship seems to have emerged from the period when many were writing first that Islam was a great ideological barrier to communism or similar movements in the Middle East, and later that Islam and Marxism were so similar in many ways that one might lead to the other. The politics of the past decade have shown that the religiosity of the Muslim masses is no more a barrier to radical politics than the Catholicism of the Italian or Latin American masses, and rather that radical political activity is inspired much more by political, social, and economic circumstances than by religious ones. The religiosity of the masses and the continued influence of religious leaders of various kinds may discourage radical politics among them to a degree, but history has shown that Islam can as easily be adapted to equalitarian and even revolutionary interpretations as Christianity. In other words, one should not equate the religiosity of the Muslim lower classes with unbending traditionalism, fatalism, or conservatism, or assume that meaningful social change can arise only from the Westernized and largely secularized elite. What does appear to retard reformist or revolutionary change in many Muslim countries is the gap between the urban Westernized elite and the masses, whose respective values, mores, and belief systems often differ widely.

It is to be hoped that the studies in this volume will give the Western or Westernized reader a more comprehensive understanding of the role of Islam and its institutions in the lives of modern Muslims. While both the ulama and the popular religious orders have declined from their earlier comprehensive roles in society, neither group can be dismissed as currently insignificant or without interest. And for the historically minded, the varied roles played by religious groups in recent centuries offer innumerable examples of human adaptation to a changing social universe, and of the ways in which different groups have encouraged or resisted change.

Part I

Scholars: The Ulama

1 | Some Observations on the Development of the Ottoman Learned Hierarchy

RICHARD REPP

ONE OF THE CHIEF DIFFICULTIES in writing about Ottoman governmental institutions lies in the fact that the empire lasted for some six centuries and that during much of that time many of its institutions were in the process of evolving from relatively simple beginnings toward more and more complex entities, at first to meet increasingly complex problems of administration created by a rapidly expanding empire, later, in many cases, as the result merely of self-perpetuating, and essentially sterile, bureaucratic proliferation. In writing on a given Ottoman institution, then, one is forced in some degree to limit one's approach in order to keep the subject to a manageable size. Among writers on the Ottoman learned hierarchy, for example, Gibb and Bowen, in their chapters on the religious institution in *Islamic Society and the West*,[1] have confined themselves largely to a description of the learned hierarchy in the eighteenth century, by which time it had only just become fully elaborated; and relatively little attention is paid to its evolution. The most recent work on the subject, İ. H. Uzunçarşılı's *İlmiye Teşkilâtı*,[2] is a mine of valuable information and references, particularly for the period from the middle of the sixteenth to the eighteenth century; but it is rendered somewhat difficult of use from the point of view of the evolution of the hierarchy as a whole by the fact that the author's approach is only superficially systematic. It is hoped in this article to trace briefly the earlier development of the hierarchy, from roughly the mid-fifteenth to the mid-sixteenth century; to try to isolate from the welter of detail some of the underlying principles of the hierarchical structure; and, finally, to make some general remarks on the strengths and weaknesses of the system.

Until the time of Mehmed II (855–886/1451–1481) it is difficult to speak of a learned hierarchy since the practice of reserving the individual offices

[1] H. A. R. Gibb and H. Bowen, *Islamic Society and the West* (hereafter Gibb and Bowen), I, part 2 (Oxford, 1957), esp. chap. ix–xi.

[2] İ. H. Uzunçarsılı, *Osmanlı Devletinin Ilmiye Teşkilâtı* (hereafter *İlmiye Teşkilâtı*) (Ankara, 1965).

of the state to men of a particular background and training—whether to slaves of the Palace School system, to the ulema, or to men of the bureaucratic profession (*kalemiyye*)[3]—had not yet developed to any very great degree. During the first half of the fifteenth century, for example, though slaves had come to man a large part of the standing army and to hold the lesser vizierates, no slave had held the office of Grand Vizier; and it was only after the fall of Constantinople, and the consequent fall of the Grand Vizier Çandarlı Halil Pasha, that one was to do so. This Çandarlı Halil Pasha was one of a family of statesmen, four members of which had held the Grand Vizierate for much of the century preceding the accession of Mehmed II; and these men had also held, prior to their appointments as vizier, the offices of *ḳâḍî* (kadı) and *ḳâḍî al-ʿaskar* (ḳazasker), the latter term meaning, literally, "judge of the army." The appointment of a slave to the Grand Vizierate in 857/1453, however, set the seal on the tendency to man the highest offices of the central administration, the vizierates, with slaves; and though it was by no means unheard of for a member of the ulema thereafter to hold a vizierate, one begins to see the development of a hierarchy more or less confined to members of the ulema, the highest offices in which, known as *mevleviyet*s (that is, offices held by *molla*s),[4] were an end in themselves and not mere stepping-stones to high office in other areas such as the central administration. Symbolic, perhaps, of the acquiescence of the ulema in this new order is a remark attributed to Molla Aḥmad b. Ismâʿîl b. ʿUt͟hmân al-Gûrânî (Molla Gürânî), Mehmed II's *k͟hwâja* (hoja). When, shortly after Mehmed II came to the throne, he offered Molla Gürânî a vizierate, the latter is reported to have refused, saying: "Those servants and slaves who are in thy palace serve thee only that they may, in the end, obtain the vizierate. Were the vizier to come from other than their number, their hearts would turn from thee and the business of thy government would become disordered."[5]

[3] See generally N. Itzkowitz, "Eighteenth Century Ottoman Realities," *Studia Islamica*, XVI (1962), 73–94.

[4] Though the term *mevleviyet* at certain periods also included high-ranking professorships and certain other posts, it is used here to indicate 300- and 500-akçe *kadılıks* (as distinct from the *ḳaḍâ* (*kaza*) *kadılıks*, i.e., those of the basic administrative districts of the empire, which carried salaries not exceeding 150 akçe and which one might term "local" *kadılıks*) and the *kazaskerliks*. The office of Mufti of Istanbul, the highest-ranking office of the hierarchy from at least the late sixteenth century, seems not to have been included in the designation *mevleviyet*. To avoid needless circumlocution I have adopted the Turkish words *kadılık* and *kazaskerlik*, signifying the office and functions of a kadı and a kazasker, respectively.

[5] ʿIṣâm al-Dîn Aḥmad b. Muṣṭafâ b. K͟halîl, known as Taşköprüzâde (d.

The first clear-cut rules regarding the organization of the ulema would seem to be those found in the *Ḳânûnnâme* (*Kanunname*), or code of laws, attributed to the latter years of the reign of Mehmed II.[6] The principal provisions pertaining to the structure of the learned profession lay down that a candidate for office, a *mulâzım* (mülâzim), shall first teach at a

968/1561), *al-Shaḳâ'iḳ al-nu'mâniyya*, printed in the margin of Ibn Khallikan's *Wafayât al-a'yân* (2 vols.; Bulaq, 1299/1881–82), I, 144. This work, hereafter "Taşköprüzâde," was translated into Turkish by Molla Mejdî al-Edirnewî (d. 999/1590–91) with the title *Ḥaḳâ'iḳ al-Shaḳâ'iḳ* (Istanbul, 1269/1852), hereafter referred to as "Mejdi": the quotation is to be found in a slightly extended form on p. 104 of Mejdi. The most important work written as a continuation to the *Shaḳâ'iḳ* is the *Ḥadâ'iḳ al-Ḥaḳâ'iḳ* (Istanbul, 1268/1852) by New'î-zâde 'Aṭâ'î (d. 1045/1635) (hereafter Ata'i), which extends from the point at which Taşköprüzâde stops, in the middle of the reign of Süleyman (1520–1566), into the reign of Murad IV (1623–1640). These three works comprise the biographical sources mentioned below, and all biographical information is drawn from them unless otherwise noted. To facilitate reference to the sources I have generally given scholar's names in their fully transliterated forms in the first instance.

6 *Tarih-i Osmani Encümeni Mecmuası* (hereafter *TOEM*), no. 13, *ilâve* (Istanbul, 1330/1912), esp. p. 20. K. Dilger (*Untersuchungen zur geschichte des osmanischen Hofzeremoniells* [Munich, 1967], esp. pp. 14–36) challenges the traditional dating of the composition of the *Kanunname*, namely the latter years of the reign of Mehmed II (1451–1481). Having demonstrated the existence of a number of anachronisms in the text, he concludes that the *Kanunname* contains a number of sixteenth-century alterations and additions and that any provision of it must be treated with reserve and checked against other sources before being accepted as being genuinely of the time of Mehmed II.

In regard to the provisions concerning the learned profession which follow in the text, there seems to be good reason for supposing them to be basically genuine, despite certain problems: e.g., Dilger is very possibly right in regarding the term *Sahn* as a sixteenth-century usage and therefore an anachronism. But, as will be noted below in the text, a survey of the careers of scholars in the biographical sources indicates that something very like the provisions of the *Kanunname* were in operation by at least the early sixteenth century. While the sources are not sufficiently detailed to confirm the operation of them in every detail, at the same time they do not cast doubt on any detail. It is impossible to date the provisions with absolute confidence, but in favor of dating them in the reign of Mehmed II is the fact that Sultan Murad III, in a firman sent to his Grand Vizier in 985/1577 in connection with reform of the learned profession, speaks of "the ancient law (*kanun*) of Sultan Mehmed Gazi" (see *İlmiye Teşkilâtı*, pp. 71, 241). It thus seems likely that Mehmed II promulgated *some* legislation concerning the learned hierarchy, if not these actual provisions. A further point suggesting that these provisions, if not actually written in his reign, were in any event written not long after his death is the fact that the medrese attached to the mosque of Bayezid II in Edirne, completed in 893/1488 and of higher rank than the Sahn, would almost certainly have received some mention in any provisions pertaining to the learned profession written subsequent to that date.

20-akçe *madrasa* (medrese), that is, one at which the stipulated salary of the professor (*mudarris/müderris*) is 20 akçe daily, the akçe being the standard Ottoman silver coin; and shall then proceed to advance by 5-akçe stages (e.g., to a 25, then to a 30-akçe medrese, and so on) until he reaches the 50-akçe medreses of which there are three classes: *khârij* (hâriç), *dâkhil* (dâhil), and the *Ṣaḥn* (Sahn). The last of these classes is the famous *Ṣaḥn-i thamân*, the eight medreses built round Mehmed II's mosque in Istanbul; the mosque itself was completed in 875/1470–71, and the medreses presumably at about the same date. After reaching the Sahn, the highest of the 50-akçe medreses, the scholar may then become a 500-akçe kadı and thence kazasker.[7]

These provisions define the basis for the highly complex *cursus honorum* of the learned profession which finally became fully elaborated only in the early eighteenth century. The principle is fixed that a scholar aspiring to high office must first teach at a graded series of medreses, one after the other, and that only when he reaches a certain grade does he become eligible for the great offices of the learned hierarchy, the mevleviyets, which are in their turn graded. The biographical sources for this period are not, unfortunately, sufficiently detailed to allow a close analysis of the degree to which the system was adhered to in the first half of the sixteenth century, but the broader outlines may certainly be perceived and seem to confirm that the provisions of the *Kanunname* were operating by the early years of that century. It is, for example, rare, though not unknown, to find the holder of an important kadılık who has not taught at the Sahn;[8] and such a one will invariably have taught at other important

[7] Although hâriç and dâhil professors received the same salary as Sahn professors, and their professorships, like those of the Sahn, were considered mevleviyets, the *Kanunname* twice states that it is from the Sahn that one ascends to become a 500-akçe kadı, the Ayasofya medrese being the only other medrese distinguished in the same way. There can be little doubt, particularly in the light of the biographical information (see below), that the Sahn was already considered a class apart from, and above, the other two. Such certainly was the case in the fully developed hierarchy. The identification of the 500-akçe kadılıks mentioned in the *Kanunname* presents a real difficulty. The whole question of the salaries of the holders of the highest mevleviyets in the early days of the empire is a vexed one, but it seems likely that to speak of a 500-akçe kadılık in the time of Mehmed II is anachronistic. According to M. T. Gökbilgin, the kadı of Edirne received only 300 akçe at the beginning of the tenth/sixteenth century ("Edirne" in *EI*², II, p. 686*a*); and if Edirne were not a 500-akçe kadılık it is difficult to imagine what would be, unless it were the kadılık of Istanbul alone. See also Dilger, *op. cit.*, pp. 25–26.

[8] E.g., Molla Zeyrekzâde (d. 1532–33): Taşköprüzâde, I, 467–469; Mejdi, p. 326.

medreses. Likewise it is extremely unusual to find a kazasker who has not held an important kadılık;[9] and again, the exceptions will have held other important offices such as that of preceptor (Hoja) to the sultan.

The later development of the system, which continued down to the eighteenth century, is essentially no more than an elaboration of these basic principles. As time went on, and the sultans who succeeded Mehmed II built their own medreses, the Sahn slipped from its position as the most important class of medreses, and, in the fully elaborated hierarchy, is only the sixth of twelve grades. The first to supplant it as the final stepping-stone to the highest offices of the learned profession seems to have been the *altmışlı* (60-akçe) class, of which the founder members were imperial medreses built by Mehmed II's immediate successors, such as the medrese attached to the mosque of Bayezid II in Edirne (completed in 893/1488); that attached to the mosque built by Kanunî Süleyman for his son S̲h̲âhzâde Mehmed (the Şehzâde medrese, completed in 954/1547); and that built by the same sultan for his father, Selim I, apparently around 955/1548.[10] Though the medrese of Bayezid II in Edirne was originally a 50-akçe medrese like the Sahn, it appears to have been ranked above the Sahn in the sense that the müderrises appointed to it were normally promoted from the Sahn; it did not, however, constitute a prerequisite to the holding of the highest mevleviyets in the first half of the sixteenth century. But from the middle of the sixteenth century—perhaps, indeed, as a result of the building of the Şehzâde medrese and that of Selim I—these three medreses, together with such others as the Ayasofya medrese and the medrese of Murad II in Bursa, seem to have come to form a distinct class of medreses, one rank higher than the Sahn and generally carrying a salary of 60 akçe. Teaching in one such medrese also appears to have become, from about the same time, a generally recognized prerequisite to the holding of the highest learned offices.

[9] E.g., Molla Mirem Çelebi (d. 1524–25): Taşköprüzâde, I, 492–494; Mejdi, pp. 338–339.

[10] For the medrese of Bayezid II, see M. T. Gökbilgin, *Edirne ve Paşa Livâsı* (Istanbul, 1952): text, pp. 357 ff.; facsimiles, pp. 90–91. For the Şehzâde medrese, see Ata'i, pp. 14, 243: the first müderris, appointed at the commencement of the building of the medrese, around 950/1543–44, received 50 akçe; The second, appointed in 955/1548, received 60 akçe. The medrese of Selim I is described in the *Seyâhatnâme* of Evliya Çelebi, Vol. I (Istanbul, 1314/1896–97), p. 315. The date for it is established by Taşköprüzâde's statement that the first müderris there was Molla S̲h̲ams al-Dîn Aḥmad al-Germiyânî, known as Küçük Şems, who came to it from the Sahn (Taşköprüzâde, II, 122; Mejdi, p. 500); and by Ata'i's statement that Küçük Şems was replaced at the Sahn in the course of 955/1548 (Ata'i, p. 14).

Süleyman's own medreses, built round his mosque in Istanbul and completed by 966/1559, were to form the top rungs in the fully elaborated hierarchy of medreses, though they seem not to have achieved exclusive claim to this preeminence immediately. A glance at the careers of nine of the ten Muftis of Istanbul—the official also known as the Shaikh al-Islam—who held the office between 1580 and 1622[11] and whose teaching careers fall in the latter half of the sixteenth century, after the building of the Süleymaniye medreses, will give an idea of the teaching background apparently considered essential to give one a chance of eventual appointment to the highest learned office: all nine men taught at the Sahn and subsequently at one of the 60-akçe medreses built prior to the building of the Süleymaniye medreses, for example, the Şehzâde medrese; two of the nine then went directly to their first mevleviyet (early on in the period, in 1566 and 1573, respectively), while six taught at one of the Süleymaniye medreses[12] and one at the medrese of the mother of Murad III in Üsküdar (the Atik Valide medrese) before being appointed to their first mevleviyet. The careers of other scholars of the period who reached the highest mevleviyets likewise suggest that by this time teaching on at least two levels of medreses beyond the Sahn had become customary, the top level being composed of the Süleymaniye medreses and later imperial medreses, such as those of Selim II and Murad III.[13]

The elaboration of the medrese system was accomplished not only by the addition of new grades but also by the division of existing grades. Thus the hâriç and dâhil grades of Mehmed II's time and the later altmışlı grade were each divided into two, termed in each case *ibtidâ* and *hareket*,

[11] Hoja Sa'd al-Dîn is omitted, as his career is anomalous. After teaching at the Sahn he became the sultan's Hoja, in which capacity he served two sultans, Murad III and Mehmed III.

[12] One of the six also taught subsequently at the medrese of Selim II in Edirne.

[13] A law purportedly reflecting the practice of the time of Süleyman (see *İlmiye Teşkilâtı*, pp. 273–276: the law is contained in a late seventeenth-century anthology, however, and references in it to the kadılık of Kamaniçe/Kamenets suggest that its present form, at least, dates from sometime in or after 1672) indicates that professors of dâhil, *Musila-i Sahn* (a separate rank interposed between the dâhil and Sahn ranks) and Sahn medreses might, because of poverty, choose to become kadıs; and in that case they were to be given low-ranking mevleviyets such as the kadılıks of Chios, Kayseri, or Manisa. While it was theoretically possible that such men might rise to the highest offices of the learned hierarchy, a survey of the careers of scholars in the latter half of the sixteenth century seems to indicate that this rarely happened and that such men generally spent the rest of their lives in relatively low-ranking mevleviyets. It would seem that the higher one rose in the medrese system, the better one's chances of receiving the highest learned offices.

for example, *ibtidâ-i dâhil* and *hareket-i dâhil.* Whether this division of the grades constituted anything more than an administrative move to attempt to solve the problem of a supply of müderrises far in excess of the number of medreses is very much to be doubted.

As the *Kanunname* laid down the principles of the gradation of medreses and the necessity of working one's way up, teaching in the various grades, before becoming eligible for high office in the learned profession, so also it established the principle of the gradation of the mevleviyets, differentiating various grades of kadılıks basically according to the importance of their locations, and placing the office of kazasker above them all. Inevitably the grades of important kadılıks grew more numerous as the number of kadılıks increased with the addition of the conquered territories, but the basic rule remained that one moved through successive grades of kadılıks until one arrived at the office of kazasker. The latter office was divided into two at the end of Mehmed II's reign, one for Rumelia and one for Anatolia, the former being the senior. For a short period in the reign of Selim I (918–926/1512–1520) there existed a third kazaskerlik, for the Arab and Persian lands, but this was, after a few years, combined with the kazaskerlik of Anatolia. One substantive addition to the system as envisioned in the *Kanunname* was the absorption of the office of Mufti of Istanbul into the learned hierarchy and the establishment of it at the head of the hierarchy, above the kazaskerlik of Rumelia. In the *Kanunname,* the Mufti, like the sultan's Hoja, is accorded enormous prestige, but neither office is included in the hierarchical structure. While the Hoja remained essentially outside the hierarchy, the Mufti was gradually drawn into it during the sixteenth century and, by the end of the century, his had clearly become the highest office in the learned profession.[14]

Several other provisions of the *Kanunname* are worth remarking upon, if only to avoid giving the impression that the establishment of a hierarchy for the ulema meant that a scholar, once enmeshed in its toils, had no option but the long grind to the top of that particular profession. It is clear from the *Kanunname* that the movement of scholars into other fields than the learned profession is envisioned: if a candidate for office in the learned profession, that is, one who has completed his medrese training, wishes to enter a military career instead, he is to be given a fief yielding 20,000 akçe; dâhil and Sahn professors and 300-akçe kadıs may

[14] I hope in the near future to publish the results of research on the origins and development of the office of Mufti in which this movement will be traced.

hold the office of *defterdar* and the first two may also become *nişancı*; and 500-akçe kadıs may become *beylerbeyis*.[15] To give but one example as an illustration of such crossing of career lines one might cite the career of Ja'far Çelebi b. Tâjî Bey (d. 921/1515) who left medrese teaching to hold the office of nişancı twice and was then elevated to the kazaskerlik of Anatolia. Though the possibility is not mentioned in the *Kanunname*, it was certainly still possible in these relatively early days for a member of the ulema to rise to the Grand Vizierate, for example, Çandarlızâde Ibrahim Pasha, the son of Halil Pasha, who held the office from 1498 to 1499, and Piri Mehmed Pasha, Grand Vizier from 1518 to 1523.

What then were the hurdles facing a young man aspiring to a scholarly career in the early sixteenth century? Obviously he had first to complete his medrese education, though neither the *Kanunname* nor the biographical sources give much guidance as to precisely what stages he had to pass through. While the biographical sources normally mention the professors from whom the student received lessons, they rarely mention the medrese at which the professor was teaching, so that it is extremely difficult to follow a student from medrese to medrese. Though Taşköprüzâde names his teachers and the works he studied under them in his autobiography appended to the *Shaḳâ'iḳ*, even he does not give the medreses in which he studied. This would seem to reflect the fact that what was learned, and from whom it was learned, was considerably more important than where it was learned. Nonetheless, it seems likely that the course of studies was so arranged that the students would pass through the same grades of medreses as those in which they would later teach: such would in any case seem to have been the practice in later times.

Having completed his education, the young scholar then became a mülâzım, that is, a candidate for office. Until near the middle of the

[15] *TOEM*, *ilâve*, pp, 14, 20, 21. The *defterdar*, or "register-keeper," was the chief finance officer, while the *nişancı*, the affixer of the royal cipher, had the power to examine and, if necessary, correct the official decrees on which he traced the royal cipher, in order to bring them into harmony with existing decrees (or, alternatively, to alter existing decrees to accord with the new ones). The *beylerbeyis*, literally "commanders of the commanders," were governors-general of the provinces of the empire, the most notable being the *beylerbeyi* of Rumelia. The offices of the defterdar and the nişancı later became more or less the preserve of the *kalemiyye*, the bureaucratic profession: see Itzkowitz, *op. cit.* Some of the details in this passage of the *Kanunname* may well be anachronistic in respect of the time of Mehmed II (see n. 7 above, for example), but the passage as a whole represents kinds of movement not uncommon in his time as well as later.

sixteenth century the enrollment of a medrese student who had completed, or nearly completed, his studies as a candidate for office and the subsequent appointment of him to a post seems to have been rather a disorganized process. Ata'i[16] writes that before the great Ottoman jurist Abu 'l-Su'ûd Efendi (Ebüssu'ûd Efendi: d. 982/1574) became kazasker of Rumelia, an office he held from 1537 to 1545, no attention had been paid to the registration of mülâzıms, and that, consequently, each student was being appointed to his post in a different manner. As a result of complaints by a group of students that Ebüssu'ûd Efendi's colleague, Muḥyi 'l-Dîn S̲haik̲h̲ Muḥammad b. Ilyâs (Çivizâde), the kazasker of Anatolia, was preventing them from becoming enrolled for appointment to office, Sultan Süleyman charged Ebüssu'ûd Efendi with looking into the matter. In doing so, the latter established the basic rules that brought some order to the method of appointment of scholars to their first posts. It became the rule, for example, that the kazaskers should keep a separate register specifically for the purpose of enrolling mülâzıms. In order to get his name on the books, however, it seems to have been necessary for the medrese student to obtain the backing of a high-ranking member of the ulema. The various high officers of the learned profession appear to have been given the right at intervals to invest a stipulated number of students, whether their own or those of others, with the right to become enrolled as mülâzıms. Ebüssu'ûd Efendi fixed the interval at which this investiture of students as mülâzıms, called a *nöbet*, might take place, namely once in seven years, though this interval was by no means always maintained in later times. He also stipulated the number of students to whom each officeholder of the learned profession might grant the right to become mülâzıms; and though none of these figures are given, it would appear that from 973/1566 down to Ata'i's own day the kazaskers might each, on such occasions, invest ten students as mülâzıms, the kadıs of Istanbul, Bursa, and Edirne five each, and the others of the highest rank of kadıs three each.[17] In addition to this more or less regular investiture, there seem to have been investitures on a number of special occasions such as the accession of a sultan or a great victory. On such occasions the Mufti and the Hoja, for example, were each allowed to invest as many as twenty students with the right to become mülâzıms.

The system of investing mülâzıms thus developed would seem to have provided the state with a means of controlling both the quality and the quantity of the intake of students into the learned profession. The need

16 Ata'i, p. 184.

17 *Ibid.*, pp. 186, 243.

for the recommendation of a high-ranking scholar provided a control on the quality of the intake—as long, of course, as the scholar were reasonably honest—while the quantity could be controlled by altering a number of factors, for example, the period at which the regular investiture (nöbet) took place, the number of ceremonial occasions on which special investitures might occur, or the number of students the holder of any given office might invest as mülâzıms. Interesting, though extremely belated, attempts to control both the quality and the quantity of mülâzıms are represented by two decrees of the year 1715, by which time the system had very nearly completely broken down. Indicative of what a degenerate state the practice of investing mülâzıms had come to is the fact that it is considered a reform that it should be inquired of the intending mülâzım how old he is, under whom he has studied, and what he has studied. In a second decree, aimed at reducing the swollen numbers of mülâzıms, it is stated, among other provisions, that the Mufti, who had formerly been allowed to invest sixteen students with the right to become mülâzıms on taking up his post, will henceforward be allowed to invest only three.[18]

To return to the earlier period, however, one finds that once the mülâzım was enrolled, he waited his turn until a post fell vacant. After the reorganization, this part of the process seems to have worked relatively smoothly, but injustices appear to have occurred in the comparative chaos of the earlier period. Not only may one cite the case of the group that felt itself to have been ill-treated at the hands of Çivizâde, but also the experience of Molla 'Abd al-Ḳâdir (Kadirî Çelebi), a Mufti in the time of Süleyman, who spent nine years in great hardship as mülâzım before receiving an appointment, probably at the beginning of the second decade of the sixteenth century.[19]

On enrolling, the student chose which area he preferred to work in, whether the European or Asiatic part of the empire, and signed on with the appropriate kazasker. He also had to make the more momentous choice of whether he wished to become a müderris or a kadı: at this stage of his career he would, of course, become a kaza kadı (local kadı). As noted above, one had to teach through the various grades of medreses before becoming eligible for one of the high-ranking official posts. The grades

[18] Mustafa Raşid, *Raşid Tarihi* (Istanbul, 1282/1865), IV, 48–50. See also *İlmiye Teşkilâtı*, pp. 49–51.

[19] Maḥmûd b. Sulaymân al-Kaffawî (d. 990/1582), *Katâ'ib a'lâm al-akhyâr*, Esad Efendi (Süleymaniye) MS 548, fols. 64v–65r. I should like to take this opportunity to thank the authorities of the Süleymaniye Library for making this MS available to me.

of the kaza kadılıks formed a unit in themselves, however,[20] and one did not normally ascend from one of them to a mevleviyet. In choosing a kaza kadılık, then, a student was in effect shutting himself off from the high offices of state and dooming himself to a lifetime of service in the local kadılıks unless he could somehow get back into the medrese stream.

It is difficult to find figures for the income of the kaza kadıs in the early days, but it seems likely that they were better off than their low-ranking medrese colleagues. In other words, the career of the kaza kadı was probably more remunerative in the short run, though offering much more limited prospects in the long run. It is certainly true that if a low-ranking müderris wanted to change over to the career of kaza kadı, he was immediately better paid: a provision of the *Kanunname* states that if a 20-akçe müderris in the *içel* (a term applied to medreses in the cities and environs of Istanbul, Bursa, and Edirne) were to become a kadı, he was to be given a 45-akçe kadılık.[21] Illustrative of the workings of this process is the career of Molla Muṣṭafâ b. 'Alî, known as Molla Bostan. Having become mülâzım in 932/1525–26, he was appointed in 935/1528–29 to a medrese in Bursa with a salary of 25 akçe. Poverty, however, forced him to abandon teaching and become a kaza kadı, in which capacity he served in several towns. About the year 944/1537–38, the two kazaskers, Ebüssu'ûd Efendi and Çivizâde, the latter a teacher of Molla Bostan's, spoke well of him in the presence of Sultan Süleyman; and as a result of their intercession, and of the sultan's interest in a monograph that Molla Bostan had recently written, it was decreed that he should be appointed to a medrese. In the event, he was given a 40-akçe medrese, from which he rose by degrees through the medreses and the mevleviyets eventually to hold the office

[20] To give examples from a later period, one might cite Serez, Silistria, and Kaffa as kadılıks of the highest rank of kaza kadılıks: see *İlmiye Teşkilâtı*, p. 92 n. 2.

[21] *TOEM, ilâve*, p. 20. I have here adopted the traditional interpretation of the term *içel* in this context, as defined by the historian 'Âli (d. 1008/1599–1600) (see *İlmiye Teşkilâtı*, p. 57). While one cannot totally reject the contention of Dilger (*op. cit.*, pp. 28–29) that *içel* here means the sanjak İçel (the province including Silifke), his argument on this point seems unpersuasive. One would be hard pressed to explain why the sanjak of İçel—which had little significance in respect of the medrese system—should be singled out for special mention not only in the *Kanunname* but also, for example, at three places in the text of a draft law presented by a committee of the ulema to Sultan Mehmed III in 1006/1598 (see *İlmiye Teşkilâtı*, pp. 243–246: on one occasion the term is opposed to *kenar*, "edge, border"). That the term *içel* as defined by 'Âli was current in the time of Mehmed II needs substantiation, but there seems to be no good reason to suppose that it was not.

of kazasker of Rumelia from 1547 to 1551. Of interest in this story is not only the fact that he was forced by poverty to abandon teaching and become a kaza kadı but also that he was able to reenter the medrese stream. It would seem, however, that it was only by the intercession of the two kazaskers, and, indeed, by virtue of an imperial decree, that he was able to do so.

An insight into the workings of the learned profession, of a kind all too rarely offered by the early sources, is to be found in an anecdote concerning the appointment of Molla S̲hams al-Dîn Aḥmad b. Sulaymân b. Kamâl Pasha (Ibn Kemal), one of the most famous of Ottoman scholars, to his first post.[22] In 908/1502–3, when he sought his first appointment, the kazasker of Rumelia was Muḥammad b. Muṣṭafâ b. al-Ḥâjj Ḥasan (Hajji Hasan-zâde), and the kazasker of Anatolia was 'Abd al-Raḥman b. 'Alî (Müeyyedzâde), an old friend of Ibn Kemal's family. When Ibn Kemal presented himself to Hajji Hasan-zâde and requested that he be appointed to the Taşlık (Ali Bey) medrese in Edirne which was then vacant, Hajji Hasan-zâde urged him to give up the thought of receiving a medrese and to accept an appointment to a kaza kadılık instead. Ibn Kemal sought the advice of Müeyyedzâde who counseled him to feign acceptance of Hajji Hasan-zâde's proposal; and when, on the next day, the latter petitioned the sultan, Bayezid II, to appoint Ibn Kemal to a kadılık, Müeyyedzâde intervened, speaking highly of Ibn Kemal's abilities and asking that he not be wasted in a kaza kadılık, but rather that he be given the vacant Taşlık medrese so that he might busy himself with the pursuit of learning. Bayezid II was won over by Müeyyedzâde's arguments and not only appointed Ibn Kemal to the Taşlık medrese but also charged him with writing a history of the Ottoman dynasty in Turkish to serve as a companion piece to that being written in Persian by Idris Bitlisi.

'Âli sees in this attempt by Hajji Hasan-zâde to induce Ibn Kemal to accept a kaza kadılık an example of a means whereby he was able to maintain himself in the office of kazasker for twenty-five years, first in that of Anatolia and then in that of Rumelia. Controlling the nominations to all learned appointments in whichever of the areas he was then kazasker, he would urge young scholars to enter the relative dead end of the career of

[22] This anecdote is to be found first, and in fullest form, in the *tad̲hkira* of Aşik Çelebi (British Museum, Or. MS 6434, fols. 37r–37v), and, in more summary form, in Mejdi, p. 384, and 'Âlî, *Kunh al-ak̲hbâr* (British Museum, Add. MS 10,004, fols. 140v–141r). My thanks are due to the authorities of the British Museum for making these MSS available to me.

kaza kadı and thereby prevent them from passing up through the ranks of the medreses to become candidates for mevleviyets and thus rivals to his own position.

Ibn Kemal's further career may serve as a useful summary of the state of development of the learned hierarchy in the first half of the sixteenth century. Having taught in six different medreses, the last two of which were the Sahn and the medrese of Bayezid II in Edirne, he became kadı of Edirne in 921/1515 and kazasker of Anatolia in 922/1516. Removed from that office in 925/1519, he spent the next seven years teaching in the Darülhadis medrese in Edirne (with 100 akçe) and, for the second time, in the medrese of Bayezid II. He ascended to the office of Mufti of Istanbul in 932/1525–26, in which post he remained until his death in 940/1534.

Compared with the careers of later scholars, Ibn Kemal's is a relatively simple one. The Süleymaniye medreses, of course, had not yet been built, and Mecca and Medina, the kadılıks of which were to form a separate grade, just below the kadılık of Istanbul, in the eighteenth century, only came into Ottoman hands while Ibn Kemal was kazasker of Anatolia. Quite apart from offices that did not yet exist, however, even by the end of the sixteenth century it would have been unusual for a scholar not to have held one other kadılık before the kadılık of Edirne; not to have held the kadılık of Istanbul before the kazaskerlik of Anatolia; and not to have held the kazaskerlik of Rumelia before the office of Mufti of Istanbul. Nonetheless, a pattern is discernible in the career of Ibn Kemal, a pattern that allows one to perceive the basic structure of the hierarchy as it existed in later times.

It remains to touch briefly upon the strengths and weaknesses of this organization of the learned profession, this creation of a hierarchical structure regulating the careers of scholars with a thoroughness unprecedented in Islamic states. There can be no question that in the great days of the empire, notably in the sixteenth century, the system produced superbly trained scholars, of nearly uniform education and experience, who were on the whole disposed—or at least not unwilling—to work with the secular officials of the state to create a viable polity. Whereas in former times the ulema and the secular authorities had often been at odds, the Ottoman ulema, by the sixteenth century, were for the most part so trained and oriented as to play a large part, together with the sultans themselves, in bringing about what one might regard as a major achievement of the empire, namely the endowment of Islamic law, in its Hanafī form, "with the highest degree of actual efficiency which it had ever possessed in a society of high material civilization since early 'Abbāsid times."[23]

This relative cooperation between the ulema and the secular authorities was not achieved without some difficulty, without overcoming certain deep-seated prejudices. Taşköprüzâde's grandfather (d. 879/1474–75), for example, refused to take up an appointment at the newly built Sahn for fear of becoming caught up in distracting ambitions for personal glory. He also warned his son, Taşköprüzâde's father, never to become a kadı, as a result of which the latter refused an appointment as kadı of Aleppo.[24] In like manner, when Molla Gürânî was asked why a noted shaikh visited Molla Muḥammad b. Ferâmerz (Molla Hüsrev: d. 885/1480) but not him, he replied: "He does right in that, for Molla Hüsrev is a scholar noted for his knowledge and works, the visiting of whom is necessary. Though I too am a scholar, I mix with sultans, wherefore the visiting of me is not fitting."[25] Similar feelings to those of the shaikh doubtless inspired the contemporary biographer of the great Ebüssu'ûd Efendi, who writes: "There was in him an excess of complaisance and softness toward men of government."[26] Yet there is little doubt that Ebüssu'ûd Efendi will be remembered longer as the scholar who "succeeded in bringing the *ḳānūn*, the administrative law of the Ottoman Empire, into agreement with the *sharī'a*."[27]

While the organization of the learned hierarchy thus at least for a period worked to the advantage of the state by providing it with a steady supply of well-trained scholars, the simple fact of the thoroughgoing organization of the ulema carried with it the seeds of considerable trouble for the state. The creation of a learned "establishment" tended to intensify the natural conservatism of the ulema, whether in such matters as the subjects that might be taught in the medreses[28] or in regard to innovations in general. Likewise, the definition of success in the learned field in terms of money and power, a definition implicit in the very process of establishing a graded hierarchy, created the climate for precisely the sort of corruption—the sale of offices, the nepotism, and so on—that afflicted other governmental institutions.

[23] J. Schacht, *An Introduction to Islamic Law* (Oxford, 1964), p. 89.

[24] Taşköprüzâde, I, 189–190, 614; Mejdi, pp. 140, 392.

[25] Taşköprüzâde, I, 148; Mejdi, p. 108.

[26] Munuḳ 'Alî, *al-'Iḳd al-manẓûm*, a continuation of Taşköprüzâde, also published in the margin of the *Wafayât*: II, 449.

[27] Schacht, *op. cit.*, p. 90.

[28] See Gibb and Bowen, I, part 2, 147–152.

A particular curse on the learned profession came to be the preferential treatment given to the sons of the holders of the high learned offices which soon reached scandalous proportions. Though the sons of holders of such offices are allotted pensions in the *Kanunname* of Mehmed II,[29] the practice of allowing them to skip grades in the hierarchy seems not to have grown up until the mid-sixteenth century.[30] It then became the rule, for example, for sons of kazaskers to be appointed directly to a 40-akçe medrese on becoming mülâzıms, and for sons of Muftis and Hojas to be appointed directly to hâriç and even dâhil medreses. In the course of the latter half of the sixteenth century, this compromising of the rigid principles of the hierarchy progressed so far that by the last decade of the century the historian 'Âli could write: "[the sons of the holders of high learned offices] need not move along the path of education: that is, without following a course of studies in any medrese, the way is opened to them to become mülâzım while in the cradle and to receive a professorship when they learn to speak. On reaching the age of puberty they set off on the road to an important kadılık, and until their beards begin to grow, they go from post to post and medrese to medrese. Once their beards begin to grow, they obtain a 500-akçe mevleviyet. In the unlikely event that they pick up a book, it will only be a commonplace book, an anthology, or a collection of lyric poems."[31] So deeply entrenched had this practice become by the early eighteenth century that the decree of 1715 attempting to reform the practice regarding mülâzıms[32] specifies that a son of one of the ulema need only be asked the name of his father. This invasion of the learned profession by the ill-qualified, or unqualified, was not, of course, confined to the sons of the ulema. Koçu Bey writes that by his time (1631) the clerks of vaivodes and *subaşıs* as well as many of the common people were buying the right to become mülâzım for five or ten thousand akçe.[33]

By means such as these, then, the integrity of the hierarchical structure became thoroughly corrupted and at least the upper ranks of the ulema, the "official" ulema, had, by the eighteenth century, become as incapable of teaching as the Janissaries had of fighting. Like the Janissaries, moreover, they had become an enormously powerful, conservative pressure group within the state, with a vested interest in maintaining the status quo.

[29] *TOEM, ilâve*, p. 21.

[30] Apparently with the sole exception of the descendants of Molla Fenârî (d. 834/1431) who were, on becoming mülâzıms, appointed directly to 40-akçe medreses. On what follows, see generally *İlmiye Teşkilâtı*, pp. 67–75.

[31] Cited in *İlmiye Teşkilâtı*, pp. 69–70.

[32] See above, p. 26.

[33] *Risale-i Koçu Bey* (Istanbul, 1277/1861), p. 11.

Ironically it was the very cohesiveness created by the hierarchical structure, which had yielded great benefits to the state in the sixteenth century, particularly in the administration of law, which from at least the eighteenth century on lent such power to the efforts of the ulema to block often necessary reforms and innovations.

2 The Ottoman Ulema and the Tanzimat

RICHARD L. CHAMBERS

In the Ottoman context, the term "ulema" denoted those men who had not only studied in medreses and received diplomas (*icazetler*) signifying that they had acquired a portion of religious learning but had then secured appointment as mosque functionaries, teachers, jurisconsults, or judges. They were members of the learned or religious profession (*tarik-i ilmiye*), holding patents of office, ranks, and titles peculiar to their career. Their names were inscribed in the official ulema ledgers and were removed only when they, for whatever reason, ceased to be counted among the learned officialdom.

The ulema were an exceptionally privileged and powerful estate in traditional Ottoman society. As members of the ruling *askerî* class, they were exempt from taxation. Unlike their fellow askerîs in the civil and military bureaucracies, they had never had the status of "slaves of the Porte" (*kapıkulları*) and thus their personal estates were not subject to confiscation by the state upon their deaths but could be passed on to their heirs. Their financial position was further strengthened by the vast religious endowments (*evkaf*) which they supervised and administered.

The ulema comprised the majority of the educated Muslim population of the Ottoman Empire. They staffed the mosques, mektebs (elementary schools), and medreses, were responsible for educating the Muslim community, served as the judges in the courts of Holy Law (Şeriat), and administered as well the *kanuns* (edicts) of the Sultans. From the early days of the Empire, the mektebs and medreses had provided the state with literate men to work as scribes and officials in the government bureaus, although "on the job" training was available in the bureaus as well. High-ranking ulema sat in the Imperial Divan and held positions in the Palace which often gave them unusual access to the sovereign himself. The Chief Mufti (Şeyhülislam) was considered on a par with the Grand Vezir (Sadrazam). He could, and on occasion did, issue a legal opinion (*fetva*) which served as a restraint upon the Sultan's sovereign will.

By the eighteenth century, the ulema had reached an apex of privilege, affluence, and political power. A relatively small group of families dominated the upper echelons of the religious hierarchy and constituted the nearest thing to a hereditary aristocracy known in Ottoman history. Many of them held high political posts. This, together with the breakdown of the slave (*kapıkul*) system and the increasing incidence of paşas' sons entering the ulema corps in order to qualify for the privilege of passing on property to their heirs, resulted in a blurring of the traditional line of demarcation between ulema and "Men of the Sword." These close connections of the upper ulema with the Palace and the Porte gave them an identity of interests while estranging even more the leaders of the religious establishment from its rank and file. The lower ulema and the medrese students (*softas*) envied and resented this privileged group of Great Mollas and expressed their antagonism by turning against all authority.[1]

The disunity in ulema ranks, the competition among more and more candidates for the limited number of top religious posts, the growing corruption, nepotism and intrigue that this competition bred, and the resultant widespread decay in moral fiber and quality of learning took their toll. Toward the end of the eighteenth century, the ulema were showing signs of strain and of weakness.[2] The purchase of diplomas and posts by unqualified men had created a class of "official ulema" (*ulema-i resmiye*) who enjoyed the privileges while lacking the attributes of the "career ulema" (*ulema-i tarik*) who had studied and earned the right to be called "possessors of knowledge."[3] The presence of "official ulema" within the corps of medrese teachers further diluted the quality of the already circumscribed religious curriculum of the medreses. The combination of these developments lost for the ulema, in particular the upper echelon, some of the trust and respect of the common people which they had traditionally enjoyed. It became evident in the reigns of Selim III and Mahmud II that the ulema, although still a force to be reckoned with, were too divided and compromised to offer sustained resistence to the will of such reform-minded Sultans.[4]

In his well-documented study, Uriel Heyd has described how the ulema

[1] Uriel Heyd, "The Ottoman 'Ulemā and Westernization in the Time of Selīm III and Maḥmūd II," in Uriel Heyd, ed., *Studies in Islamic History and Civilization* (Jerusalem, 1961), p. 72.

[2] *Ibid.*, pp. 77–78.

[3] Richard L. Chambers, "Ahmed Cevdet Paşa: The Formative Years of an Ottoman Transitional" (unpublished Ph.D. dissertation, Princeton University, 1968), p. 43; Şerif Mardin, *The Genesis of Young Ottoman Thought: A Study in the Modernization of Turkish Political Ideas* (Princeton, 1962), p. 219.

[4] Heyd, "The Ottoman 'Ulemā," p. 79.

responded to the attempts of Selim and Mahmud to reform and modernize the Ottoman Empire. Exploding the myth that the Muslim men of religion stood united and of one mind in opposition to all change, Professor Heyd concluded that "the leading 'ulemā in Selīm's and Maḥmūd's time were not farsighted enough to realize that the Westernizing reforms supported by them would eventually destroy the Islamic character of the Ottoman State and society."[5]

During the succeeding reform period known as the Tanzimat (1839–1876), the ulema continued to lose ground on every front. With some notable exceptions, they were excluded from political leadership roles and reacted negatively and defensively to the secularizing tendencies of the Tanzimat reforms. But neither the further decline of the ulema nor the Tanzimat itself can be appreciated without reference to the fundamental changes wrought in the Ottoman system by Selim and Mahmud. In the light of the work of Uriel Heyd, Niyazi Berkes, Bernard Lewis, and others, present purposes may perhaps be served by summarizing four aspects of these earlier reforms which had a direct bearing upon the position of the ulema in the Tanzimat.

First, political power in the Ottoman Empire always implied possession of, or access to, military support. In the seventeenth and eighteenth centuries, the ulema and the Janissaries had frequently found it expedient to set aside their mutual animosities and cooperate in order to preserve their traditional vested interests.[6] Mahmud's destruction of the Janissary Corps in 1826 and its replacement by a Western-style army left the ulema without a similarly conservative military ally. The nearest thing to a military force they could muster during the Tanzimat was the mob of undisciplined softas and assorted discontented elements of the Istanbul populace. These were no match for the regular government troops.

Second, the ulema corps had always enjoyed administrative autonomy vis-à-vis the Palace and the Porte, subject only to the Sultan's prerogative to appoint and dismiss its chief, the Şeyhülislam. Control of evkaf revenues made it, likewise, economically independent. By giving the Şeyhülislam an official residence and setting up a department of the Chief Mufti (Bab-i Meşihat or Fetvahane), Mahmud infringed upon the administrative autonomy of the ulema. He thus initiated the process of bureaucratizing the religious establishment and of making a distinction between affairs of state (*devlet*) and those of religion (*din*).[7] This worldly-religious dichotomy

[5] *Ibid.*, p. 96.
[6] *Ibid.*, pp. 79–80.
[7] Bernard Lewis, *The Emergence of Modern Turkey* (London, 1961), pp.

became a prominent feature of the Tanzimat.[8] Furthermore, Mahmud's creation of a Directorate (later Ministry) of Evkaf by consolidating the various existing supervisory agencies as a government department opened the door to state control of evkaf revenues and ultimately to the diversion of a portion of these to state purposes. This undercutting of their economic base was a severe blow to the ulema.[9]

Third, the civil bureaucracy was reorganized and upgraded by Mahmud to become the principal agency for making and executing government policy, subject to his approval. The legal fiction of the kapıkul system ended when Mahmud abolished the practice of confiscating the estates of officials upon their death. For the first time, civil officials could legally bequeath their material goods to their heirs and became the equals of the ulema in this respect. Greater job security and regular salaries were intended to make the bureaucratic career more attractive and the bureaucracy more efficient.[10]

Fourth, new schools for the military and the bureaucracy were opened by Selim and Mahmud. The Translation Bureau (Tercüme Odası) set up in the Sublime Porte in 1833 soon became a foreign language school, and many of its graduates were assigned to the secretariats of Mahmud's embassies in European capitals where they were able to continue their studies of Western languages and sciences. The need for military officers, bureaucrats, and statesmen who were acquainted with Europe and with European languages, especially French, served to emphasize how inadequate and out of touch with reality and the times the traditional religious educational system was. A new educated elite was gradually being produced in the government schools and bureaus, and it was this elite which dominated the political scene during the Tanzimat to the virtual exclusion of the typical medrese graduate.[11]

By the beginning of the Tanzimat in 1839, the process of change had so altered the shape of Ottoman institutions and so reoriented the Empire's course of development that a return to the past was impossible. Of

95–96; Niyazi Berkes, *The Development of Secularism in Turkey* (Montreal, 1964), p. 98.

[8] Berkes, *Development of Secularism*, p. 109.

[9] Lewis, *Emergence*, p. 92; Richard L. Chambers, "The Civil Bureaucracy: Turkey," in Robert E. Ward and Dankwart A. Rustow, eds., *Political Modernization in Japan and Turkey* (Princeton, 1964), pp. 317–318.

[10] Chambers, "The Civil Bureaucracy," p. 305; Roderic H. Davison, *Reform in the Ottoman Empire 1856–1876* (Princeton, 1963), p. 28.

[11] Chambers, "The Civil Bureaucracy," p. 305; Lewis, *Emergence*, pp. 82–87, 116.

the several medieval orders, the Janissaries had been destroyed, the local notables (*ayan* and *derebeys*) crushed, and the Palace and Porte radically overhauled. Only the ulema survived relatively unchanged in organization and outlook, despite a diminution of their autonomy, wealth, prestige, and political power. Only they had successfully resisted Mahmud in continuing to wear their medieval attire. Their turbans and flowing gowns became a symbol of ulema conservatism and set them apart as a class of Muslim "clergymen" in a state and a society that was becoming less Islamic and more secular.[12] Although seldom openly fanatic, the ulema as a group maintained a fierce pride in their faith and in their privileged position in Muslim society and opposed innovation, particularly in their own ranks.[13]

This stubborn defense of established tradition, together with the ignorance and shortsightedness of the majority of the ulema, explains in large part the lack of any efforts to reform the medreses.[14] By the 1840s, a thorough traditional education was available only to the exceptional student of independent means, unusual ability, and strong motivation. He was obliged to choose his teachers carefully, to take private lessons from ulema holding official posts outside the educational system, and to augment the meager medrese curriculum by studying such subjects as literature, poetry, and Persian in dervish tekkes and the homes of lay poets. He could learn French only in secret and at the risk of severe criticism since the knowledge of that infidel language was regarded as incompatible with ulema attributes.[15]

The economic impact of the West upon the rural Ottoman economy was being acutely felt by the 1840s and 1850s. Despite the fact that the medreses were also feeling the pinch of rising prices and diversion of some evkaf revenues, their endowments still provided at least a subsistence living for many of the impoverished peasant youths who were coming to the cities in large numbers. This influx of displaced peasant boys into the urban medreses more than offset, at least in numbers, the defections among medrese students to the new secular schools.[16] Their presence, however, lowered still more the quality of scholarship in the medreses while reinforcing attitudes antithetical to the Tanzimat. The most promising and open-minded of the teachers and students, finding the atmosphere of the

[12] Berkes, *Development of Secularism*, p. 124.

[13] Davison, *Reform*, p. 67.

[14] *Ibid.*, p. 68; Berkes, *Development of Secularism*, p. 176.

[15] See my article, "The Education of a Nineteenth Century Ottoman *Âlim*, Ahmed Cevdet Paşa," to appear shortly in *International Journal of Middle East Studies*.

[16] Berkes, *Development of Secularism*, pp. 142 and 176.

medreses frustrating and incongenial, were lured away by the advantages of the new government schools.

The efforts of the Ottoman government to improve primary education were to no avail owing to the intransigeance of the ulema who controlled the existing primary schools (*sıbyan mektebs*). A start was made during the Tanzimat in setting up a new level of secondary schools (*rüşdiyes*) to bridge the gap between religious primary education and secular higher education. Five rüşdiyes had been opened in Istanbul by 1850, and subsequently a number of others were established in the capital and in provincial centers. But whatever benefits derived from them could not compensate for the failure to improve the primary schools which continued to provide the sole educational experience of all except the privileged few. Not much progress could be expected at a time when the study of maps was banned in primary schools and the maps destroyed because it was said that the children were being taught drawing.[17]

The rüşdiyes did, however, create a demand for professional teachers and thus led to the establishment of normal schools, one for men (Darülmuallimin) in 1848 and another for women (Darülmuallimat) in 1870. The first graduates of the Darülmuallimin were all former medrese students and were inculcated with the conservative reform philosophy of the school's director, Ahmed Cevdet.[18] He was himself a product of the medreses and at that time still a member of the judiciary branch of the corps of ulema, although closely associated with and strongly influenced by Reşid Paşa and his reformist circle.

Cevdet Paşa is the most famous but by no means the only one of a number of ulema who made significant contributions to secular education during the Tanzimat. Comprehensive proposals for meeting the educational needs of the state were drawn up by a temporary commission appointed by Sultan Abdülmecid in 1845. A leading member of that commission was Arif Hikmet Bey Efendi who was elevated to the post of Şeyhülislam the following year and continued to show a benevolent interest in the development of state schools.[19] It was he who persuaded Cevdet to accept the directorship of the Darülmuallimin and membership in the Council of Public Education. These were the first of a long line of civil posts held by Cevdet in his long career as âlim and vezir.[20]

[17] Chambers, "Ahmed Cevdet Paşa," pp. 106–108.

[18] Berkes, *Development of Secularism*, p. 175.

[19] Chambers, "Ahmed Cevdet Paşa," p. 103.

[20] *Ibid.*, pp. 110–113.

Without exhausting the list of ulema concerned with secular education, mention should also be made of Hayrullah Efendi, Selim Sabit Efendi, and Hoca Tahsin. Hayrullah Efendi followed in the footsteps of his father and uncle, Abdülhak Molla and Mustafa Behçet, both ulema who were closely associated with Mahmud II and his reforms in the field of medical education.[21] Hayrullah Efendi studied in the medrese and entered the ulema ranks, but he was also graduated from the Military Medical School. This famous historian and statesman, while maintaining always his official ulema status, devoted most of his life to government service, held various high posts in the Ministry of Education, served as one of the presiding officers of the Ottoman Academy of Learning (Encümen-i Daniş), and was Ottoman ambassador in Tehran when he died in 1866.[22]

Hoca Tahsin, a talented young medrese teacher, had served as the tutor of Hayrullah Efendi's sons. When Hayrullah, then Deputy Minister of Education, went to Paris in the early 1860s to acquaint himself with the French educational system, he arranged for Hoca Tahsin to be appointed to the staff of the Ottoman School (Mekteb-i Osmanî) in Paris. Hayrullah's sons were enrolled in French schools but continued to receive religious instruction from Hoca Tahsin who also acted as imam of the Ottoman embassy and taught Turkish and religious sciences to the Muslim students of the Ottoman School.[23] While in France, Hoca Tahsin studied mathematics and the natural sciences and was on friendly terms with the Young Ottomans (Yeni Osmanlılar). In 1869 Hoca Tahsin was sent back to Istanbul to accompany the body of Fuad Paşa who had died in Nice. The following year he was appointed as the first director of the new Ottoman university (Darülfünun), but his scientific experiments and his outspoken liberalism earned him the suspicion of the conservative ulema. They managed to secure his dismissal and somewhat later the closing of the university. To Hoca Tahsin goes the credit for the first Turkish treatise on psychology and the first Turkish book on modern astronomical theories addressed to a popular audience as well as a Turkish translation of Constantin François Chasseboeuf de Volney's *Loi Naturelle*.[24]

[21] Heyd, "The Ottoman 'Ulemā," p. 67.

[22] Richard L. Chambers, "Notes on the *Mekteb-i Osmanî* in Paris, 1857–1874," in William R. Polk and Richard L. Chambers, eds., *Beginnings of Modernization in the Middle East: The Nineteenth Century* (Chicago, 1968), p. 325.

[23] *Ibid.*, pp. 325–326.

[24] *Ibid.*, p. 325. For a detailed and authoritative account of the incidents involving Hoca Tahsin, Cemaleddin Afganî (Jamal ad-Din al-Afghani) and

The predecessor of Hoca Tahsin at the Ottoman School was Selim Sabit Efendi. He also was medrese trained but had studied in the Darülmuallimin before going to Paris. Like Hoca Tahsin, he showed an interest in modern science and mathematics and learned French. Selim Sabit Efendi returned to Istanbul in 1862 and, after working in various government bureaus, was appointed vice-director of the Galatasaray Lycée. He later taught in the Darülfünun and the Darülmuallimin, served as a member and then as president of the High Council of Education, and was the author of a number of textbooks on pedagogy and other subjects.[25]

More examples might be added to this list of Tanzimat ulema who contributed to educational modernization, but perhaps these will suffice to illustrate a point. None of them could be considered the typical medrese product of the time. Şeyhülislam Arif Hikmet Bey Efendi represents a continuation into the Tanzimat of the same tradition of liberal or enlightened ulema who supported the reforms of Selim and Mahmud. In fact, he was the son of Ibrahim Ismet Bey Efendi, one of the leading ulema of the time of Selim III and Ottoman plenipotentiary at the Sistova peace conference in 1791. As the title following their names implies, these men were descended from paşas of vezir rank.[26] Arif Hikmet was a distinguished scholar, author, and poet and displayed definite leanings toward the Nakşıbendî order to which his father had belonged.[27] It is significant that Cevdet Paşa, certainly one of the most brilliant and erudite Ottomans of the nineteenth century, considered the line of truly learned ulema to have come to an end with the death of Arif Hikmet Bey Efendi in 1859.[28]

The other men mentioned above were of a younger generation and had supplemented their medrese training by acquiring some knowledge of the West and its science and learning. In the case of Cevdet, this knowledge was largely second hand. He never left the Ottoman Empire nor studied in one of the new schools, but he learned to read French on his own and described his association with Reşid, Fuad, and the other Tanzimat reform leaders as a new educational experience.[29] Cevdet also made

---

the Darülfünun which have generally been reported and interpreted inaccurately, see Berkes, *Development of Secularism*, pp. 180–188.

25 Chambers, "Notes on the *Mekteb-i Osmanî*," pp. 324–325.

26 Heyd, "The Ottoman 'Ulemā," p. 83.

27 Chambers, "Ahmed Cevdet Paşa," pp. 86–87.

28 *Ibid.*, p. 67; Mardin, *Genesis*, p. 219.

29 Chambers, "Ahmed Cevdet Paşa," p. 88.

the acquaintance of a number of prominent Europeans resident in Istanbul and discussed with them all manner of topics, not excluding religion.[30] Hayrullah Efendi, Hoca Tahsin, and Selim Sabit Efendi, as we have seen, had a more direct acquaintance with things Western gained through formal education in one of the modern schools as well as residence and study in France.

Of the five, only Cevdet formally severed his connections with the corps of ulema and became a bureaucrat with the rank of vezir. He did so reluctantly in 1866 when an express order of the Sultan left him with no alternative.[31] Yet the careers of these men were devoted in large measure to the service of state (devlet) as distinct from religion (din), and their activities contributed to the expansion of the secular arm of the state into an area traditionally reserved for the ulema.

More surprising than the fact that such men as these helped to create a modern, secular educational system is the apparent unconcern and lack of serious opposition to its creation which was shown by the conservative majority of the ulema. Professor Berkes has argued convincingly that these "custodians of tradition" ignored the new secular higher schools as being "outside their own realm and, perhaps, as ephemeral, worldly institutions expedient to the needs of secular life."[32] So long as the medreses held a monopoly on the traditional religious sciences (*ilm*), the new schools were welcome to the modern secular sciences (*fen*). Only when the Darülfünun was opened and it was announced that such traditional sciences as *fıkh* and *kalam* would be included in its curriculum did the ulema react. Most of the students for the university were taken from the medreses, and the director was an âlim. The conservative Şeyhülislam, Hasan Fehmi Efendi, saw the university as the medrese's real rival and succeeded in destroying it in the early 1870s.[33]

This same Şeyhülislam opposed the *Mecelle*, a Western-style codification of a part of Şeriat law which was the culminating achievement of the Tanzimat in legal reform. In this area, too, it was Sultan Mahmud who

[30] On his acquaintance with the French ambassador, M. Moustier, for example, see *ibid.*, pp. 168–169.

[31] *Ibid.*, pp. 172–173. Recurrent rumors that Cevdet aspired to the post of Chief Mufti had become an insupportable embarrassment to his principal patron of that time, Grand Vezir Fuad Paşa, and his obligatory transfer to the civil bureaucracy put the rumors to rest once and for all. For additional details, see *ibid.*, pp. 163–164 and 169–172.

[32] Berkes, *Development of Secularism*, p. 187.

[33] *Ibid.*, pp. 180–188.

had established the guidelines and begun the process of change. Just as he had helped to popularize the concept of *maarif*, the learning of things unknown, as a challenge to the traditional ilm of the ulema,[34] in law Mahmud became identified with the concept of *adalet* (justice), distinguishable from both Şeriat and kanun.[35] Whereas Şeriat was the divine law that formed the basis of the traditional Muslim system of life, and kanuns were edicts of the Muslim ruler concerning matters beyond the scope of the Şeriat (but theoretically in accordance with it and with its spirit), neither allowed for equality among Muslims and non-Muslims before a common law. That is precisely what adalet, as used by Mahmud and the Tanzimatists, did imply. Moreover, it recognized, at first implicitly but later explicitly, a source of legislation other than God and the Muslim ruler. "With Mahmud's initiative, . . . the medieval conception of the temporal law as an expression of the 'will' of the ruler, or as an affirmation of local customs and usages or of Islamic practices, tended to give way to a new conception in which an impersonal legislative agency in law-making was recognized by enacting regulations not according to religion or tradition, but according to the requirement of 'reason.' "[36]

It was this concept of adalet which permeated the Tanzimat Charter or Hatt-i Şerif of Gülhane of 1839, despite the lip service it paid to the Şeriat. Lawmaking by special councils and commissions, some of them inherited from Mahmud's reign, became the characteristic feature of the Tanzimat. In the permanent councils, the ulema were represented on a limited scale even in the last years of Mahmud's reign, sometimes only by the mufti of the council who led prayers and occasionally was called upon to clarify a point of Holy Law.[37] It was the new educated elite, products of the secular higher schools and the Translation Bureau, who dominated the councils and made the laws.

The first legal codification of the Tanzimat was the Penal Code of 1840. It was prepared and promulgated by the Supreme Council of Judicial Ordinances (Meclis-i Vala-yi Ahkâm-i Adliye), affirmed the equality of all Ottoman subjects before the law, and was influenced by French law. Its provisions, however. were drawn mainly from the penal law of the Şeriat and, perhaps to give it the appearance of being within the tradition of kanun-making, it was called Ceza Kanunnamesi. The novel aspects of this code drew no fire from the ulema. On the other hand, they reacted strongly when Reşid Paşa presented to the Supreme Council in 1841 a new

[34] *Ibid.*, p. 99.
[35] *Ibid.*, pp. 94–95.
[36] *Ibid.*, p. 133.
[37] Heyd, "The Ottoman 'Ulemā," p. 84.

commercial code derived almost exclusively from French commercial law. When asked whether it conformed with the Holy Law, Reşid made the mistake of replying, "The Holy Law has nothing to do with the matter." With cries of "Blasphemy!" the ulema forced suspension of the code and the dismissal of Reşid.[38]

When he became Grand Vezir five years later, Reşid Paşa moved more cautiously. He saw the advisability of finding şerî examples or precedents with which to defend his program against the charge that it was not in conformity with the Holy Law. Having no medrese training and being unfamiliar with the intricacies of the şerî sciences, Reşid requested the Bab-i Meşihat to assign him an intelligent, learned, and open-minded âlim who would be, in effect, his legal consultant and advisor. The man chosen for this task by Şeyhülislam Arif Hikmet Bey Efendi was Ahmed Cevdet.[39] Thus began the long and close association between Reşid and Cevdet.

The remarkable career of Cevdet in the field of legal codification and judicial reform did not begin, however, until 1855. The Crimean War had focused European attention on the Ottoman Empire and had expanded commerce greatly. The mixed courts handling lawsuits under the European-inspired Commercial Code of 1850 could not accommodate the increasing number of cases brought to them, and Europeans did not want to use the şerî courts in view of their restrictions on non-Muslim evidence. There was talk of translating French law into Turkish and applying it in the courts. The ulema objected, ostensibly on the grounds that changing the basic law of a nation would be destructive of that nation and pursuing such a course would not be lawful. The Europeans then suggested that the Ottomans expose their law to view and let the Europeans see it and explain it to their subjects.[40]

The ministers agreed to the suggestion and appointed a commission of Muslim jurists (ulema) to write a book "concerning the transactions section of the science of jurisprudence" (*ilm-i fıkhın muâmelât kısmına dâir*). It was to be written in a simple style of Turkish which everyone could understand and was to be called *Metn-i Metin*.[41] The commission held its first session on November 2, 1855, under the chairmanship of

[38] Lewis, *Emergence*, pp. 107–108.

[39] Chambers, "Ahmed Cevdet Paşa," pp. 85–86.

[40] *Ibid.*, p. 150; Berkes, *Development of Secularism*, pp. 166–167.

[41] Chambers, "Ahmed Cevdet Paşa," p. 151; Berkes, *Development of Secularism*, p. 167.

Rüştü Molla Efendi, a member of the High Council of the Tanzimat (Meclis-i Âli-i Tanzimat) with the rank of *kazasker* (second only to that of Şeyhülislam within the ulema hierarchy). Tahir Efendi, *kadı* of Istanbul, Hüsam Efendi and Ali Ratib Bey, members of the Council of Education (Meclis-i Maarif) with the judicial rank of Istanbul, and Cevdet Efendi were appointed to serve on the commission. These men spent considerable time consulting books on jurisprudence and writing a summary of their subject; but before *Metn-i Metin* was completed, the commission was disbanded.[42]

Cevdet subsequently was appointed to commissions that produced the new Imperial Penal Code of 1858 and the Imperial Land Code of the same year. The former was based principally on French law, but the Land Code was produced by applying Western methods of classification and codification to traditional law collected on a selective basis and adapted to the contemporary situation. Cevdet later published these and other laws and regulations drawn up by the Tanzimat Council in a volume called *Düstur*.[43]

The idea of adopting the French Civil Code had been toyed with since the beginning of the Tanzimat. It was finally set aside in 1868 when Cevdet Paşa was appointed to head a commission for the compilation of a civil code based firmly on the Şeriat. He had been transferred two years earlier from the corps of ulema to the bureaucracy, exchanging his religious rank of kazasker for the secular rank of vezir. In 1868 he was made president of the Council of Judicial Ordinances (Divan-i Ahkâm-i Adliye), successor to the old Supreme Council as the state's highest judicial organ and, in reality, an embryonic Ministry of Justice.[44]

Cevdet's considerable experience, especially his work on the *Metn-i Metin* commission which he considered the direct forerunner of the *Mecelle* commission,[45] was put to good use. Between 1869 and 1876, the commission produced sixteen volumes of the *Mecelle*. This was accomplished despite interruptions and opposition. Şeyhülislam Hasan Fehmi Efendi, who led the opposition, was concerned primarily with the question of jurisdiction. He argued that any such compilation of Holy Law should be a function of his office, not of the secular Ministry of Justice.[46] In April 1870, he man-

42 Chambers, "Ahmed Cevdet Paşa," p. 151.

43 *Ibid.*, pp. 153–154.

44 Berkes, *Development of Secularism*, pp. 166–167; Davison, *Reform*, pp. 240–241, 253–255.

45 Chambers, "Ahmed Cevdet Paşa," p. 151.

46 Berkes, *Development of Secularism*, p. 169.

aged to secure Cevdet's dismissal and to have the *Mecelle* commission transferred to the Fetvahane.[47]

The sixth volume of the *Mecelle*, prepared and published under this new arrangement, evoked such severe criticism that in August 1871 the commission was removed from the Şeyhülislam's charge and Cevdet was reinstated as its chairman. He immediately had all copies of the controversial sixth volume confiscated and destroyed and a completely new volume prepared in its place.[48] Work on the *Mecelle* continued under Cevdet's direction until 1876, but in Abdülhamid II the conservative ulema found an ally. The commission became inactive and was finally dissolved in 1888, having codified only the transactions section of the Holy Law. The very core of the Şeriat, family, marriage, and inheritance laws, was left untouched.[49] The ulema, who had put up hardly more than a token show of resistance until the legal reforms threatened their jurisdiction over the Şeriat, fought the *Mecelle* as they had fought the secular university. In both cases, they won short-lived victories.

The Tanzimat thus produced not an integration of tradition and modernity but a series of dichotomies with ill-defined limits and conflicting interests. There were secular law codes, codified Şeriat and uncodified Şeriat, statutory courts and courts of Holy Law, a Ministry of Justice and the office of the Şeyhülislam. These differentiated legal systems overlapped and contradicted one another at many points, but the sum effect was a dramatic curtailment of the legal jurisdiction of the ulema through successive reinterpretations of what was "religious" and what was "worldly."

Even more damaging to the Muslim religious establishment in the long run was the degeneration of the medreses. Fundamentally out of tune with the times, lacking intellectual vitality and integrity, suffering from the diversion of much of their wealth and many of their most promising men to the "worldly" realm of the state, and unable to compete with the new secular schools, the medreses became impotent citadels of reaction. The rival educated elites produced by the dual school systems seemed incapable of mutual understanding or cooperation. The ulema, still tied to the political system which was dominated by the new elite coming from the secular schools, were not free to pursue an autonomous development and incapable of resisting steady encroachments upon their traditional spheres of influence and activity.

[47] Ali Ölmezoğlu, "Cevdet Paşa," *İslam Ansiklopedisi*, Vol. III (Istanbul, 1945), p. 116.

[48] *Ibid.*

[49] Berkes, *Development of Secularism*, p. 169.

The majority of the ulema shut themselves off from the contemporary world in their medieval medreses and courts of Holy Law. Only the exceptional ones such as Cevdet would admit the inevitability, much less the desirability, of change and attempt to reconcile tradition and modernity by building bridges between the two. The Darülmuallimin and the rüşdiyes are examples of such attempts in the field of educational reform, just as the Land Code of 1858 and the *Mecelle* represent similar efforts in the legal sphere.

But such men were too few and the results of their labors too limited. The dichotomies of the Tanzimat persisted; its inconsistencies and contradictions begged resolution. Disillusioned by the failure of the Tanzimat to find efficacious remedies for the Ottoman Empire's ills and disenchanted by the constitutional trend of the late Tanzimat era, even such men as Cevdet found a congenial refuge in the absolutist, tradition-oriented regime of Abdülhamid II.

The ulema enjoyed one last period of official approbation under this regime which stressed traditionalism, anti-Westernism, and pan-Islamism. But it was the *tarikats* (Sufi orders) and the "men of religion" from outside the ulema ranks—*şerif*s, *seyyids*, *nakib*s, and *amīr*s—who grew and flourished as the chief beneficiaries of Abdülhamid's policies.[50] Even in that reactionary political atmosphere, the ulema were unable to reverse the process of decline and deterioration which began to affect their corps in the eighteenth century and was exacerbated by the reforms of Selim, Mahmud, and the Tanzimat. Compromised by association with the Hamidian despotism, this last of the medieval Ottoman orders clung to an attenuated existence under the Young Turks.

Defeat in World War I, enemy occupation, and dismemberment of the Ottoman Empire were followed by a successful struggle to establish a new Turkish nation state. In the secular republic fashioned by Mustafa Kemal Atatürk, the ulema as an estate with official status and with distinctive dress, ranks, titles, and privileges was abolished along with the caliphate, the medreses, the Şeriat, and the dervish orders. Yet the ulema, the Şeriat, and the dervishes have continued to make their presence felt among the Muslim masses of the Turkish Republic.

50 *Ibid.*, p. 258.

3 The Religious Establishment in Husainid Tunisia*

LEON CARL BROWN

IN THE EARLY DECADES of the nineteenth century Tunisia, like most of the Muslim lands washed by the Mediterranean, possessed a still largely intact traditional Islamic society and polity that were soon to be challenged with increasing intensity by the attraction of European

* This contribution represents a slightly modified version of a chapter in my forthcoming book on Tunisia in the age of Ahmad Bey (1837–1855).

Since this chapter draws so heavily upon the excellent chronicle and biographical dictionary of Ahmad ibn Abi Diyaf (hereafter Bin Diyaf), a few remarks about this remarkable man and his work are in order. Bin Diyaf (1804–1874), the son of an important government scribe, was himself brought into the ranks of the Husainid scribal bureaucracy at an early age in 1827. He was soon promoted to the post of private (or secret) secretary, a position he held under successive beys until his retirement only a short time before his death.

His thorough training in the traditional religious studies and his equally thorough mastery of the customary notions of bureaucratic practice in combination with his access to the inside story of political developments in nineteenth-century Tunisia and his undeniable perceptiveness and intelligence make his work an invaluable historical source. An extra bonus to the later scholar, Bin Diyaf became a partisan of Western-inspired reforms. Bin Diyaf not only reconstructs the story as seen from within. He reveals himself and, through him, the agonies and hopes of his generation and class. A heightened appreciation of the ideological confrontation between traditional Islam and the intruding West necessarily results.

Bin Diyaf's work, *Ithaf Ahl al-Zaman bi Akhbar Tunis wa 'Ahd al-Aman*, has been edited and published in eight volumes by the Tunisian Secretariat of State for Culture and Information (1963–1966). The first six volumes are a history of Tunisia since the Muslim conquest, but Bin Diyaf's account is quite summary until the beginning of the Husainid dynasty (1705). The heart of his great history begins with the Husainids and is especially rich for that long period when he himself was active in government service. The last two volumes contain biographies of leading statesmen and religious figures who died between the years 1783 and 1872. (The sample used for this chapter is confined to the years 1814–1872 in order to give greater weight to Bin Diyaf's firsthand knowledge). Since these biographies are numbered consecutively, the biography number (instead of volume and page number) has been used in the notes. (Biographies 1–196 appear in Volume VII, biographies 197–407 with one appendix in Volume VIII.)

ideas and the threat of European force. The study of Tunisia's response to this intrusive outside force—what an earlier generation of writers referred to as westernization and is today described as modernization or development—can best be understood when related to that already established societal pattern, itself the product of an over twelve-centuries-old connection between Tunisia and Islamic culture. The following pages seek to explain the role of one important group in the Tunisia of this last age before the impact of the West effectively challenged and then finally broke down the venerable traditional Islamic synthesis of state and society. The group to be considered are those who were professionally concerned in several different capacities as spokesmen for Islam. The large body of persons who answered this description might best be labeled "the religious establishment."

The religious establishment was the one group in Husainid Tunisia, aside from the state, whose activities and influence transcended the small units of families, tribes, quarters, and guilds within which most of daily life was circumscribed. Even the state itself played a less comprehensive role in comparison with this establishment, for it chose to remain aloof from society to the extent possible, but the other had roots—and influence—in every part of Tunisia.

Who were the members of the religious establishment and how did they fit into daily life? One can begin to answer these questions by imagining what kind of contacts an average Tunisian might have had with the religious establishment in those days. As a young boy, he attended a kuttab or primary school where, sitting cross-legged on the floor and forming with his fellow students a semicircle around his shaikh, he wrote out Koranic verses on his slate, and by dint of endless repetition committed them to memory.

If he proved to be an apt pupil or his family had the means, he might go on to higher education, study under the ulama at Zitouna mosque in Tunis, or perhaps in equivalent mosque schools in such larger towns as Kairouan or Sfax. If he came from the provinces to study, he would probably live in a madrasa where students were housed and often a certain number of courses given, although the more important courses were usually held in the major mosque. There was a resident director of the madrasa (the shaikh), and occasionally a few other members of the ulama class were housed there as well. (Thus, it was somewhat like the traditional college system of Oxford and Cambridge.) If he continued his studies successfully for many years (eight to twelve, or even more in some cases), he could himself eventually become an alim (pl., ulama) and thereby enter the ranks of the religious establishment. Or, as a literate educated Muslim, he would also have the opportunity to begin his apprenticeship as a government clerk. Few, however, got that far, and the average Muslim's education did not go beyond the kuttab.

At some time in his life, the average Muslim might need to bring some legal matter before a shari'a court presided over by a qadi. It might be a problem of divorce, inheritance, guardianship of an orphan, dispute over property, contracts, or a debt or the desire to establish a trust fund (waqf or habus, gallicized habous); but whatever the issue, he would have to rely on the corps of adls or shahids.[1] Many of these adls or shahids were merely persons recognized by the court as meeting the Islamic requirements for giving testimony (e.g., mature age and an honorable reputation), and these individuals were not necessarily members of the religious establishment as defined here.[2]

A small group, however, had received a higher education, were trained in Islamic law, and in some cases had earned the rank of ulama. They were competent to serve the dual role of lawyer and notary, and in many cases they were able to settle minor legal matters outside the courts. They earned their living in this manner, and can justly be called members of the religious establishment. If the case was at all complex or difficult, it is quite likely that the average Muslim would have solicited the service of one such professional shahid.

The qadi would decide the case but he might prefer to refer a difficult problem to the mufti (jurisconsult) for his opinion. Also, the private Muslim—confused by the applicable Islamic ruling covering some aspect of daily life—might well address himself to the mufti seeking his advisory opinion (fatwa).

On Friday, the average Muslim would attend the mosque service in his village or the quarter of his town and hear the weekly sermon given by the khatib. The khatib was usually also the imam (prayer leader), which is to say he was the principal religious official of the mosque. In the larger mosques there might be several other religious officials as well, such as the mu'adhdhan (muezzin) to give the call to prayer from the minaret, the

[1] Men officially recognized by the court as competent to give testimony (for the shari'a courts accepted only competent oral testimony, not documentary evidence, as proof).

[2] A brief summary of the usual requirements is to be found in the article "shahid," *Shorter Encyclopaedia of Islam* (hereafter *SEI*), ed. H. A. R. Gibb and J. H. Kramers (New York, 1965).

deputy imams. (Zitouna had three regular imams, plus imams for special services such as the imam al-tarawih—the special prayers performed during the night of Ramadan),[3] and the chief of the Koranic reciters, shaikh al-qurra.[4] When there was a death in the family the average Muslim might also hire one of the professional Koranic readers to come to the house and recite portions of the Koran during the period of mourning.

The average Muslim found much of his social life bound up with the religious establishment. Mosques were not only houses of prayer but also places to come for quiet conversation with friends. Even more important as a social center were the many zawiyas (lodges) of the brotherhoods. Brotherhoods were organized around the pious founder always deemed to have been a saint (wali). Many of the more important brotherhoods had been in existence for centuries (like the Qadiriyya and the Shadhiliyya founded in the twelfth and thirteenth centuries, respectively), but new brotherhoods organized around a new charismatic leader were always in process of formation. Two destined to play an important role in the history of Islamic Africa were springing up at that very time, the Tijaniyya in Algeria and the Sanusiyya in what is now Libya. Both, especially the former, had some influence in Tunisia.

There were also scores of zawiyas having only a local influence. To develop into a proper brotherhood the founding zawiya needed to create its own ritual, often bordering on heterodoxy, and establish affiliate zawiyas elsewhere, in which case the shaikh of the parent group (whether the founder or a successor) would authorize a disciple to become the shaikh of the new branch. Many of the local zawiyas never expanded to create other branches or to establish formal rituals and systems for initiating new members. These were not, strictly speaking, brotherhoods at all, but they played a social role similar to the more elaborate brotherhoods. In all instances, large or small, the founder directed the zawiya during his lifetime and then passed on the leadership to his designated heir, almost invariably in the case of the smaller local zawiyas a son or member of the family. Also in all groups, whether new brotherhoods, single zawiya, or those possessing a widespread network of branches, the current leaders were believed to possess baraka (or special powers of intervention with the divine).

[3] See the article "Tarawih," *SEI*.

[4] For example, one Muhammad al-Saffar (d. 1806) held this office while serving also as imam al-tarawih (Bin Diyaf, biography no. 183). Muhammad al-Shatyawi (d. 1833) held jointly the office of chief Koranic reader and shahid of Zitouna mosque's wafq funds (*ibid.*, no. 200).

In the zawiya a man could participate in the religious ceremonies (dhikr) special to each brotherhood, and out of this experience he could establish a sense of intimacy and common bond with a small number of fellow disciples. The zawiya was a mixture of many things—religious society, fraternity, mutual aid association, and club. It was a place where a man buffeted about by seemingly hostile fate, hounded by enemies, creditors, or tax collectors, could achieve a feeling of security, both psychologically and physically—for many of the zawiyas were recognized by the government as asylums, and a fugitive or criminal who sought refuge there would not be molested as long as he stayed within its confines. The rare brotherhood member who traveled could also find friends and lodging for the night by seeking out his brotherhood's zawiya in other towns or villages, even in other countries, for the larger brotherhoods extended all over the Muslim world.

In addition to these several formal functions noted, members of the Tunisian religious establishment, and especially the ulama class, had great prestige and high social standing in several informal ways. The ulama were counselors to the people. Their advice was accepted with due respect or at least not openly flouted. The ulama were deemed models of proper social behavior. Their habits of speech, dress, and behavior were accepted as the ideal especially by the nongovernmental urban classes. For all these reasons they tended—more than any other class—to set the tone for what was considered proper behavior.

Such were the major ways in which the activities of the religious establishment touched upon the daily lives of Tunisians. By comparison with other occupations in Tunisia, governmental or private, the religious establishment loomed large both in its undoubtedly high social standing and in the sheer weight of its numbers. Given the scarcity and unreliability of statistical data it would be hazardous and in itself not very meaningful to risk an estimate of the total number of persons belonging to the religious establishment as defined here, but the following random figures might help to give a general idea.

The city of Tunis had roughly three hundred mosques and two hundred zawiyas.[5] The judiciary in Tunis was composed of two qadis—one Hanafi and one Maliki—and as many as seven muftis—two Hanafi and up to five Maliki. This group plus the qadi of Bardo (the Bey's palace complex located near Tunis) made up the majlis al-shari'i which met with the Bey

[5] Shaikh Muhammad Bayram V, *Ṣafwat al-I'tibar bi-mustawda' al-Amṣār wa al-Aqṭār* (2 vols., Cairo, 1302/1884), I, 122 (hereafter Bayram V).

every Sunday to render justice.[6] There were also certain special judgeships such as the qadi al-farida (specializing in the Islamic law of inheritance),[7] and the qadi bil-mahalla (who, as the name suggests, accompanied the mahalla, the tax-collecting military expedition). There were also nine areas outside the capital, usually major cities or towns, which had their own majlis shari'i with a membership of at least two muftis and a qadi.[8] In addition four places had both a qadi and a mufti.[9] The approximately forty-seven other qaidal districts each had a single qadi.

There seems to have been a recurring problem about an excessive number of shahids or adls authorized to testify before the courts.[10] Early in the reign of Muhammad Bey (1855–1859) there were six hundred shahids in Tunis alone, and the Bey ordered the number reduced to two hundred in Tunis and an appropriate number elsewhere.[11] The reduced number was probably in line with the actual need for shahids, and further it seems reasonable to assume that bona fide members of the religious establishment with appropriate legal training were the last to be cut. Probably not all the remaining two hundred were ulama or even persons having at least a few years of higher education in religious and legal studies. Still, if only fifty of the two hundred fit that category and may thus properly be included within the religious establishment, the number is fairly impressive, and there would be a corresponding number to be found in the provinces.[12]

[6] *Ibid.*, II, 3, and Robert Brunschvig, "Justice religieuse et justice laique dans la Tunisie des Deys et des Beys, jusqu'au milieu du XIXe siècle," *Studia Islamica*, XXIII (1965), 27–70, at pp. 47–48 (citing *Kitāb al-Bāshi*).

[7] See Bin Diyaf, biography no. 103.

[8] These areas were Kairouan, Sousse, Monastir, Sfax al-A'rāḍ, Tozeur, Nefta, Le Kef, and Beja (see Bayram V, II, 124).

[9] Nabeul, Maḥdia, Djerba, and Gafsa (*ibid.*).

[10] The excess of shahids and the political action to reduce the authorized number is a not unfamiliar theme in Islamic history. We are told that Baghdad in 300/913 had 1,800, but in 383/993 their number was cut to 303. See A. Mez, *Renaissance of Islam* (London, 1937), pp. 228–229. Also, in Mamluk Cairo the qadis were regularly ordered to cut down the roster of authorized witnesses (I. Lapidus, *Muslim Cities in the Late Middle Ages* [Cambridge, Mass., 1967], p. 137). Other references and a brief discussion of this subject are to be found in Jeannette Wakin, *Islamic Legal Documents* (State University of New York Press, in press).

[11] Bin Diyaf, IV, 193–194, and VIII, 125. See also Brunschvig, "Justice," pp. 57–58.

[12] Out of the 134 members of the ulama class who figured in Bin Diyaf's biographies for the years 1814–1872, 21 worked at some time in their careers as shahids and 32 (including 10 of the shahids) in tawthiq (other forms of notarial work and public letter-writing). Since Bin Diyaf's biographies include only the most notable ulama and since notarial work was considered a *pis aller* for those ulama who lacked the means

Estimates of the number of members of the religious establishment engaged in education are even more impressive. Bayram V lists the total number of teachers at Zitouna as 102 of which 42 might be considered as composing the regular staff. Bayram's information describes a period long after the reforms and rationalization of Zitouna instituted by Ahmad Bey (1837–1855), but there seems to be no reason for assuming that the total number of teachers had appreciably changed. The student body was composed of approximately 800 students. There were also about fifteen madrasas in Tunis each offering one or two courses, and courses were given in a few other mosques in the city. (As already indicated these madrasas were mainly used to house students enrolled at Zitouna and elsewhere. Such students were not in addition to the 800 listed as studying at Zitouna.)

There were, Bayram adds, about 111 kuttabs (primary schools) with some 3,500 students. (Admittedly, this average of almost 32 students per teacher seems exorbitantly high. Evidence for a later period and from other parts of the Arab world, plus the known dimensions of many surviving rooms known to have served as kuttabs, suggests that the number of students was more likely to range between 5 and 20 at the most.)

Outside Tunis there were few establishments of higher education. Most were concentrated at the venerable religious city, Kairouan, but there were also mosque schools in a few of the larger cities such as Sfax and Sousse. In addition, there might be found "a bit of reading, writing, and jurisprudence (fiqh)" taught in some of the zawiyas spread around the countryside.[13]

As for Koranic schools in the province, Bayram insisted that no village was without its kuttab. He estimated that perhaps twelve thousand students attended primary schools outside Tunis. The latter figure, even if exaggerated, would account for several hundred kuttab teachers throughout the entire country. Not all the kuttab teachers, however, would be automatically included in the religious establishment as defined here. Indeed, the majority should be excluded, for they had little or no higher education and were barely capable themselves of reading and reciting the Koran.[14]

---

to earn their living otherwise (a fact that emerges from occasional statements in the biographies), it seems reasonable to assume that at least 50 members of the religious establishment were earning their living as shahids in Tunis alone at any given time during the first half of the nineteenth century.

[13] The quoted material as well as the educational statistics are from Bayram V, II, 126.

[14] The paragraphs above which attempt to illustrate the size of the religious establishment are not concerned

The religious establishment was large, widespread, and its members engaged in a variety of different tasks; but for all that, and largely as the result of their formal training, it was amazingly cohesive and uniform, possessing an identical body of skills, attitudes, and prejudices. Virtually all its membership had passed through a similar long period of apprenticeship in Islamic higher education, studying the same subjects and usually reading the same texts whether in Tunis, Kairouan, Sfax, Sousse or, for that matter, Fez or Cairo. Admittedly, many of the walis (saints) who founded zawiyas or whose devoted followers later founded zawiyas around their tombs were usually men of very modest education, but often the sons and successive generations (if the zawiya survived and remained in the control of the same family) managed to spend a number of years in higher education and even in some cases to become ulama. (A number of zawiyas in the remoter parts of the beylik seem to have remained for generations in the hands of families with little or no formal education, but their standing in the religious establishment can be compared with that of the less competent kuttab teachers. They both represented the outer fringe, neither fully integrated nor fully accepted.)

I. The Ulama

It was the ulama class who formed the core of the Tunisian religious establishment and served as guardians of the Islamic high cultural tradition. At the same time, the factors making for uniformity and a strong sense of group identity were most markedly in evidence among the ulama. As a group they were characterized by a similarity of class background, continuity from generation to generation with the same families providing recruits to the principal ulama positions, and a decided urban bias.

The biographies included in Bin Diyaf's great work contain several interesting facts about the ulama recorded as having died between the years

---

with that elusive factor, the *quality* of education. This subject is briefly treated below. It might be interesting to record that the celebrated political tract *La Tunisie Martyre* (1920) which had an important formative influence in the establishment of the Destour Party relied largely on Bayram's figures (with some subtle changes) to paint the picture of a pre-Protectorate golden age (pp. 34–37). This is understandable in a political tract, but in fairness to Bayram's reputation as a scholar and accurate observer it should be noted that he saw the kuttabs in a different light. The student, he observed, might remain ten years and still not know how to read and write well. Even the best students got no farther than memorization of the Koran.

1814 and 1872. Before proceeding to a consideration of the ulama class during this period, as reflected in Bin Diyaf's biographies, a few words about methodology and some of the possible weaknesses in this approach are in order.

Bin Diyaf's biographies for these years include 143 persons who can be readily identified as ulama, but 6 of these men died too young to establish themselves in any career (they were included as sons of famous families), and they are excluded from some of the breakdowns in order to avoid unnecessary distortion of the results. Only the ulama are included in this sample. This arrangement creates certain inconsistencies, for a few of the walis or descendants of saintly families are excluded even though they clearly fit into the definition of "religious establishment." The several members of saintly families who received a higher education are included. The other saints are excluded from this sample because those who did not receive the orthodox formal training of the ulama class are not readily comparable with the latter in several of the items being considered. The role of the brotherhoods and the overall importance of mysticism within the religious establishment are considered later.

To forestall any possible misinterpretation it should be emphasized that the separate analysis of mysticism and the brotherhoods on the one hand and the ulama class on the other should not be construed as implying any rigid institutional separation or antipathy dividing the two groups. On the contrary, a careful study of this period in Tunisia (and there is very good reason to assume in other parts of the Muslim world as well) reveals the intimate connections between the brotherhoods and the "orthodox" ulama.

Further, Bin Diyaf's biographies, like all such biographical collections, represent only the leadership; and as a man who spent his entire career in Tunis, Bin Diyaf obviously knew the leading personalities of the capital much better than those of the provinces. If it were possible to include in the sample a representation of middle- and lower-level members of the ulama, the results would surely be different. One can assume that there would probably be a higher percentage of ulama having provincial and/or nonurban origins, there might be appreciably greater social mobility, and quite likely at the bottom of the scale a number of part-time religious careers would be found (e.g., a kuttab teacher, imam, or Koranic teacher who earned part of his livelihood in business or agriculture).

In any event, the findings based on an analysis of Bin Diyaf's biographies may be considered to reflect accurately the situation of the religious *leadership* in the ulama class during these years; and, used cautiously, they should contribute to an understanding of the religious establishment as a whole.

Where did the ulama come from? Where did they receive their higher education, and where did they spend most of their careers? Table 1 presents the findings based on the 105 biographies in which Bin Diyaf provides such information. One point that could have been anticipated is revealed by these figures. The heaviest concentration of ulama leadership was found in Tunis, the political capital, principal religious center, and only large city in the entire country. Obviously, there was little incentive for a member of the ulama class born and educated in Tunis to seek employment elsewhere.

TABLE 1

ULAMA ORIGINS, EDUCATION, AND CAREER LOCATION

	Tunis	*Kairouan*	*Sfax*	*Sousse*	*Monastir*	*Kef*	*Gabes*	*Beja*	*Testour*	*Tabursuq*	*Msakin*	*Manzil Tamin*	*Fez*	*Tribal Origin*	Total
BIRTHPLACE	54	12	11	5	3	4	1	1	1	1	2	3	2	5	105
RECEIVED HIGHER STUDIES IN TUNIS	54	2	4	2	1	4	1	1	1	1	2	3	1	5	82
SPENT ALL OR MOST OF CAREER IN TUNIS	54	1	2	0	0	3	1	1	1	1	2	2	2	4	74

Instead, one would expect the capital to be the lodestar of the aspiring young provincial. Here, however, the results to be derived from Bin Diyaf's biographies are somewhat surprising. Several of the leading provincial ulama received their higher education in their hometowns. This statistic is, of course, especially clear in the case of Kairouan, the only religious center in the country which could claim to rival Tunis, but even provincial cities with less claim to a tradition of higher religious studies—like Sousse, Sfax, or Monastir—educated many of their own religious notables.

Nor did the best of the provincial religious leaders tend to leave their hometowns after being educated to seek a career in Tunis. Of the thirty-one religious figures cited by Bin Diyaf who came from the more important provincial towns of Kairouan, Sfax, Sousse, and Monastir only three made their careers in Tunis.

On the other hand, a very high percentage of those born in the smaller towns or in a tribal environment were educated in Tunis and remained there for their later careers. The man from a small town or tribe who had shown the intellectual capacity and the patience to complete his studies and join the ranks of the ulama must usually have felt, quite understandably, that he could hardly give full scope to his new skills in his home region.

The exception was rare enough to be commented upon. A certain Salih b. Abd al-Jabbar of the Farashish tribe had studied both in Tunis and at al-Azhar in Cairo, but then he returned home for "he enjoyed living among his own tribesmen, mixing with his brothers in the shadow of his own tent, more than being absorbed in the refinement of life in Cairo."[15] As a result, "even the herdsman among his people began to read the Koran." He was clearly a model to be admired but was seldom emulated by those having the opportunity to remain among the "refinements" of Tunis. One can feel reasonably certain that the tribes and small towns were served (if at all) by religious figures having a more modest training and less exposure to a wider world.

In Bin Diyaf's list of ulama biographies almost 50 percent (51 of 105) were born outside Tunis. Given the distortion to be expected from Bin Diyaf's greater familiarity with the ulama of Tunis, this is an imposing provincial representation demonstrating quite clearly that the unifying force of the Islamic high cultural tradition was constantly at work throughout the country.

It is intriguing to speculate why the leading ulama of Kairouan, Sfax, Sousse, and Monastir cited by Bin Diyaf chose to stay at home. The avenue of advancement in Tunis was not closed to them. The statistics from other small provincial towns and the tribes prove that the Tunis religious establishment was always open to an infusion of new blood from outside. Indeed, it was possible to rise from modest provincial origins to a commanding position in the Tunis religious elite in one generation.[16]

In most cases, they probably decided to stay at home for several interrelated reasons. Since they were known in their hometowns advancement

[15] Bin Diyaf, biography no. 115.

[16] The two most striking examples were the celebrated Shaikh Ibrahim al-Riyahi, chief Maliki mufti and imam of Zitouna, who was born in Testour; and the man who assumed most of al-Riyahi's duties after his death, Shaikh Ahmad b. Husayn, born in Le Kef. In fact, Shaikh Ahmad was living in Le Kef when the Bey invited him to succeed Shaikh al-Riyahi following the latter's death (*ibid.*, nos. 74 and 401).

was easier than in Tunis. This implies that ambition could be satisfied at home and such seems to have been the case. These places were urban agglomerations that, in spite of their small populations, were genuine towns instead of villages. Kairouan was the oldest Muslim city in North Africa, and its religious leaders would have felt almost a sense of betrayal in leaving their hometown for anywhere else. Sfax was the leading port and commercial center after Tunis. Also, Sfax, Sousse, and Monastir were all towns servicing the inhabitants of the sahil (Tunisia's eastern coastal plain) which had been for centuries the region with the most durable and cohesive social structure in the entire country.

In these towns an urban tradition and a deeply rooted local pride could combine to induce ambitious local talent to stay at home. Further, the traditional conservatism that characterized all elements of Tunisian society helped to keep in existence these long-established local religious elites as sons followed fathers in the same profession.

This latter point raises an important cluster of questions that deserve separate treatment: How many of the persons in Bin Diyaf's list had fathers who had been members of the religious establishment? How many had sons who followed them in the same careers? Is there any discernible pattern of previous family occupations for those who entered the ulama ranks? What careers were adopted by those who dropped out of the ulama class?

In ninety-six of his biographies of ulama for the time period under examination Bin Diyaf indicated the father's occupation (see table 2).

TABLE 2

MEMBERS OF THE ULAMA CLASS BY FATHER'S OCCUPATION

Origin	*Religious establishment*	*Old family*	*Political*	*Katib*	*Tribal*	*Other*	*Total*
TUNIS	49	5	1	3			58
PROVINCES	15	8	1		3	1[a]	28
NOT SPECIFIED	7	3					10
TOTAL	71	16	2	3	3	1	96

NOTE. The classifications used in tables 2–4 reflect an attempt to exploit, without distortion, the often very general terminology used by Bin Diyaf in his biographies. "Religious establishment" is used as already defined in this chapter. "Old family" includes leading businessmen, tax and concession farmers, and nontribal families with a regional sociopolitical power base (as the Jalulis in Sfax or the Murabits in Kairouan). "Political" refers to those directly involved in civil or military command functions, thus excluding both the katibs (government clerks) and the religious functionaries (e.g., qadis and muftis). "Tribal" indicates pastoralists and transhumants.

[a] Father was a perfumer from Fez.

Seventy-one fathers were themselves members of the religious establishment, mostly ulama. Six of the seventy-one had fathers who were in charge of family zawiyas but who seem not to have had formal religious training equivalent to that of the ulama class.[17]

In fifty-two of Bin Diyaf's biographies of ulama, information is given on what occupation the son(s) followed (see table 3). Forty-five of the sons

TABLE 3

MEMBERS OF THE ULAMA CLASS BY OCCUPATION OF THE SON(S)

Origin	*Religious establishment*	*Katib*	*Political*	*Old family*	*Total*
TUNIS	31	5[a]	1[b]		37
PROVINCES	11			1	12
NOT SPECIFIED	3				3
TOTAL	45	5	1	1	52

[a] In two cases other sons became ulama (see Bin Diyaf, biographies nos. 151 and 350).
[b] The son became shaikh al-madina in Tunis (see *ibid.*, no. 143).

themselves became ulama. There are three instances where *at least* a three-generational continuity (grandfather-father-son) of ulama may be noted, and only three cases noted where a son whose father and grandfather had been ulama adopted another profession (see table 4). The latter group all became katibs (government clerks) and in one of the three cases other siblings became ulama.

TABLE 4

OCCUPATIONS OF THE SONS OF ULAMA WHOSE FATHERS WERE ALSO ULAMA[a]

Origin	*Religious establishment*	*Katib*	*Total*
TUNIS	25	3	28
PROVINCES	5		5
NOT SPECIFIED	2		2
TOTAL	32	3	34

[a] I.e., Third generation ulama.

This marked conversatism and continuity in choice of family occupation held true for both Tunis and the provinces. Tables 2–4 serve to clarify these findings. Although it cannot be claimed that the figures in tables

[17] Three of the six were from the same family, al-Bahi. Of the remaining three one each was from Tlili, Azuz, and Bin Maluka religious families (*ibid.*, nos. 161, 211, 231, 353, 288, and 337).

2–4 present a representative sample or a scientifically controlled random sample[18] it is interesting to convert them into percentages (see tables 5–7; figures do not always add up to 100 because of rounding).

The wide difference between Tunis and the provinces in the number of ulama whose fathers were also in the religious establishment (84 prcent and 54 percent, respectively) may be more apparent than real (see table 5). Bin Diyaf probably had less firsthand knowledge about the families

TABLE 5
MEMBERS OF THE ULAMA CLASS BY FATHER'S OCCUPATION
(In percentages)

Origin	*Religious establishment*	*Old family*	*Political*	*Katib*	*Tribal*	*Other*
TUNIS	84	9	2	5		
PROVINCES	54	29	4		11	4
NOT SPECIFIED	70	30				
ALL TUNISIA	74	17	2	3	3	1

of provincial ulama, and the large proportion of provincial ulama listed as springing from "old families" with no further details given (29 percent as opposed to only 9 percent in Tunis) may well include many whose fathers were themselves members of the religious establishment.[19] The information in table 6 supports this interpretation. The sons of the provincial ulama would usually have been actively embarked on their own careers at the time Bin Diyaf was writing, and thus better known to him. The percentage of sons of ulama following their father's profession is even higher for those with roots in the provinces than those long established in Tunis (92 percent to 84 percent [see table 6]).

TABLE 6
MEMBERS OF THE ULAMA CLASS BY OCCUPATION OF THE SON(S)
(In percentages)

Origin	*Religious establishment*	*Katib*	*Political*	*Old family*
TUNIS	84	14	3	
PROVINCES	92			8
NOT SPECIFIED	100			
ALL TUNISIA	87	10	2	2

[18] The figures are based on (1) information given explicity by Bin Diyaf, supplemented by (2) what can reasonably be inferred from the context, and (3) other sources, especially Shaikh Muhammad Naifur, *'Unwān al-Arīb*.

[19] Of the eight provincial ulama whose fathers' occupations are ob-

TABLE 7

Occupation of the Sons of Ulama Whose Fathers Were Also Ulama[a]
(In percentages)

Origin	*Religious establishment*	*Katib*
TUNIS	89	11
PROVINCES	100	
NOT SPECIFIED	100	
ALL TUNISIA	91	9

[a] I.e., Third generation ulama.

In any case, the dominant position of the two categories—religious establishment and old family—as the normal occupation of both ancestors and descendants of ulama is striking for both Tunis and the provinces. Indeed, the family's previously established high social standing is attested to in almost every case where Bin Diyaf offers any information on the family background. The movement from katib to alim (or vice versa) entailed, other things being equal, only a slight change in social prestige usually in favor of the latter. It was more nearly a lateral movement within the same social class.

The two Tunis ulama whose fathers had been in "political" careers could hardly be described as social parvenus either. One boasted a grandfather who had been a major military figure in the service of Ali Pasha (reigned 1735–1756).[20] The other sprang from a notable family of Le Kef long noted for its political service, and it was with him that the "family moved from political to religious leadership."[21]

This leaves only the three ulama of tribal origin unaccounted for (aside from the alim whose father had been a perfumer in Fez, but it might be observed that this occupation was traditionally one of some social standing). These three, including the celebrated Shaikh Ibrahim al-Riyahi, appear to be the only examples within this sample of parvenus.[22]

scured in the vague category of "old family" four were from Kairouan, two from Sfax, and one each from Sousse and Monastir (*ibid.*, nos. 130, 178, 229, 333, 125, 189, 195, and 113 respectively).

[20] Ali al-Tamimi (*ibid.*, no. 298).

[21] Ahmad b. Husain (*ibid.*, no. 401). A more literal translation would refer to a change from "customary" (urfiyya) to "shari'a" leadership, but the general sense is better conveyed in the translation given. For a general treatment of the interrelationship between non-Islamic, customary matters, and canonical shari'a rules in Islamic theory and practice see the article "'Urf" in *Encyclopaedia of Islam*, 1st ed.

[22] According to his son's biography, al-Riyahi's grandfather had been a Koranic teacher among the Riyah tribesmen. His father, whose occupation is not mentioned, had moved to

The above information suggests that the ulama class—or at least its upper ranks—may not have offered too many opportunities for upward social mobility. The point is sufficiently important to warrant further examination even though it must be in large measure speculation based on fragmentary data.

It must be remembered that Bin Diyaf does not give information identifying the family background or place of origin in all his biographies; and it may properly be assumed that in many cases a discreet silence on the matter indicates that the alim in question came from humble stock. (For a cultured Muslim such as Bin Diyaf in Tunisia of that period it would have been unseemly to call attention to a man's modest origin just as it would have been unthinkable not to have mentioned a creditable family background.)

An attempt to estimate the percentage of those born in Tunis who advanced socially by becoming ulama might offer the best opportunity for relative precision, for Bin Diyaf would have known the family background of those born and living in Tunis. It has already been seen that Bin Diyaf provided information on the family background of fifty-eight ulama born in Tunis, and all of them represented a previously established high social position:

Fathers were ulama	48
Old family	6
Fathers were katibs	3
Fathers in political career	1
Total	58

There are only four other ulama for the time period covered who are known or can reasonably be assumed to have been born in Tunis. It is quite likely that none of the four came from families of any previous social standing, although in one case Bin Diyaf refers to the man following

Testour where Ibrahim al-Riyahi was born in 1180. See 'Umar al-Riyahi, *Ta'-Ṭīr al-Nawaḥī by-Tarjamat al-Shaikh Sidi Ibrāhīm al-Riyāḥi* (2 vols.; Tunis, 1320/1902–1903), Vol. I. There is also no mention of al-Riyahi's father in Bin Diyaf (biography no. 74) nor in Shaikh Muhammad al-Naifur, *'Unwān al-Arīb 'amma Nasha'a bil-mamlaka al-Tūnisiyya min 'ālim adīb* (2 vols.; Tunis, 1351/1932–1933), II, 90–97. Salih Bin Abd al-Jabbar was the tribesman from the Farahish who has already been mentioned as having studied in Tunis and al-Azhar before returning to teach in his own tribe. Nothing seems to be known of his father. Had he been a tribal shaikh, Bin Diyaf would almost certainly have mentioned it (see *ibid.*, no. 115). Ahmad al-'Awadi was a tribesman of modest background from the Constantine (Algeria) area (*ibid.*, no. 173).

a good pious life "in accordance with the tradition of his family"[23] and another of the four may well have been the son of a minor saintly figure.[24] Another of the four named Smith (al-Haddad) became something of an expert on the histories of important Tunis families.[25] Quite possibly here was a man assiduously applying himself (whether consciously or not is immaterial) to the task of integrating himself and his descendants into the Tunis elite by showing an appropriate appreciation of its traditions.

In addition to these four there are a total of twelve ulama about whom no information is given concerning their place of origin or family background. Assuming the two extreme possibilities that none or all of this group were from Tunis, one would then arrive at the following: Between 6 percent and 22 percent of the ulama listed in Bin Diyaf's biographies who were born in Tunis during the time period studied seem to have appreciably bettered their social position by becoming ulama.[26]

Probably some point in between the two extremes is closest to the truth and one might advance the estimate, with all due reservations, that perhaps one man in seven from among the ulama born in Tunis was an example of upward social mobility via the religious establishment. For the lesser members of the ulama class in Tunis and for the provinces in general, it may be assumed that the percentage of upward social mobility would not have been less and was more likely considerably greater. By modern standards, this infusion of new blood might be considered very low, but for so traditional a society as Husaynid Tunisia, it is not an unimpressive figure.

Even granting a healthy margin of error for such crude estimates, the ulama class still appears as the institution in Husainid Tunisia offering the greatest opportunity for both geographical and social mobility to the largest number of Tunisians. In its recruitment of new members just as in its social role, the ulama class played a well-nigh unique role of both leaven and cement for Tunisian society.

The entrenched ulama seem to have permitted without mental reservation competent newcomers to join their ranks. There is no indication of old religious families showing prejudice against a newcomer qua newcomer or attempting to block his advancement. The major difficulty was

[23] Shaikh Muhammad 'Abbas (see *ibid.*, no. 309).

[24] At least the name so implies—Ali b. Yusuf al-Darwish al-Hanafi (see *ibid.*, no. 272).

[25] *Ibid.*, no. 318.

[26] That is, either a total of 62 (58 plus 4) or 74 (58 plus 16) from which in either case 58 can be accounted for as having come from families already well established socially.

that the newcomer as a relative unknown needed to catch someone's eye. He required a patron or a sponsor. Shaikh Ibrahim al-Riyahi, for example, considered emigrating to another country because he was not earning a decent living as a teacher, and only the timely intervention of the minister Yusuf Sahib al-Tabi insured that al-Riyahi's talents would remain in the service of Tunisia.[27]

If it sometimes took a bit of luck in addition to talent to enter the upper ranks of the ulama, there can be no doubt that, once established, a man or his descendants—if they chose to follow the same profession—could easily remain in good standing. Bin Diyaf's repeated references to the son's "following in the father's footsteps" or to "perpetuating his name" underscore the continuity of professions within the same family; and the almost invariable pattern of praiseworthy descendants of ulama, which seems to defy experience or common sense for any society, can best be explained as reflecting Tunisian society's implicit assumption—the son of an alim who followed in the same profession inherited his father's social standing.

For example, the son of an old religious family in Sousse who received only "a bit of learning" nevertheless became mufti in his hometown. His son also became an alim.[28] Only certain egregious acts sufficed to remove the favorable prejudice with which a man born into the religious establishment began his career, but the descendant of even the oldest religious family could lose this inherited prestige.

Perhaps the most striking case was Abu al-Ghaith al-Bakri, descendant of the family that had provided the principal imam of Zitouna Mosque in unbroken succession for over 190 years.[29] His father, who had been poorly qualified for this lofty position, was the last of the family to be appointed imam, but the son might still have managed to maintain or even recoup the declining family prestige. Instead, "lacking anyone to admonish and raise him" after the death of his father, he decided to go into governmental (makhzan) concession farming.[30]

Even worse, he sold habous properties attached to the Bakri family zawiya, thus accelerating both the social and economic decline of that once famous zawiya. It was the custom for government ministers to rise in honor of the zawiya shaikhs but when this unfortunate man appeared

[27] *Ibid.*, no. 74.

[28] Abdullah al-Hidda (see *ibid.*, no. 320).

[29] *Ibid.*, no. 71.

[30] *Ibid.*, no. 138. He assumed the concession farm of the ulfa and the ghaba (provision of fodder and olives).

before Larbi Zarruq, the latter remained seated while observing, "We used to rise to greet you out of respect for your ancestors, but since you were not satisfied to follow in their way preferring instead governmental positions you must become as other men of government acting as they do without any other distinction."[31]

Muhammad al-Kawwash, son of the famous Salih al-Kawwash, offers another example. Bin Diyaf deplored that "as with certain sons of the distinguished he wanted to be at once as great as his father,"[32] which was not possible. There seems to have been more to the story than Bin Diyaf cared to relate, for at some time after the death of his father, Muhammad al-Kawwash was even stripped of his adala (i.e., he could not give testimony in court or carry out other functions of the adl).

He was later restored to the adala and thus had the opportunity to earn a living in the following way: When the celebrated minister Yusuf Sahib al-Tabi finished building his mosque in the Halfawin area of Tunis, he chose the then quite young Muhammad Bayram III as khatib, but the latter's father, Bayram II, protested that the appointment was not fitting as long as "the son of Salih Kawwash" remained stripped of the adala that he lived on. Whereupon Yusuf Sahib al-Tabi caused Muhammad al-Kawwash to be returned to the ranks of adls.[33]

Apparently, everything possible was done to aid "the son of Salih al-Kawwash." Even his father's former students helped out financially, but to no avail. Surviving documents reveal him as tenaciously remaining in the house reserved for the shaikh of the al-Muntasariyya mosque (the post long held by his father) despite the pressure on him to move exerted by the new appointee.[34] The unfortunate man died of the plague at a relatively early age in 1232/1816–17.

The poor fate reserved for Abu al-Ghaith al-Bakri and Muhammad al-Kawwash proved to be quite exceptional. Normally the sons stayed in the same profession and the entrenched family position seemed to be a more important consideration than the variations of talents which one can expect to distinguish the several generations of any family. This is not to deny that there was always room for new blood in the ulama class. Indeed, there was always room at the top, but the continued importance of such families as Bayram, Barudi, Mahjub, and al-Rassa offered the more dominant pattern of family continuity, a condition that probably

[31] *Ibid.*
[32] *Ibid.*, no. 94.
[33] al-Naifur, *'Unwān al-Arīb*, II, 69–70.
[34] *Ibid.*

prevailed both down the ranks of the ulama and out from Tunis into the major provincial centers.

What were some of the dominant group values and mores of the ulama in Husainid Tunisia? Undoubtedly, they placed a great value upon strict observance of the traditionally established behavior patterns. An alim was, of course, expected to live an exemplary life in conformity with the precepts of Islam and thus free of any breath of scandal, but this was only the beginning.

He should affect a certain gravity at all times, avoid the popular cafes, and not let himself be seen in public laughing, speaking in a loud voice, or eating. In his speech he was expected not only to avoid the trivial and the evanescent in favor of weightier matters but also to adopt a more formal, classical Arabic than that used by the man in the street.

The ideal alim could adorn his discussion with appropriate citations from the Koran, hadith, and the principal religious authorities. The ability to turn a phrase was highly valued, and the alim who could write poetry and was familiar with the secular Arabic literature earned additional esteem.

An elaborate code of politesse governed his daily contact with others and with his fellow ulama. Among the factors that contributed to the informal hierarchy of precedence among the ulama were respect for sharifs, venerable families, age in general, and for one's former teachers. Failure to observe the last rule caused quite a flutter in the ulama dovecotes in 1836.

A qadi, one Muhammad al-Bahri, was overruled in a legal point by his former teacher, Shaikh Ibrahim al-Riyahi. The qadi insisted on presenting his argument before the Bey and the majlis al-shari'i. When he went so far as to demand the Bey's permission to read certain citations supporting his argument, al-Riyahi could stand no more, retorted, "Stop! Impudent person," and insisted on resigning. Only with difficulty were the Bey and others eventually able to soothe al-Riyahi's ruffled feelings.[35]

Questions of precedence and offended dignity could easily arise. When Muhammad al-Shadhili al-Muaddib, then Third Imam of Zitouna, was appointed mufti, he refused to walk behind the Second Imam, Mahmud Muhsin. With the help of several mediators, the dispute was amicably settled "as usually happens among the distinguished."[36] Custom was

[35] Bin Diyaf, III, 214–216, and Brunschvig, "Justice," p. 58.

[36] Bin Diyaf, nos. 372 and 384.

upheld. The order of precedence of the three Zitouna imams was not to be related to the other positions the incumbents might hold, but Shaikh Mahmud Muhsin graciously agreed not to walk ahead of al-Muaddib.

Another incident involved the haughty behavior of Shaikh Muhammad b. Salama. He did not bother to invite all members of the majlis al-shari'i, as custom and courtesy required, to hear his final lecture in a special series of lectures at Zitouna. As a result, the meeting was boycotted by the ulama, and Shaikh Muhammad became even more incensed when the Bey refused to intervene. Relations between Shaikh Muhammad and his colleagues remained tense until they all happened to be gathered at the funeral of Shaikh Ibrahim al-Riyahi's son. There Shaikh Muhammad told the assembled mourners that he and his fellow ulama as men devoted to religious knowledge were expected to show brotherhood and forgiveness. "I bear witness to God that I forgive all of you," he added, and asked that they do the same for him. This gesture was highly appreciated by the ulama and good relations were immediately restored.[37]

As in any comparable institution there were many personal rivalries and considerations of amour propre, but the ideal man of religion was expected to rise above such things. It was especially commendable to acknowledge a mistake and accept being overruled (a difficult step to take as the incident concerning Ibrahim al-Riyahi suggests). Bin Diyaf praises the mufti Husain al-Barudi who was willing to reverse a decision already made after being shown it was wrong.[38]

Muhammad Za'fran, qadi of Monastir, realized the error in one of his judgments fully two years later and reversed himself. The man affected by the change then took his case to the majlis al-shari'i meeting in the presence of the Bey, but the majlis upheld the qadi and praised him for preferring the right over "personal considerations."[39]

Always acting as a counterweight to pretension and pride of place among the ulama was that basic principle of Sunni Islam which posited the equality of all believers before God. The most educated alim felt obliged to respect the pious asceticism of the unlearned man and was prepared to believe that God, in His wisdom, inspired the acts of the majdhub[40] wali. Even among the ulama themselves there was a point

[37] *Ibid.*, no. 296.
[38] *Ibid.*, no. 297.
[39] *Ibid.*, no. 114.
[40] Majdhub, possessed; the customary term used to describe those whose aberrant behavior is interpreted as a sign of holiness or a special relationship with the Divine.

beyond which the usual considerations of family, education, and native ability seemed insignificant. Shaikh Muhammad Mzali, in an argument with the qadi of Monastir, Shaikh Hasan al-Khairi, asked "Whom did you study under?" apparently in a not too subtle gesture of belittling the man's formal training. Shaikh al-Hasan retorted, citing the Koran, "Fear God and He will teach you." Mzali, to his credit, admired this response and praised the qadi.[41]

The ulama class was the one group that could be considered as representing the conscience of the community, but as a general rule they were extremely circumspect in the specific actions they took in fulfillment of this lofty role. Their cautious relations with government are considered separately below, but even in their dealings with private individuals the ulama were more likely to convey their approval or disapproval by a subtle gesture, a veiled reference in a sermon or an avoidance of further contact with the transgressor. It was the rare alim who took individual action beyond what was strictly required of him in his official capacity to right public or private wrongs. The exceptions to this unwritten rule of prudence were noted with approval—the venerable Islamic principle to "command the good and proscribe the evil" never lost its force as an ideal—but the few incidents of this kind cited by Bin Diyaf and the general context in which they took place leave no doubt that the chronicler is describing the seldom-to-be-attained ideal, not the norm.

For example, when Shaikh Muhammad al-Mana'i saw a crowd dragging the body of the assassinated minister Yusuf Sahib al-Tabi through the streets he grabbed his sword and rushed out to stop them. Only the forcible intervention of his neighbors, fearful for his safety, held him back.[42] Al-Mana'i was of tribal origin (Drid), however, and his response may well be interpreted as that of a tribesman rather than a long-urbanized member of the ulama class.

Shaikh Hasan al-Sharif[43] also reacted bravely and decisively when presented with a crisis. A woman whom a Turkish soldier was forcibly carrying through the street clutched pleadingly at the shaikh's arm. He immediately intervened, and when insulted by the soldier, Shaikh Hasan took him to the Dey accompanied by the perfumers from the Suq al-'Attarin (where the incident took place) who wanted to insure the shaikh's safety. Presenting himself before the Dey, he insisted that the soldier be held in

[41] *Ibid.*, no. 113.

[42] *Ibid.*, no. 194.

[43] Whose appointment as imam of Zitouna brought to an end the Bakri family's long monopoly of this post. See above p. 64.

prison until the Bey himself was informed. Hamuda Bey ordered the soldier to be executed that very day.[44]

The same Shaikh Hasan al-Sharif was accosted once by a female slave who claimed to have been mistreated and asked him to intercede with her master so he might agree to sell her. The shaikh insisted on being taken at once to the man's house in Bab Suwayqa, reputed to be the tougher, lower-class suburb of Tunis. (The master was himself a "nobody"[45] not known for his wealth. This single shred of evidence offers a suggestive insight to the pattern of slaveholding at that time.) The master upon seeing Shaikh Hasan al-Sharif before his own house took fright and cried out, "Oh Sidi, if you had sent for me I would have come to you," and freed his slave on the spot.[46]

These were the exceptional cases. Normally the ulama were content merely to set a good example. The story told of Bayram II depicts the classic exemplar. His barber, long accustomed to a stony silence on the part of his customer, was pleasantly surprised when one day Bayram II greeted him cheerfully and asked about his family. When the barber asked why the sudden change, Bayram II replied that he had now resigned his post as qadi. While he was qadi it would not have been seemly for him to have "contacts with people." This might have jeopardized his impartiality, but now he was free to resume his regular social relationships.[47]

The ulama expressed the conscience of the community in muted terms and along conservative lines, but when they spoke it was with more than the voice of blind traditionalism. There was a certain flexibility in their

44 *Ibid.*, no. 71. This forcible abduction of a female in broad daylight which Shaikh Hasan thwarted, unusual enough for any settled urban environment, is jarringly out of line with what one would expect in a traditional city such as Tunis. Obviously an extreme example, the incident suggests at the same time the wide gulf separating the ethnically distinct military from the native society of Tunis.

45 Min 'aamat al-naas.

46 *Ibid.*, no. 72. Shaikh Muhammad al-Bahri bin Abd al-Sattar also freed a female slave who came with physical proof that she had been beaten by her master, but he—as a qadi holding court—was acting in a more customary manner (see *ibid.*, no. 234). These two references leave the larger issue of slavery and the law at that time tantalizingly vague. Since Bin Diyaf found these two incidents noteworthy, can it be assumed that slaves rarely made such appeals to the courts or that courts rarely decided in favor of the slaves? A careful sifting of the available evidence plus a diligent search for hitherto unexploited material could certainly produce an excellent monograph on this important but largely neglected subject. On the general subject of slavery in Islam see the excellent article by Robert Brunschvig, " 'Abd" in *Encyclopaedia of Islam*, 2d ed., with several references to Tunisia.

47 The story is cited in the biography of his brother, Mustafa Bayram (see Bin Diyaf, no. 404).

stand. Tactically, this flexibility saved them from confrontation (and possible defeat) with political authority or public opinion, but another consideration probably motivated them as well. The challenge of being able to find a plausible loophole or of treating a case according to different principles leading to a quite different judgment was ever present among trained Islamic juridical scholars in Husainid Tunisia as elsewhere.[48] The result could often be a juxtaposition—confusing to the modern mind accustomed to positive law enacted by the political sovereign—of rigorously applied general principle and practical expediency, or of apparently inescapable judgments accompanied by a not always logically consistent escape clause.

In the plague of 1783, Hamuda Bey ordered the clothing and effects of those who died of the disease to be burned, but the mufti, responding to the hue and cry of those affected, claimed that this was unlawful. Man, he argued, should submit to God's will. In any case, he continued, if it were deemed medically advisable the heirs who were deprived (including widows and orphans) were entitled to compensation. When the clamor continued against the measure, Hamuda backed down.[49]

What was the relative prestige accorded the several different kinds of positions an alim was qualified to fill? The muftis and the leading qadis clearly rated high on the social scale, but there was nevertheless a certain lingering suspicion about such positions whose incumbents were beholden to government and obliged to concur in, or at least overlook, its actions which violated the shari'a.

At the other end of the social scale were those for whom Bin Diyaf often felt compelled to offer an explanation—the ulama who became notaries

[48] As has often been observed, it is in this loving regard for the intricacies of "the Law" that Islam and Judaism are so similar, and at the same time so readily distinguishable from the Christian tradition.

[49] Bin Diyaf, II, 14–15. Here, indeed, one discerns more than blind traditionalism in the face of a modern public health measure. The mufti was willing to accept the measure provided those affected should receive just compensation for any loss sustained by state action aiming to advance the public good. Nothing could be more "modern" than this legal principle. It might even be argued that the Husainid state structure—with no mechanism for such compensation—was more archaic than the body of Islamic law defended by the qadi. One would like to have fuller information on such seemingly banal incidents. Did the mufti really think the burning was prohibited by Islamic law and mention compensation merely to avoid an overly abrupt confrontation with political authority? What exactly provoked him to take a stand on this issue? To what extent did public opinion play a role?

or went into business for a time. Economic circumstances obliged them. Otherwise, Bin Diyaf strongly implies, they would have preferred to remain in teaching or some other "purer" religious calling.[50]

Higher education seemed to offer the best opportunity for complete devotion to religious studies without distraction from either the world of business or government, but there were other drawbacks in teaching. It was not especially remunerative. It has already been noted that Ibrahim al-Riyahi had almost decided to emigrate, despairing of ever being able to earn an adequate salary as a teacher.[51] Shaikh Ahmad Zaruq al-Kafi taught for a time but then became a shahid in order to earn a living.[52] Even the celebrated and beloved teacher Hasan al-Sharif became a teacher almost by accident—only after the chief katib (scribe) who was jealous of him spread false stories which caused him to lose his job as katib.[53]

Also, against the handful of excellent teachers who were accorded the highest esteem was a much larger body of lesser lights whose native talents were hardly adequate to overcome the baleful effect of a jejune system of rote learning. The system, common to higher education throughout the Sunni Islamic world until quite recent times, has been often described and deplored, but perhaps the stifling dullness of the system can best be sensed by reference to the pedagogical technique of one man who dared to be different, the famous Shaikh Hasan al-Sharif.

"He used to joke with his students during the lessons lest they become bored. If one of his students asked a question, he would pay attention to him and then, repeating what has been asked in a clearer fashion, ask his students, 'Can any of you think of the answer?' If one of them answered, he would again listen to him carefully and then repeat the answer as well. This was done to train his students in discussion while taking delight in their excellent qualities. If one of the students deviated from the rules of polite scholarship, he would interrupt the discussion, answer the student and then return to his lectures."

Creditable but hardly noteworthy, the modern reader might be inclined to say, but it is illuminating to see how Shaikh Hasan al-Sharif's own peers reacted at that time. "Some of his colleagues reproached him that such ways were not appropriate to the dignity of shaikhs, but he answered,

[50] See, for example, Bin Diyaf, nos. 156, 322, 355, 393, 214, 380, and 384.

[51] See above, p. 64.

[52] *Ibid.*, no. 187; al-Naifur, *'Unwān al-Arīb*, II, 83.

[53] Bin Diyaf, no. 72 and al-Naifur, *'Unwān al-Arīb*, II, 73.

'You take pleasure in cockfights. I enjoy battles among men using their intellects as swords.' "[54]

In another sense, any attempt to determine the relative prestige of the different positions open to ulama is condemned to at least partial failure. The effort to establish so neat a scale reflects the values of a different age and another culture. The leading members of the religious establishment in Husainid Tunisia were those who held, or were given the opportunity to hold if they so chose, several leading posts at the same time—teachers, muftis, imams, or qadis. Then, they could vary the emphasis they cared to place on one or the other aspect of their multiform careers according to their own interests.

Next down the scale were those who although given fewer choices were still able to devote full time to teaching, preaching, or the law. Then came those who, passed over for the leading positions, earned their living as notaries, lawyers, habous administrators, functionaries in lesser mosques, and teachers in the less imposing madrases.

Beyond this point one moves outside the religious establishment as here defined—meeting, on the one hand, those who although trained in religion had ceased to be members of the establishment as a result of entering business or the clerkly profession and, on the other, the lower ranks of teachers in the elementary schools, minor mosque functionaries, and religious administrators who, lacking the complete ulama training, never fully belonged.

Even in this less orderly picture of social ranking, one must leave room for considerable change and mobility. A certain Muhammad al-Qabaili abandoned teaching to enter business. Later, he was appointed to the prestigious post of mufti by Ahmad Bey.[55]

The Ulama and Government

The precise relationship between government and the ulama in the world of Sunni Islam remains a matter of some controversy among scholars. Certain scholars have been impressed by the similar training and sense of

[54] Bin Diyaf, no. 72. Even if he could not convince his colleagues Shaikh Hasan al-Sharif was in accord with an eminent predecessor among Tunisian scholars, Ibn Khaldun, who observed, "The easiest method of acquiring the scientific habit is through acquiring the ability to express oneself clearly in discussing and disputing scientific problems. . . . Some students spend most of their lives attending scholarly sessions. Still, one finds them silent. They do not talk and do not discuss matters. More than is necessary, they are concerned with memorizing" (*The Muqaddimah*, trans. F. Rosenthal. Bollingen Series [New York, 1958], II, 429).

[55] Bin Diyaf, no. 322.

corporate identity which bound together the ulama. They have noted a major theme to be found in the biographical literature of saints and scholars—the pious man of God standing up to the corrupt governor and obliging him to change his ways. As a result, this school of thought, without overlooking the formal ties between government and the ulama, has emphasized the latter's role as a mediating agency between government and people. Other scholars, especially those engaged in the complex task of discovering how Ottoman government actually worked, have emphasized the broad governmental functions fulfilled by the religiously trained. Some in this latter school would even question the validity, or usefulness, of presenting the matter in terms of a religious group separate from government.

Most scholars on both sides would agree that little progress can be made in resolving the issue until more circumscribed studies of the religiously trained and their relations with government for specified times and places are forthcoming. The following is a brief interpretation of what seems to have been the situation in Husainid Tunisia in the early decades of the nineteenth century. Given the shared legacy of political and religious institutions it would be surprising if the Tunisian pattern did not offer many similarities with other parts of the Ottoman Empire. This was probably especially true in Arabic-speaking portions of the Empire where a native, Arabic-speaking religious elite was in a position to assert its separateness and relative independence from the government.

Also, one might expect the similarities to be more striking between Tunisia and other autonomous or semiautonomous parts of the Empire as Egypt, Tripolitania (until 1835), and Algeria (until 1830). The work done to date on Egypt[56] suggests that government-ulama relations were sufficiently comparable with those in Tunisia for one to speak of a single generic pattern, although the timing of changes in the modern era was often different. For example, the great change began with the French occupation in 1798 and the subsequent rise to power of Muhammad Ali in 1805. It would be completely unwarranted, however, to assume a single Sunni Muslim pattern of government-ulama relations (or even a single Ottoman pattern) and then use isolated evidence from scattered times and places to document the a priori assumption.

The ulama in Husainid Tunisia had a strong sense of their own cor-

[56] See, for example, Afaf Loutfi el-Sayed, "The Role of the 'Ulama in Egypt during the Early 19th Century," in Peter M. Holt, ed., *Political and Social Change in Modern Egypt* (London, 1968).

porate identity separating them from government and, for that matter, from other elements of Tunisian society. The religiously trained did not become government ministers or a fortiori military leaders, nor did their sons aspire to enter these professions. Nor was there a flow in the other direction from political to religious careers. The few exceptions to be found in Bin Diyaf's biographies are listed in a manner that makes it quite clear that they were exceptions. To move to and from an ulama position and clerkly profession was not really an exception but only a broader extension of careers open to the religiously trained. To speak of an ulama class in Tunisia at this time is not only a useful way to divide up Tunisian society for purposes of analysis. The ulama class was a living reality.

Although possessing a sense of separate identity, the ulama were closely tied to government. The Bey not only had the formal authority to appoint and dismiss muftis, qadis, madrasa shaikhs, imams, and even, for that matter, shaikhs of zawiyas. He actively intervened in the exercise of this authority. Since government did not usually care to concern itself with such details the ulama exercised a relatively broad de facto autonomy, but it could be disrupted at even the most insignificant level if the Bey or one of his subordinates chose to act.[57]

The ulama carefully avoided conflict with the government and the government with somewhat less care adopted the same position. When a dispute did flare up between an alim and the government, the matter was almost invariably resolved by the alim's withdrawal or dismissal. At other times, the government would arbitrarily intervene to dismiss or even imprison a religious functionary. In no such case did the ulama as a group, or any appreciable number, offer resistance, active or passive, to governmental authority.[58] They might advise, cajole, serve as intermediaries, or

[57] On the general subject of the courts the reader's attention is directed to the excellent article, already cited several times, by Robert Brunschvig, "Justice religieuse et justice laique dans la Tunisie des Deys et des Beys, jusqu'au milieu de XIX siecle," pp. 27–70.

[58] The customary apolitical stance of the ulama seems to have saved them at times from the suspicion of plotting against the government in circumstances that could otherwise have proved embarrassing. For example, the Turkish soldiers who attempted a coup d'etat against Mahmud Bey in 1816 rounded up the majlis al-shari'i and forced its members to draft and then sign a document replacing the ruling Bey by his brother, Ismail. (This proved an unfortunate choice for those in revolt. Ismail refused to turn against his brother.) The abortive coup was soon suppressed, but at no time either during or after the incident did the Bey or his entourage show any suspicion concerning the conduct of the majlis al-shari'i. Also, aside from making it clear that they would use force if necessary, the Turkish soldiers in revolt

withdraw from governmental affairs to show their disapproval. An especially bold alim might even make cautiously elliptical allusions in a sermon to governmental actions he disapproved.[59] These were the limits of confrontation. These were nothing comparable with the major *institutional* conflicts that pitted church against state in Europe.

Such were the general principles governing relations between government and the ulama in Husainid Tunisia. Reference to a few specific examples may help to clarify just how things worked in practice. There are several known cases of the Bey's arbitrarily dismissing high religious functionaries. In 1814, soon after the assassination of Uthman Bey, Shaikh Muhammad b. Bakir was removed as imam of a small mosque (Masjid bayt al-basha) since he had been close to Uthman Bey. Shaikh Ali al-Darwish took his place.[60]

Some fifty years later Muhammad al-Sadiq Bey dismissed Shaikh Mahmud al-Ubbay from his post as imam of Sahib al-Tabi mosque (which had been held by his father before him) because he concluded the Ramadan ceremony before the arrival of the Bey, having been misinformed that the Bey had canceled his decision to attend and had returned to Bardo.[61]

An even more outrageous example concerned the mufti Ismail al-Tamimi who was dismissed and banished in 1820 allegedly because certain slanderers informed the Bey that he was prophesying the end of the regime.[62]

It is noteworthy that other members of the religious establishment apparently did not protest these arbitrary acts. Their acquiescence in the first case seems somewhat more understandable. A new Bey who had come to power by way of assassination would feel politically insecure and want only loyal followers preaching in the mosques. Their position in the case of Shaikh al-Tamimi is less easily justified.

Shaikh al-Tamimi was himself, as mufti, a member of the majlis al-

---

throughout the affair showed toward the majlis al-shari'i members a special consideration not granted to their other prisoners from among the civil and military administration (see Bin Diyaf, III, 117–119).

59 For example, the 1845 sermon by Shaikh Ibrahim al-Riyahi protesting the oppressions of the Bey's concession monopolies (see *ibid.*, IV, 82). The sermon is also included in the works of al-Riyahi collected by his son (see al-Riyahi, *op. cit.*, II, 30–31).

60 Bin Diyaf, III, 106.

61 *Ibid.*, no. 398.

62 Apparently, this was a conveniently vague accusation to bring against an alim. The faqih Ahmad bin Rajib, one of those imprisoned following the execution of Larbi Zarruq, was accused of stargazing (*ibid.*, III, 140).

shari'i. Mahmud Bey had dismissed and banished him without prior investigation,[63] and when he announced his decision to the majlis al-shari'i, not a single member registered a protest or even requested further information concerning the case.[64] In passive resistance, at least, each religious dignitary asked to replace al-Tamimi could have respectfully declined. Nothing of the sort occurred. Shaikh Muhammad Mahjub took Shaikh al-Tamimi's place as mufti and member of the majlis al-shari'i.[65]

The Bey also intervened to settle disputes among religious functionaries. In 1818, Mahmud Bey dismissed the qadi of Sousse because he and the mufti of Sousse were deadlocked in a bitter quarrel that threatened to stop the regular process of justice in that area. The majlis al-shari'i in Tunis was ordered by the Bey to write a letter to the two parties admonishing them to mend their ways, but when this proved of no avail, dismissal by the Bey seemed the only possible solution.[66] This was an example of a very beneficial exercise of beylical authority, but it does at the same time underscore the direct authority of the Bey in religious matters and the absence of institutionalized structures to settle such disputes without reference to the Bey.[67]

The Beys, as already noted (see above p. 52), could be equally arbitrary in controlling the number of adls; and as is seen below (p. 86) they played a decisive role in the appointment and dismissal of zawiya shaikhs. The Beys possessed and exercised a broad power of appointment and dismissal in virtually all religious and educational offices.

These examples of arbitrary beylical authority can be matched by as many cases of prudence on the part of the Beys in order to avoid controversy. Shaikh Muhammad al-Naifur was dismissed as qadi for the mahalla during the time of Ahmad Bey because he rashly sentenced a leading officer to imprisonment. The Bey of the Camp, Muhammad Bey, sent someone to persuade the qadi to back down since he could not imprison

[63] *Ibid.*, pp. 132–133. The Bey rescinded the banishment (to Mateur) after one month, and almost four years later he reinstated al-Tamimi as mufti (*ibid.*, p. 146). Mateur is a mere 42 miles northwest of Tunis. One can speculate that had Shaikh al-Tamimi been a potentially dangerous political prisoner, the Bey would have wanted to send him farther away. This not being the case, banishment to a modest provincial town of no intellectual pretensions such as Mateur was apparently deemed punishment enough for an alim.

[64] *Ibid.*, p. 132.

[65] *Ibid.*, p. 133.

[66] *Ibid.*, no. 314.

[67] The Bey seems to have had a hand even in matters settled amicably by the ulama. When Mustafa Bey learned of the dispute over precedence among two imams of Zitouna (see above p. 66) he sent Bin Diyaf and the qadi Muhammad al-Bahri b. Abd al-Sattar to mediate (see *ibid.*, no. 384).

one of his chief military leaders. Al-Naifur retorted, "I have done what was required of me. Now it is up to him [the Bey of the Camp] to imprison him or not as he chooses."[68] Obviously, such a stiff-necked legist would not do as qadi of the mahalla, and he was dismissed when the mahalla returned to Tunis. Even so, he was in no way penalized or disgraced. He was later appointed qadi in Tunis and eventually became mufti.

Another example of beylical prudence may be attributed to Mustafa Bey who presented what appeared to be a reasonable request to the qadi Muhammad b. Hamida bin al-Khoja. The Bey wanted to build a house for his favorite minister Mustafa Sahib al-Tabi on property that was held in habous, and he proposed to place another property in habous in exchange for release of the former (a process acceptable in Hanafi law provided the two properties in question are of equivalent value). The qadi refused, however, and Mustafa Bey reluctantly accepted the adverse verdict "as was his wont in shari'a judgments."[69]

Indeed, as more evidence is slowly accumulated, the emerging pattern of relations between political authority and the ulama appears increasingly subtle and nuanced. Although politically quiescent and readily cowed into submission on certain matters, the ulama were, nevertheless, far from being passive instruments of beylical power to be used as the Bey saw fit. In addition to the two cases cited above there are many other examples of ulama risking governmental disfavor in order to stand by their convictions. Shaikh Hasan al-Sharif's bravery in accosting a Turkish soldier who was abducting a woman and personally bringing him to justice has already been cited.[70] Acting on the orders of the Bey, Larbi Zarruq in 1232/1816–17 attempted to get the leading Zitouna shaikhs to stop teaching many of their courses at the Yusuf Sahib al-Tabi mosque (the founder of the mosque that bore his name having been assassinated at the instigation of Larbi Zarruq only two years earlier). They agreed to teach at both Zitouna and the Sahib al-Tabi mosques but refused to abandon the latter. Shaikh Muhammad al-Fasi, the first to speak, pointed out that the Bey had the right to withdraw his stipend as a teacher at Zitouna but "he has no right to prevent me from disseminating religious science is a mosque devoted to the worship of God." Both shaikhs Ahmad al-Ubbay and Ibrahim al-Riyahi concurred, and each alluded to the late Yusuf Sahib al-Tabi's per-

[68] *Ibid.*, no. 339. al-Nayfur had apparently not wanted the job in the first place, and he accepted only after strong pressure from his mentor, Shaikh Muhammad Bayram III. Possibly, this was his way of getting out of an unwanted governmental assignment.

[69] *Ibid.*, no. 350.

[70] See above, p. 68.

sonal regard for them. "But for him the Bey would not even know my name," al-Riyahi added. These were sentiments that it took some courage to express before Larbi Zarruq.[71]

Shaikh Ibrahim al-Riyahi was once summoned to appear before Husain Bey. Everyone except the members of the majlis al-shari'i was expected to kiss the Bey's hand, and at that time al-Riyahi was not yet a member of the majlis al-shari'i. When the Bey extended his hand to be kissed, the shaikh grabbed it and shook hands with him instead. Husain Bey was both surprised and irritated, but he let the incident pass without comment.[72]

The sense of personal and professional pride is also noticeable in the story concerning the appointment of Shaikh Muhammad al-Rassa (from the venerable al-Rassa family that had provided imams of Zitouna before the Bakris) as qadi al-farida and shahid of the bait al-mal[73] (replacing his late father). One day the minister Shakir Sahib al-Tabi said to him jokingly, "The bait al-mal is in your hands and the hands of the Agha. You pay what you wish to the state." Al-Rassa responded haughtily, "The treasury is in the hands of the Agha. He is closer to you than I am. You promoted me as shahid for what is collected, not what is spent. Since you now have some doubt as to my trustworthiness, look for someone else." Bin Diyaf's father explained to Shakir that al-Rassa was from a family that would not tolerate such banter. Shakir tried, using Bin Diyaf's father as intermediary, to get al-Rassa to reconsider, but in vain.[74]

Yet another aspect of personal honor and a sense of propriety as understood by the religious establishment are revealed in the story of Shaikh Ahmad al-Barudi who refused a gift of money sent to him by Yusuf Sahib al-Tabi. He informed the messenger that he might have accepted a horse (*sic*—hardly a trifling gift) or something to eat as a gift, but not money. Bin Diyaf's father, realizing Yusuf Sahib al-Tabi's inadvertent blunder, re-

[71] Bin Diyaf, III, 122–124, and biography no. 331.

[72] al-Naifur, *'Unwān al-Arīb*, II, 90–97.

[73] The two jobs were apparently usually held by the same person who by the nature of the work was a member of the religious establishment (see Bin Diyaf, nos. 103, 144, 133, and 397). It would seem from the context that the qadi al-farida supervised the canonically fixed distribution of estates, especially those coming before the bait al-mal (see, in this conection, the article "Fara'id" in *SEI*). According to Charles Monchicourt (*Documents historiques sur la Tunisie* [Paris, 1929], p. 28n) the bait al-mal was entitled to receive the money of those dying without heirs and to receive the equivalent of the male heir's portion for those leaving only female heirs. The money was used to cover the expenses of burying indigents, circumcizing the poor, and arranging for the marriage of girls.

[74] Bin Diyaf, no. 397.

turned the money himself, explaining to the minister, "This man Shaikh al-Barudi sees you as a friend and an equal. He would not even mind revealing to you his needs, but you send him money by way of Qasim the Doorman without even including a letter." Bin Diyaf's father then induced Shaikh al-Barudi to write the minister listing some of his needs. Thus, the original purpose was eventually achieved in a fashion acceptable to all.[75]

A sense of honor that could easily slip into disdain, professional pride, prudence in the face of power which at times smacked of cowardice but was occasionally relieved by individual acts of courage and conviction—such were some of the confusing features discernible in the ulama's relations with government. Largely beholden to government for their very livelihood, they never really resisted the system, yet they never completely surrendered to it either.

As for the Beys, they honored leading ulama, attended their funerals, built mosques, madrasas, and zawiyas in their memory, made a show of seeking their counsel and deferring to their judgment, but they maintained effective control in their own hands, and from time to time they arbitrarily intervened in important or petty matters as if to make it quite clear where ultimate power and authority resided.

II. Mysticism, Brotherhoods, and the Religious Establishment

The subject of mysticism and the brotherhoods should be approached with caution, for few matters so readily lend themselves to distortion through simplification or anachronistic reasoning. The general Arabic word for Islamic mysticism—Sufi—may evoke memories of the great intellectual and moral giants of Islam such as Ibn al-Arabi or al-Ghazzali or it may instead suggest connotations of primitive folk religion replete with amulets, exotic ceremonies, and semiliterate "holy men." This confusion is unavoidable for Islamic mysticism or Sufism has always contained both elements—a sophisticated intellectualism within the framework of esoteric doctrines as well as the crude manifestations of popular religion.

The problem of presenting a balanced interpretation of Sufism is rendered even more difficult today because many, perhaps most, Muslim intellectuals now regard Sufism and the brotherhoods with the same condescension that the men of the eighteenth century Enlightenment in Europe

[75] *Ibid.*, no. 82.

reserved for the Middle Ages. Such a view is the legacy of the Wahhabiyya and Salafiyya movements, for in modern times the puritanical reformism within Sunni Islam, sparked by Ahmad ibn Abd al-Wahhab and continued by Shaikh Muhammad Abduh and his followers, has succeeded in changing radically the venerable medieval adjustment between orthodoxy and mysticism, between the learned legal tradition under the guardianship of the ulama and the illuminist tendencies associated with Sufism. In tactical terms, modern Islamic reformism was able to achieve this goal by eventually winning over the ulama class while at the same time seeking battle with and usually defeating the leadership of the traditionally Islamic brotherhoods.[76]

This modern theological struggle that pitted ulama against the brotherhood leadership must not be accepted uncritically as the norm for earlier periods of Sunni Islamic history in Tunisia or elsewhere. Of course, there was always the possibility of friction between representatives of the learned, legal tradition and advocates of illuminist mysticism, and such conflicts occurred not only in the formative periods of both Sunni orthodoxy and of Sufism but also later from time to time as the career of Ibn Taimiyya (1263–1328) so readily illustrates. Nevertheless, the extreme positions of a few bold leaders either on the side of legalistic orthodoxy or illuminist mysticism must not obscure the more normal pattern of an easy adjustment between orthodoxy and mysticism, between ulama and Sufi shaikhs.

Husainid Tunisia in the early nineteenth century was still living in the period of accommodation between orthodoxy and mysticism. This is not to suggest that the Wahhabi movement which had originated in the Arabian peninsula during the previous century was unknown in Tunisia. No movement that had captured Medina and Mecca as the Wahhabis had done in 1804 and 1806, respectively, could pass unnoticed in other parts of the Muslim world. Indeed a Wahhabi letter appealing to other Muslims had reached the beylik, and Hamuda Bey had summoned the ulama to write an appropriate response in order to provide guidance to the

[76] The argument set forth represents a simplification, and thus necessarily only an approximation, of a much more complicated reality. There were certain reformist brotherhoods. Muhammad ibn Abd al-Wahhab and Muhammad Abduh were themselves influenced by Sufism in their early training. Even so, it is believed that the approach suggested here is basically accurate and provides a workable conceptual framework for interpreting general Sunni Muslim developments since the late eighteenth century.

people.[77] Judging from the rebuttal written by the ulama's spokesman it would appear that the Tunisian ulama were unimpressed by the Wahhabi theological arguments while they were scandalized by the sack of the Holy Cities and by a doctrine that authorized warfare against fellow Muslims who would not freely accept Wahhabi principles.

The ideological revolution of Islamic reformism, initiated in modern times by Wahhabism, would eventually make itself felt in Tunisia as in other parts of Sunni Islam, but during the early decades of the nineteenth century, there was as yet no discernible evidence of such influence.

The pattern of accommodation between legalistic orthodoxy and illuminist mysticism in Husainid Tunisia was thorough and consistent both on the level of theology and in the specific institutional and personal relationships that characterized daily life. Both ulama and people accepted the idea of intercession between the individual believer and Allah, and it appeared thus perfectly consistent that such persons—or "saints"—should be granted a special veneration. Even after their death what could be more normal than that the believer would want to offer prayers at their tombs? A prayer was more likely to be heard by the Deity if transmitted through the channel of a person whom He had singled out for His special favor. Both ulama and people also believed that God could and did intervene to change the normal order of events in this world.

God was not the transcendent deity of the post-Enlightenment West. He was immanent and His ways inscrutable. He might work through an ignorant peasant or even a madman, a man or a woman. The believer should approach the possibility—indeed the likelihood—of Divine intervention in daily life with a sense of awesome reverence.

With this attitude of mind it was obvious that institutionalized mysticism could hardly be dismissed as heterodox. The attempt to understand God's will through the mystical ritual (dhikr) of a religious brotherhood was not seen as being in conflict with the formal requirements of Islamic law (shari'a).[78] It was simply another and complementary manner in which

[77] The Wahhabi letter and the response of Shaikh 'Umar b. Qasim Mahjub (see Bin Diyaf, no. 60) is to be found in Bin Diyaf, III, 60–75. Bin Diyaf also mentions that Shaikh Ismail al-Tamimi wrote a book in refutation of the Wahhabi principles entitled *al-Manh al-Allahiyya fi Tams al-Dallāla al-Wahhābiyya* (The Divine Gift Obliterating the Errors of Wahhabism).

[78] Although, of course, those who pushed matters to extremes could create a conflict, for example, by arguing that gnosis (ma'rifa) superseded the shari'a or, on the other hand, that the shari'a forbade mystical attempts to understand God's will.

finite man attempted to establish a proper relationship with his God.[79]

Consistent with these theological assumptions, a highly trained Muslim savant did not need to have any mental reservations about acknowledging the saintliness of an unlearned man. Even a mufti, the leading authority on the shari'a law, might well desire to round out his religious life by membership in a brotherhood. Most members of the ulama class looked with a favorable eye upon Sufism and were themselves members of one or more brotherhoods. Shaikh Ibrahim al-Riyahi, for example, was a leading member of the Tijaniyya brotherhood and largely responsible for its rapid growth in Tunisia.[80]

Only the disapproval or hesitations of the ulama class might have dampened the ardent will to believe in miracles and to seek refuge from an uncertain world in saintly men and women possessing the power of intervention with the Deity (baraka). Given approval by the ulama class, the full institutional organization of Islamic mysticism was assured. Virtually every Tunisian Muslim had his saint, usually the shaikh of an Islamic brotherhood.

Brotherhoods were, in a sense, one of the most effective leveling agencies of Tunisian society, for in a brotherhood dhikr the Bey and his lowliest subject, the rich man and the poor, were on the same plane. At the same

79 The interpretation given above must not be seen as an attempt to advance, without further demonstration, the hoary idea that Islam is especially conducive to resignation and fatalism in the world. Of course, the Muslims of Husainid Tunisia, ulama and people, took thought of the morrow. They expected the sun to rise each morning. They planted and reaped according to the seasons. In the present age, the existence of an underdeveloped world parts of which are Christian, Muslim, Buddhist, or Hindu should suffice to discredit the notion that Islam—or any other religion—is the crucial factor in social change. It is equally important not to err in the other direction. Clearly, a religious value system not only reflects the collective assumptions and aspirations of a given society. It also creates and shapes those assumptions and aspirations. Nothing would be more logical than that there should be certain religiously fashioned differences between, for example, the Muslim peasant and the Christian peasant or the Muslim businessman and the Confucian businessman, and these differences should have their impact on the social, economic, and political institutions of a given culture. It is equally apparent that no a priori, simplistic formula (and, a fortiori, no monocausal theory) will be able to capture the essence of these subtle differences.

80 See Jamil Abu-Nasr, *The Tijaniyya: A Sufi Order in the Modern World* (London, Oxford University Press, 1965), pp. 82–83. Note also the highly critical account of al-Riyahi's adherence to the Tijaniyya to be found in Muhammad al-Bahli al-Niyāl, *al-Haqīqa al-Tārīkhiyya lil-taṣawwuf al-Islamī* (Tunis, 1384/1965), pp. 329–333, where it is suggested that al-Riyahi embraced the new brotherhood for prestige and worldly gain.

time, the equalitarian aspect of brotherhood organization must not be exaggerated. The very normal human tendency for persons of similar background and social standing to band together was always at work. The urban bourgeoisie were usually to be found in certain brotherhoods, the peasants in others. The learned man would obviously feel more at home in a brotherhood that offered a sophisticated doctrine and was more thoroughly in the mainstream of Sunni Muslim universalism. Such a man might be drawn to the Shadhiliyya, Qadiriyya, or—beginning in the nineteenth century—the Tijaniyya brotherhoods. On the other hand, a provincial man of no formal education might feel more satisfied by venerating a local figure whose piety or whose reported miracles attested to his saintliness and his baraka.

The beys themselves played a role in maintaining the importance of the saints and the brotherhoods. Most of the beys were members of at least one brotherhood. Ahmad Bey, for example, was an active member of the Shadhiliyya. When the Shaikh of the Shadhiliyya brotherhood, al-Shadhili bin al-Muaddib, died in 1847, Ahmad Bey was among those carrying his coffin in the funeral procession "just like any other member of the brotherhood."[81] Ahmad also visited the tomb of the brotherhood's founder (Sidi Abu al-Hasan Ali al-Shadhili, known locally as Sidi Bel Hasan [d. 1258]), before leaving on his state visit to Paris in 1846 and upon returning safely to Tunisia.[82]

The beys respected the tradition that made many zawiyas inviolate asylums for fugitives from justice, and most of them built tombs, madrasas, or zawiyas for their favorite saints. Mahmud Bey, for example, was remembered for renovating the tombs of many saints. His successor, Husain, built the zawiya for Sidi Muhammad al-Bashir, and Ahmad's father, Mustafa Bey, built a tomb and dome in honor of the "possessed" (majdhub) saint, al-Sayyid Hasan bin Maskat.[83] The registers of treasury expenses for the years between 1252 and 1258 (1836–1842) even reveal a modest monthly stipend to four Sufi shaikhs.[84]

[81] Bin Diyaf, IV, 112.

[82] *Ibid.*, pp. 96 and 111.

[83] al-Baji al-Mas'udi, *al-Khulaṣā al-Naqiyya fi umarā, Ifriqiyya* (Tunis, 1283/1866–1867), pp. 142, 144, and 145. Bin Diyaf, no. 165.

[84] These were Ali b. Ziyad (four piasters per month), Mahraz b. Khalf, Ali 'Azur, and Muhammad bu (*sic*) Hadid, all receiving eight piasters per month. (Tunis, Archives Generales Tunisiennes, registres 453, 463, and 470 [hereafter AGT]). Since these years span the reigns of Mustafa Bey and Ahmad Bey it would seem that these were customary grants that had perhaps been in existence for many years. Mahraz b. Khalf was a descendant of the celebrated Sidi Mahraz (Abu Muhammad Mahraz al-Saddiqi, 340–413/951–1022)

As a natural result of this consideration granted them by the state many of the saints and brotherhood leaders were pushed forward into a position of some political importance. Since the powers of baraka were believed usually to be passed on from father to son certain families—or in some cases even parts of tribes (like the Awlad Sidi Tlil)[85]—continued to enjoy political power. They might serve as advisers to tribal shaikhs, qaids, or even the beys themselves. Often they would act as intermediaries between governmental authority and the people. The support of a Sufi shaikh might assure an uncontested collection of taxes due or facilitate the recruitment of young men for the new regular army.

The potential political importance of a saint or Sufi shaikh is illustrated by the life of Muhammad al-Bashir.[86] This man, born in Algerian Kabylia, came to Tunis to study and remained to teach. Later he went into religious retreat, and he soon achieved fame as a saint. Mahmud Bey sent his two sons, Husain Bey and Mustafa Bey, to study under him, and Mahmud himself was in the habit of visiting him in times of need, as before leaving on the tax-collecting military expedition (mahalla). More important, Muhammad al-Bashir, himself a Zwawa Berber tribesman, became the patron saint of the many Zwawa living in Tunisia most of whom served in the military, just as many of their fellow tribesmen served in the Algerian army (the Gallicized Zouaves, a name recognizable to students of French military history, reveals the Zwawa origin). Indeed, in the first third of the nineteenth century the Zwawa (or Zouaves, to use the more familiar spelling) accounted for one-third to one-half the infantry in the Bey's army (the Turks providing the remainder). It was almost legendary that if any Zouave swore by Sidi Bashir, he would certainly keep his word. Sidi Bashir died in 1827 and was succeeded as leader of the zawiya by a nephew, but in the late 1860s, Bin Diyaf could write that "To this day they [the Zouaves] seek baraka in his clothing and rosary."[87] It can be well imagined how important it was to the beys to keep in the good graces of the man

---

honored as the patron saint of Tunis. According to tradition, he founded the Jewish quarter (hara) of the city. The beautiful mosque of Tunis named in his honor is a much later structure dating from c. 1675. See al-Niyal, *op. cit.*, pp. 182–185; Bin Diyaf, nos. 96 and 97; and George Marçais, *L'Architecture Musulmane d'Occident* (Paris, 1954), p. 463. Ali 'Azuz (d. 1122/1710–1711) founded a zawiya in Zaghwan. See al-Niyal, *op. cit.*, p. 298, and Bin Diyaf, no. 211. Muhammad bu Hadid has not been identified.

85 Cf. Henri Duveyrier, *La Tunisie* (Paris, 1881), p. 101.

86 For whom Husain Bey built a zawiya.

87 Bin Diyaf, no. 165.

(or his successors) who commanded the religious fealty of so important a part of the army.

The activist Sufi shaikh is equally well illustrated by Mustafa bin Azuz (d. 1866) of the well-known Sufi family with a parent zawiya in Biskra (Algeria). He was instrumental in spreading the Rahmaniyya brotherhood in Tunisia, had a fine reputation in the western regions of the beylik, was well regarded by Ahmad Bey, and in the last years of his life played a leading role in putting down the 1864 revolt.[88] Bin Diyaf, certainly far from naïve politically, viewed Mustafa Bin Azuz essentially as a religious figure who necessarily had some political influence. "There is," Bin Diyaf observed, "no severity in his tariqa [brotherhood] except for whoever wants to become completely absorbed in Sufi practices and seclusion. He commands the people to carry out the obligation of prayer and to say 'There is no God but God' whenever possible." Yet to the French consular authorities Mustafa Bin Azuz was one of the most active agents sending contraband gunpowder into Algeria.[89] There is no reason to doubt either appraisal of Mustafa Bin Azuz. It is, rather, more important to realize that in the context of Husaynid Tunisia these "religious" and "secular" activities by a regional Sufi leader were not viewed as contradictory or discordant.

The beys were respectful of the moral influence, so readily convertible into real political power, held by the saints and brotherhood leaders, and where possible without derogating from their own political authority they showed them deference and special consideration. There were limits, though, and when necessary the saints and Sufi leaders were, like the ulama class, treated as subjects who must be made to realize where political sovereignty resided. In 1837, for example, Shakir Sahib al-Tabi organized a military expedition to put down the revolt led by a zawiya shaikh in that area. The considerable political power this shaikh had previously exercised by virtue of his friendship with Allalah b. Qaji, half-brother of Husain Bey and Mustafa Bey, had been lost with the rise of Shakir. Irritated to find that he had lost his special standing, he led other dissident elements into revolt. The revolt was crushed with no special mercy or consideration shown for his Sufi calling.[90]

[88] *Ibid.*, no. 370. See also B. Slama, *L'Insurrection de 1864 en Tunisie* (Tunis, 1967), *passim*, for a more critical view of his role in the 1864 revolt.

[89] Report of eleve-consul Tessot, May, 1853 in the Archives of the French Ministère des Affaires Etrangères, *Memoires et Documents* (Tunis), vol. 8.

[90] Bin Diyaf, III, 217.

The beys also used their power to appoint zawiya shaikhs as an instrument of political control. If a certain zawiya shaikh became too obstreperous it was not difficult to find a rival member of the same family who would willingly assume the job. The bey obviously could not destroy the real personal power of a Sufi religious leader by an official decree appointing someone else, but quite often the question of who possessed commanding moral authority within a brotherhood or at a single zawiya was not that clear-cut. In such cases, the bey's ability to grant or withhold legal recognition—with which went the legal right to collect and dispense the monies paid into the brotherhood or zawiya by its living members or as a result of trust funds (wafqs or habous)—was sufficient to assure compliance.

Indeed, even a most un-Machiavellian bey who might desire nothing more than to leave the brotherhoods free to engage in their religious activities (admittedly a somewhat idealized and hypothetical situation) would be dragged willy-nilly into the politics of zawiya leadership. In the Tunisian archives is a document drawn up during the reign of Muhammad al-Sadiq (1859–1882) setting out the conflicting claims of two families to the rights over the zawiya of a certain Sidi Umar b. Hijla. Each family's claims are buttressed by beylical decrees going back to the reign of Ali b. Husain (1759–1782). It seems likely that the document was originally drafted by a qadi or perhaps by a katib at Bardo as a succinct legal brief to aid the reigning bey in deciding the case of a zawiya about which apparently neither he nor his predecessors were especially well informed or even overly interested—so long as its members did not disturb the peace.[91]

[91] AGT, dossier 987, cahier 81 bis (decrees nominating zawiya shaikhs). This dossier, containing several score decrees for the period of the early and mid-nineteenth century, is tantalizingly incomplete and it would be impossible to estimate on the basis of this evidence alone how many decrees of nomination to zawiya leadership a bey normally issued in a year, the average tenure in office, the number dismissed (and why) as opposed to those who held their positions until death, and so on. The surviving decrees are sufficient evidence to corroborate strongly what was already believed to be the case—that zawiya leadership tended to stay in the same family. The dossier also indicates the existence of three separate officers in a zawiya—shaikh, wakil, and nazir. The shaikh was, of course, the leader of the zawiya, but the precise distinction between wakil and nazir is not clear in this context. Was the wakil the deputy and administrator while the nazir was the supervisor or auditor? This would fit with an acceptable translation of the two terms in this context, but little more clarification can be offered from the internal evidence. There are several examples in which the appointee was named to two of the three offices. Wakil and nazir were the most common, but the combination of shaikh and wakil as well as shaikh and nazir is also to be found. For the later period of Muhammad al-Sadiq's reign a large proportion of lower-grade army

The legalistic orthodoxy represented by the ulama and the illuminist doctrines of Sufism could also achieve a working accommodation in Husainid Tunisia because there was a marked tendency for the two elements to be espoused by the same religious figures. The ulama class and the Sufis were not really separate but complementary religious institutions. They were inextricably blended together. Most of the ulama, as has already been mentioned, were members of a brotherhood, and several—including the most important, like Shaikh Ibrahim al-Riyahi—played an active role in spreading the doctrines and increasing the membership in one or another of the brotherhoods. In some cases it is meaningless to classify a religious figure as a Sufi leader rather than a member of the ulama class (or vice versa). A good example was a certain Ali al-Nuri (d. 118/1706–7) who had studied in Tunis and Cairo before returning to his hometown of Sfax where he "founded a madrasa for students and a zawiya for murids (disciples of a Sufi order) from which sprang a great number of both the ulama and the brotherhood leaders of the Sahil."[92]

There were always individual Muslims, often with little or no formal religious training, who had a mystical experience and became recognized as possessing baraka. Such persons might collect a faithful following and perhaps found a zawiya, thus beginning the process of creating a new brotherhood in their own lifetime. Or perhaps the zawiya would be created around the saint's tomb following his death. To this extent, the spontaneity of mystical leadership would seem to be clearly distinguishable from the formal training required to achieve standing in the ranks of ulama. Yet, even in such cases the apparently clear distinction between Sufi and alim evaporates as one follows the careers of the zawiya founder's descendants. Time and again they will be found to have received the formal education of the ulama class before returning to assume leadership of the family zawiya.

Nothing could have been more natural, for two interrelated reasons. The family zawiya usually served as a school in addition to a meeting place for mystical exercises. Of course, a primary school teacher did not require the long training necessary for becoming an alim. A rudimentary knowl-

officers appear to have received appointments as wakils. This may well be one more sign of Muhammad al-Sadiq's tendency to concentrate public office and its prerogatives in the hands of officialdom at the capital to the detriment of provincial leadership—one of the causes of the 1864 revolt. On this subject see Slama, *L'Insurrection de 1864, passim*, and Pierre Granchamp, *Documents relatifs a la revolution de 1864 en Tunisie* (2 vols.; Tunis, 1935).

92 al-Niyal, *al-Haqīqa al-Tarikhiyya*, p. 319.

edge of reading and writing adequate to guide the rote memorization of the Koran would have sufficed, and in many cases that was all the intellectual baggage the primary school (kuttab) teacher brought with him, whether his school was connected with a zawiya or not. Nevertheless, the prestige of the zawiya was enhanced to the extent that it offered a more impressive formal education.

Also, the descendant's claim to have inherited the saintly founder's baraka was always subject to the pragmatic test. He might not be as mystically inclined as his father or earlier ancestor. His personality could well be different. Whatever the situation his claim to a share of the original saintliness. and thus to the devoted loyalty of the zawiya disciples, could only be enhanced by the rigorous formal training of the ulama class. In Weberian terms the routinization of the baraka in a saintly family was thus assured, and at the same time the possibility of institutional rivalry among the ulama class and the zawiya leadership was largely avoided. The celebrated al-Bahi family illustrates this tendency at work.

The al-Bahi family traced its genealogy back to the Prophet Muhammad. The founder of the family zawiya in Tunis, Shaikh Ahmad al-Bahi,

The al-Bahi Family

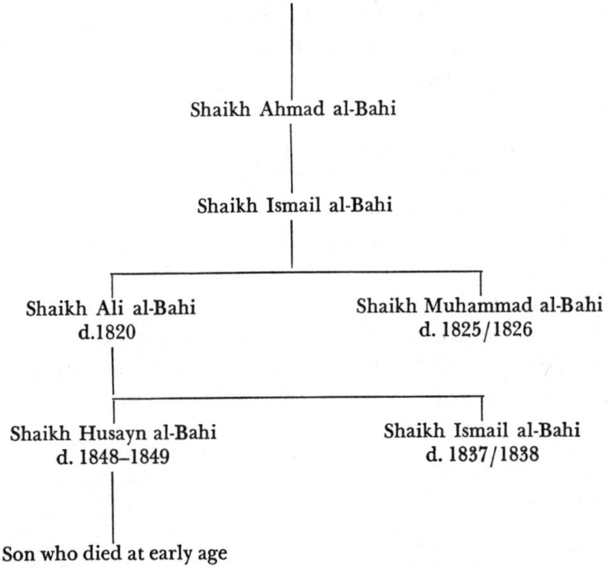

Source: Bin Diyaf Biography nos. 124, 151, 231, 288.

lived in the first half of the eighteenth century. He was venerated by the people of Tunis, believed able to perform miracles (dhu kiramat), and at the time Bin Diyaf was writing (the 1860s) people still sought baraka at his tomb. The extent of his formal education is unknown, and it may well have been scant.

His son, Ismail, was sent to study in Djerba for nine years at the zawiya of the saint Ibrahim al-Jumni. Then he returned to teach in his father's zawiya in Tunis. Thus far the Sufi tendency clearly overshadowed all else, for Shaikh Ahmad al-Bahi, living in Tunis where the best institution of orthodox higher Islamic studies in North Africa—Zitouna—was located, nevertheless chose to send his son to be educated at the foot of another Sufi saint. Ismail's son, Ali, studied "the essentials" (ma la budda minhu) under his father. Ali's younger brother Muhammad al-Bahi, however, received a rigorous formal education under the leading ulama of the day.

In the next generation, Ali's two sons, Husain and Ismail, both received the same thorough education which qualified them to join the ranks of the ulama. The zawiya remained in the hands of the family with leadership passing in succession to the eldest lineal male descendant. It was still a zawiya in the customary mystical sense of the term, just as al-Bahi remained a saintly family, but they were also now an ulama family even with intermarriage into other old ulama families. (Husain al-Bahi married the daughter of his teacher Muhammad al-Bahri b. Abd al-Sattar.)[93] Attention might also be called to the al-Mahrizi and al-Talili families who showed a similar development.[94]

A statistical indication of this tendency for Sufi and saintly families to join the ranks of the ulama can be seen in the twenty biographies given by Bin Diyaf[95] of persons who can be primarily identified as saints or Sufis (thus excluding those already included on the ulama list who had strong connections with Sufism).[96] Of the twenty subjects who fit this classifica-

[93] Bin Diyaf, no. 288. See also, for the al-Bahi family, *ibid.*, nos. 124, 161, and 231.

[94] See especially *ibid.*, nos. 321 (Khalf al-Mahrizi) and 253 (Muhammad al-Shafi'i al-Talili).

[95] For the same time period used in analyzing the ulama, those persons who died between 1814 and 1866.

[96] Reference to ulama closely linked with Sufism may be found in Bin Diyaf, nos. 92, 309, 313, and 321. As already suggested this classification into separate lists of ulama and Sufis is necessarily somewhat arbitrary at times. For example, Shaikh Muhammad 'Abbas (*ibid.*, no. 309) studied under all the major ulama of Tunis, he was deemed one of the leaders of the Hanafi rite in Tunisia, and he became imam of al-Qasba mosque. Yet, according to Bin Diyaf, "it was said that he had power over the spirits (yatasarrafu fi al-jann), and people sought him out to obtain

tion, ten can clearly be qualified also as ulama. In several of the other cases, it cannot be excluded that they might have had an education equivalent to that of the ulama class, but Bin Diyaf is silent on the matter.

Only two clearly did not have such formal educational background. One, Sulaiman al-Arusi, was a descendant of the famous saint Sidi Ahmad b. Arus (d. 868/1463) and Bin Diyaf notes tersely that the only respect and glory accorded to him was "derived from the baraka of his ancestor."[97]

The other, Ali al-Mazaghini, was a tribal shaikh, and perhaps he should not be classified as *primarily* Sufi or saint. He was believed to have the miraculous power of prophecy,[98] and he deserves mention in this category if only as a good example of how it was believed that anyone, regardless of background or formal training, might be given supernatural powers.

The mystical aspects of Sunni Islam, in short, were thoroughly and smoothly integrated into the fabric of life in Husainid Tunisia. The Sufis and saints were part of the religious establishment, and there were no appreciable institutional or ideological disputes dividing ulama from Sufis and saints, for indeed often the same persons filled both roles.[99] Virtually every Muslim Tunisian belonged to a zawiya, and the influence of the Sufis and saints was undoubtedly pervasive.

This section opened with a warning about the difficulties facing the scholar who would treat mysticism and the brotherhoods, and it would be well to close with equal caution. European literature of Islamic society has often stressed the explosive potential for insurrection and revolutionary violence likely to be unleashed by some God-intoxicated provincial mystic, and the difficulties encountered by European colonial administrations in Muslim lands suffice to explain this viewpoint. Yet, this interpretation is at best a distorted simplification of a much more complicated reality. In times of stress, social breakdown, or foreign threat, any resistance in a still largely theocentric society would likely take on a religious coloration, led not by the urbanized judge or teacher but by someone more in the vision-

---

his baraka for various purposes, to cure their illnesses, and for expiatory deeds."

[97] *Ibid.*, no. 175. For information of Sidi Bin 'Arus see R. Brunschvig, *La Berberie Orientale sous les Hafsides* (Paris, 1947), II, 341–351, and al-Niyal, *al-Haqīqa al-Tarīkhiyya*, pp. 273–274.

[98] Bin Diyaf, no. 247. The term used is "al-kiramat mulawwana bilmaqamat," but all the kiramat cited are those of prophecy.

[99] Only one reference noted in Bin Diyaf's long chronicle prefigures what might be called the salafiyya position. Shaikh Muhammad bin al-Tahir bin Mas'ud once insisted to the young Bin Diyaf who wanted to study mysticism with him that only 'ilm was the proper tariqa (*ibid.*, no. 101).

ary or messianic tradition. Who would be more likely to dream dreams or see visions than an activist thoroughly indoctrinated with Sufi illuminist doctrines?

This is all logical and consistent with what has often happened in Sunni Islamic society—especially, one might add, in North Africa,[100] but it does not describe at all the pattern of what actually happened in Tunisia during the early and middle years of the nineteenth century. Instead, Sufis and saints fitted into the over-all religious institution and, as such, played an important role in socializing the Muslim masses and mediating among discrete parts of society and between society and the state. Rather than providing a focal point for coalescing the several parts of Tunisian society together into a new working synthesis to meet the challenge of a new world, the Sufis and saints played an important role in preserving the existing balance of stability-in-stagnation that characterized Husainid Tunisia.

[100] To name only the more important in North Africa, the rise of the Fatimids, Almoravids, Almohads, the sixteenth-century resistance of sharifs and Sufis to Portuguese and Spanish incursions into Morocco, and the Qadiriyya connections of Algeria's Abd al-Qadir.

4 The Moroccan Ulama, 1860–1912: An Introduction*

EDMUND BURKE, III

IT IS ONE of the curiosities of the generally very complete French literature on pre-Protectorate Morocco and Moroccan society that there has been no treatment of the ulama, as such. If we consider that the literature is otherwise exceptionally full on all aspects of Islam in Morocco, down to detailed studies of the most insignificant religious brotherhood, then this deficiency becomes even more mysterious. It is certainly not because there were no ulama in Morocco, for the sources are full of references to them. Nor is it because the Moroccan ulama played only an insignificant part in the turbulent years prior to the establishment of the French protectorate (1900–1912). For in fact, as this paper seeks to demonstrate, they were the leaders of the movement aimed at resisting the French conquest. How then do we explain this paradox? The beginnings of an explanation, I would suggest, may be found in a consideration of the position the ulama occupied in Moroccan society. For individual members of the ulama were often also sharifs (descendants of the Prophet), leaders of religious brotherhoods, or descendants of local saints, and these ascribed positions often seemed more important to French investigators than did their membership in the ulama. It is precisely the characteristics of Moroccan society which determined that the Moroccan ulama would tend to act less as a corporate group, and more in terms of the conflicting pulls and strains of Moroccan popular Islam. An examination of the situation of the ulama in early twentieth-century Morocco should therefore start with a brief survey of the Moroccan style of Islam.

The Moroccan Style of Islam

In order to discuss the position of the ulama in Moroccan society it is advisable first to place them in the context of the distinct Moroccan blend

* The research on which this paper is based was conducted while the author was in Morocco and France under the auspices of a National Defense

of sharifism, saint worship, and popular Islam. For the nature of Moroccan society and especially the Moroccan style of Islam are sufficiently different from that of many other Middle Eastern countries to require some elaboration. Only when the full extent to which popular Islam influenced the behavior of even the supposed preservers of "high Islam" in Morocco is grasped, will it be possible to move on to a consideration of the responses of the ulama to the far-reaching economic, social, and political changes that shook the foundations of Moroccan society from 1860 to 1912.[1]

The characteristics of Moroccan society as it existed on the eve of French conquest were formed during the turbulent years 1500–1650. As a result of the multiple crises of these years, a new Moroccan cultural synthesis of tribalism and popular Islam gradually crystallized. The medieval Islamic synthesis, which included an urban, high Islamic culture and a sedentary peasantry, and was based on close ties of trade and mutual advantage with the Arab East, Europe, and Africa, gradually crumbled. In its place there emerged a stalemate society in which the radiating influence of urban civilization was sharply reduced by the massive influx of Berber tribes from the Sahara, the reassertion of sharifism as a principle of religious legitimacy, and the rise of politico-religious maraboutic (saintly) lineages in the rural areas. The destruction of the old civilization stemmed from the convergence of four major crises. These were: (1) the invasion of Spanish and Portuguese "crusader" forces, (2) the encroachment of the Ottomans upon Algeria and their attempts to seize Morocco, (3) the onset of the Berber encroachments into central Morocco which upset the balance of settled life, and (4) the emergence of sharifian dynasties, the Sa'adian and the 'Alawī, and the crystallization of Moroccan popular Islamic culture.[2]

Education Act–related Fulbright-Hays Fellowship (1965–1967) and a subsequent research trip in the summer of 1969. The conclusions, statements, and opinions made in the article are those of the author and in no way obligate the Fellowship Program.

1 Parts of the following exposition have previously appeared in altered form in my "Morocco and the Near East: Reflections on Some Basic Differences," *Archives Européennes de Sociologie*, X (1969), 70–94.

2 On the crises of the sixteenth century, see Auguste Cour, *L'établissement des dynasties des Chérifs au Maroc* (Paris, 1904); Fernand Braudel, *La Méditerranée au temps de Philippe II* (Paris, 1949); Pierre Boyer, "Contribution à l'étude de la politique religieuse des Turcs dans la régence d'Alger," *Revue de l'occident Musulman et de la Méditerranée*, I (1966), 11–50; and Marcel Lesne, "Historique d'un groupement berbère: les Zemmour" (Paris, 1959), thèse complementaire pour le doctorat ès Lettres, Paris.

By 1650 the essential traits of early modern Morocco had come together to form a new and precarious balance between rural, popular culture and the higher urban culture represented ideally by the ulama. In this mixture the folk components tended to dominate. If we consider this new Morocco in comparison with the Ottoman Empire at the end of the nineteenth century, a number of striking differences between the two emerge. Contrary to the situation that prevailed in the Near Eastern heartland, Morocco lacked some of the features of the Ottoman domains, such as a docile peasantry fixed to the land, a class of absentee urban-dwelling landholders, a highly ramified government bureaucracy, and large agricultural villages as the characteristic pattern of rural settlement. There were, in brief, very few of the links between town and tribe, city and country which one might expect to find in most parts of the Ottoman Empire during the same period. As a result of this situation the collection of taxes, corvée labor, the military impressment of civilians, and the growing involvement of the Moroccan central government in the lives of its subjects all were rendered difficult. Prior to 1912 there were no schools on the Western model for Muslims (although Jews benefited from the efforts of the Alliance Israelite Universelle) in Morocco, few newspapers, no railroads, few paved roads, or bridges, little wheeled traffic, and no industry that went beyond the level of artisanry. In Morocco, where intermediary groups and institutions were relatively scarce, much of the burden of integrating the society was borne by religion, since it was one of the few things that most men had in common. Trade and commerce, and to a lesser extent the central bureaucracy or *makhzan,* also helped bind the national society together. A more detailed examination of the Moroccan style of Islam may help to illustrate further how it helped to integrate the various segments of Moroccan society.

The new style of Islam which evolved in Morocco during the crises of the fifteenth century was marked by a much heavier emphasis upon popular religious practices than had previously been the case in Morocco. The much weakened position of the central government (the makhzan) and the decline of the cultural influence of the cities in the following centuries were one aspect of this transformation. Instead there developed a new Moroccan Islam based upon sharifism, the worship of popularly acclaimed saints, and the proliferation of religious brotherhoods.[3] Belief

[3] For a fine picture of the emergence of this new style of Islam, see Alfred Bel, *La Religion Musulmane en Berbérie,* Vol. I (Paris, Paul Geuthner, 1938), pp. 357–407. See also Edouard Michaux-Bellaire, "Islam marocain"

in such practices as *'ar* sacrifice (a kind of conditional curse, employed to constrain someone to grant a special request), *baraka* (literally, "blessing," the recognition that an individual possesses a special divine charisma), and religiously sanctioned pacts of mutual protection, were widespread. They enabled groups and individuals to conduct face-to-face relationships beyond the bonds of kinship, and thus aided the conduct of trade. Such manifestations were not unknown in the rest of the Middle East. But significantly in the Moroccan case saint worship, the notion of *baraka*, venerations of sharifs, heterodox religious brotherhoods, and *'ar* sacrifice all acquired a political signification to accompany their religious one.

In addition to the ulama, there are at least three other indigenously recognized kinds of men of religion in Morocco, namely, saints, sharifs, and members of Sufi orders. Although these have often been treated as separate statuses within the society, in fact, as we shall see, none of them represents a real corporate group, and an individual could combine more than one role at a time. From the possibility of cumulating religious and other kinds of identities, an individual Moroccan could broaden his sphere of action, and enlarge his circle of potential patrons and clients. Since the whole man was never defined solely by any one of his affiliations, except contextually, the difficulties of analysis become very great. It is in this way that the impact of popular Islam upon even the Moroccan ulama must be approached. A brief examination of each of the three major kinds of men of religion may help make this more explicit.

The descendants of popularly acclaimed saints, known as Awlād Sayyid, or, more colloquially as marabouts (from *murābiṭ*, "tied," i.e., tied to God or vice versa) served as arbitrators of disputes, arranged for the payment of blood money, and helped provide assistance to merchants traveling under their protection in the countryside.[4] In the rural society of Morocco, where suspicion of strangers and the blood feud were rife, saints served to make normal social intercourse possible beyond the bonds of kinship. In return for the services that they provided, the holy lineages received offerings proportional to their help. Saints were widely dispersed throughout the countryside, generally settling near the borders between

---

and other essays in *Archives Marocaines*, XXVII (1927) (hereafter cited as *A.M.*); Edward Westermack, *Ritual and Belief in Morocco* (2 vols.; London, 1926); and Edmond Doutté, *Notes sur l'Islam maghrébin: Les Marabouts* (Paris, 1900).

[4] On the worship of saints in Morocco, whom Bel has called in a striking phrase, "les hommes-fetiches," in addition to the above see Ernest Gellner, *Saints of the Atlas* (Chicago: University of Chicago Press, 1969).

tribes or tribal factions where they could best serve. The ability to provide for travelers and those in need or the shrewd settlement of disputes could give a saint a reputation for possessing baraka, which would further enhance his position vis-à-vis his clients. Not all saints were successful—indeed the supply exceeded the demand, and it was not unusual for saintly lineages who had lost their following to be absorbed into the tribal society. Saints also tended to specialize in certain functions, ranging from exorcism or the sale of amulets to cure sterility, to playing a manifestly political role. Saintly lineages and saints' tombs existed in profusion in the cities as well as the countryside. The descendants of saints were visited by all classes. Moroccan cities were in fact known by their patron saints. For Fez it was Mawlāy Idrīs, for Tetuán, Sīdī 'Alī Mandarī, and for Marrakesh, the Seven Saints (Sab'a al-Rijāl). Upon entering a city, a traveler was expected first to pay his respects at the tomb of the patron saint before going about his business.

Sharifism is a second important aspect of Moroccan popular Islam. There was a great proliferation of sharifism in Morocco, with three major lines of descent from Ḥasan ibn 'Alī being especially numerous, namely the Idrīsīs, the 'Alawīs, and the Qadirīs.[5] The reemphasis upon the principle of sharifism as a means of legitimizing rule which occurred after the rise of the Sa'adian dynasty (1510–1659) and their successors the 'Alawīs (1659–present) produced one of the paradoxes of western Islam, 'Alid dynasties which were also strongly Sunni.[6] There is some evidence that the Ottomans may have initially confounded the rise of the Moroccan Sa'adians and 'Alawīs which threatened their expansion to the west with the no less remarkable rise of the Safavis in Iran at about the same time. Both movements grew out of similar circumstances, the recrudescence of heterodox Sufi brotherhoods, saint worship, and sharifism. Both posed a potential threat to the legitimacy of the Ottoman state by their 'Alidism since the Ottoman sultans were not of sharifian descent. They also were rivals for political power in the outlying regions of the empire. The nature of the dispute between the Moroccan 'Alid dynasties and the Ottomans in Algeria has not yet been clarified.

Sharifism in Morocco, as we have seen, assumed a political significance to accompany its religious one during the upheavals of the fifteenth century. But the importance of sharifs in Morocco went beyond this. Sharifs represented a kind of nobility of blood who exercised their influence at

[5] On the branches of sharifs in Morocco, *EI*[1], s.v. "Morocco."

[6] On this period, see Cour, *op. cit.*

all levels of the society. The shrine of Mawlāy Idrīs at Fez and the Idrīsī sharifs who were associated with it constituted a pervasive force in Fāsī society. Since the Idrīsī sharifs were the most numerous and most deeply rooted of all the sharifian groups in Morocco, they were a powerful check upon the centralizing ambitions of the 'Alawīs.[7] Since many of the members of the ulama of Fez and the other major cities of Morocco claimed sharifian descent, their position was thereby strengthened.

Being a sharif entitled one to tax immunities, justice by one's peers, and in the case of certain prominent sharifian families, made one eligible for pensions and grants of the usufruct of land (known as *'azīb*, pl. *'azabā*) or buildings by the makhzan. Idrīsī sharifs also received an annual share in the offerings made at the shrine of Mawlāy Idrīs located in the Jabal Zarhūn, outside of Fez. Yet there were also begger sharifs, and sharifism was thus no guarantee to wealth, power, or high status. Certainly the fact that the sultan of Morocco claimed to be a sharif greatly enhanced his position in the eyes of his subjects. If however he lacked the necessary political skills or a strong personality his descent alone could not make him an effective ruler. Like the popularly acclaimed saint, in a sense, the sultan lived as a kind of outsider in Moroccan society, while his influence derived from his willingness and ability to use the social leverage inherent in his position. In the circumstances of precolonial Morocco, in which the cities were in decline and the tribes a continuing source of disorder, the sultan found himself ruling less as a chief executive and decision maker and more as an interest broker for the various factions of the kingdom, obliged by circumstances to play a perpetual balancing act.

A third major component of Moroccan Islam were the Sufi brotherhoods, or *ṭuruq* (sing., *ṭarīqa*).[8] For the purposes of our analysis here, what was significant about the religious brotherhoods was that in addition to their spiritual role of introducing their members to a mystical path or way that placed them in a close personal relationship with God, the brotherhoods also provided yet another means of crosscutting local ties and providing an individual with access to a wider range of potential allies. Further, because the head of the order generally was the chief source of spiritual legitimation of the authority of the heads of the local chapters of the brotherhood, the political potential of the brotherhoods was often

[7] The Idrisi sharifs are discussed by G. Salmon, "Les Chorfa Idrisides de Fès," *A.M.*, III (1904), 425–453.

[8] On religious brotherhoods see especially Georges Drague (pseud. for Georges Spillman), *Esquisse d'histoire religieuse du Maroc* (Paris, 1956).

considerable. It is wise, however, not to exaggerate the political power of the brotherhoods, for it in fact was most often circumscribed by the constant pull of local and regional loyalties. In general those ṭuruq which were centered upon the cities tended to be more hierarchically organized and centralized, while the rural orders tended to be more diffuse, and more given to heterodox practices. Urban brotherhoods tended to draw their adherents from specific segments of urban society, with the Tijānīya, for example attracting merchants and lower government officials, the 'Aynaynīya drawing on the higher echelons of government, and the Kattānīya recruiting its members among some of the disaffected lower religious groups, and among the floating populations of the city. In the rural areas Sufi orders tended to draw their adherents from particular tribes or regional groupings. The fact that members of the ulama were often also strong supporters of particular religious brotherhoods could have a strong impact upon both their theological orientation and their political preferences.

The net effect of the unique Moroccan blend of tribalism and popular Islam upon the Moroccan state, was to produce a society that was noted for its flexibility and malleability, well adapted to dealing with the changes that every society experiences, the cyclical occurrence of droughts and abundance, the ebb and flow of the fortunes of men. Only when the direction of these changes became fixed in one direction, as they did after 1859 and the outbreak of the Hispano-Moroccan War, did this cultural synthesis begin to break down. Then the Moroccan ulama, and the government, or makhzan, began to undergo a series of changes that considerably altered their power and influence. Yet although the ulama were ultimately considerably affected by the forces unleashed by European commercial and political penetration of Morocco, they continued to be powerfully influenced by popular Islamic beliefs and institutions. The remainder of this essay is devoted to an examination of the position of the ulama in Moroccan society, and the impact upon them of the economic, political, and social changes of the latter half of the nineteenth century and the first part of the twentieth.

The Position of the Ulama in Moroccan Society

Our analysis of the Moroccan style of Islam has stressed the fact that in spite of superficial resemblances between Morocco and the Ottoman Empire, there were many important differences that set the two apart. Much the same comment can be made about the position of the ulama in Moroccan society. Superficially there were many similarities between the ulama of Morocco and those of the Ottoman Empire.[9] That is to say, in Morocco there was the usual panoply of judicial and educational officials which one would expect to find in a Muslim country, and they were arranged in a roughly hierarchical organization. Although there was no Chief Mufti or Shaikh al-Islām in Morocco who headed the religious institution as there was in the Ottoman Empire, the principal religious official in Morocco, the Chief Qadi of Fez (Qāḍī al-Quḍāt) was a very important man. He appointed the qadis of all the cities of Morocco, named the professors and teachers at the Qarawīyīn mosque university (the center of higher learning in Moroccan Islam), and controlled the *ḥubus* (or *waqf*) properties of the city of Fez (which gave him access to substantial wealth). He jealously guarded his position from the centralizing attempts of the makhzan. As the first religious official of the country, one might think of him as being roughly equivalent to the Ottoman Shaikh al-Islām. But once again Moroccan appearances are deceiving. There was in fact no clearly separate religious institution in Moroccan society, and the Chief Qadi had no direct control over the manner in which provincial qadis conducted their office, and he did not function as a court of higher appeals for the country. Access to lesser judicial office was not controlled by the Chief Qadi, but instead was most often dependent upon personal and local ties with the particular individual qadi.[10] Access to teaching jobs in the Qarawīyīn was largely by cooptation within the old-boy network, again decisively influenced by personal ties.[11]

The office of mufti was of lesser importance in Morocco than in the Ottoman Empire. Early in the nineteenth century muftis had been ap-

[9] That is, with the portrait of the ulama of the Ottoman Empire presented in H.A.R. Gibb and Harold Bowen, *Islamic Society and the West,* Vol. 1, part 2 (London, 1957), pp. 81–113.

[10] Although named by the Chief Qadi, local qadis were in fact invariably of local origin, and were often elected by the local ulama and notables, with the Chief Qadi merely adding official approval. See, for example, the case of Tahamī al-Filāl cited in Muḥammad Ibn Dāwūd, *Mukhtaṣar Tarīkh Tiṭāwin,* Part 2 (Tiṭāwin, 1375/1955), p. 266.

[11] J. Berque, "Ville et Université, Aperçu sur l'histoire de l'Ecole de Fès," *Revue historique de droit française et étranger* (1949), pp. 64–114, on the history of the Qarawīyīn. On access to teaching jobs, A. Péretié, "Les madrasas de Fès," *A.M.*, XVIII (1912), 314–315, 328–330. Also Roger Le Tourneau, *Fez Avant le Protectorat* (Casablanca, 1949), pp. 214–215.

pointed by the sultan, but the Sultan Mawlāy 'Abd al-Raḥmān (1822–1859) appears to have stopped appointing them. Though the practice was resumed under his successors, the function of rendering judicial opinions, save on matters of public policy (an important exception) in Moroccan Malekite Islam, was handled chiefly through references to compendia of *fatwas*, such as the famous *Kitāb al-Miyar* of al-Wansharisī (834–914).[12] The sultan did retain the practice of consulting the ulama for opinions on matters where their approval might be beneficial in the implementing of a particular policy. Although the ulama in such situations rarely delivered judgments that contradicted the outcome the sultan desired, there were instances when the ulama dared to oppose the ruler. One such instance related by the Moroccan historian al-Nāṣirī was the opinion given by the ulama of Fez in response to a question of the Sultan Ḥasan I (1873–1894) as to whether the sale of tobacco, *kīf* (cannabis) and other stimulants by government monopoly was licit or illicit. To the astonishment of Ḥasan I, the ulama ruled that the practice (which had been followed by several sultans) was not permitted.[13] This was, however, an unusual outcome and was noted as such at the time. More generally characteristic was a high degree of cooperation of the ulama in the desires of the sultan. The kind of formalized check-and-balance system represented by the idealized Gibb and Bowen version of the Ottoman Ruling Institution and Religious Institution is quite foreign to nineteenth-century Moroccan realities.

Not only was there no religious institution, per se, in Morocco in the sense that there was no separate bureaucratic hierarchy of religious officials controlled from the top, it is even possible to say that the ulama as an identifiable corporate group did not exist in Morocco. Only if the term is restricted in its employ to refer to the seventeen to twenty major professors (*'ulamā al-kibār*) at the Qarawīyīn university (a limitation that considerably distorts the way the term is actually used) is it possible to distinguish a clearly defined group of ulama. Otherwise, some of the lesser professors might not be counted as belonging to the ulama while qadis, prominent sharifs, heads of religious brotherhoods, and individuals known for their piety and learning might well find their way into the group. The ulama acted as a corporate entity only when drawing up and signing the *bay'a* or act of allegiance to a new sultan, or when giving a formal legal

[12] On the influence of al-Wansharīsī, see Berque, 'Ville et Université," pp. 89–90.

[13] Aḥmad ibn Khālid al-Nāṣirī al-Salāwī, *Kitāb al-Istiqṣā lī Akhbār Duwwāl al-maghrib al-Aqṣa* (Casablanca, 1956), IX, 192–193, trans. E. Fumey, *A.M.*, X (1907), 356–358.

opinion (fatwa) on an important question which had been addressed to them by the sultan. There was no recognized head of the corps of ulama, and no internal organization such as might be present in a craft guild, for example.[14] Until 1900 the Moroccan ulama manifested no tendency to act corporately, or to intervene in politics. We shall see below how the changed circumstances after the death of Ḥasan I (1894) gradually drew the ulama into group action in the political sphere.

Except in times of tension, then, the notion of ulama in Morocco was quite fluid, and highly contextual. In general, the fact that an individual had studied at the Qarawīyīn university or one of the universities in the Middle East was often an important route to later recognition as being an alim. But personal connections, such as being the *kātib* (or secretary) of a wellborn qadi were often enough subsequently to propel an individual into this status. The case of the historian Aḥmad ibn Khālid al-Nāṣirī, who was employed for most of his life as an *amīn* (government customs agent), yet was accounted a member of the ulama of the provincial city of Salé, shows some of the variety that can be found among the members of the Moroccan ulama. In the Ottoman Empire it would have been impossible for a government official and nonacademic scholar like al-Nāṣirī to have been recognized as an alim. The importance of context in Morocco may come out more clearly in the following example. If we compare a list of the professors at the Qarawīyīn in 1905 with a list of men recorded as signing fatwas as members of the ulama of Fez during the same period, a considerable discrepancy can be observed. Some of those listed as professors did not sign the fatwas, while a number of others who were neither judges nor teachers did.[15] This suggests that as with other Moroccan indigenously created social categories, the status of alim was contextually defined. With further study it might be possible to probe the maximum and minimum boundaries defining membership in the ulama.

Since most if not all the members of the Moroccan ulama possessed other social identities as sharif, landowner, and so forth, it is by no means

[14] R. Le Tourneau, *La vie quotidienne à Fez en 1900* (Paris, 1965), p. 158.

[15] The list of professors at the Qarawīyīn may be found in Péretié, *op. cit.*, pp. 344–345. A list of individuals signing a fatwa condemning the rebel, Bou Hamara, may be found in "Lettre des Oulama de Fez," trans. Viala, *Bulletin de la Société de Géographie d'Oran*, XXIII (1903), pp. 254–255. See also the names indicated in "Proclamation de la déchéance de Moulay 'Abd al 'Azīz et de la reconnaissance de Moulay 'Abd el Hafiz par les Ouléma de Fès," trans. E. Michaux-Bellaire, *Revue du Monde Musulman* (hereafter cited as *R.M.M.*), V (1905), 426–427.

certain that their status as alim was the most important one in directing their actions in any given instance. Take, for example, a man like the Qarawīyīn professor and mufti Mahdi al-Wazzānī who was simultaneously, as it were, a prominent member of a saintly lineage (the house of Wazzan), an Idrīsī sharif, leader of a religious brotherhood (the Wazzānīya), a judicial official, a teacher, a landowner (he owned land among the Ḥiyāna tribe north of Fez) and no doubt a businessman as well. To define fully the social nexus in which this man lived it would also be necessary to specify his personal ties and his marriage alliances. To attempt to estimate which of the many interests that had a claim on a man like al-Wazzānī was decisive in influencing a particular action of his is clearly a very complex matter. Yet this is the kind of analysis that is necessary if we are ever to be able to get behind such stereotypes as "the ulama did thus and such." For every member of the ulama had many roles in Morocco, and the difficulties of getting concerted action from such a group are evidently all but insurmountable. We would need to know in such instances whether those participating did so as members of the ulama, or whether their action was instead a cloak for business interests, sharifian privileges, or one of their other subsidiary "identities." One must constantly refer to the particular context in order to gain a fuller appreciation of which role is being emphasized by an individual.

If one studies the career patterns of members of the Moroccan ulama in the late nineteenth century, one of the things that emerges is the considerable mobility that individuals possessed, physically, in their movements from city to city, socially, in the rapid rise and fall of individual careers, and occupationally, in the career lines they followed. An example may help bring out some of these factors. 'Abdullāh ibn Khaḍrā was born and raised in the city of Salé. He then studied in the Ottoman Empire (where is uncertain), and returned to Morocco while still a young man. Soon after his return the sultan Ḥasan I indicated that he would receive candidates for a number of government positions that needed to be filled, and in 1296 A.H./1878, Ibn Khaḍrā journeyed to Marrakesh with the historian al-Nāṣirī to try his luck. When his turn came to be received, he recited a poem in honor of the sultan which so captured the latter's fancy that he allowed Ibn Khaḍrā to name his reward. The young scholar requested the authorization to deliver fatwas and a *ẓahīr* (dahir) assuring him honor and respect. He was given both of his requests and appointed to teach in the mosque of Ibn Yūsuf in Marrakesh, with a salary paid by ḥubus revenues. Later on he was appointed to a position in the financial ministry as an amin for government expenses, in which post he served for a year. Soon thereafter, and while still a young man, he was appointed qadi of Marrakesh, and worked to eliminate the bribery and corruption that had flourished under the previous occupant of that office. This inevitably made him many powerful enemies in the city, and he was forced to resign. For about the next fifteen years of his life he served as a customs agent (amīn) in a number of Moroccan port cities. Finally he was appointed Chief Qadi of Fez (the last to serve in that office) and taught at the Qarawīyīn university. His reputation for honesty and learning was further enhanced during his stay in that office.[16]

The following points should be noted in this brief biography. First of all, the fact that Ibn Khaḍrā was of provincial origin made him a bit of an anomaly among the professors at the Qarawīyīn, as did the fact that he had studied in the Ottoman Empire. It will be noticed that Ibn Khaḍrā began his career as a teacher, and was then successively financial agent, judge in a provincial city, customs agent, and finally Chief Qadi of Fez, freely crossing from government service to the judiciary and back with little apparent logic or purpose. Further investigation of the case of Ibn Khaḍrā would probably reveal the crucial importance of personal ties in his advancement. This may also provide a partial explanation for the erratic course of his career. One of the things that a consideration of his career suggests is how much a part of government service a "religious" career like that of a judge appears to have been in Morocco in the nineteenth century. The differences between the Moroccan practice and that of the Ottoman Empire where the careers were kept much more rigidly separate are striking.

While the primacy of the ulama of Fez on political questions is a well-established principle of Moroccan history, one must not lose sight of the surprising vigor of the ulama of some of the provincial cities of the realm. Since during the late nineteenth century the court was frequently in residence in Marrakesh when it was not at Fez, the ulama of that city acquired a considerable reputation of their own. The patronage of the court and the proximity to the halls of power evidently had much to do with this development. After the death of Mawlāy al-Ḥasan in 1894, the effective rule of Morocco fell to the Grand Vizier and Regent, Sī Aḥmad ibn Mūsā.

[16] The career of Ibn Khaḍrā is discussed in Kenneth Brown, "The Social History of a Moroccan Town: Salé, 1830–1930," unpublished Ph.D. dissertation, University of California, Los Angeles, 1969, pp. 320–321.

Bā Aḥmad, as he was known, had a strong personal preference for Marrakesh over Fez and the court was in continuous residence there from 1897 until 1902. During this period the Fez region gradually slid into insecurity and neglect. The importance of the ulama of Marrakesh rose as a result, a fact we see reflected in the comments of the biographer of Muḥammad ibn 'Abd al-Kabīr al-Kattānī, (a member of the Fez ulama) about his visit to Marrakesh during this period.[17]

An indication that where political matters were concerned the ulama of Fez were not the only force in the kingdom can be found by consideration of the early moments of the Ḥafīẓīya movement of 1907–1908. When Morocco began to drift further under French control after the Algeciras conference, a considerable amount of internal opposition to the continued rule of the sultan 'Abd al-'Aziz (1894–1908) developed. The campaign for the deposition of 'Abd al-'Azīz centered upon Marrakesh, where the backing of the great tribal barons of the Western High Atlas was assured. It was the ulama of Marrakesh who took the lead by announcing on August 16, 1907, a formal opinion that 'Abd al-'Aziz must be deposed, and that his brother 'Abd al-Ḥafīẓ was qualified to replace him. They first signed the *bay'a* (oath of ratification) of 'Abd al-Ḥafīẓ, and their example soon attracted imitators among the ulama of the other cities of the realm.[18] It was therefore not only the ulama of Fez who could be political leaders. While the fate of the Ḥafīẓīya movement was evidently decided less by the stand taken by the ulama, than by the presence of some of the most powerful elements of Moroccan society among their ranks, it is clear that the decision of the ulama of Marrakesh formally legitimized rebellion in this instance on the grounds that the present sultan was incompetent to defend Islam from its enemies.

The vigor of the ulama in other provincial cities in the latter half of the nineteenth century is no less well attested. In addition to Fez, the other *ḥaḍrīya* towns in Morocco (in which the Andalusians expelled from Spain had settled) Tetuán, Tangier, and Salé all possessed well-developed traditions of learning. All showed signs of intellectual ferment and activity during the period. The city of Salé may be taken as typical of this group. The famous historian Aḥmad ibn Khālid al-Nāṣirī was from Salé,

[17] Muḥammad Bāqir al-Kattānī, *Tarjama Shaykh Muḥammad al-Kattānī al-Shahīd* (n.p., 1962), pp. 79–81.

[18] The Ḥafīẓīya is discussed in more detail below. On it, for example, A. G. P. Martin, *Quatre Siecles d'histoire marocaine* (Paris: F. Alcan, 1923), pp. 447–495.

as was the Chief Qadi of Fez Ibn Khaḍrā. Numerous other important writers, judges, teachers, and government officials in pre-Protectorate Morocco also came from this city.[19]

In the wake of this evidence, it is probably time to reconsider the prevailing tendency among historians of Morocco to perceive events from a Fez-oriented viewpoint. Since the seat of government was often at Fez, the Qarawīyīn university was the only institution of higher learning in Morocco, and the shrine of Mawlāy Idrīs and the presence of many influential sharifs all were concentrated upon Fez, there was considerable ground for this opinion. As a result of this, however, insufficient account is taken of the mobility that existed within the ulama and the existence of a number of important provincial centers of religious learning.

Social and Economic Changes and Governmental Reforms, 1860–1912

Since the Moroccan ulama were not a corporate group under ordinary circumstances, but instead were drawn in a number of different directions by the other positions and roles they filled in Moroccan society, their initial responses to the social and economic changes that began to shake the country after 1859 were characteristically diffuse. Only toward the end of the century, as the impact of these changes and of makhzan attempts to respond to them by reforming and centralizing the instruments of government began to impinge more directly upon them, did the Moroccan ulama begin to drift into a confrontation with the state. Since the reforms not only threatened the privileges and position of the ulama, but also provided them with new opportunities to increase their wealth and power, the impact of these changes was not as keenly felt as it might have been. Only after 1900 when a new challenge, that of the French colonial offensive, was added to the confusion of rapid social and economic change did the ulama begin to emerge as the spokesmen of national independence against the weak rule of 'Abd al-'Azīz (1894–1908). For the moment our concern is with the ways in which governmental reforms affected the position of the ulama. The next section examines their responses to the threat of French imperialism after 1900.

Although the image of pre-Protectorate Morocco which has been enshrined in the historical literature is one of an unchanging medieval

[19] Brown, *op. cit.*, pp. 305–310.

Muslim state, it is important to realize that Moroccan sultans of the nineteenth century were seriously concerned about the changes that began to threaten the Moroccan position during the course of the century. A series of important efforts at reforms can be traced from the reign of Muḥammad IV (1859–1873) to that of ʿAbd al-Ḥafīẓ (1908–1912). For the most part these reforms were unsuccessful, owing to the lack of human and financial resources in the Moroccan government to press them through to a conclusion, and to the obstacles posed by poor internal communications, tribalism, and well-entrenched interest groups. Among these interest groups, the various religious brotherhoods, local saints and sharifs, and an independent judiciary and educational system were among the most important. It is therefore no wonder that reforming sultans from Ḥasan I (1873–1894) onward were drawn into attempting to reduce the power and influence of the religious groups. This necessarily eventually brought the government into conflict with the ulama, since the members of the ulama were also sharifs, saints, and heads of religious brotherhoods. The attempts of the government to centralize the bureaucracy and reform it along Western lines was another source of conflict, insofar as the judicial and education systems were part of the bureaucracy. Owing to the delicate nature of tampering with the privileges of the ulama, the sultans adopted a policy of only gradually seeking to extend the control of the government over the judiciary and the Qarawīyīn university.

Until the reign of Ḥasan I there had been only one qadi of Fez al-Bali (old Fez), and he was the Chief Qadi. The appointment of the other qadis of Morocco was traditionally vested in his hands, giving him considerable control at least in theory over the system of religious courts. Mawlāy al-Ḥasan took a first step to whittling away the powers of the Chief Qadi by appointing a second qadi to share jurisdiction over Fez al-Bali. The principal qadi became known as the *qāḍī al-jāmiʿ*.[20] This situation persisted until 1906 when the last Chief Qadi, ʿAbdullāh Ibn Khaḍrā, died. The office was drastically altered by the sultan ʿAbd al-ʿAzīz. The old title was abolished, and a new one, "Nāib al-makhzan fī Aḥkām al-Sharīʿa" (Representative of the Makhzan for Shariʿa Judgments), was given to his successor ʿAbd al-Salām al-Hawārī. The new title in effect undermined the independent position of the Chief Qadi as the chief interpreter of the religious law in the kingdom. In addition, from this point onward the Qadi al-jāmiʿ was no longer permitted to appoint the other qadis, as this

[20] Péretié, *op. cit.*, pp. 315–316, 329–330.

function was taken over by the sultan. Henceforth he could only propose names for nomination to the sultan, who was under no obligation to accept his suggestions.[21]

Similar developments marked the limitation upon the Chief Qadi's authority in the realm of education during the reign of 'Abd al-'Azīz. The sultan officially took over the headship of the Qarawīyīn university, and deprived the qadi of the right to appoint professors and approve their advancement in grade. Again, the qadi was allowed only to propose names for nomination as teachers in the university, whereas formerly there had been no direct controls upon his conduct in this area. Still, radical as these changes were, too much should not be made of them. There is no evidence that the government sought to intervene directly in an attempt to influence the behavior of either judges or professors. No program was laid down, no provision for regular inspection was made of the way in which these individuals conducted their official functions.[22] The effects of government centralization efforts upon the Moroccan ulama were therefore only marginal, at best.

More important as a source of conflict between the ulama and the government was the attempt on the part of the sultans to restrict the right of mosques and religious shrines to accord sanctuary to criminals and political opponents of the makhzan. The first shadowy beginnings of this policy stretch back into the reign of Mawlāy Sulaymān (1792–1822). It was Mawlāy Sulaymān who first attempted to put Wahhabi ideals into practice in Morocco. He launched a campaign against the worship of saints, and strove to prevent religious shrines from granting protection to refugees from makhzan justice.[23] Under Mawlāy al-Ḥasan this trend continued.

Perhaps the most famous example of the makhzan drive against the right of shrines to accord sanctuary occurred in October of 1902, when 'Abd al-'Azīz intervened to arrest a tribesman who had killed an English tourist, even though the man was formally under the protection of the shrine of Mawlāy Idrīs at Fez. Since this shrine was the holiest one in Moroccan Islam, and its guardians and patrons were the Idrīsī sharifs, the incident was particularly serious. When the sultan had the murderer put to death soon thereafter, he drove into opposition the guardians of the

21 *Ibid.*
22 *Ibid.*, pp. 315–316, 318–320.
23 Jamil Abun-Nasr, "The Salafiyya Movement in Morocco: The Religious Bases of the Moroccan Nationalist Movement," in Immanuel Wallerstein, ed., *Social Change: The Colonial Situation* (New York: John Wiley and Sons, Inc., 1966), pp. 492–493.

shrine and many prominent Idrīsī sharifs (a number of whom were members of the ulama of Fez). The appearance of a pretender to the throne in the hills to the north of Fez soon thereafter placed the regime in considerable jeopardy. The pretender, who was named Abū Ḥimāra (generally rendered in the French version, Bou Hamara), linked up with the defenders of the shrine for several months. Only after his defeat by makhzan forces in January of 1903 did the custodians of Mawlāy Idrīs renounce their attempt to overthrow 'Abd al-'Azīz, largely, it might be added, from disappointment with the qualifications of Bou Hamara for the position. The rebel continued to plague Moroccan governments until his capture in 1909, but he no longer posed a serious threat to the regime after 1903.[24] In subsequent years 'Abd al-'Azīz was even able to obtain a fatwa from the ulama of Fez which was sharply critical of Bou Hamara.[25] The incident undoubtedly contributed to the weakening of the support of many among the ulama of Fez for 'Abd al-'Azīz, and helped pave the way for his eventual deposition.

In addition to the attack upon the right of sanctuary, there was a general tendency on the part of Moroccan sultans from as far back as the reign of Mawlāy Sulaymān (1792–1822) to inveigh against the abuses of popular saint cults and the heterodoxy of certain Sufi brotherhoods. In a country where the power of the sultan was fragile even in good times, and where localized saints and *ṭuruq* were able to develop strong local roots and acquire a large and devoted clientele, such groups were potential threats to the control of the government, and blocks to its centralizing drive. Where Idrīsī sharifs were involved, in particular, the makhzan had to be very discreet, for the Filālī (Alawi) dynasty had never been fully accepted by them, and there was always a danger that an Idrīsī sharif might develop a sufficient following to be tempted to compete directly against the government. There were thus ample reasons for the government to feel the need of a policy that reduced the attractiveness of the local saint cults and religious brotherhoods to the people.

As in the case of the suppression of the right of sanctuary at Mawlāy Idrīs at Fez, where members of the ulama were also patrons of the shrine, makhzan attempts to circumscribe the influence of the brotherhoods could

[24] On the origins of the revolt of Bou Hamara, and the breaking of the right of sanctuary of Mawlāy Idris see René Pinon, *L'Empire de la Méditerranée* (Paris, 1904), pp. 153–157. Also, Eugène Aubin (Descos), *Le Maroc d'aujourd-hui* (Paris, 1904), pp. 108–131, and *Afrique Française* (1902), p. 395.

[25] A translation of the fatwa appeared in *Afrique Française* (1903), pp. 225–226.

and did excite the opposition of those members of ulama who were also members of particular religious brotherhoods. There was, for example, persistent friction between Mawlāy al-Ḥasan and the head of the Wazzānīya ṭarīqa, Mawlāy 'Abd al-Salām, in the 1880s growing out of French efforts to utilize the sharif of Wazzan (who was a French protégé) to further their imperial ends, and the attempts by Mawlāy al-Ḥasan to reassert makhzan control over them.[26] An antibrotherhood policy was never consistently pursued by Ḥasan or his successor, however, for the dangers of failure were too great. Perhaps the most notable instance of the attempted crackdown on the Sufi orders came early in the reign of 'Abd al-Ḥafīẓ. In 1908–1909 this sultan, who had become attracted to Salafīya by the desire to counteract the excesses of the religious brotherhoods, launched a broad-gauge attack on three of the most important brotherhoods in the north of Morocco. He published a pamphlet violently attacking the Tijānīya order, arrested and killed the head of the Kattānīya, and sought to restore makhzan authority in the city of Wazzan, headquarters of the Wazzānīya, which had enjoyed a de facto autonomous control over its internal affairs for many years.[27] As with the case of 'Abd al-'Azīz's suppression of the right of sanctuary of Mawlāy Idrīs, this series of actions by 'Abd al-Ḥafīẓ incited considerable opposition among the ulama of Fez (as well as other cities) who happened to be affiliated with these brotherhoods. But in this case 'Abd al-Ḥafīẓ possessed great prestige as the sultan of the *jihād*, owing to his recent leadership of the resistance against the French in the Chaouia (1907–1908), and was in a much stronger military position. Thus there were fewer signs of opposition by the ulama. Subsequently, many withdrew into a sullen neutrality and refrained from supporting the sultan when he later got into difficulties with the tribes around Fez in 1911.

Discussion of the makhzan attempts to crack down on the abuses of the saint cult and the heterodoxy of religious brotherhoods leads to yet another aspect of the way in which the reforms policy of the sultans manifested itself, namely, through government patronage of religious scholars

[26] On this episode see Jean-Louis Miège, *Le Maroc et l'Europe* (Paris, 1961–1963), IV, 44–81.

[27] On 'Abd al-Ḥafīẓ's attack on the religious brotherhoods, see the following: France, Archives, *Ministère de la Guerre. Maroc. Série C-22*, Mangin, "Notice sur Sidi Mohammad el Kettani," March 25, 1909 (hereafter cited as *Guerre*); Great Britain. Archives, *Foreign Office. 413/54*, Lister to Grey, March 7, 1911, No. 40 (hereafter cited as *F.O.*). Also Abun-Nasr, *op. cit.*, p. 98; *Guerre. Maroc. Série C-22*, Mangin to Guerre, July 2, 1909, no. 58.

who favored the purification and reform of Moroccan Islam. Ḥasan I inaugurated this policy by his support of 'Abdullāh ibn Idrīs al-Sanūsī, a proponent of the Islamic reformist movement known as Salafīya. In the 1870s after a period of time studying at universities in the Middle East (including at al-Azhar), al-Sanūsī returned to Morocco to take up a position teaching at the Qarawīyīn. He was also appointed a member of the royal learned council, with whom the sultan studied theology and jurisprudence. But the time was not yet ripe for the widespread acceptance of Salafīya ideas in Morocco, and al-Sanūsī met with such strong criticism from the ulama of Fez that he soon found his position there untenable and returned to the Middle East.[28] Mawlāy al-Ḥasan had not seen fit to battle the ulama of Fez on behalf of his protégé. Only after the accession of 'Abd al-'Azīz was al-Sanūsī able to return to Morocco, retiring to Tangier.

A second scholar who appears to have exercised considerable influence upon not only Ḥasan I, but also 'Abd al-'Azīz and 'Abd al-Ḥafīẓ, was the Mauritanian figure Mā al-'Aynayn. While not a Salafī, Mā al-'Aynayn was convinced of the need to purify the religious brotherhoods of their heterodox practices, and to suppress many of the excesses of the saint cults. He preached the unification of the religious brotherhoods into one, his own. By this, and his leadership of resistance to French imperialism in Mauritania, he succeeded in attracting the interest of Mawlāy al-Ḥasan. Makhzan patronage of Mā al-'Aynayn continued until his death in 1910, and both 'Azīz and Ḥafīẓ were considerably influenced by many of his ideas.[29] Under 'Abd al-'Azīz the 'Aynaynīya brotherhood enjoyed a vogue among the high makhzan officials.[30] Mā al-'Aynayn was widely respected among the Moroccan ulama as an eminent scholar and religious figure, and he occasionally assisted in the deliberations of the ulama in the rendering of legal opinions. The most notable instance of this was Mā al-'Aynayn's chairmanship of a panel of the ulama who investigated charges of heterodoxy against Muḥammad ibn 'Abd al-Kabīr al-Kattānī.[31]

Under Mawlāy 'Abd al-'Azīz there were further efforts on the part of the makhzan to patronize members of the ulama who supported the program of reforms which the government had embarked upon. 'Abd al-'Azīz

[28] Abun-Nasr, *op. cit.*, p. 494.

[29] Julio Caro Baroja, "Un Santon Sahariano y su familia," in *Estudios Saharianos* (Madrid, 1955), esp. pp. 295–326. Also Paul Marty, "Les Fadelia," *R.M.M.*, XXXI (1915–1916), 160–166.

[30] al-Moutabassir, "Ma el Ainin Ech Changuity," *R.M.M.*, I (1907), 348. Aubin, *op. cit.*, p. 231.

[31] al-Kattānī, *op. cit.*, pp. 85–86.

relied upon al-Mufaḍḍal al-Sūsī, a Marrakesh faqih, and the qaḍi of Fez al-Jadid (new Fez), Muḥammad al-'Iraqī, for support for his attempt to introduce a major tax-reform program.[32] Under 'Abd al-Ḥafīẓ, Abū Shu'ayb al-Dukkālī served as a major advisor on religious policy. Al-Dukkālī, who has been referred to as the Moroccan Abduh, was born in the countryside outside of the city of Safi on the Atlantic coast of Morocco, and studied for many years in the Middle East. He was recalled to Morocco by 'Abd al-Ḥafīẓ in 1907, and appointed to teach at the Qarawīyīn. There he reintroduced the teaching of *tafsīr* (exegesis), while also serving as a religious tutor to the sultan and a member of the royal learned council. It was under his influence that 'Abd al-Ḥafīẓ launched the campaign against the religious brotherhoods in 1908–1909 noted above. Al-Dukkālī lived long enough to become the teacher of many of the founders of the Salafīya movement in Morocco and many of the first nationalists.[33]

The conflict between the state and the ulama had other aspects besides the religious policy of the sultans and their attempts to centralize the bureaucracy. One of the most significant was the opposition of the ulama to government-sponsored tax reforms including the introduction of new taxes, the elimination of tax exemptions, and the reform of inefficiencies in the collection of the old taxes. The economic changes of the second half of the nineteenth century, which included runaway inflation, a huge war debt and reparations charges, and the absorption of Morocco into the world capitalist system, forced the government to seek to upgrade the efficiency of the bureaucracy, and to become increasingly ruthless in the collection of taxes. Since the ulama included many individuals who benefited from tax exemptions and other privileges from the government, a move to restrict these privileges would incite much opposition. Many members of the ulama of Fez and other Moroccan cities had business relations with the merchant bourgeoisie, if they were not themselves from merchant families.[34] An effort by the makhzan to introduce such new taxes

[32] France, Archives, *Ministère des Affaires Etrangères. Maroc. Politique Etrangère. Dossier General, II*, Gaillard to Saint-René-Taillandier, July 25, 1902 (annex to Tangier dispatch of August 2, 1902) (hereafter cited as *M.A.E.*).

[33] On al-Dukkālī cf. Abun-Nasr, *op. cit.*, pp. 494–496. Also J. Berque, "Ça et là dans les débuts du reformisme religieuse au Maghreb," *Études d'Orientalisme dediés à la memoire de Levi-Provençal* (Paris, 1962), II, 480–483.

[34] Muḥammad Ibn Dāwūd (*op. cit.*) cites a Faqīh Abū 'Abdullāh Muḥammad al-Najjār who earned his living as a merchant (pp. 325–326). Many of the ulama of Fez came from bourgeois families well known for producing merchants as well as scholars.

as the market tax, or *maks* (a tax on the entry and exit of goods from the cities), or to establish new government monopolies thus risked stirring up opposition among the ulama as well as the bourgeoisie.

After 1860, the Moroccan government in fact moved to establish market taxes and to do away with many of the privileges and tax exemptions enjoyed by prominent sharifs and religious personalities. The sultans tended to proceed cautiously in the implementation of this policy, since the ulama tended to join forces with the merchants, and to become the leaders of the opposition. Several times during the period demonstrations forced the government to back down from announced tax policies. There were riots at Fez in 1894 when Mawlāy al-Ḥasan restored the maks (gate tax),[35] further disturbances in 1902–1903 when ʿAbd al-ʿAzīz sought to introduce the *tartīb* (a new universal tax on agricultural products from which no exemptions would be granted),[36] and still further disturbances in 1908 when ʿAbd al-Ḥafīẓ restored the maks and government monopolies at Fez after his accession.[37] But contrary to the Iranian pattern of the alliance of bazaar and ulama referred to elsewhere in this volume, the Moroccan government was generally able to keep the two groups divided.

The attempts of the makhzan to extend its control over the judiciary and the educational system, and parallel efforts to reduce the privileges of well-entrenched religious interests should ordinarily have led to strong protests by the ulama. That it did not owed partly to the multifaceted interests of the ulama, which meant that the group as a whole was never directly threatened, and partly to the gradual way in which the government pursued its policy. Only after 1900, as the sultans became more desperate in their attempts to deal with the rapidly deteriorating situation, did they abandon this gradual approach and begin directly to challenge broad segments of the ulama. There was, however, another reason why at least until 1900 the government was not brought into conflict with the ulama: they were among the chief beneficiaries of the modernization of the state bureaucracy.

The makhzan had originally been staffed and run by members of the privileged military tribes (*jaysh*, or in the French version, guich.) But other than a talent for intrigue most of these individuals possessed few

[35] Nāṣirī, *op. cit.*, pp. 129, 136–137, trans. Fumey, *op. cit.*, pp. 279–280, 291–294.

[36] On the *tartīb* see Aubin, *op. cit.*, pp. 253–256.

[37] The difficulties of ʿAbd al-Ḥafīẓ are treated in *Afrique Française* (1908), pp. 250–251.

qualifications for their posts. The declining economic position of Morocco after 1859 required that many new posts as tax administrators, customs officials, and the like be created by the makhzan to extract the maximum revenues possible. Since the jaysh bureaucrats were lacking in the necessary skills to staff such positions, the sultans were compelled to look elsewhere to fill them. The graduates of the madrasas and the Qarawīyīn university comprised one of the few sources of qualified individuals, and thus there was a heavy influx of intellectuals into government service, many of whom maintained their connections with the religious teachers who had formed them, and like Ibn Khaḍrā moved freely from the office of amīn to that of a qadi or a teacher.[38] In this way the ulama came to play an important role in the modernization schemes of the government, providing the cadre for the transformation of the makhzan.

The bulk of these new officials came from Tetuán, Salé, and Fez, the traditional seats of bourgeois culture and learning in Morocco. Personal connections, rather than ability, seem to have been a major factor in the recruitment of new personnel. A study of the amīns from the city of Salé has clearly demonstrated the importance of such links.[39] Service as an amīn was an important source of patronage, payoffs, and graft, and seems to have been instrumental in the rise of a new class of wealthy men in Morocco between 1890 and 1910. Finally, as was observed above in our study of the career patterns of members of the ulama, a number of important members of the ulama of Fez, as well as those of the provincial cities, rose to the rank of qadi through service in the government financial administration.

Although most of the amīns were drawn from the merchant class and had no aspirations toward eventually becoming recognized as members of the ulama, the fact that at least some of the ulama were given access to power in the state may help explain the relative absence of a prolonged and bitter conflict between the state and the ulama prior to 1900. Using their connections in the government, members of the ulama could seek to resolve their difficulties and soften the effect of government policy. They therefore did not have to band together to oppose makhzan measures that threatened their interests.

[38] On the influx of intellectuals into the government, see Aubin, *op. cit.*, pp. 190, 194, 207. Also Brown, *op. cit.*, pp. 305–307, 325–326.

[39] Brown, *op. cit.*, pp. 315–318, 326–331.

The Political Role of the Moroccan Ulama, 1900–1912

The attempt by successive Moroccan sultans in the latter half of the nineteenth century to extend the control of the government over the state apparatus and to introduce reforms would not of itself have resulted in the stimulation of strong opposition from the ulama. The reforms themselves were rarely vigorously applied, and few of them directly disturbed the interests of the ulama as a group. Even when the pace of reform increased after 1900, and the ulama found themselves more in the line of fire, it is uncertain whether this fact alone would have generated more than vocal protests. To understand the sudden crystallization of the ulama of Morocco as the leaders in the opposition to the government of 'Abd al-'Azīz in the years 1900–1908, some consideration must be given to their ideological role in the Moroccan state. For it was largely because of the position of the ulama as the holders of the symbols of legitimacy and the guardians of the interests and independence of the Moroccan state, that they became involved in the struggle against a government which by its reform policies threatened their interests, and by its foreign policy toward Europe threatened national independence.

As elsewhere in the Muslim world, in Morocco it was the scholars of the Koran, the traditions, and the holy law, who were charged with the task of preserving the purity and integrity of the faith. The ulama served as watchdogs over the Islamic cultural heritage, and guaranteed that it would be passed on from one generation to another intact and free of contamination. More importantly, it was the ulama in Morocco who retained the chief symbols of legitimacy in the state, and who as the guardians of the interests of the people had the power to depose one sultan and proclaim a successor should a ruler waver in the performance of his essential duties. The preservation of the independence of the *dār al-Islām* against the unbelievers was the first duty of the *amīr*. Should a sultan prove himself unenergetic in the performance of this task, then the ulama were expected to take steps to see that another, more worthy sultan was placed upon the throne.[40] In addition, the sultans often consulted the ulama on important issues of the moment. It was the ulama of Fez who ordinarily served as the highest body to which important matters of public policy could be referred for judgment. But if the court happened to be located

[40] Martin, *op. cit.*, pp. 456–458.

in another of the capital cities of Morocco, a sultan could address his request for a formal legal opinion to the ulama of that city. It was the ulama who issued fatwas on important issues of the moment, such as whether Muslims who collaborated with the Christians against Islam could lawfully be dispossessed or not, whether the government could maintain a monopoly on the sale of tobacco and kīf, and whether tax reforms were lawful or not. It was also the ulama who were charged with the drawing up of the bay'a, the official ratification of a new sultan. In Morocco, the bay'a retained some of the quasi-democratic associations that it had held under the first caliphs, although it was not the instrument of popular sovereignty some have claimed it to have been.[41]

For most of the nineteenth century it was less the threat of European invasion which upset the Moroccan ulama than it was the insidious side effects of European commercial penetration, especially in the port cities. There it seemed to many of the ulama all manner of vice and immorality flourished unchecked, and the inroads of European stimulants were most marked. The ulama, of whom al-Nāṣirī may be taken as representative, manifested alarm at the increase in alcoholism and drug addiction in the ports after 1860.[42] Tangier, being the major part of the realm and the center of the diplomatic interchange between the makhzan and the powers, was viewed as contaminated beyond hope of redemption by the presence of a large resident European population. It appeared to learned and pious Moroccans as the fountain of iniquity, much celebrated in pessimistic verse.[43] Even the spread of the habit of drinking tea in Morocco was seen as something subversive. The sharif Muḥammad ibn 'Abd al-Kabīr al-Kattānī was so alarmed by the development of tea consumption among the Moroccan elite that he forbade it to the followers of his religious brotherhood. He saw in the spread of tea (and sugar, its essential companion in the Moroccan method of preparation), the beginning of a European take-over of the Moroccan economy, and a prelude to colonization.[44] A concern for the economic independence of the country was a trend in the thinking of the ulama which was heightened by the series of loans in which the Moroccan government engaged after 1900.

Prior to 1900, the Moroccan ulama had not shown much desire vig-

[41] Such as the exaggerated claims of Mohamed Lahbadi, *Le Gouvernement marocain à l'aube du XXe siècle* (Rabat, 1958), pp. 41–60.

[42] al-Nāṣirī, *op. cit.*, pp. 193–199, trans. Fumey, *op. cit.*, pp. 358–368.

[43] See for example the anonymous poem in "La corruption des moeurs à Tangier," P. Paquignon, trans., *R.M.M.*, VII (1909), 23–38.

[44] al-Kattānī, *op. cit.*, pp. 93–94.

orously to assert their duty to defend the cause of national independence. When, after the French invasion of Algeria in 1830, the ulama of the city of Tlemcen addressed a request for Moroccan support to the ulama of Fez they were turned down.[45] The Moroccans similarly showed little strong desire to support the Algerian resistance leader 'Abd al-Qādir, although in both instances they were overruled by the Moroccan sultan. Neither the Moroccan defeat at Isly by the French (1844), nor the Hispano-Moroccan War of 1859–1860 stimulated the ulama of Fez to demonstrations of especial zeal. Rather, they remained attached to an essentially conservative strategy of avoiding unnecessary entanglements with European powers, apparently banking on Morocco's relative isolation to preserve it from attack. Since the nineteenth-century sultans maintained a diplomatic policy aimed at playing off the powers against one another, the ulama could rest content that national interests were being attended to and that their intervention was unnecessary. While the nineteenth-century Moroccan sultans limited their attempts at reform to the army, and did not attempt more than limited reforms in other spheres, there was little reason for the Moroccan ulama to oppose the government directly. Even the religious policy of Mawlāy al-Ḥasan had been relatively cautious—he had acquiesced in the dismissal of al-Sanūsī from the Qarawīyīn, for example, and had proceeded slowly in his campaign to limit the right of local shrines to accord the privilege of sanctuary to fugitives from makhzan justice.

After the death of Ḥasan I (1894), however, circumstances changed. With the French invasion of the Touat oasis complex in the central Sahara (1900), the diplomatic stalemate was broken, and Morocco had to confront the direct threat of French imperialism. At the same time the vigorous reform policy of 'Abd al-'Azīz and his bold religious policy threatened many of the traditional interests of the ulama. The combination of these factors soon produced a much more activist Moroccan ulama, led by the ulama of Fez. Since the court was in residence at Fez for most of the period 1900–1912, the makhzan was placed under the direct surveillance of the ulama of Fez, a fact that further encouraged the emergence of the Fāsī ulama as the defenders of national independence and of the interests of the merchant class.

Reactions to the conquest of Touat among the Moroccan population as a whole were mild. Given the relative isolation in which most rural Moroccans lived, there is no reason to have expected otherwise. But among

[45] al-Nāṣirī, *op cit.*, pp. 26–27, trans. Fumey, *op. cit.*, pp. 132–133.

the ulama on the contrary, there was considerable alarm expressed at Fez and elsewhere. An indication of the views of the ulama is provided by the anonymous author of the *Ḥalāl al-Bahīya.* He has nothing but scorn for the mild diplomatic protests of the government of 'Abd al-'Azīz. A real Muslim government, he makes it plain, would have been ashamed to appeal to the Christian powers for assistance, when the only proper response was a military one. Another indication of the extreme displeasure of elements of the Moroccan elite with the policy of the government on the French seizure of Touat is the strange death of the Moroccan envoy to the powers, who "accidently" suffocated to death at Tangier in a *ḥammām* (bath), soon after delivering the makhzan's pro forma diplomatic protest.[46] When the government of 'Abd al-'Azīz continued to place its trust in the efficacy of diplomacy as a means of dealing with the French colonial offensive along the Algerian border, and even signed accords with the French in 1901 and 1903 which the ulama regarded as a sellout, opposition began to develop and spread.

The active opposition of the ulama was finally stimulated in 1903 when the government of 'Abd al-'Azīz initiated a program of radical internal reforms which directly threatened the privileges of the ulama, and seemed likely to give Great Britain a dominant position in Moroccan affairs. Taken in conjunction with the weak response to French military incursions along Morocco's Algerian frontiers, it demonstrated the dangerously weak status of the government. The attempted application of a new universal tax, the *tartīb,* from which no exemptions would be granted, struck at the root of sharifian privileges.[47] At the same time, the swarm of speculators and confidence men around the royal court and the unpredictable ways of the young sultan gravely alarmed the ulama. With pressures building up, the breaking of the right of sanctuary of Mawlāy Idrīs and the rise of Bou Hamara galvanized the ulama into open opposition for a time, and served as an indication of their new political role. While the fears of Bou Hamara were still high they induced the sultan to expel his European entourage to the coast, where they would be safer. Although some of them returned when the emergency was over, European influence was never again as strong upon the young sultan as it had been. British influence in the makhzan underwent a sharp decline, and the

[46] "Un opinion marocaine sur la conquête du Touat," trans. G. Salmon, *A.M.*, I (1905), 416–424. On the *Ḥalāl al-Bahīya* cf. E. Levi-Provençal, *Les Historiens des Chorfa* (Paris, 1922), pp. 371–372.

[47] On reactions to the *tartīb,* see Aubin, *op. cit.*, pp. 254–256.

British were forced to abandon their strong support of reforms. Under heavy fire from the ulama and his enemies within the makhzan the chief supporter of British interests in the government, the royal favorite Mahdī al-Munabbhī, was compelled to resign. In order to preserve his life, he had to go on a lengthy pilgrimage to Mecca and the Near East.[48]

The ulama of Fez were drawn into still more direct conflict with the government following the signing of a loan agreement between a consortium of French banks and the makhzan in 1904. The terms of the loan, which included the giving of 60 percent of the customs revenues as security, seriously compromised Moroccan economic independence. When this was accompanied by the news of the Franco-British Accord (under the terms of which Great Britain renounced its claims to Morocco in return for a free hand in Egypt), the dangers of a French protectorate suddenly became acute. The French government followed up its gains by making preparations for its minister at Tangier, Georges Saint-René-Taillandier, to present a comprehensive program of reforms to 'Abd al-'Azīz early in 1905.[49]

The resistance of the ulama to further French encroachment increased in the summer of 1904 after the return from the Middle East of a number of Moroccan pilgrims, including the sharif Muḥammad ibn 'Abd al-Kabīr al-Kattānī.[50] Under the leadership of al-Kattānī, the ulama of Fez issued a fatwa in which it denounced the government policy of hiring European advisors to help reform the makhzan and the army. The need for these advisors, they asserted, had not been demonstrated. For the most part, they went on to say, Moroccans were perfectly capable of performing the tasks that the Europeans had done. Where advisors were genuinely needed, there were Near Eastern Muslims who were capable of imparting the necessary skills and knowledge. Accordingly, they suggested that the makhzan dismiss all of its European personnel, and hire Egyptians and Turks to take their place.[51] Under heavy fire at Fez, the makhzan issued orders that the European advisors to the government should cease their work, and that qualified Muslim replacements be hired. News of this dramatic turnabout reached Tangier on December 17, on the eve of the

[48] Pierre Guillen, *L'Allemagne et le Maroc* (Paris, 1967), pp. 619–620.

[49] On the French reform program see France, *Documents diplomatiques. Affaires du Maroc, 1901–1905*, Vol I, no. 209.

[50] *M.A.E., Maroc. Politique Etrangère. Rélations avec la France*, XV, Saint-René-Taillandier to Delcassé, Dec. 10, 1904, no. 248. Also, A. Terrier, "La Crise marocaine," *Questions diplomatiques et coloniales* (1905), p. 4.

[51] "Le Fetoua des oulama de Fès," *A.M.*, IV (1905), 141–143.

departure of the Saint-René-Taillandier mission to Fez.[52] French Foreign Minister Delcassé became very upset when he heard the news, and issued orders to his Minister in Tangier to threaten to withdraw all French nationals living in Fez, preparatory to a break in relations. In the meantime, he urged Saint-René-Taillandier to bribe as many of the prominent individuals at Fez as possible.[53]

Although strong French diplomatic pressure eventually secured the rehiring of the fired Europeans, the Saint-René-Taillandier mission continued to Fez under a cloud. The ulama continued to agitate against further concessions to France. Led by al-Kattānī, they were instrumental in getting 'Abd al-'Azīz to convoke a *majlis al-a'yān* composed of notables drawn from Fez and the other cities of Morocco to consider the French reform proposals on behalf of the nation.[54] Al-Kattānī consistently supported a hard-line policy, and insisted on the willingness of the Moroccan people to defend themselves if necessary. He also drew a lesson for the sultan from a comparison between the Bey of Tunis, who compromised away the independence of his state, and the Ottoman sultan, who knew when to stand up for the rights of his nation.[55] The end result of this sort of agitation was that when the French mission finally reached Fez at the end of January, they were faced with a Moroccan demand that all proposals be presented to the majlis, rather than to the sultan in private. Only as the Moroccan intention to remain firm became clear in January did the German government begin to make its first overtures of support to 'Abd al-'Azīz.[56]

The Fez elite, and the ulama as well, were divided on how far they could go in resisting the French demands. But under the pressure of the militant group among the ulama, led by Muḥammad al-Kattānī, the makhzan remained firm. With strong German backing for its position, the makhzan was able to maintain its opposition despite heavy French pressure. Al-Kattānī was kept in touch with the state of French public opinion through his agent in Paris, 'Abd al-Ḥakīm al-Tūnisī.[57] The land-

[52] France, *Affaires du Maroc, 1901–1905*, Vol. I, no. 210. Also Saint-René Taillandier, *op. cit.*, p. 214.

[53] Cited in Guillen, *op. cit.*, p. 827.

[54] On the *majlis al-a'yān* cf. Saint-René Taillandier, *op. cit.*, pp. 237–238. Also 'Alāl al-Fāsī, *al-Harakat al-Istiqlālīya fī al-maghrib al-'Arabī* (Marrakesh, 1948), pp. 106–107.

[55] *M.A.E., Maroc. Politique Etrangère. Rélations avec la France XV*, Saint-René-Taillandier to Delcassé, Dec. 10, 1904, no. 248.

[56] On the German support of the Moroccan resistance, cf. Guillen, *op. cit.*, pp. 816–827.

[57] *M.A.E., Maroc. Politique Etrangère. Rélations avec la France XVI*, Saint-René-Taillandier to Delcassé, March 2, 1905, no. 18 bis.

ing of Kaiser Wilhelm at Tangier on March 31, 1905, placed German opposition to the French reform proposals on public record for the first time, and exposed Delcassé's miscalculations. The opposition of the ulama at Fez had made the French position vulnerable, and the strong support of Germany enabled Morocco to defeat the French reform proposals. Had they been implemented they would have amounted to a disguised form of protectorate. On May 28, 1905, 'Abd al-'Azīz announced the decision of his government to the French Minister with the words, "It has not been possible for His Majesty to oppose the people. . . ."[58]

Although the first direct political intervention of the Moroccan ulama had been successful, the verdict of the Algeciras Conference went against Morocco. In effect, the French reform proposals were given an international sanction and the French position of predominance in Moroccan affairs was confirmed. Despite an attempt by the militant faction at Fez to get the government to reject the Algeciras Convention, the government signed the agreement. By this act it definitively alienated itself from many of the ulama and leaders of Moroccan society and lost much popular support. A conspiracy began to develop which had as its object the deposition of 'Abd al-'Azīz, and the substitution of his more anti-French brother, Mawlāy 'Abd al-Ḥafīz, as sultan.[59]

The final effort of the ulama to intervene directly in politics grew out of the increasing opposition to the pro-French policy pursued by 'Abd al-'Azīz after the signing of the Algeciras Convention. When the sultan issued a strong statement condemning the tribes involved after the attack upon the workers of Compagnie marocaine at Casablanca in July 1907, and went on to justify French military intervention to restore order, the point of no return was finally reached.

On August 17, 1907, the ulama of Marrakesh in the presence of Madanī al-Glawī and an impressive group of Glawa warriors formally issued a proclamation deposing 'Abd al-'Azīz and elevating 'Abd al-Ḥafīẓ to the throne. The text of the bay'a of 'Abd al-Ḥafīẓ makes clear the reasons for this act lay in the inability of the previous sultan to perform his duty of defending the state from French aggression.[60] The loss first of Touat, then parts of the southeastern frontier, then Oudjda, and finally Casablanca and the Chaouia to French forces of occupation left them no choice but to select a ruler who would seek to redress the balance.

[58] Saint-René-Taillandier, *op. cit.*, p. 301.

[59] On the development of the Ḥafīẓīya see Martin, *op. cit.*, pp. 415–446.

[60] See Martin, *op. cit.*, pp. 451–455, for the text of the fatwa of the ulama of Marrakesh in French translation.

Thus began a bitter, protracted one-year struggle between the supporters of 'Abd al-'Azīz and the supporters of 'Abd al-Ḥafīz. Moroccan society became polarized as the two factions maneuvered for position. With the French invasion of the Chaouia serving as rallying point for a jihād against the French, and with 'Abd al-'Azīz irrevocably identified in the minds of the people with France, the result was largely a foregone conclusion. Although the struggle persisted for a year owing to French backing of 'Abd al-'Azīz, most of the major towns and the most militarily significant tribes had gone over to 'Abd al-Ḥafīẓ by January 1908.

On January 4, 1908, the ulama of Fez, after having refrained from taking sides in the conflict between the two sultans, acceded to popular pressure and signed the documents deposing 'Abd al-'Azīz, and proclaimed 'Abd al-Ḥafīẓ. From the picture that one can gather of the political atmosphere at Fez from August 1907 to January 1908, the city was in constant turmoil as the partisans of 'Abd al-Ḥafīẓ, led by Muḥammad al-Kattānī, systematically terrorized the families of all those suspected of relations with 'Abd al-'Azīz.[61] By November al-Kattānī and his supporters both in the ulama and in other walks of life had successfully constituted themselves as an armed militia against rumors that the army of 'Abd al-'Azīz was on its way to retake Fez. By early January the pressure upon the segment of the ulama which still maintained a nonpolitical stance became too much and they agreed to sign the bay'a of 'Abd al-Ḥafīẓ. The bay'a itself was drawn up by Sī Aḥmad ibn al-Mawāz, and included a number of conditions which the new sultan was to be required to fulfill.[62] When the supporters of 'Abd al-Ḥafīẓ showed themselves reluctant to commit themselves to any conditions without prior approval, al-Kattānī made an effort to divert the bay'a to himself, since he was willing to abide by the militant conditions. This attempt failed, but the entire incident remains obscure.[63]

61 A unique view of the political climate at Fez during this period by an eyewitness to the events can be found in A. Maitrot de la Motte Capron and Dr. Trenga, "Journal d'un Correspondant de Revolution," *Bulletin de la Société de Geographie à Alger* (1936), pp. 14–62, 133–192.

62 A complete text of the *bay'a* of the Fez ulama can be found in 'Abd al-Raḥmān ibn Zaydān, *Itḥāf a'lām al-nās bī jamāl akhbār ḥāḍirat Miknās* (Rabat, 1929), Vol. I, pp. 448–453. See also the discussion in 'Alāl al-Fāsī, *Ḥafriyāt 'an al-ḥaraka al-dustūrīya fī al-maghrib qabla al-ḥimayā* (Rabat, n. d.), pp. 20–23. For other versions of the conditions, see al-Kattānī, *op. cit.*, pp. 199–200, A. Maitrot de la Motte Capron and Dr. Trenga, *op. cit.*, p. 22, and E. Michaux-Bellaire, "Une tentative de revolution idrisite à Fès," *R.M.M.*, VII (1909), 394.

63 There is a difference of opinion

While we do not know all that we would like to about the bay'a of 'Abd al-Ḥafīẓ by the ulama of Fez, several points stand out. The first is that for almost six months the ulama of Fez, and Fez society more generally, were sharply polarized over the issue of deposing 'Azīz and proclaiming Ḥafīẓ. A group within the ulama, led by al-Kattānī but undoubtedly including other important names as well, agitated publicly against 'Abd al-'Azīz, and succeeded in creating a very tense, near revolutionary situation at Fez. Collaborators and would-be collaborators became the object of threats. The militant segment of the ulama went beyond threats to attempting to mobilize the lower classes and the floating populations of Fez into demonstrations against former ministers and their families suspected of retaining contact with 'Abd al-'Azīz. This direct intervention of a segment of the ulama into the political arena represented a sharp break with the traditions of an earlier age, and marks the apogee of the political action of the ulama. Their motives in doing so were derived from their sense of duty to see that Islam (in this case the Moroccan state) would be defended by a strong amīr, one who was not afraid to lead the jihād against France if such proved necessary.

After the success of the Ḥafīẓīya revolution, the ulama of Fez and other cities once again withdrew from the center of the stage. By the time that Morocco became a French Protectorate in 1912, the ulama's early zeal was spent, and, resigned to disaster, they made no protest. Several among their number provided money and information to the tribes during the May siege of Fez, but essentially their political effort had run its course. Morocco became a French protectorate in spite of their best efforts.

Conclusion

The ulama of Morocco present an interesting case study in politicization of an apparently noncorporate and apolitical group. The structural position of the Moroccan ulama was considerably vaguer than the more rigidly hierarchical Ottoman ulama, or even the ulama of Iran. Since the Moroccan ulama did not represent a distinct corporate group in Moroccan

---

over what al-Kattānī was up to. Michaux-Bellaire ("Une tentative de revolution," pp. 393–423) places a strongly anti-Kattānī emphasis on this incident. For a more favorable view, see al-Kattānī, *op. cit.*, pp. 196–201. It is important to emphasize that the available evidence, both Arabic and French, makes it clear that al-Kattānī was not alone in urging the signing of the *bay'a.*

society even under ordinary circumstances, their emergence as leaders in the opposition to French penetration and governmental reforms after 1900 might at first appear incongruous. They possessed neither a developed identity as a group, nor a tradition of intervention in the affairs of state. Apparently vulnerable to government efforts at centralization and reform by virtue of their internal divisions and varied personal interests, the ulama of Morocco nonetheless were able to surmount all apparent obstacles to cooperative action. Here the Moroccan tendency for each man to occupy a number of different roles appears to have worked to the advantage of such cooperation. Since the ulama had diversified interests, they were better able to reflect popular grievances against the government. Reforms that affected merchants, sharifs, or qadis affected the ulama as well. The impact of a number of reforms on different segments of the Moroccan population tended to be cumulative upon the ulama.

During the nineteenth century most government reform efforts were confined to the army, and had relatively little effect upon the ulama. The sultans were rarely prepared vigorously to assert their authority for fear of provoking serious unrest among the population. Then too, not all the reforms worked against the interest of the ulama. The elaboration of the financial bureaus of the makhzan required a considerable number of new functionaries, and these were drawn from among the graduates of the madrasas and the Qarawīyīn university, as well as from the merchant class. Since the reforms tended to have a differential impact upon the Moroccan ulama, they alone were not likely to provoke a united opposition, although they might elicit occasional grumblings and displeasure within the group.

The foreign policy of the nineteenth-century sultans received on the whole the support of the Moroccan ulama. Both Muḥammad IV and Ḥasan I maintained a strong domestic military posture, coupled with a foreign policy calculated to preserve Moroccan isolation and play off the powers against one another. So long as no one power wanted Morocco badly enough to force the issue, and risk a possible European war, the stalemate could continue. But by 1900 this set of diplomatic circumstances no longer pertained, and there was growing restiveness among colonialist circles in France over Morocco. At this moment, the Moroccan government passed into the hands of the young and inexperienced 'Abd al-'Azīz, following the death of the Regent Aḥmad ibn Mūsā.

Under 'Abd al-'Azīz, the makhzan adopted a vigorous tax reform policy which threatened the financial interests of the sharifs, while at the same time launching a campaign to control the ulama, and abolish the right of religious shrines to accord sanctuary to fugitives. These measures incited considerable opposition among the ulama, and produced a potentially delicate political situation for ʿAbd al-ʿAzīz. What crystallized the ulama into united opposition to the government however, was the total failure of the foreign policy of the government, which rapidly drifted into the hands of the European financiers, while French military incursions along the frontier went unchecked. In the face of the steady loss of territory along the southeastern border zone, and the great increase in European influence at Court, the ulama were provoked into action. After the Entente Cordiale and the major loan of 1904 Morocco seemed easy prey to Delcassé and the French. The threat posed by the French reform proposals of 1905 provided the catalyst that finally stimulated the ulama to intervene directly in the political arena. Buffeted by government reform attempts, and alarmed at the growing powerlessness of the makhzan, their ideological role as guardians of the national spirit of independence led them to take action. They continued to remain in a state of alert until a new sultan who seemed more committed to fulfilling his duties as amīr and defending Morocco was placed upon the throne. Thereafter, their duty done, the Moroccan ulama once again receded into the background.

5 | Profile of a Nineteenth-Century Moroccan Scholar*

KENNETH BROWN

> The scholar walks along the street, his eyes lowered, his prayer rug under his arm. Unctious, his step expresses disdain for the sights of the world about him. Rather it seeks and obtains the advantageous veneration of the masses. This devoted teacher has been attached always, by a thousand-year tradition, to the affairs of the city. Only rarely has he given himself over to brutal asceticism or ill-bred pendantry. The master of religious science is at the same time the master of the right tone. His slippery courtesy, his nerves of old city dwellers, his ruse of an old courtier, his attachment to ornamental velvets and the sculpted plasters of magnificent houses, make him the intellectual champion of a culture that expresses itself equally well by the erudition of the scholastic, the fine hand of the craftsman, or the succulence of its cuisine. Everything beyond is no more than barbarism. This personality was shaped within the horizons of the city. . . . It became so expressive of a distinctive character—one on the defense and under the attack of time—that it became almost unintelligible to the outsider.[1]

The role of the scholar in nineteenth-century Morocco and, more generally, the roles that the ulama fulfilled in that society remain enigmatic. Were these men, as some have claimed, stereotyped products of an immutable and stagnant system of education, conservative guardians of a religious tradition, obstructionists in the face of the forces of change? Or were they, despite appearances, men of their times with identifiable social roles and with hopes and visions for the future. The rich and still largely unexploited Moroccan sources for this period offer the possibilities for a more judicious—if still preliminary—appraisal than has yet been made of who the ulama were and what they knew and did. Furthermore, these

* I wish to thank the Center for Middle Eastern Studies at the University of Chicago and the Social Science Research Council for affording me the time to study and write about some of the matters touched upon in this essay and to express my gratitude to Lloyd Fallers for his helpful criticism.

[1] J. Berque, "Ville et Université: Aperçu sur l'histoire de l'École de Fès," in *Revue Historique du Droit Français et Etranger*, XXVII (1949), 107.

sources can be complemented by our increasing knowledge of nineteenth-century Moroccan society. This essay is an attempt to clarify some of our notions about the ulama. Its method is twofold: (1) to present the profile of a particular Moroccan scholar of the late nineteenth century, both on the basis of internal sources and from what is known about the changing context of his social milieu, (2) to suggest how this milieu helped to define the functions fulfilled by the ulama.

Aḥmad b. Khālid an-Nāṣirī

an-Nāṣirī, because of his compendium history of Morocco, is one of the best known of the nineteenth-century ulama.[2] He was born in 1834 in Salé, a city renowned for its intellectual heritage, and died there in 1897. His father, Khālid, had moved to Salé from Tamgrūt—a town in the Dra' valley reputed for the tomb of its seventeenth-century patron saint, Shaikh Muḥammad b. Nāṣir, and for the mother lodge of the Nāṣiriyya religious order that he made flourish there.[3] As a descendant of Shaikh Muḥammad, Khālid an-Nāṣirī was acknowledged in Salé as a saintly man of the Nāṣiriyya order. His reputation and personal qualities, wealth (from trade and property), and kinship alliances made it possible for him to become a respected and integrated member of the city's community.

Where the life of Khālid evinces geographical mobility, that of his son can be taken to illustrate upward social mobility—the former was a holy man, the latter a scholar. The younger an-Nāṣirī received a traditional religious education.[4] After memorizing the Koran according to the several methods of recitation, he studied the religious sciences. His teachers for these subjects were reputed scholars who had studied in the Qarawiyin mosque in Fez—the most prestigious center of higher learning in Morocco. Under their guidance an-Nāṣirī studied an imposing number of

[2] *Kitāb al-istiqṣā li-akhbār duwal al-Maghrib al-Aqṣā*, 1st ed. in 4 vols. (Cairo, 1924); 2d ed. with additional notes and a prefaced biography of the author by two of his sons, in 9 vols. (Casablanca, 1954–1956). A French translation of the 1st ed., with the exception of part of vol. 2, appeared in *Archives Marocaines*, IX–X (1906–1907) and XXXI-XXXIV (1923–1936). For an analysis of the book, and of Moroccan scholarship in general, cf. E. Lévi-Provençal, *Les historiens du Chorfa* (Paris, 1920).

[3] G. Spillman (pseud. Drague), *Esquisse d'histoire religieuse du Maroc: Confréries et zaouias* (Paris, 1951).

[4] Cf. Lévi-Provençal, *op. cit.*, pp. 10 ff.; E. Michaux-Bellaire, "L'enseignement indigène au Maroc," *Revue du Monde Musulman*, XV (1911), 422–452; L. Mercier, "Les mosques et la vie religieuse à Rabat," *Archives Marocaines*, VIII (1906), 99–198.

classical Islamic subjects: commentaries on the Koran, the traditions and biography of the Prophet, Islamic law, Arabic language and grammar, rhetoric, logic, dialectic theology, and Islamic philosophy. Later, on his own, he studied Arabic works on the natural sciences (particularly mathematics and physics), geographies and histories, and acquainted himself with classical Arabic literature, as well as with the pre-Islamic poets. Moreover, he is said to have read widely among the modern scientific and literary editions and translations then emanating from Cairo. By the time he reached his thirties, an-Nāṣirī's erudition and mastery of the religious sciences and his gifts of intelligence and eloquence had earned him the respect of his fellow citizens in Salé. Having assumed the prestigious and distinguished status of a member of the ulama, he was able to earn a livelihood (in addition to the income from whatever land he had inherited) as a modest official in the law court and as a mosque teacher, both positions being financed out of funds from Salé's foundation of pious endowments (*ḥabūs*). The professional education of an-Nāṣirī had now made available to him an administrative function and a specific style of life.

Soon after the beginning of the reign of Mawlay al-Ḥasan I (1874–1894), an-Nāṣirī entered upon a career of government service. The appointment of learned men to positions in the *makhzan* (central government administration) was an old tradition in Morocco. Such appointments began to be more widely practiced during the latter half of the nineteenth century.[5] This expansion of the government bureaucracy favored the ulama of those cities reputed for their urban tradition—Fez, Tetuán, Rabat, and Salé. an-Nāṣirī, initially reluctant to abandon his studies and teaching for a government career, nevertheless followed a path already well trodden by the ulama of Salé. In addition to his learning, two other interrelated factors recommended appointment: administrative experience on the local level and ties of kinship and friendship with important personalities of the city. After having served as a notary in the court of Salé, and then assistant to the qadi, he was named administrator of the ḥabūs. The last appointment was closely related to the ascendancy to the office of qadi of his father-in-law and former teacher. Thereafter, an-Nāṣirī became the constant companion of the qadi, his kinsman and patron, accompanying him during his travels to various cities of the kingdom.

[5] Cf., J.-L. Miège, *Le Maroc et l'Europe*, Vol. III (Paris, 1962), pp. 124–125; M. Lahbabi, *Le gouvernement marocain a l'aube du XXe siècle* (Rabat, 1958), p. 158; E. Aubin, *Le Maroc d'aujourd'hui* (Paris, 1908), pp. 209, 247 ff.; R. Le Tourneau, *Fès avant le protectorat* (Casablanca, 1947).

These travels provided opportunities to meet and impress contemporary ulama and notables and to widen thereby the horizons of his knowledge and contacts. All these factors helped an-Nāṣirī to enter the patronage system of the administration and to gain the government appointment that he secured in 1875.[6]

For the next twenty years this scholar from Salé served either as notary or chief agent of customs in Fez, Marrakesh, Essaouira (Mogador), El Jadida (Mazagan), Casablanca, and Tangier. Although there is no indication in the sources of the particular income that an-Nāṣirī derived from these positions, it can safely be assumed that, like his contemporary customs agents, he gained relatively large material benefits. These agents were among the "bankers" of the makhzan, those who provided the treasury with loans as they were needed. The abuses of this financial system were belatedly recognized, and attempts at control and reform were made, but without much success. A good share of the wealth and influence belonging to certain urban families in Morocco originated from within that system, and in this respect Salé was no exception.

an-Nāṣirī made his fortune (not, however, at the expense of his continued learning) and retired to Salé. There, in the comfortable surroundings of his house and among his books, he spent the last years, until his death in 1897, reading, writing, teaching, and in religious devotion, interrupted only by the exigencies of requests by the authorities for judicial opinions.

The principal biographer of an-Nāṣirī was his student and compatriot from Salé, Muḥammad b. 'Alī ad-Dukkālī (1868–1945). Unfortunately, the complete biography that ad-Dukkālī wrote has been lost, but a eulogy for his teacher which appeared in another of his works is printed in the introduction to the second edition of an-Nāṣirī's compendium history.[7] Now, writing biographies of scholars and religious personages was an act of piety whose primary aim was to glorify the religious elite and to awaken imitation and emulation of them. This art of hagio-biographical literature, highly developed and widespread in Morocco, was inseparable from the science of *nasab*, or genealogy. Individuals were identified in terms of

[6] The system of patronage in Morocco, like its counterpart in the Ottoman Empire, had no stigma attached to it and was a means for advancing one's career in the bureaucracy. Cf. R. Chambers, "The Education of a Nineteenth Century Ottoman Alim: Ahmed Cevdet Paşa." Forthcoming in *International Journal of Middle East Studies.*

[7] Vol. I. Introduction, pp. 44 ff.; ad-Dukkālī's life and work are treated in my *The Social History of a Moroccan Town: Salé, 1830–1930* (in preparation).

their lineages and their virtues were described with an elaborate vagueness. The phrases used in these panegyrics were cultural glosses that served to place the scholar or holy man in his rightful category and to establish his position therein.

ad-Dukkālī begins his eulogy of an-Nāṣirī with a string of titles reflecting his knowledge of the religious sciences: "Master, scholar, omniscient, professor, excellent" (*ash-shaikh, al-'allāma, al-mushārik, al-ustādh, al-fāḍil*). He proceeds to establish the genealogy—"an-Nāṣirī al-Ja'farī," viz., a descendant of the saint Ibn Nāṣir and of Ja'far, Son of Abū Ṭālib, the paternal uncle of the prophet Muḥammad—and to praise it (in rhymed prose): He is from a House of majesty and religion (*min baiti jalālatin wa-dīn*), of deep and solid rooted nobility of genealogy and of virtue (*sharaf*, 'solid' nobility in the sense of high birth, i.e., the glory, honor, and dignity transmitted by illustrious ancestors to their descendants; *nasab wa-ḥasab*, aspects of nobility, *nasab* denoting distinguished kinship descent, *ḥasab* referring to the virtues or glorious acts by which an individual or his ancestors acquired nobility). The members of that House have inherited glory both by newly acquiring it and by heritage, and they have embellished it from generation to generation (*yatarathūna 'l-majda ṭarīfan wa-talīdan wa-yatawashshiḥūnahu wālidan wa-walīdan; al-majd* is here a synonym of *sharaf; ṭarīf wa-talīd* means newly acquired and its opposite—old and long possessed; *wālid wa-walīd*—father and son—playfully complete the rhyme).

After this grandiloquent eloge of noble origins, the biographer bestows special honor and dignity on his subject by stating that he, among his illustrious ancestors, was a wonder unto himself. As for the personal qualities of the deceased, the biographer exalts by confessing inability to describe his subject's perfection (*kamāluhu*, the sum characteristics of ideal manhood). Then follows a series of religious and moral qualities that his life had exemplified: intelligence and noble-mindedness (*dhakā' wa-nubl*, the latter containing within itself the sense of elegance and aristocracy, as well as that of acute mental discernment); scientific attainment and excellence (*taḥsīl wa-faḍl; taḥsīl* is the accumulating of knowledge and respect for suitability and conformity; *faḍl* contains, again, the idea of nobility, aristocracy, bounty, and erudition); a high-mindedness that scorned acts of negligence (*himmatun nākabati 's-suhā*); an exactness in the knowledge to which he devoted his intellect (*taḥqīqun fī l-ma'ārifi badda fīhi 'n-nuhā*). He excelled in the instrumental sciences, and was a master at them (*atqana 'l-'ulūma 'l-ālatiyyatà fa-kāna fīhā imāman*); he distinguished the intended meanings from their opposites (*ḥarrara 'l-mā-qāṣida min siwāhā*, i.e., the genuine sense of things from the spurious). He was a complete human being (*fa-huwa insānun kāmil*). The biographer then catalogues additional qualities of his subject; only a few of the terms that he uses need detain us here: the deceased was omniscient (*mushārik*), that is, he had acquired knowledge (*muhaṣṣil*) and was equally well versed in various sciences (*muḍṭali'un munṣifun fī 'ulūmin shattā*). Moreover, he was among those who possessed the ideal virtues (*min dhawī 'l-murū'āt*, viz., the characteristics of a courtly gentleman) and preserved the religious prescriptions (*wa-'l-iḥtifāḍi bi-'r-rusūmi 'd-dīniyya*).

The Moroccan biographical literature of the ulama is steeped in this terminology and these images. Drawing upon and modeled after the dominant attitudes of medieval Muslim society, it portrays the scholar as a normative pattern of human character and activity. This typology and the cultural category of the ulama implicit in it represent one conception of nineteenth-century social stratification in urban Morocco. It tells us, in effect, that scholars belonged to the highest social rank, and that reverence and respect belonged to those of noble descent, piety, and learning. The career of an-Nāṣirī and knowledge about social and economic life in nineteenth-century Morocco suggest quite another model for perceiving the function and status of the ulama than the one offered by his biographer.

Social Mobility and Networks of Alliances

There is ample evidence to show that religious learning in Morocco and the prerogatives that might accompany it were not the ascribed birthright of men who belonged to a hereditary or otherwise exclusive social group. Where the descendants of the Prophet or of holy men inherited the *potentiality* of religious prestige, the ulama had to acquire the tools and skills of learning to reach the same goal.[8] That the "miraculous" and learned capacities sometimes coalesced in certain individuals is important, but it has been oversimplified and overemphasized. "Lineages of erudition" (*buyūt al-'ilm*) were the exception among the ulama rather than the rule. Descent along agnatic lines, whether of holy man or scholar, was most often vaunted ex post facto, as justification and reaffirmation of a status

[8] An interesting contrast are the Sayyids of southern Lebanon whose authority on religious matters rests on descendance, not acquired knowledge. Cf. E. L. Peters, "Aspects of Rank and Status among Muslims in a Lebanese Village," in J. Pitt-Rivers, ed., *Mediterranean Countrymen* (Paris, 1963), pp. 159–200.

already achieved. Learning, in particular, was the fief of no social group or groups. The "chain of science" from master to disciple was a spiritual genealogy independent of lineal descent. Although access to the requisite religious education of the ulama came most easily to the sons of the wealthy and learned, the biographies of scholars indicate the wide variety of their social origins. High status could be and often was achieved through learning by individuals whose social background was quite modest.

Lack of stringency in the notion of preconceived rights coupled with a growing measure of social fluidity during the nineteenth century made religious learning an important vehicle of upward mobility. an-Nāṣirī was a first-generation scholar, as well as a first-generation Salétin. His father's migration to Salé and integration into its society illustrate both the geographical mobility of Moroccans and the open-endedness of urban society. Arguments for the saintly genealogy of the family were produced later, to buttress a social ascent already accomplished. It was only in 1881, at the age of forty-six, that an-Nāṣirī completed a work that sought to demonstrate the Sharifian origin of his forefather, Ibn Nāṣir. In writing this book, his evident ulterior motive was to establish his own religious nobility. Genealogical research and genealogical fiction consolidated the entrenched social position of the scholar.[9]

If learning provided the possibilities for upward social mobility, the path was long, tortuous, and arduous. At best, an aspiring student had the opportunity to be in daily, intimate contact with the city people—the scholars, merchants and artisans, and the elite of the countryside. The example par excellence was the university community of the Qarawiyin in Fez, where the student, during his quest for God and an orthodox culture, perfected and internalized the good manners of the city dweller and contracted friendships that might serve him well in his later years.[10] Here, again, the case of an-Nāṣirī—a man who through the friendship of his teachers found both a means to his livelihood and ties of kinship.

[9] Cf. *Ṭal'at al-mushtarī fī 'l-nasab al-Ja'fari* (lithographed in Fez, n.d.); summarized by M. Bodini, "La zaouia de Tamgrout" in *Archives Berbères,* III (1918), 259–296. On the weaknesses of the "pseudo genealogy," cf. Lévi-Provençal, *op. cit.,* p. 354. Even the biographer ad-Dukkālī nowhere explicitly recognizes his subject as a descendant of the Prophet's blood. During the early period of Islam, the Ja'farīs were sometimes considered *ashrāf,* but later the only legitimated descendants were the sons of 'Alī.

[10] Phrases of Berque from his excellent study of the Qarawiyin, *op. cit.,* p. 104. The acquisition of urban behavioral patterns is developed at length in Brown, *op. cit.*; cf. R. Le Tourneau, *La vie quotidienne à Fès en 1900* (Paris, 1965), pp. 183 ff.

The pattern of crosscutting ties that one finds commonly in nineteenth-century Moroccan society was seldom fortuitous. Friendships, kinship ties, patronage coalitions—both permanent and temporary—were closely studied and manipulated for the social, economic, and political effects that they might produce. These networks of human relations provided crucial mechanisms for upward social mobility, particularly for the ulama. The individual scholar was potentially a valuable ally, because he might lend prestige, legal and religious knowledge, and powers of social arbitration to other men. That does not, of course, mean that the religiously learned formed an elite group among themselves.

The conceptions of status level and stratum solidarity that one finds in the written sources are formalized and ideologized; vague and loose categories, they resemble what Lloyd Fallers has called "secondary cultures of stratification," that is, values and beliefs about stratification which are opposed to basic values that give rise to stratification in the first place. For example, the public glorification of achievement may be combined with an absorbing interest in genealogy and symbols of ascribed status.[11] Such a perception of stratification is seen in the remarks of ad-Dukkālī: "The rural way of life *(al-bādiya)*", he writes, "differs from the urban way of life *(al-ḥaḍāra)*. The former is practiced by peasants and the poor and needy of the city; the latter includes the learned, gentlemen farmers, craftsmen and merchants, builders, officials and those with lineages."[12] The composition of the "cosmopolitan" urban population is characterized largely in terms of certain economic groups that share a basic life style. In contrast with this rather rigorous model of stratification, there is another much more loosely defined pattern of social organization. Here, the most important structural feature is a multiplicity of networks of specific and conditional relations among individuals of differing cultural and social backgrounds.

The nineteenth-century biographers offer precious little information about this mode of social organization in which diffuse and crosscutting ties among individuals formed multiple coalition groups. These were loosely knit networks of relations—sometimes overlapping, sometimes conflicting—between patrons and clients. Usually, they were conditionally based on contract, and only sometimes reinforced by the accumulation of

[11] Lloyd A. Fallers, "Social Stratification and Economic Processes," in M. J. Herskovits and M. Harwitz, eds., *Economic Transition in Africa* (Evanston, 1964), p. 121.

[12] Muḥammad b. 'Alī ad-Dukkālī, *Itḥaf ashrāf al-malā bi-ba'ḍ akhbār ar-Ribāṭ wa-Salā* (Salé, 1895), MS no. D11, Archives Générales, Rabat.

more specific ties, such as kinship. Given the fluidity of social life and the accompanying possibilities for upward mobility, such coalitions performed especially important functions. The clients of a man of relative authority helped to define, strengthen, and often justify his social status. When a man achieved high status, he, in turn, had to create his own clientele and to satisfy its needs for goods, services, or sponsorship. In such a system the scholar was a valuable auxiliary to the men of power. His influence might further the interests of his patron and, perhaps, eventually allow him to rise to a position of relative independence.[13]

Economic Rewards and Forces of Change

The biography of an-Nāṣirī shows the posts to which men of learning might aspire. Appointments to these posts involved a mechanism that still has not been studied systematically. Theoretically. all governors, jurists, teachers, and religious dignitaries were government officials, appointed directly by the sultan by means of of a *ẓahīr*, or official document bearing the seal of the sultan. In reality, the type of coteries described above usually influenced or controlled these appointments through the sponsorship of a candidate by his patron. Here, we are concerned in particular with the customs agents (*umanā'*). Their appointment occurred in the following manner: every year certain local governors and judges (largely those of Fez, Tetuán, Salé, and Rabat) submitted a list of the outstanding merchants and ulama of their cities to the Ministry of the Treasury. From these lists the agents were chosen. Judging by a letter from a qadi of Salé to the vizier, candidates had to satisfy these formal and explicit criteria: they were to be righteous and pious men, brought up in an atmosphere of learning and steadfast religion, yet clever and familiar with practical matters.[14] In effect, then, the qadi was able to nominate any experienced scholar whom he might choose.

During the late nineteenth century, Moroccan bureaucracy expanded quickly in response to the development of urban capitalism and an econ-

[13] The theoretical literature to help us define these urban social relations is very slight. The excellent article by Jeanne Favret, "Relations de dépendance et manipulation de la violence en Kabylie," in *L'Homme*, VIII (1968), 18–44, and Eric R. Wolf's, "Kinship, Friendship and Patron-Client Relations in Complex Societies," in M. Banton, *The Social Anthropology of Complex Societies* (London, 1966), pp. 1–20, have been useful.

[14] Muḥammad 'Awwād to al-'Arabī b. al-Mukhtār, Jan. 23, 1849, unpublished letter in Archives du Ministère des Affaires Administratives, Rabat; on the appointments of various officials and questions relating to the delegation of powers, cf. Lahbabi, *op. cit.*, pp. 77 ff., 128 ff.

omy geared toward large-scale importation. Numerous ulama found government employment (particularly in the posts), and they were drawn thereby into the main currents of Moroccan commerce. Besides social status and direct economic rewards, these posts offered to the customs agents opportunities to become directly and actively engaged in commercial activities.[15] Thus, the religious education of the ulama now became more than preparation for a *waẓīfa,* or government employment in the administrative service. In the late nineteenth century emergence of a new urban bourgeosie and a socio-economic ethic that despised neither commerce nor speculation, the involvement of the ulama and their allies was profound.

Hand in hand with administrative, economic, and social developments came the beginnings of the great shocks of the modern world—the shaking of the foundations of traditional culture and the Western threat to cultural autonomy. Especially sensitive to these unsettling times were the ulama who served in the port cities. The lifetime of an-Nāṣirī spanned a period of ephemeral prosperity, from 1852 until 1872, and a long depression that began thereafter (and ultimately led to the Moroccan crisis and—fifteen years after his death—to the loss of Moroccan independence). In his writing, an-Nāṣirī sometimes looked beyond immediate economic and political affairs and problems and considered their cultural consequences. Near the end of his history of Morocco, he shows the extent to which overall economic life had been steadily undermined by contact with the European countries. He goes on to warn the reader:

> The reason for this [economic crisis] is in what we have said. The more the intermingling and contact with the Europeans, the more it will increase; and as they lessen, so will it. The proof of this is in the fact that the people of Morocco have had least contact with them of all the nations [of Islam], and that is why the prices are lower, the standard of living higher, the way of dressing and customs further away from those of the Europeans. For these reasons their [the Moroccans'] religion is whole, as everyone knows, in contrast with Egypt, Syria, and other lands. Indeed, what we have heard about them deafens the ear![16]

[15] This is apparent in the reform of 1862: the customs system was reorganized, the agents forbidden to participate in any commercial activities in the cities *where they served,* and monthly salaries fixed at 90 douros for agents and 20 douros for notaries (cf. Miege, *op. cit.*, pp. 124–25, and an unpublished letter from the Sultan Sīdī Muḥammad to Aḥmad as-Simlālī in El-Jadida, March 31, 1862, in Archives du Ministère des Affaires Administratives, Rabat).

[16] an-Naṣīrī, *op. cit.* (Cairo ed.), IV, 279.

For the scholar, the most striking consequence of European domination over neighboring Algeria had been moral corruption and irreligion among its Muslim inhabitants.[17] Social and economic changes had brought personal advantages to the Moroccan ulama and had allowed them to become part of a new urban bourgeosie. But they feared the price of change. In an inherently ambiguous situation, they profited from the opening up of Morocco to new forces, yet, at the same time, their primary task—as defined by themselves and by society—was to represent and to defend what had been handed down by history: the moral conscience of the Muslim community and its traditional culture.

Further passages in an-Nāṣirī's work indicate the extent to which he felt that Morocco's identity—its religion, culture, language, and independence—was challenged by the European nations: his description of the symptoms and effects of cholera epidemics and droughts and his discussion of the quarantine practiced by the Christians—which he rejects for its "temporal and spiritual disadvantages," its harmfulness to normal trade, and its undermining of resigned confidence (*tawakkul*) in God, particularly among the masses who, deluded by appearances, are apt to fall into heresy and anarchy;[18] his support for the creation of a regular standing Moroccan army—whose soldiers should be "instructed in religious ideology as well as warfare, so that they protect Islam rather than undermine it";[19] his opposition to the request by the European ambassadors to establish railway and telegraph systems in Morocco—"the worst of evils, the Christians have put to trial (*ajrabū*, literally, affected with mange) other lands and wanted to try this happy country that God has kept pure hitherto from their pollution" (*danas*, sullying, defilement—of a garment, a man's honor, or his disposition);[20] his repudiation of what he considers to be the European concept of "liberty"—on the grounds that it represents only libertinism, licentiousness, and anarchy, and that it abolishes the "rights" of God and parents and the quality of "humaneness."[21] To judge these statements

[17] *Ibid.*, pp. 217–218, "moral corruption," *al-fasād*.

[18] *Ibid.*, III, 93 ff.; "anarchy," *al-fitna*, literally, temptation.

[19] *Ibid.*, IV, 222 ff.; and they should learn the qualities of "virtue, dignity, modesty," *al-murū'a*, *al-ḥayā'*, *al-ḥishma*.

[20] *Ibid.*, p. 254; the images also have connotations of ritual pollution: "*an-naṣārā ajrabū sā'ir al-bilād fa-arādū an yajrabū hadhā 'l-qatra 's-sa'īda alladhī ṭahharahu Allah min danasihim.*"

[21] *Ibid.*, pp. 227 ff., "liberty" *al-ḥuriyya*; on its connotations in Islamic thought, cf. F. Rosenthal, *The Muslim Concept of Freedom* (Leiden, 1960), esp. p. 99, and the article "Ḥurriyya" in *Encyclopedia of Islam*, 2d ed.; "rights," *ḥuqūq*, i.e., legal rights or

simply as an ostrich-like, negative, defense of a traditional way of life is not an adequate interpretation of an-Nāṣirī's position, nor of those taken by his contemporary ulama. We should not ignore the positive aspect of intransigent pride that opposed colonialism out of both religious and patriotic considerations.

Furthermore, it should be noted that the scholars of nineteenth-century Morocco tried to a certain extent to have a voice in defining the options and decisions of policy open to the makhzan. For example, in 1885 the sultan Mawlay al-Ḥasan requested from the ulama legal advice concerning the persistent demands by Europeans for concessions that would improve their trading privileges. Obviously, it was hoped that the legal reasoning of the ulama would support concessions by the makhzan. an-Nāṣirī put his erudition and knowledge of the intricacies of Islamic law to the service of the sulṭan's policy in regard to this question. Yet even in his support, his despondency found expression. He argued that there was no sense in prohibiting the sale of goods to the Christians nor in attempting military resistance to them, because while they were strong and prepared, the Muslims were weak and confused: "I swear," he laments, "that in mixing and coming together with them, great harm is done to us. But it is less in comparison with the harm of war. . . . Every man knows that peace is preferable to war."

This discussion of the inequality of military power is in answer to people who cry out for *jihād* against the Europeans. an-Nāṣirī holds the warmongers responsible for internal dissension, describing them as the ignorant masses who do not know what wars are about, but only seek anarchy for its own sake. Pointing out that numbers of soldiers do not win wars, the scholar warns the sultan that there are no substitutes for the unity of purpose best accomplished by a commander (*ḍabiṭ*) and a code of regulations (*qanūn*). If these are not to be instituted, there must at least be perspicacity in religion, strength of belief, harmony among the Muslims, zeal for the homeland and the household (*al-waṭan wa-'l-ḥarīm*), intelligence and practice in warfare and the intrigues of the polytheists. Meanwhile, war is unthinkable; people have become so weak and concerned with their food, drink, and clothing that there remains no difference between them and their women. To make war is to welcome anarchy

claims and their corresponding obligations according to Islamic law (such as prayer, fasting, Koranic punishments, parental authority); "humaneness," *insāniyya*, i.e., the essence of man, viz., to be virtuous and reject vices.

and to offer the enemy a path to the ports and the taking as booty of women, wealth, and blood.[22]

There is a tone of guarded assertiveness in the opinion that an-Nāṣirī expresses to the sultan in his Response. Filtered through legalistic casuistry and plaints of despair, the ulama try to influence the policies of the central government by proclaiming their view of the fundamental social and cultural values of the Muslim community.

The Status of the Ulama and the Nature of the Makhzan

Supreme authority in nineteenth-century Morocco lay in the hands of the sultan of the Alawite Sharifian dynasty. The Moroccan kingdom represented, at once, a religious and political system. Its claim to sovereignty and legitimacy was twofold: by the genealogical charisma (as descendants of 'Alī) of its sultans and by the *bai'a*—the collective and formal acknowledgments of certain representatives from among their subjects.[23]

That the ulama might jeopardize the accession of a new sultan by actually withholding acknowledgment was a theoretical possibility. More real was their capacity to validate claims of a pretender. The *bai'a* deserve our attention here, for the privilege of drawing up these documents belonged to the outstanding personages of the various cities and tribes of the kingdom, especially to their ulama.[24]

The *bai'a* was indeed ceremonially and symbolicly significant. It projected an image of legitimization by contract whereby the sultan was recognized and acclaimed in a formal sense by the religious scholars of the various communities of the kingdom. This makhzan tradition and policy of formal investiture served, in turn, to enhance the prestige of the

[22] *Ibid.*, pp. 268 ff.

[23] For an excellent discussion of the distinctiveness of the Moroccan monarchy, cf. C. Geertz, *Islam Observed* (New Haven, 1968), pp. 75 ff.

[24] The extent of the participation of rural communities in this practice remains obscure. On the role of the ulama in the countryside, see last note below. Although the acts were drawn up by the ulama, the signatories were more varied. For example in Salé, they included descendants of the Prophet (*ash-shurafā'*), the elite (*al-aṭrāf*), notables (*al-a'yān*), merchants (*at-tujjār*), scholars (*al-'ulamā'*), those of known families (*dhawū 'l-buyūt*), holy warriors (*al-mujāhidūn*), and people of judgment and solid opinion (*dhawū 'l-aḥkām wa-'l-ṭawr at-rāsikh*). In a *bai'a* from Rabat: "The Muslim community of Rabat—elite and masses, our saints—descendants of the Prophet, jurists, scholars, students, holy warrior captains of the army and navy, and craftsmen."

ulama as experts in the Divine Law, as spokesmen for the moral conscience of the Islamic community, and as arbiters between ruled and rulers. The relationship between government and ulama was one of mutual support which expressed itself in various other symbolic and real forms: frequent official delegations of the ulama to the sultan; visits and demonstrations of respect by the sultan or high-ranking members of his entourage to well-known scholars; requests by the sultan for advice and judicial opinions; the entrusting of young members of the royal family and retinue to the ulama for the purposes of education; the appointment of ulama to religious, educational, and administrative posts.

All these practices served to strengthen the hand of the religiously learned and to make them appear, individually and collectively, as extremely important figures within a society saturated by theological considerations and values. The ulama fostered a view of themselves as the experts and guardians of the Divine Law, those whose task was to defend, maintain, and perpetuate its foundations and proofs of faith. Clerks, jurists, theologians, and teachers, they felt, moreover, that it was natural that they should provide the manpower for the judicial, financial, and administrative organization of a state based on the precepts of the revealed religion of Islam. Both the ideology of the dynasty and its conduct toward the ulama seemed to confirm this self-image.

In the late nineteenth century this natural alliance and mutual solidarity between the sultans and the ulama may have become increasingly strained. The documents that might permit us to describe and analyze these tensions have hardly begun to be exploited. If one finds in an-Nāṣirī's work glimmerings of recalcitrance, there are elsewhere, and slightly later, at the turn of the century, signs of a resistance by some of the ulama that was religious, intellectual and, by implication, political. The activities of the Committee of Notables of Fez, the judicial opinions of the ulama, the program, career, and ultimate assassination of Muḥammad b. ʿAbd al-Kabīr al-Kattānī—all may be interpreted, as they have elsewhere in this book (chap. 4), as assertions of the independence of the ulama vis-à-vis the central government and as an early stage of political nationalism. If, indeed, the stances taken by some of the ulama reflect a relative independence, what, it may be asked, were its causes and potential consequences? A plausible explanation is predicated on the role of the ulama as the conservative guardians of faith, tradition, and style of life: motivated by their fear of change, the ulama spoke out and acted in defense of the old values and ways. With the growth of European involvement in

Morocco and the subsequent tentative moves toward reforms by the government, the ulama were awakened to a resistance that was, on the whole, negative, and sterile.[25]

Such an explanation emphasizes the inherent conservatism of the ulama—the role that they had played in preserving a civilization intact. In itself, however, the explanation does not sufficiently account for much of the biographical data that we have on the ulama. The intellectual horizons of the Moroccan scholars of the nineteenth century, as we have seen, were expanding. Contact with the modern world was not confined to administrative and economic activities in the ports. Beyond these, the ulama found the capacities and premises of another civilization. To be sure, men like an-Nāṣirī perceived European civilization as a threat to their own. But more important is the fact that this contact incited him into a kind of dialogue, and that he was led thereby to participate in the early stages of that process of self-analysis which, in its further development, marked both the cultural renaissance and political nationalism of Morocco.[26] The stake of the ulama in political developments during this period of stress and change did not as we shall see, leave them the peaceful respite of stagnation and conservatism.

The Functions of the Ulama

Religious life in the cities of nineteenth-century Morocco seemed marked by calm piety and lack of religious conflicts.[27] Indeed western Islam had long been untroubled by those schisms, heresies, or even the plurality of law schools found to the east. This state of affairs, at least on the surface, neatly accorded with that Islamic view of the world in which between individual believer and the all-inclusive solidarity of *umma* (the community of believers), there was no legitimate or permanent group whose characteristics were exclusivity, solidarity, or hostility to others.[28] Nonetheless, nineteenth-century Moroccan society—however loosely structured—had its pattern of organization; nexus of patron-client relationships or

[25] This is the hypothesis suggested (to be sure, with much reservation) by Miège, *op. cit.*, IV, 135 ff.

[26] Cf. the passing, almost hidden, remarks by Lévi-Provençal on the late nineteenth-century cultural stirrings in Morocco, *op. cit.*, pp. 349–350, which have awakened little curiosity.

[27] Le Tourneau, *Le vie quotidienne à Fès en 1900*, p. 291.

[28] Cf. the criticism by Hourani of L. Massignon's analysis of the role of Islamic guilds, in "The Islamic City in the Light of Recent Research" in A. H. Hourani and S. M. Stern, eds., *The Islamic City* (Oxford, 1970), p. 14.

coalition groups which centered around prominent individuals were, as I have shown, the basic constituents of the social fabric.

It is difficult to know with certainty the extent to which these relationships and groupings permeated all of a given urban society. Evidence from Salé suggests that people there conceived of all human relations and associations in this manner. Moreover, according to their conceptions, these coalitions interlocked in such a way that no individual was permanently excluded from access to the elite of the community. That is to say, clientele groups—in their interrelationships and interdependencies—contained individuals of varying degrees of power and wealth. To some extent, then, the social structure of the Moroccan town was vertically oriented.

Yet, apparently in contrast with this principle of organization, we find another conception of the social system, one articulated in terms of the cultural evaluation of others. According to this view, society was perceived as being divided by a horizontal barrier drawn between those who practiced the urban way of life (*al-ḥaḍāra*) and those who did not. This distinction was sometimes expressed in the familiar classical terms of *al-khāṣṣa* (upper class, educated) and *al-'amma* (the common mass of the people).[29] Here the rubrics al-ḥaḍāra and al-khāṣṣa include those of the urban population who shared a particular cultural orientation and form of social behavior. It was a cultural category and not a social group with qualities of homogeneity or exclusiveness. To a large extent these categorizations were the work of and were most staunchly defended by the ulama. Moreover, they clearly reflected the staunch advocacy of literacy and learning by the ulama as those qualities which best defined the urban way of life.

In Islam there had been no synods or councils to define and interpret the meanings of orthodoxy. Rather, it was left to normative religious practices of the majority at a given time and place to determine those definitions and interpretations. In medieval Muslim society the dominant attitudes had favored the scholar as a model of human character. In nineteenth-century Morocco, the ulama sought and were often given control of the religious life of the community, in accord with that divine positive law (*al-sharī'a*) that they had mastered through their studies. They conceived of their function in society as guardians of the heritage of Islam and the Muslim way of life, that is, of a law that embraced the civil as well as the religious life of the faithful. Ultimate truth and goodness, the mean-

[29] Cf. H. A. R. Gibb and H. Bowen, *Islamic Society and the West*, Vol. I, Part II (London, 1957), p. 81.

ing of life and man's identity, were embodied in the law as defined by the ulama. Spiritual or material practices considered inimicable to that law were to be actively opposed. Most often, this meant that the ulama found themselves committed to normative religious practices and symbols, at the same time that they were engaged in protecting and restraining the common masses from harmful ideas and activities.

Thus, learning was usually, if not always, put to the service of the powerful. an-Nāṣirī, to be sure, criticized in no uncertain terms the signs of moral corruption and religious limpness of his times—wine, tobacco, slavery—manifestations not confined to the masses.[30] More common. however, is his exaltation of the urban elite and their way of life and his denigration of the ignorant lower classes. Moreover, his vehement attacks against the leaders and adepts of certain religious orders suggest more than just an attitude of social superiority or religious admonition. By his impassioned testimony we are led to postulate that the vague, culturally defined, horizontal barrier across society was hardening into a self-conscious and antagonistic tension along class lines and that the unstable conditions of the period made the ulama apprehensive lest they lose their favored status in society and their hold over the masses.

Granted, not all the ulama opposed all the religious orders. an-Nāṣirī, himself, was a proud descendant of the founder of an order that was highly respected throughout Morocco, including Salé. For the people of the city, the Nāṣiriyya represented an "orthodox," "proper," "decent" order; and, indeed, a marriage party, celebrating in the streets of Salé, would lapse into reverent silence as it passed before the lodge of the order. There were also other "orthodox" orders in the city, most of them founded during the nineteenth century: the Tijāniyya, Darqāwiyya, and Kattāniyya. These were frequented by the cosmopolitan inhabitants of the city, including the ulama. Indeed, one of the leading scholars of Salé, Ibn Mūsā (d. 1328/1908), was the disciple and successor of the famous Sufi and alim al-'Arabī b. as-Sā'iḥ, shaikh of the Tijānī lodge in Rabat. Later, he was buried in the Darqāwī lodge of Salé, just as the qadi of Fez 'Abd Allah b. Khadrā' (d. 1309/1891) (also originally from Salé) had been interred in the Nāṣirī lodge of Fez.[31] These "orthodox" and respectable orders of the cities were largely frequented by the staid and dignified urbanites, for purposes of learning, social intercourse, and reaffirmation of their sense of religious probity. The scholars did not condemn these

[30] an-Nāṣirī, *op. cit.*, III, 62–65.

[31] 'Abd al-Ḥayy al-Kattānī, *Fihris al-Fahāris* (Fez, 1932), II, 276.

people or their practices. Their attacks were aimed at the common people who attended orders that provided their adepts with ecstatic mysticism, sometimes laced with military and political overtones.[32]

an-Nāṣirī's views point to the existence of important social cleavages along the lines of these religious orders. In a manuscript entitled *The Exaltation of the Grace of God by Support of the Sunna,*[33] he set himself to exposing the errors of certain religious orders and their heterodox followers who had introduced innovations into Islam. In this work he argues that the only way in which progress might be achieved among the Muslims would be by their return to the sources of religion. When the book had been completed and read, some of the supporters of the orders wrote to the Sultan demanding that the author repudiate his charges. an-Nāṣirī's refusal to disown what he had written was not contested, but it may explain the fact that his book was not printed.[34]

In his history of Morocco, an-Nāṣirī assailed some of the religious orders because of the way in which their followers related to the shaikhs. He claimed that these groups of adepts believed that their shaikh alone was able to benefit or harm mankind. Their activities had become a matter of zealous partisanship (*fa-sāra 'l-amar 'aṣabiyyan*) and sectarianism (*at-tashayyu'*), and they conflicted with the basic tenets of Islam—the unity of the Community and the unique existence of God. an-Nāṣirī goes on to argue that for real Muslims those individuals of great intuition or piety, such as the shaikhs of the orders, should be considered simply "as the teeth of a comb"—collectively beloved because of and for the sake of God.[35]

To the spirit of the ulama, the people who indulged in the ecstatic producing practices of "seance", and the like, represented an ignorant and dangerous element of the population. an-Nāṣirī describes how these "common people" (*ṭaghām,* the most wretched of people, the low, ignoble, stupid) take over lodges in the name of a shaikh and then turn them into mosques of prayer in which they sing and dance to the accompaniment of

[32] Le Tourneau, *La vie quotidienne à Fès en 1900,* p. 287, where the social origins of the followers of various orders in Fez are clearly distinguished.

[33] *Ta'thim al-munna bi-nuṣrat as-sunna.* MS no. D530, Archives Générales, Rabat. Cf. esp. pp. 127 ff.

[34] an-Nāṣirī, *op. cit.,* IV, 145–46; on the "permanent vein of reformism" in Moroccan history, cf. J. Berque, *Al-Yousi* (Paris, 1958), p. 123. On modern reformism in Morocco, see A. Hourani, *Arabic Thought in the Liberal Age, 1798–1939* (London, 1962), pp. 37–38; J. Abun-Nasr, "The Salafiyya Movement in Morocco: The Religious Bases of the Moroccan Nationalist Movement," in *St. Anthony's Papers No. 16,* Middle Eastern Affairs, No. 3 (London, 1963), pp. 90–105.

[35] an-Nāṣirī, *op. cit.,* I, 63 ff.

musical instruments. The animosity of the scholar toward the followers of these orders and the way in which he conceives of his own role in relation to them are clearly articulated by an-Nāṣirī in the following passage: "If someone who seeks to make them aware of their true welfare calls to them while they roam about in this state of confusion, they do not listen; they do not perceive the error (*al-ḍallāl*) in this state of evil! No, they believe that they are closer to God! May God raise them from their ignorance!" Elaborating on the ignorance, uselessness, and sinfulness of these common people, an-Nāṣirī mentions visits and pilgrimage fairs (*mawāsim*) to the tombs of saints, carried out in imitation of customs attached to the pilgrimage to the holy Ka'ba of Mecca. In the final analysis, such people are not considered as true believers and are accused of manifestly partaking in polytheism.[36]

Now these pronouncements by the ulama about the religious practices of their contemporaries may well be sound from the point of view of Muslim theology or religious reformism. Seen as religious ideology, however, as they must be in an analysis of social forces, these judgments are indexes of socio-economic functions and interests. During the late nineteenth century, Moroccans lived through a period of political, economic, and social uncertainties and changes. On the one hand, popular religious orders such as the 'Aisāwa, Ḥamādsha, and Qādiriyya seem to have held an increasing attraction for the poor and disoriented and offered to them both psychological refuge and emotional exaltation. On the other hand, the ecstatic activities of these orders held no fascination for the urban groups that profited from this period of instability. On the contrary, these groups feared and opposed the undisciplined common people and the religious orders that allowed them to give vent to their feelings. The ulama were the spokesmen for the people of the city in these matters. It was left to them to counteract and control, by virtue of religious prestige and by way of censure and propaganda, the "antisocial" and potentially threatening behavior of the masses and their popular religious leaders.[37]

The popularity of these orders offended not only the ulama's view of orthodoxy; it challenged the respect and influence enjoyed by scholars among men of power. The high positions that the professionally learned had attained in society, owing to their expertise and success as custodians

[36] *Ibid.*

[37] Cf. the suggestive remarks by Berque in *Al-Yousi*, p. 123, on the psychological aspects of adhesion to the orders by the masses and the "missionary" reaction (rather than "fraternal correction") of the scholars.

of the revealed religion, could only be maintained as long as the ulama retained their image as the best defenders of true faith. Their attacks against the innovations and heresies of the masses thus enhanced and justified their role as religious leaders who were forever seeking to reinforce the moral fiber of the Muslim community. In effect, by siding with the cosmopolitan against the common people, the ulama were protecting class interests. Orthodoxy and a superior socio-economic status were mutually sustaining.

The attitude of the ulama toward the Western nations was consistent with their position vis-à-vis the masses. They wanted to maintain the material benefits gained through the economic penetration of Europe, but not at the price of Western political or cultural domination. It was an attempt to preserve a status quo that was to their advantage, by posing as the defenders of the community from within and from without. To some extent the ideas of these nineteenth-century Moroccan scholars are predecessors of the two tendencies that were to characterize the development of much of modern Islamic thought—internal reform and external defense. But as ideas they had little effect on the sweep of events leading to the French Protectorate. For the ulama were neither able to counteract the gradual weakening of the authority and prestige of the monarchy, nor were they able to control the actions of the common people or of the European nations. Their failure to assert themselves as a coherent group or to significantly influence the flow of history at that moment should not surprise us. The ambiguities of their functions in society, the lack of a clearly defined status as a group, the readiness, indeed need, to seek worldly advantages, left the ulama too deeply enmeshed in the affairs of society. Weak, dependent, and compromised, they were, like the government and the rest of the population, equally submerged by the fatality of colonialism.

Conclusion

The education, social ties, economic activities, and ideas of an-Nāṣirī have been viewed within certain contexts of nineteenth-century Moroccan society—the social and economic mobility, the relationship between groups, the forces of change. His life has served us as an example of what the ulama might hope to, and often did, achieve in the way of prestige, wealth, and influence. What has not been dealt with adequately, so far (except by implication), is the fact that the very fluidity of Moroccan society provided only for the upward mobility of individual scholars and not for the ascent of a coherent group of religiously learned men bound by mutual interests.

The absence of an ascendant, corporate group of scholars can be partly explained by the characteristics of urban social organization. Yet, even when secondary cultural categories began to harden into a more stratified social system, the ulama shared in some sort of status level but did not themselves form a group apart. To some extent, the very definition of just who were the ulama was not clear. Scholars were not designated by a degree, or in any other formal way. Rather, the popular linguistic usage by the consensus of one's contemporaries determined those who were to be included by that term of address and reference. This meant that the separate and sometimes divergent milieus and communities of which Moroccan society was composed often designated the ulama according to their own idiosyncracies. Thus, for example, Fez (itself no homogeneous society) was jealous and parsimonious in naming its own ulama, much less those of the other, less cosmopolitan, cities. Where there was no formal recognition of individual ulama or overall identification of them by consensus, one could hardly expect to find a coherent group. Certainly the organized status of the canon lawyers in medieval Christian Europe, to take one example, finds no counterpart in traditional Morocco, or for that matter, it would seem, in any traditional Islamic society.

A further and complementary explanation for the absence of a corporate group of ulama lay in the fact that learning was in no way a monopolistic affair. Koranic schools and "centers of advanced studies" (ranging from dismal prayer rooms to the sumptuous Qarawiyin mosque) were open to those who felt the desire and ambition to frequent them. When a man emerged from his studies, he was considered at least by some people to have grasped a measure of religious science. To be sure, the level of education that a man attained was sometimes influenced by the traditions, wealth and ambition of his family, but many who came to be called ulama were of humble origins. This lack of differentiation seems to have bothered the biographers, for we find that they laboriously and carefully tabulate the genealogies and exact qualities of each scholar whom they describe. These distinctions usually indicate the scholar's origins, the contents of his storehouse of knowledge, what characterized him as a teacher and, finally, what were his personal qualities.[38]

[38] The Moroccan biographical literature is very rich. In these remarks I have drawn, in particular, from my own work on Salé and its historians and from Lévi-Provençal's *Les historiens du Chorfa*. On the lack of a struc-

The terminology of the biographers is important in another respect, for it offers an insight into the ulama's view of themselves. Essentially, it is a terminology that emphasizes the qualities of men as teachers and as ideal models of behavior. In their own self-image the ulama were responsible for the education and moral fiber of their coreligionists. This responsibility was theirs, they believed, because they were links in a chain, liaisons to the authorities of religious knowledge and moral behavior and, ultimately, to the Prophet of the Muslim community. In practice, many of the functions performed by the ulama in their society were an affirmation of their own self-image. Given charge of their own vision, they sought to insure the continuity of the religious community by propagating their knowledge and by morally defining the values and ideals that in their view constituted the Islamic way of life. Moreover, and herein lies the source of the ambiguous situation of the ulama, religion and politics in the Sharifian empire of Morocco were so inextricably tied that religious knowledge provided a stepping-stone to administrative positions and to relative wealth.

In nineteenth-century Morocco the learned reached positions of high status because of the nature of the administration, and because religion permeated the society in which they were the religious experts. The functions performed were themselves prestigious and opened the way to wealth and influence. Yet, neither by education nor function, and despite the brilliance and integrity of outstanding individuals, did the ulama form a group able to influence decisively the tenor or direction of Moroccan history at the close of the century.[39]

---

tured, exclusive system of education, see A. Bel, *La religion musulmane en Berbérie* (Paris, 1938), pp. 373 ff.

39 Postscript. There is much more to be said about the ulama of the countryside. This essay has relied predominantly on material concerning the urban ulama. Sources for a complementary study of the role of ulama in the countryside (particularly the cultural history of the Moroccan south) remain unexploited. The studies of R. Montagne (*Naissance du prolétariat marocain* [Paris, 1950], pp. 31 ff.) and J. Berque (*Structures Sociales du Haut Atlas* [Paris, 1955], pp. 315 ff.) call attention to the juridic and spiritual roles of the clerical families whose teachings produced a latent millenarism. Recently published works by al-Mukhtār as-Sūsī emphasize the importance of zawiya villages in the Sus, the prestige and protection that their scholar communities enjoyed, and the sometimes passive, sometimes active role of the ulama in entourages of local caids (cf. *al-Ma'sūl* [Casablanca, 1966], VI, 155 ff.; *Ilīgh* [Rabat, 1966], pp. 263–264). All this suggests that the scholars of nineteenth-century Morocco were honeycombed throughout the country. To what extent their various functions resembled one another and their individual lives were historically significant remains a problem for further study.

6 The Ulama of Cairo in the Eighteenth and Nineteenth Centuries*

AFAF LUTFI AL-SAYYID MARSOT

IN THE INTRODUCTION to his chronicles, *Ajaib al-athar fi'l tarajim wa'l akhbar,* Abd al-Rahman al-Jabarti in 1820 set forth a remarkable self-image of the ulama and of their place within the Muslim ethos. According to his account God created mankind in five categories of descending importance. In the first category were the prophets who were sent to reveal God's message to mankind and to show the world the path of righteousness. In the second category were the ulama who are the heirs and the successors of the prophets, "the depositors of truth in this world and the elite of mankind."[1] Below them in rank were the kings and other rulers, and below them ranked the rest of mankind in two last categories.

Such a glorified image of the ulama was not entirely a product of Jabarti's fantasy or ego, but was indeed grounded in Muslim ethics, and it serves to explain the special position the ulama occupied in their society. For where all men are enjoined to obey a moral imperative, "command good and set aside evil," for themselves and their circle, it was the duty of the ulama to see that this was carried out by the whole of society. They were the purveyors of Islam, the guardians of its traditions, the depository of ancestral wisdom, and the moral tutors of the population. The ulama who did not even form a priestly caste attained a position of moral and social superiority on the basis of their profession as doctors of the law and of their preoccupation with "the words of God" which regulated the

* Earlier and more expanded versions of parts of this paper have appeared in "The Role of the *'ulamā'* in Egypt during the Early Nineteenth Century," in *Political and Social Change in Modern Egypt,* P. M. Holt, ed. (London, 1968), pp. 264–280; "The Beginnings of Modernization among the Rectors of al-Azhar," in *Beginnings of Modernization in the Middle East,* William R. Polk and Richard L. Chambers, eds. (Chicago, 1968), pp. 267–280; "A Socio-Economic Sketch of the 'Ulamā' in the Eighteenth Century," paper read to the colloquium commemorating the millenary of Cairo, 1969, to appear in the *Mélanges du Millénaire du Caire,* 1973.

[1] 'Abd al-Raḥmān al-Jabartī, *'Ajā'ib al-athār fi'l tarājim wa'l akhbār* (Cairo, 1882), I, 7.

gamut of relationships between individuals and between them and their Maker. The rest of Muslim society acquiesced in the special standing of the ulama, as did indeed the rulers, in theory, if not always in practice. For though one would like to believe that the "pen is mightier than the sword" the facts showed that the ruler who had the sword at his side was the more powerful until he lost that sword. Physical coercion was more forceful than moral sanctions. Hence the growth of a Sunni tradition of submission to authority no matter how tyrannical, with the concomitant fear of anarchy implicit in the Sunni aversion to revolution. Nevertheless the ulama's moral influence throughout the Muslim world won them a virtual immunity from arbitrary punishment by the rulers,[2] and at times they braved the wrath of the rulers and used their moral sanctions to thwart tyrannous measures as I show below.

The high ulama of Cairo were those who had an official position either in the learned orthodox hierarchy or in the Sufi mystical one. And while the lines between the two were by no means rigid, for there were rectors of al-Azhar who were also heads of Sufi brotherhoods, like the eminent Shaikh al-Hifni (or al-Hifnawi [d. 1761]) who was head of the Khalwatiyya order, there were also heads of Sufi orders who did not necessarily qualify for the title of alim. Thus there were ulama who were predominantly identified with the Sufi hierarchy, and others who were predominantly identified with the orthodox hierarchy. Among the regular ulama, that is, belonging to the orthodox hierarchy, we have the rector of al-Azhar, the leading religious dignitary in Egypt. (The grand Qadi who was appointed from Istanbul and was an Ottoman does not fit the description of Egyptian ulama.) Then came the heads of the schools of law, the muftis, some of the heads of the twenty-five colleges, or *riwaqs*, of al-Azhar, and some of the senior teachers. Although there were numerous other teaching establishments in Cairo—Jabarti gives us the names of some twenty madrasas and an equal number of mosques—al-Azhar dominated the professional scene completely, and in fact dominated the whole establishment of ulama in the country. Exact figures for the number of ulama in al-Azhar in the eighteenth century are nonexistent. M. de Chabrol gives an estimate of thirty to forty, others have gone up to a hundred.[3] Of that number only

[2] H. A. R. Gibb and H. Bowen, *Islamic Society and the West* (London, 1950), I, Pt. II, 111; also Jabarti, *op. cit.*, III, 266.

[3] See J. Heyworth-Dunne, *An Introduction to the History of Education in Modern Egypt* (London, 1968), p. 29. Also M. de Chabrol, "Essai sur les moeurs des habitans modernes de l'Egypte," *Description de l'Egypte: Etat Moderne* (Paris, 1832), II, 67.

a small percentage qualify as high ulama, that is, as men who were powerful and influential among the ruling circle and the population. We can therefore, and somewhat arbitrarily, divide the high ulama into poor and pious intellectuals, respected for their rectitude and learning, and having or not political influence, and wealthy men, possessing character and influence and perhaps learning as well. For quite often wealth, when it was not inherited, came as the result of connections with the ruling elite.

The second group comprised the Syndic of the Notables, *naqib al-ashraf,* and the titular heads of two Sufi orders, Shaikh al-Bakri who was shaikh of the Bakri order, and Shaikh al-Sadat who was head of the Wafai order. Naqib al-ashraf in the past had been nominated from Istanbul but from the seventeenth century onward he was usually a member of either the family of al-Bakri or of al-Sadat, and was chosen by the previous incumbent who nominated his successor before his death. A man named al-Sayyid Umar Makram had occupied the position from 1793 to 1809, but on his exile by Muhammad Ali the position reverted once again to the Bakri family. Both the family of al-Bakri and al-Sadat were *ashraf,* descendants of the Prophet, and were contenders for the title of *shaikh mashayikh al-turuq al-sufiyya,* principal coordinator of all the mystical orders in the country. Which means that he not only led the orders during ceremonies, but appointed their heads, and also had a hand in choosing the rector of al-Azhar.[4] These two positions, naqib and shaikh al-mashayikh, explain why the two families formed a virtual hereditary aristocracy when their orders, the Bakri and Wafai, were not the most numerous or even the most popular in the country. The titular heads of these families, that is, *shaikh al-sijada,* were without doubt the two richest ulama in Egypt, and the two most powerful. For it was estimated that in times of crisis the Sufi orders could call upon seventy to eighty thousand men.[5] It is no exaggeration to say that every man in Cairo, and probably in Egypt, was a member of at least one Sufi brotherhood, for the orders performed a vital social as well as a religious function. The *maulids* or festivals connected with the orders were also of economic importance. For example the city of Tanta which was a commercial center, commemorated three annual maulids for saints, *auliya,* which brought thousands of people from all over the country to attend the celebrations, and also to trade. (It is estimated that in recent years the number of people who flocked to Tanta to

[4] For full details respecting these functions see, Muḥammad Tawfīq al-Bakrī, *Bait al-Saddīq* (Cairo, 1905).

[5] Stanford J. Shaw, *Ottoman Egypt in the 18th Century* (Cambridge, Mass., 1962), pp. 22–23, English text.

attend the maulid of al-Sayyid al-Badawi exceeded the million mark.) Cairo celebrated a saint's maulid at least once a month, although some maulids were naturally of more consequence than others, and attracted more attention. The birthday of the Prophet, *al-maulid al-nabawi* was the most important and was celebrated by Shaikh al-Bakri. This was followed by the maulid of the Prophet's grandson al-Husain, which was celebrated by Shaikh al-Sadat.[6] These events were of such importance and magnitude that they warranted the presence of the wali, the Ottoman governor, and of the ruling Mamluk Beys. Aside from the maulids, the brotherhoods met regularly to recite prayers and perform the *dhikr* which was the bond that created solidarity between the members of the brotherhood.

Jabarti in his biography of Shaikh Abu 'l Anwar al-Sadat (d. 1813) wrote that men worked for him without wages, considering it a major sin, *min al-kabair,* to be paid for such an honor. He somewhat acidly adds that al-Sadat had become so glorified that once when a *khatib* in a mosque had lavished praise on him, Jabarti overheard a man muttering that they should now kneel and worship his eminence.[7] If we set aside Jabarti's sarcasm, the picture that emerges from his long account of Shaikh Abu 'l Anwar is that of an extremely influential man, who was excessively wealthy, and who was involved in every major political event in the country, whether at the time of the Mamluks, under the French occupation, or even under Muhammad Ali. To a lesser extent so was Shaikh al-Bakri.

The basic functions of the ulama were to teach Islam and interpret it, that is to be the teachers, lawyers, qadis (judges), and religious mentors. But since almost every aspect of daily living was regulated by the *shari'a* (holy law), or required a ruling in the light of the shari'a, the services of the ulama became necessary in every walk of life, political, social, and economic, and they were called upon to play a vast variety of parts.

Politically they were required to serve on the diwan in a consultative capacity along with the other communal leaders and the military. But that was not their most important political role; frequently they were called upon to act as emissaries, and even as ministers plenipotentiary with full powers of negotiation. Ibn Khaldun's historic meeting with Tamerlane in 1401 was not the first or the last such instance, and the eighteenth and early nineteenth centuries in Egypt abound in occasions when the high ulama were involved in negotiations between warring Mamluk factions,

[6] 'Alī Mubārak, *al-Khitat al-Tawfīqiyya fī Misr al-Qāhira* (Cairo, 1888), I, 90, and III, 73.

[7] Jabartī, *op cit.,* IV, 192.

and between the Mamluks and the Porte.[8] Moreover they acted as a court of appeal in quarrels of a political nature, and even as a sanctuary for the persecuted.[9] One facet of the ulama's political role was to make, or at least to manipulate, public opinion thereby serving as a channel of communication between the rulers and the ruled; the reverse process was also practiced, and the ulama, albeit less frequently, communicated the will of the people to the rulers. And while they were generally keepers of the peace, they could turn into leaders of the mob.[10] In times of crisis, when the central authority was weak, or when the Beys were at loggerheads with the Ottoman authorities, which occurred fairly frequently in the eighteenth century, it was not unusual for the Beys to beg the ulama to help them preserve the peace and keep the population tractable.[11] It was equally not unusual for al-Azhar University to be used as a rallying point for the mob. A drum sounded from its minarets signaled danger and summoned all from the neighboring *suqs* (bazaars) to gather posthaste; the gates of the university were then closed, and the ulama led the mob in a demonstration. More prosaically but equally effective as an instrument of public opinion was the use of the *minbar* (pulpit), especially during the Friday prayer when the *khutba* (sermon) reached a wider audience than on weekdays, and could be, and indeed was, used to diffuse political opinions as well as moral exhortations.

Economically the ulama filled the role of administrators. They managed the wealth of minors and orphans, of schools, mosques, hospitals, and above all managed the funds of charitable endowments, the *awqaf* (pl. of *waqf*) which by the nineteenth century covered under one-fifth the total cultivable land, around 600,000 faddans,[12] and which included perhaps a higher proportion of real estate and other forms of urban property. They were also involved in every form of commercial transaction since all sales, purchases, and transfers of property had to be authorized by the qadi and in the presence of the *shahid* (witness). They frequently acted as bankers and were entrusted with the safekeeping of valuables and had charge of whole families when the head was away, including families of

[8] The Mamluks were a military oligarchy of Turco-Circassian origins who ruled Egypt from 1250 until the Ottoman conquest in 1516. The Mamluk Beys regained hegemony over Egypt in the mid-seventeenth century and from then on with but a few exceptions ruled Egypt as technical vassals of the Ottoman Sultan, but with a fair share of autonomy. The Beys were grouped in various "households" or factions, and strife between them was commonplace (Jabartī, *op. cit.*, II, 79, 154, I, 288, IV, 105, *passim*).

[9] *Ibid.*, II, 23.

[10] *Ibid.*, pp. 103, 258.

[11] *Ibid.*, p. 111.

[12] *Ibid.*, IV, 141.

Mamluks.[13] A few ulama were part-time merchants and artisans. Many were men of property. At times they even doubled as tax collectors when forcible loans were imposed on the population, although they themselves were exempt from such taxations.[14]

Abd al-Rahman al-Jabarti, who is our most important source on the men of the period, supplies us with details as to the financial situation and scholarly standing of the ulama. Frequently he is critical of those men having great wealth, and of the means by which they amassed it. He himself was very rich, but he had inherited his wealth, and so his attitude might be explained as typical of the rich toward the nouveau riche, but there is more behind it. At times it savors of the disapproval of a dedicated doctor of the law for those who concentrate their talents on the attainment of worldly goods to the detriment of the life of the intellect and the spirit. Thus he writes with regret about Shaikh Muhammad al-Mahdi that he could have become a great scholar had he spent more time on his work and less at amassing fortune.[15] But the true cause of disapproval of those who amassed wealth was that they had to be connected with the ruling elite in order to acquire their riches, and a puritan note of pride creeps into his words when he describes a pious man who "had never frequented the houses of the mighty."[16] Often enough there is also a note of respect when he writes about a man who was rich, powerful, and also a noted scholar like his mentor Shaikh Murtada, for instance, who was the author of the grammatical compendium *Taj al-Arus*. He writes that the wali so respected Shaikh Murtada that when he received a missive from him he would first put it to his lips before opening it, and he would never refuse a request made by the shaikh.[17]

Given the economic situation of Egypt the ulama were financially dependent on the bounty of the ruler or of other patrons. Time and again they were to be cowed through finances. They received no cash salary for teaching, and in general were remunerated either through financial endowments (awqaf) or donations. As teachers in al-Azhar they received a ration, *jiraya*, of bread every two days, and gifts of clothing (fur pelisses) on special occasions such as feast days, the accession of a wali or of a new Sultan. A very few ulama even received a cash allowance, for instance Shaikh Murtada received 150 paras (*nisf fidda*) daily from the Porte through the good offices of the wali.[18] Every riwaq had a different ration

[13] *Ibid.*, II, 108–109, IV, 188–190.
[14] *Ibid.*, IV, 20, 62, *passim.*
[15] *Ibid.*, p. 237.
[16] *Ibid.*, p. 105.
[17] *Ibid.*, II, 203.
[18] *Ibid.*, p. 199.

of bread and staples depending on its endowment and the gifts offered to it, thus some distributed over eight hundred loaves every two days, and others eighty. (It is interesting to note that the custom of distributing loaves to students and teachers at al-Azhar continued until 1929, when more than 10,000 loaves were distributed daily.)[19] Most ulama received around three loaves, but higher ulama, such as heads of riwaqs, received some twenty or more.[20] The surplus loaves, if there were any, were therefore traded for other staples.

The ulama supplemented this ration by various means: they held additional positions in other schools or mosques, or managed to get themselves inscribed in the registers of the various regiments, which then paid them a salary,[21] or they received salaries for teaching in private houses, or for copying books, or for reciting the Qur'an, or they simply received presents from the wealthy.[22] The most lucrative source of income they could aspire to was to become *nazir* (supervisor) of a waqf. This post paid the holder a fee, and was usually accompanied by little supervision, so the nazir could dispose of the proceeds of the waqf at his own discretion and according to the individual dictates of his conscience. Jabarti writes at some length on the abuse of the awqaf by their nazirs,[23] for they frequently allowed the mosques or other buildings they were supposed to supervise to fall into disrepair while the funds were squandered. But even if one assumes that the nazir was a pillar of rectitude, as many were, the accumulation of several supervisory posts, which was a fairly common procedure among the high ulama, undoubtedly led to wealth. To give but one example, Shaikh Muhammad al-Bakri (d. 1782) who was head of the Bakri order of mystics was nazir over forty-four awqaf.[24] One of these forty-four was the waqf of Sultan al-Ashraf Barsbay (r. 1422) which was such a rich endowment that by the end of the nineteenth century it still disposed of vast sums of money. The Imam of the mosque was paid 1,000 dirhems a month and 3 rotls (pounds) of bread a day. The khatib was paid 500 dirhems a month and 3 rotls of bread a day. Nine *muazzins* each received 200 dirhems a month and 3 rotls of bread a day. A Hanafi

[19] Muhammad 'Abdullah 'Inān, *Tārīkh al-Jamī' al-Azhar* (Cairo, 1958), p. 291.

[20] *Ibid.*, p. 290.

[21] I.e., Dafṭar al-Aytām, or the registers of the regiments. For more details see my "A Socio-Economic Sketch of the 'Ulamā' in the Eighteenth Century."

[22] E. W. Lane, *An Account of the Manners and Customs of the Módern Egyptians* (London, 1849), I, 291.

[23] Jabartī, *op. cit.*, IV, 209–210, *passim.*

[24] Cairo, Maḥkama Shar'iyya Archives, MS 776/18, 18 Jamad al-Awal, 1788/1202 A.H.

teacher was paid 300 dirhems a month and the Hanbali and Shafi'i teachers each received 100 dirhems, while the Maliki teacher received 50 dirhems a month. The waqf also supported sixty-five students, so that the various services stipulated in the *waqfiyya* came to a total of 20,000 dirhems a month and over 300 rotls of bread a day.[25] And while this is an example of a very rich waqf, it nevertheless serves to point out the various possibilities open to the ulama to supplement their basic remunerations. Appointment to the supervision of a waqf, and often to any of the positions stipulated in the waqf, was naturally dependent on social connections, that is, on patronage. The ulama also acquired *iltizams* (tax farms) in the same fashion.

Our main interest in the wealth of the ulama lies simply in using it as a gauge for their political stock, for it rose when they were powerful, and fell when they were not. It is also a matter of general interest to note the different branches of Egyptian economic life which attracted the ulama and which in turn throw light on economic life in general, and on the ulama as a potential middle class. Thus we find that when the ulama acquired a little capital they first bought real estate, usually a house in which to live. According to Jabarti the more affluent, like Shaikh al-Sadat, Shaikh al-Bakari, and Shaikh al-Mahdi, had more than one house, and often housed wives in different establishments. Later on they bought houses to rent out, or tenements, warehouses, shops, baths, coffeehouses and mills, flour mills and so on.[26] They also acquired iltizams if they could, and they seem to have done that in such a widespread manner that the ulama and the women became the main *multazims* (tax farmers) in the land after the Mamluks. They also traded. In brief their sources of capital investment were diversified, as with any other canny investor, and show their links with the suq, the countryside, and of course with the ruling class who were the main source of wealth. And because of their religious calling they were immune from the confiscations and from the forced loans that the rulers regularly levied on the merchants which decimated their wealth, so that the fortunes of the ulama though perhaps less grand than those of the merchant princes, lasted for longer periods of time, and sometimes into several generations.[27]

[25] 'Alī Mubārak, *op. cit.*, IV, 58.

[26] See my "Socio-Economic Sketch of the 'Ulamā'."

[27] One example is Shaikh al-Mahdī's family, and those of al-Bakrī and al-Sādāt. The opposite case was equally true, thus Shaikh Shanan, who was described as the richest man of his age, left a fabulous fortune which was rapidly decimated by his son, who died in debt (Jabartī, I, 73).

Socially the ulama were teachers, scholars, and the intelligentsia of the day. They were scientists and mystics, humanists and artists. They comforted the bereaved, advised the high and the mighty, and on occasion protected the poor and the downtrodden. In brief they were ubiquitous, and fulfilled functions on all social levels, and had an entrée into every nook and cranny of society. The social background of the Egyptian ulama differed from that of the ulama in the rest of the Ottoman Empire, for there was no aristocratic hereditary caste of high as against lesser ulama, but rather the profession presented a case of genuine social mobility. Most of the prominent ulama were of fallah, peasant, origin as their names denote. If we glance at a list of the rectors of al-Azhar up to the nineteenth century and their places of origin we find the following:

Shaikh	*Place of origin*
al-Khorashi (d. 1689)	Abu Khorash in Buhaira
al-Nasharti (d. 1708)	Nashart
Shanan (d. 1720)	al-Jidiya
al-Fayyumi (d. 1724)	Fayyum
al-Shubrawi (d. 1756)	Shubra
al-Hifni (d. 1767)	Hifna
al-Sajini (d. 1768)	Sajin
al-Damanhuri (d. 1778)	Damanur
al-Arusi (d. 1793)	Minyat al-Arus
al-Sharqawi (d. 1812)	Tawila in Sharqiyya
al-Shanawani (d. 1817)	Shanawan
al-Arusi (d. 1830)	Minyat al-Arus
al-Damhudji (d. 1830)	Damhuj
al-Quwasni (d. 1838)	Quwasna

The only exception to that list was Shaikh Hasan al-Attar (d. 1834) who was a Cairene, and whose father was a herbalist from North Africa. Al-Attar was actually Muhammad Ali's candidate for the rectorship rather than the ulama's choice,[28] and his successors followed the previous pattern of fallah rectors.

Although other lesser ulama came from all social levels, some were sons of urban dwellers, many sons of ulama, and some sons of merchants, the striking fact remains that the leading ulama were of fallah origin. It would then seem that even though there were eminent families of ulama,

[28] For more details see my "Beginnings of Modernization among the Rectors of al-Azhar."

like the Arusi and the Adawi, yet there is no evidence that the ulama families exclusively dominated the learned institution as they did in Istanbul. Only one family, that of al-Mahdi, has produced three ulama who became rectors of al-Azhar, and that was also a fallah family in origin and, more interesting, of Coptic descent. Every generation of ulama then threw up new blood, and the test for survival in the highest ranks was ability. Incompetent ulama were physically driven away by their disgruntled students, and before any man was accepted as an alim he passed a test of endurance and ability before his peers and his students.[29] We may safely say then that the profession of alim was the most successful vehicle of social mobility for the lower classes, and especially for the fallahin.

It is also interesting that even by the nineteenth century it was the profession that remained the obvious choice in the rural areas among even the most affluent village notables for the brightest child, the weakest child, and the blind child, of whom there were all too many. The last two categories were guided into that career because they were physically unfit to follow the fallah way of life which demanded brawn, and the first because he was marked for better things and this was his entree into them. Later in the century we note that those who could afford it directed their sons into the new university and the liberal professions and above all into government service which promised security of tenure. If they had several sons then one of them might also become an alim. By the twentieth century this practice became commonplace. To give but two examples, the sons of prominent rectors of al-Azhar (who were also rivals): Shaikh al-Maraghi (d. 1946) had one son who became a judge and another a civil servant and eventually a cabinet minister. Shaikh al-Zawahri (d. 1944) had a son who became a civil servant and another the foremost dermatologist in Cairo. (Extensive work still needs to be carried out on the subject before one can draw conclusions about the trend.)

The peasant links of the ulama partly explain why by the end of the eighteenth century ulama became the largest group of multazims after the Mamluks, and also lead us to assume that their influence in the rural regions was just as powerful as in the urban, if not more so. The incident involving Shaikh al-Sharqawi is a case in point. In 1794 the multazims of Bilbais in Sharqiyya appealed to al-Sharqawi, also a multazim of the area, to oppose a new tax. Sharqawi then rector, closed al-Azhar, gathered the ulama round him, and marched to Shaikh al-Sadat's house, and there the

[29] Mubārak, *op. cit.*, IV, 36.

ulama discussed their grievances against the Mamluks in general. The crisis lasted for three days during which the mob outside al-Sadat's house daily grew in size and the Mamluks became increasingly alarmed at what looked as though it might develop into a city insurrection. Finally the ulama and the Mamluks met at the wali's house and signed a document wherein the Beys promised not to raise new taxes, and promised to deal justly with the population. The incident was a potent example of the pressure the ulama could bring to bear on the Mamluks, although never for long, and it also demonstrates the links the rural population had with al-Azhar and the ulama[30] when their interests coincided, for as multazims the ulama were often rapacious and abusive toward their fallahin as were the Mamluks.

It is therefore easy to understand the veneration that the ulama commanded from the population, less easy to understand the respect that they commanded from the rulers who were complete autocrats. As the guardians of religious lore and tradition the ulama in general represented an element of stability in times of flux and a thread of continuity in the face of all too common political disruptions. To the mass of the Egyptian population they became a constant source of succor and their natural leaders in the matters of this world as well as the next, especially since the ruling elite was formed of an alien people who did not even speak the language of the masses. We must remember, however, that any special position the ulama occupied was the consequence of a Muslim framework and could continue to survive only within a Muslim society. The rulers also played the game according to Muslim rules—even those among them who were relative newcomers to Islam—and though they frequently circumvented the ulama they would not radically change the system. (The only one who came close to doing so was Muhammad Ali.) To the rulers, therefore, the ulama represented an important tool of government in subjugating the population, and were frequently a source of advice and of consultation. To both rulers and ruled they were an objective haven which contending factions could turn to in times of stress.

It must be noted that it was a facet of the ulama's many functions to fill temporarily a power vacuum whenever one occurred, and this feature was not unique to that or any period but was a basic element of their role within the socio-political framework. The fact that similar situations had occurred in the past and were to occur in the future serves to make the point. For example, when the Ayyubid dynasty fell to the Mamluks in

[30] Jabartī, II, 258.

1250, the ulama dominated the scene to the extent than an astute and clever ruler like Baibars (r. 1260) had to submit to their dictates until he managed to assert himself fully. Later on he controlled the ulama by the simple expedient of curtailing their finances. He issued an order preventing the ulama from holding more than one teaching post at a time. Thus threatened with penury they perforce had to plead with him for permission to return to the previous system, and thereby put themselves at his mercy.[31]

The relationship between the high ulama and the Mamluks was in general an amicable one. The Mamluks respected the ulama, deferred to their wisdom, and trusted them to the extent of relying almost exclusively on them as emissaries during their frequent internecine quarrels. After the death of Ali Bey al-Kabir (d. 1773) the central power had weakened and authority had become diffused among several contenders. Power struggles culminated in the joint rule of two Beys, Ibrahim and Murad. For two decades that duumvirate, stormy and precarious a relationship though it was, managed to rule Egypt and to survive numerous attempts on the part of other Beys to displace them. They even managed to survive a punitive Ottoman expedition in 1786, until they were ultimately destroyed by Bonaparte's invasion of Egypt in 1798. The ruling Beys and their lesser rivals sought to attach the ulama to their cause through largesse: gifts, salaries, iltizams, various positions, and the ulama who were dependent on the Mamluks cooperated with them. During that period popular uprisings kindled by Mamluk abuses had become frequent, and the ulama were beginning to show a more active participation in these manifestations and in the political life of the country than they had previously done. Thus almost simultaneously the ulama gained in political authority and in riches when they realized how much the ruling elite were dependent upon them in controlling the political situation and in giving a semblance of legitimacy to their deeds. In that period the ulama enjoyed a brief "golden age" when they showed a spurt of independence, which was to become even more pronounced in 1805 as we shall see later. The ulama therefore braved the Mamluks, and restrained them when they went too far. Shaikh al-Mansafisi (d. 1775) rebuked Ali Bey al-Kabir for being rude to him;[32] Shaikh Ali al-Saidi went even further and rebuked Yusif Bey al-Kabir who had threatened him by saying, "May God curse the slave-dealer who sold you, and the person who bought you and

[31] Ibrahim Salama, *L'enseignement Islamique en Egypte* (Cairo, 1939), p. 64.

[32] Jabartī, I, 415.

made you an Amir."[33] Shaikh al-Hifni, the rector, had the power to restrain the Beys from going to battle against Ali Bey al-Kabir, and they were delayed until Shaikh al-Hifni died, quite suddenly, thereby giving rise to the suspicion that he had been poisoned by the Beys.[34] Shaikh al-Dardir, the Maliki mufti, was often used by the Mamluks as negotiator, yet when a group of people came to complain to him that a Bey had plundered the house of the head of the Bayyumi order he suggested to the mob that they march on Mamluk houses and pillage them to pay them back in their own coin, "either dying as martyrs or gaining victory."[35] Before he could put his plan into action, however, the chief of police went to Murad and Ibrahim Beys and they forced the plunderous Bey to return his booty. The list of brave stands on the part of the ulama is a long one. They even opposed the delegate of the Porte who had led an expedition in 1786 against the two Beys. The Pasha had tried to sell the wives and children of the Mamluk Beys in pique over his failure to defeat them in battle, and there he met the combined opposition of four of the leading ulama. Shaikh al-Sadat continued to oppose the Pasha when he attempted to extort Mamluk moneys that had been deposited with the alim for safekeeping. In brief the Pasha complained that Shaikh al-Sadat had so successfully frustrated him that he had "burned his heart," *ahraqa qalbi.*[36] Perhaps the high point of the ulama's opposition to the Mamluks came during a meeting of the diwan when news reached Cairo of Bonaparte's landing and of his taking Alexandria. Then they heatedly accused the Mamluks of being the sole cause of Egypt's troubles.[37] In effect this was the beginning of the end for the centuries of ulama-Mamluk cooperation.

When the French invaded Egypt in 1798 they needed the services of the ulama even more than had the Mamluks. Bonaparte considered the ulama the natural leaders of the country and described them as men who "are interpreters of the Koran, and the greatest obstacles we have met with and shall still meet with proceed from religious ideas; and . . . because these ulama have gentle manners, love justice, and are rich and animated by good moral principles . . . they are not addicted to any sort of military maneuvering and they are ill adapted to the leadership of an armed movement."[38] For these reasons he wished to use them as a political front, and his diwan was therefore composed entirely of ulama who were to help him legislate, maintain order, and act as an intermediary

[33] *Ibid.*, II, 17–19.
[34] *Ibid.*, I, 303–304.
[35] *Ibid.*, II, 103.
[36] *Ibid.*, IV, 188.
[37] *Ibid.*
[38] C. de la Jonquière, *L'éxpedition de l'Egypte (1798–1801)* (Paris, 1899), V, 597.

between the French authorities and the people. But for these very same reasons the ulama had to lead movements against the French. The fact that they were ill equipped to do so was no deterrent. Amazingly enough, the first revolt movement against the French was led by the shaikh of the riwaq of the blind.[39] The riwaq had always had a reputation for ill temper, but that was carrying imprudence too far, and the outcome was disastrous for al-Azhar was shelled and several ulama executed. The ulama were generally willing to cooperate with the French—except for Shaikh al-Sadat who refused to serve on the diwan as demeaning to a man in his position—but Shaikh al-Bakri and Shaikh al-Sharqawi were willing to join it. By pushing the ulama so much to the forefront, the French strengthened the hand of the ulama and cut the knot that had tied them to the Mamluks, thus making it easier for them at a later period, in 1805, to look elsewhere for a ruler, notably Muhammad Ali who came to power with their connivance. The French continued to show patronage to the ulama, and, more important, they instituted salaries for those serving on the diwan—a custom that met with the approval of the recipients. It is important to realize that over a century later the ulama finally received regular cash salaries for their teaching posts in al-Azhar.

The evacuation of the French troops and the advent of the Ottoman forces in 1801 which brought Muhammad Ali to Egypt, also brought chaos and bloodshed to the land. The Ottoman armies treated Egypt like conquered territory, and they, the governor, the wali, and the Mamluks jockeyed for power, ravaged the land, and forced the ulama to seek a way out of such anarchy. Led by naqib al-ashraf, the remarkable Sayyid Umar Makram,[40] who was being wooed by Muhammad Ali, the ulama decided to oust the wali and replace him with Muhammad Ali. Walis had often been ousted by the Mamluks; this was the first instance of one being removed by the ulama and in the name of the people. Understandably the man refused to take his ouster seriously. Galvanized by Umar Makram the ulama helped organize some of the guilds into combat forces, and for one glorious moment they led a popular resistance movement which the French agent described as "On voit règner le même enthousiasme qu'en France dans les premiers moments de la Révolution."[41] They then sent a

[39] The events of October 1798.

[40] Very little is known about his background. He seems to have had great powers of organization for he was able to organize the artisans into combat groups on at least three separate occasions. Muhammad Ali came to power with his help, and when Makram began to oppose him he sent him into exile.

[41] Georges Douin, *Mohamed Aly: Pacha du Caire, 1805–1807* (Cairo, 1929), p. 35.

petition to Istanbul requesting the Sultan to sanction their act and proclaim Muhammad Ali wali of Egypt, which the Porte did.

The ulama supported Muhammad Ali because he had promised to govern Egypt in consultation with them, but they were not willing to take an active share in government and at once abdicated whatever political influence they had by telling the people that they should now consult the wali not the ulama on matters political and military.[42] Muhammad Ali, like Baibars before him, knew that he had to dominate the ulama if he was to rule absolutely, and he did that by sending their leaders into exile, by abolishing the iltizam system and confiscating the awqaf, and making the ulama completely dependent on the ruler for subsistence.

The modernization of Egypt which was begun by Muhammad Ali and which flowered under Ismail (1864–1879) dealt a heavy blow to the ulama. Politically and economically they were rapidly displaced by the new bureaucracy, and the new foreign merchant class. Intellectually they were outdistanced by the new westernized intelligentsia. As secularism crept in they lost more and more of their power and authority, but nonetheless they remained a force to contend with, although it dwindled with each generation. Successive rulers realized the value of the ulama as a tool of government because of their influence on the population and on the manipulation and creation of public opinion, and continued their amicable relationship. Occasionally an alim would place the weight of his moral sanctions athwart a blatant act on the part of the ruler, but there were now other forces of restraint in the state. Thus the patronage system continued to function even throughout Muhammad Ali's period and we note continuous entries in the archives relative to monthly salaries and grants of land to the high ulama. Abbas (1849–1854) was a very pious ruler, who attended lectures at al-Azhar, but when he tried to confiscate all land belonging to Muhammad Ali he was firmly opposed by the Mufti, Shaikh Muhammad al-Mahdi. Even though he was exiled and threatened with death the Mufti held his stand and it was Abbas who finally had to give in. Ismail was the most munificent of the rulers, which explains why he was regarded by some ulama as a pious and devout Muslim in spite of all his modernizing activities—the founding of western style schools, and of Dar al-Ulum in 1872 modeled on the École Normale, and a potential rival to al-Azhar. During the Urabi revolution in 1880 one of the most powerful ulama, Shaikh al-Adawi, who had sided with the revolutionaries against the Khedive Taufiq the deposed Ismail's son,

[42] Jabartī, III, 337.

daily visited Urabi and recounted a recurring dream he had in which the Prophet appeared to him and told him that Ismail must be brought back to Egypt for he was a true Muslim ruler.[43]

A true Muslim ruler always needed the ulama, and Ismail certainly used the ulama though one would hesitate to apply to him the description of a true Muslim ruler. In the first place the ulama were useful allies, even if in the negative sense to prevent them from showing active opposition or from making adverse religious pronouncements. Earlier in his reign Ismail had needed the help of the ulama in Istanbul when he wanted concessions from the Sultan Abd al-Aziz. In a letter written to his agent in Istanbul Ismail revealed the cynical manner in which the brotherhood of the ulama could be used for the ruler's own ends. The Khedive wrote that he knew the Sultan and his mother both believed in visions and dreams, and he suggested to his agent that certain ulama and mystics might be bribed to have dreams that were favorable to his cause, and which might get his opponents dismissed.[44] Ismail was not unique in this use of the ulama for it was rumored that most Sultans used certain Sufi orders as secret informers.

Later in Ismail's reign when the European Powers began to harass him because of his financial difficulties, he needed the ulama to rally public opinion behind him in order to convince the Powers that he was in control of the financial situation. And in April 1879 Shaikh Ali al-Bakri, naqib al-ashraf, summoned the notables to a meeting at his house, and together they issued a declaration *al-laiha al-wataniyya,* the National Charter, as it was called, in support of the Khedive's financial proposals, and requested a constitutional form of government and the dismissal of the French and English Ministers in Nubar Pasha's cabinet.[45] Unfortunately for Ismail the Powers refused to recognize the proposals and sent him into exile.

If the ulama were an influential group, the question that springs to mind is why they never attempted to seize power and wield it themselves instead of passing it on to some other person as soon as they could. After all, Sufi leaders had founded kingdoms in North Africa. The answer is to be found in the very function of the ulama within an Islamic society. Their political involvement was of only secondary interest, a by-product, so to speak, of their social standing. And though they were the natural

[43] Najīb Makhlūf, *Nubār Pasha* (Cairo, n.d.), p. 147.

[44] Egyptian State Archives, Box 126, *Abhāth,* 16 Sha'bān 1283 (Dec. 1866).

[45] 'Adb al-Raḥmān al-Rāfi'ī, *'Aṣr Ismā'īl,* Vol. II (Cairo, 1932), pp. 215–216.

leaders of the people, they did not aspire to lead politically, and were never at ease in the exercise of direct power. They saw their role in society as that of governing the governors if one may paraphrase Lord Cromer who made such a form of government commonplace in nineteenth-century Egypt. Their self-image was that of the preservers of tradition, not of political innovators; tradition had decreed that though they become involved in the power process they neither direct nor lead it save indirectly. Perhaps there remained vestiges of the concept that power corrupts. They could not destroy that image of themselves, hence their limited involvement and the precipitation with which they abdicated power as soon as they acquired it. To "obey those in authority" has been followed by the ulama to the present day and in return "those in authority" have depended on the ulama in many aspects.

7 | Nonideological Responses of the Egyptian Ulama to Modernization

DANIEL CRECELIUS

THE TRANSFORMATION of Islamic society under the impact of modernization has been the major concern of scholars interested in the modern history of Islam. Until recently, however, this concern was confined to the effects of modernization, such as the disintegration of Islam's classical institutions, rather than with the motive forces of modernization, social and economic change. Nowhere has the fascination with effects been more pronounced than in the plethora of studies dealing with the attempt to reform traditional Islamic thought. Especially in the case of Egypt, which has provided a fertile field for the research scholar, has there been an incredible overemphasis upon the importance of Jamal al-Din "al-Afghani," Muhammad Abduh, and Rashid Rida. Such overemphasis is all the more remarkable when it is recognized that their combined efforts to reform Islam's classical institutions and theories ended in failure. This study therefore concentrates upon the nonideological responses of the ulama to modernization in an attempt to direct the interest of scholars away from the ideal to the real.

The ulama have been recognized as an important element of traditional Islamic government, but it has been customary to view them merely as political brokers, as representatives of the oppressed masses to the rulers. The higher ulama in Egypt have been portrayed as outsiders in the councils of the Ottoman-Mamluk rulers. Their actual role, however, was much greater than that attributed to them by scholars such as Gibb and Bowen,[1] for they shared, albeit to a lesser degree, the responsibilities and rewards of government, and comprised a native elite distinguished by position, wealth, and influence.[2] The ulama were actually an integral part of tra-

[1] H. A. R. Gibb and Harold Bowen, *Islamic Society and the West*, Vol. I, parts 1 and 2 (London, 1957).

[2] The Egyptian ulama, long neglected, have recently been the object of several studies, as it is realized they have played important political, administrative, and economic roles in addition to their roles as teachers and defenders of a corpus of religious learning. Several recent studies that devote themselves precisely to the pe-

ditional government in Egypt and formed exceptionally close political and social ties with their Ottoman-Mamluk rulers. These ties of cooperation and friendship created patterns that can only be described as patron-client relationships. The native ulama were participants in the government of the foreign military-bureaucratic elites, not outsiders, and their own influence and wealth, the well-being of their entire corps, and the influence of Islam in general depended upon the close relations the ulama were able to maintain with their powerful rulers.

Traditional government in Egypt combined the skills of several mutually antagonistic elites. The Ottoman-Mamluk military elites were responsible for the defense of Egypt and the supervision of government. With their preponderant power they dominated the wealth of the land and regulated the political life of the province. But the skills necessary to organize society below the highest levels of government were supplied by the native elites who presided over structures performing a wide range of important social, economic, political and administrative functions. It was through these native structures that the foreign ruling elites reached all levels of Egyptian society.[3]

riod of the late eighteenth century are my "The Ulama and the State in Modern Egypt," unpublished Ph.D. dissertation (Princeton University, 1967), Afaf Lutfi el-Sayed, "The Role of the *'ulamā'* in Egypt during the Early Nineteenth Century," in Peter M. Holt, ed., *Political and Social Change in Modern Egypt* (London, 1968), pp. 264–280, and Afaf Lutfi el-Sayed Marsot, "A Socio-Economic Sketch of the 'Ulamā' in the 18th Century," a paper presented to the International Colloquium on the History of Cairo (Cairo, 1969), and soon to be published under the auspices of the Egyptian government. All three portray the ulama as an element integral to traditional government and view the ulama as a native elite differentiated from the Ottoman-Mamluk elites only by degree of wealth, influence, and power.

[3] The Lybyer thesis which so neatly, but incorrectly, divided Ottoman government into a ruling institution of slaves of the Sultan and a religious institution of freeborn Muslims, each performing complementary but mutually exclusive functions, has been discarded, largely through the publications of the students of the deceased Lewis V. Thomas of Princeton University. The Lybyer thesis (see Albert Lybyer, *The Government of the Ottoman Empire in the Time of Suleiman the Magnificent* [Cambridge, 1913]) was incorporated into the Gibb and Bowen study, but has been reworked as we have learned more about the intricate patterns of Ottoman government and society in the Ottoman Empire. For a critique of the Lybyer thesis see Norman Itzkowitz, "Eighteenth Century Ottoman Realities," *Studia Islamica*, 16 (1962), 73–94. Stanford Shaw also has abandoned the rigid Lybyer division of function and groups in his publications on eighteenth-century Ottoman Egypt. See Shaw, ed. and trans., *Ottoman Egypt in the Eighteenth Century* (Cambridge, Mass., 1962), and *Ottoman Egypt in the Age of the French Revolution* (Cambridge, Mass., 1964). Though it covers the period be-

It was the merchant and religious elites who performed the indispensable integrative functions that linked society with the government of the foreign military elites. Though the populace maintained a general hostility to the foreigners, opposition was useless, for native society was without the capability to drive them from Egypt. Mutual hostility was thus held in check by the realization that the goals of all could be obtained only through mutual cooperation. Only through cooperation could the native elites draw close to the foreign elites and so enjoy the advantages of wealth and authority which they could dispense; and only through cooperation could the Ottoman-Mamluk elites enjoy in peace the many rewards that stable rule in Egypt promised.

Despite the many grievances the ulama had against their rulers, relations between the two groups were marked by harmony, not hostility. Besides the ties of mutual self-interest which bound them together, the ulama were able to establish exceedingly intimate social relations with their rulers. The ulama frequented the houses of the amirs, gave them instruction, acted as their agents and confidants, and even, on occasion, entered the harems of the amirs.[4] Egyptian ulama were able to purchase

fore the Ottoman conquest of Arab lands, Ira Lapidus's *Mamluk Cities in the Later Middle Ages* (Cambridge, Mass., 1967) argues that the ruling military elites organized government by consciously drawing to themselves the various socio-economic institutions in the Arab lands. Gabriel Baer's *Egyptian Guilds in Modern Times* (Jerusalem, Israel, 1964) demonstrates that in the nineteenth century Egyptian society was still governed through its traditional institutions, such as the guilds and the dervish orders, which performed actual administrative functions that the military elites were themselves incapable of performing. My "The Ulama and the State in Modern Egypt" also views the ulama as a socio-administrative group through which the foreign military elites governed native society, but it emphasizes the many advantages that this close relationship with the military elites brought to the ulama.

[4] The Egyptian historian 'Abd al-Raḥmān Ḥasan al-Jabarti is the most valuable source for the history of this period spanning the late eighteenth century to the rise of Muhammad Ali. Among several editions of this famous work see *Ajā'ib al-Āthār fī al-Tarājim wa al-Akhbār* (4 vols.; Cairo, 1913). Cheikh Mansour Bey and others have translated it into French as *Merveilles Biographiques et Historiques du Cheikh Abd el-Rahman el-Djabarti* (9 vols.; Cairo, 1888-1896). Following references to Jabarti are to the French translation. Jabarti remarks on numerous occasions on the close relations between ulama and their Ottoman-Mamluk rulers. Ulama were often called into the houses of the amirs to instruct their children, but it was not unusual for the mamluks or Ottomans themselves to take instruction from the ulama. Amir Ali Bey al-Daftardar, for instance, is reported to have attended lessons at al-Azhar each day (VI, 126). The ulama also shared the company of the Mamluks in frequent dhikrs, banquets, and celebrations at which singing and dancing were prominent entertainments. It was not unusual, moreover, for the

mamluks of their own, to marry mamluk women, or to grant the families of the amirs sanctuary when they were threatened.[5] It is an indication of the close ties existing between the two groups and a sign of the prestige that the religious profession still enjoyed in the nineteenth century that freed mamluks continued to enter the ranks of the ulama.[6] These close personal relationships between the ulama and the Ottoman-Mamluk

amirs to visit the houses of the ulama. Jabarti specifically says that ulama of lesser ranks frequented the houses of the well-known shaikhs in the hope of meeting high personages (IX, 43). They also handled the financial affairs of the rulers. Shaikh Yusuf, for instance, is mentioned as the wakil and katib (agent and clerk) in the house of al-Amir Ahmad Agha ibn Abdallah, the freed slave of the deceased Husain Katkhuda in a waqf document dated 1225 A.H. Egyptian Ministry of Awqaf, Qalam al-Sijillāt al-Ahlīya, Sijill 12 Ahli, Haraf B, no. 11). Jabarti mentions on several occasions that shaikhs entered the harems of their amirs (III, 267; VII, 181; VIII, 149). The famous shaikh Sulaiman al-Fayyumi, who had traveled to Istanbul to represent the interests of the amirs to the Porte and who was married to two Circassian women, was permitted into the harems of the amirs, obviously when he was an old man, and was called by the women of the harems "Abuna," our father (VIII, 234–238).

5 Shaikh al-Azhar Muhammad Shanan, Shaikh Ahmad Shanan, and Jabarti's own father are mentioned by the historian as having owned mamluks (Jabarti, I, 178; III, 187; IV, 41–42). Waqf documents I have studied in Cairo also frequently make reference to freed mamluks of the important ulama. Several of the great shaikhs at the end of the eighteenth century were married to mamluk women. Shaikh Sulaiman al-Fayyumi married two Circassian women and Jabarti's father also was connected with a mamluk family by marriage. A waqf document also identifies the wife of Shaikh Muhammad al-Amir, one of the most powerful shaikhs of his day, as Hanifa bint Abdallah al-Jarkasiyah (the Circassian), the freed slave of al-Amir Hasan Agha (Egyptian Ministry of Awqaf, Qalam al-Sijillāt al-Ahliya, Sijill 10 Ahli, Haraf B, no. 118). In times of civil war or invasion the ulama generally provided sanctuary to the female inhabitants of a house whose amir had fled and guarded the wealth of the exile (Jabarti, IX, 46). The sanctuary of a shaikh's house did not extend to the renegade amir himself, for if he sought refuge with his shaikhly friends he was usually apprehended.

6 The archives of the Ministry of Awqaf are a tremendously rich, yet untapped, source for eighteenth and nineteenth century Egyptian history. The waqf documents and registers kept by the Ministry give us a microscopic insight into Egyptian society in these centuries. To date, for instance, I have found two references in the nineteenth century of freed mamluks becoming members of the corps of ulama. One Shaikh Abdallah Agha is cited as the freed slave of Muhammad Ali Pasha (Qalam al-Sijillāt al-Ahliya, Sijill 2 Ahli, Haraf A, no. 19 [1274 A.H.]). The wakil of Salihah al-Baida, the freed slave of Nafisah al-Baida, the wife of Murad Bey al-Kabir, is identified as Shaikh Hasan al-Katib ibn Yusuf, freed by al-Sayyid Ahmad al-Bakri (Qalam al-Sijillāt al-Ahliya, Sijill 34 Qadīm, no. 28 [1237 A.H.]).

elites were advantageous not only to the ulama personally involved, but to the entire corps. It would not be exaggerating to note that the entire religious structure was dependent upon the favors and support of the ruling elites. Certainly education would not have existed on any scale comparable with that which it had attained without the generous support given it by the Ottoman-Mamluk rulers.

Every great mosque and school in Cairo, for instance, had been completed at state expense under the auspices of one or another of Egypt's foreign rulers.[7] Each structure, and the activities for which it was meant, was supported by the revenues of vast lands and properties, sometimes comprising thousands of feddans or exclusive urban property, alienated in (theoretical) perpetuity through their designation as waqf.[8] These properties supplied the revenues to pay everything from the upkeep of the buildings themselves, including repairs, floor mats, lamps, and candles, to the salaries of nazirs, imams, khatibs, muezzins, and even janitors. Teachers and students received liberal financial and material support.

But awqaf were not the only means of support for the religious community. Generous allocations from the imperial treasury and lavish gifts from their Ottoman-Mamluk patrons supported schools, mosques, tombs, fountains, public religious ceremonies, and the personnel of the corps.[9] In addition, many ulama engaged in commerce or enjoyed the rents of

---

[7] In his famous compendium, *al-Khiṭaṭ al-Tawfīqīya al-Jadīda* (Bulaq, 1887–1889), 'Ali Mubārak Pāsha noted that there were only eight mosques in Cairo where Friday prayers were said before the Circassian Mamluks came to dominate Egypt. In 1875, as a result of Mamluk support for the religious structure, there were 130! See Mubarak, I, 87.

[8] It was possible through legal manipulation for a nazir (supervisor of the waqf) to exchange (a form of selling) the property he supervised for a sum of money. In this way, legal matters aside, land or property once protected as waqf once more became the personal property of the purchaser.

[9] In her paper presented to the International Colloquium on the History of Cairo Dr. Afaf Lutfi el-Sayed Marsot mentions the generous support the ulama themselves received from the Imperial Treasury ("A Socio-Economic Sketch of the 'Ulamā' in the 18th Century," p. 2). It was possible for shaikhs to perpetrate these funds by turning them into awqaf. Shaikh Abu al-Anwar al-Sadat, for instance, created a waqf in which he listed 45 different pieces of property or monies, among which were 7 references to sums that he made waqf from various accounts. These were 178+ Uthmanis from the daftar of al-Madina, 187+ Uthmanis from the same daftar, 130 and 80 Uthmanis from the Orphans' daftar, 22 Uthmanis from the daftar of the Mustahfazan, 240 Uthmanis from the daftar of the Jawishan, and 18 breads from the daftar of the Mutaqa-'idin (see Qalam al-Sijillāt al-Ahliya, Sijill 2 Qadīm, no. 117 [1209 A.H.]).

commercial property, urban dwellings, or agricultural lands. By the end of the eighteenth century the higher ulama had even acquired control of numerous iltizams (tax farms) in their own right.

The glorious period of construction and endowments came to an abrupt end with the deaths of the amirs Muhammad Bey Abu al-Dhahab and Abd al-Rahman Katkhuda in 1775 and 1776, respectively.[10] By the end of the eighteenth century their successors had temporarily usurped the revenues of many of the awqaf which supported the religious community.[11] In the lawless period spanning the Mamluk civil wars to the rise of Muhammad Ali the ulama suffered several waves of repressions during which many of their revenues were taken outright by their rulers.[12] Yet the basic premises that underlay Islamic state and society and its centuries-long equilibrium remained unaffected by these disturbances. Before they would be driven from the seats of power and before their intimate relations with government and the ruling elites would be broken they would,

[10] Abd al-Rahman was the greatest builder of his day. According to Jabarti, he established awqaf more important than had ever existed to support the vast building program he undertook in Cairo (III, 242). He repaired or built innumerable cisterns, fountains, and bridges. His repairs to minarets, buildings, lodgings, and walls won the admiration and thanks of the entire religious community. "Only the work that he had done at al-Azhar," says Jabarti, "suffices to immortalize his memory" (III, 244). The number of major mosques alone that he built or refurbished was eighteen. If talking about zawiyas, small mosques, tombs, or schools, the number is immense (*ibid.*). Abu al-Dhahab's major undertaking was the completion in 1774 of a mosque-school next to al-Azhar which bore his name. It supported fully twenty-one shaikhs who taught in the school or performed one of the services of the mosque, had a sizeable library attached and even supported students from awqaf set aside for its purposes. The waqf in favor of this complex, 112 pages of illuminated gold leaf, is one of the fine examples of eighteenth-century Islamic manuscript illumination. It is found in the Egyptian Ministry of Awqaf, document no. 900 in the Daftarkhanah. Abu al-Dhahab, says Jabarti, was the last amir to support the ulama (III, 249).

[11] Jabarti notes with sadness that despite the 600,000 feddans of land alienated for the support of religious institutions (a figure that strikes me as exaggerated), the buildings of the religious community were all in ruin. The mosque-school of Abu al-Dhahab, for instance, and all its activities had halted only a few years after its completion. It was stripped of all its movable property and left deserted (III, 230).

[12] Ibrahim Bey, for instance, appointed himself nazir of al-Azhar and on several occasions provoked student riots by withholding their provisions (Jabarti, III, 249). Revenues were withheld from the mosques and the amirs and others tried to skimp on their obligations to equip and defend the annual pilgrim caravan to Mecca. Several were not even able to depart.

as a result of the French invasion and the destruction of the Mamluks, experience a brief period of influence and wealth unmatched in their history.

The Golden Age

The oppression and instability engendered by the Mamluk and Ottoman wars of the late eighteenth century continued throughout the French occupation (1798–1801) and into the early reign of Muhammad Ali Pasha. This period of almost uninterrupted chaos provided the ulama various opportunities to maximize their political influence and noticeably to raise their social positions through the acquisition of extravagant wealth. For a very brief period they would, in fact, experience an unprecedented "Golden Age."

Napoleon made every effort to win the friendly cooperation of the ulama, for he recognized them as the natural leaders of native society.[13] He invited them to occupy the places on the divans left vacant by the flight of the ruling elites, permitted Egyptian ulama to occupy the highest positions in the religious hierarchy which had previously been reserved for Turkish ulama, and attempted to give the general impression that the French had come to help the Egyptians achieve liberty, equality, and fraternity within a Muslim context. But promises, propaganda, and bribes failed to convince the ulama of French friendship or good will. "All this is nothing but trickery and deceit, they said, to entice us. Bonaparte is nothing but a Christian, son of a Christian."[14]

Despite their hatred of the infidels, the ulama were forced by circumstances to assume the difficult role of representing the people to the French and maintaining public order in a period of extreme tension. Their active leadership of the masses throughout the French occupation and the years

[13] "I have preferred the ulema and the doctors of the law: first, because they are the natural leaders; secondly, because they are the interpreters of the Koran, and the greatest obstacles we have met with and shall still meet with proceed from religious ideas; and thirdly because these ulema have gentle manners, love justice, and are rich and animated by good moral principles . . . they are not addicted to any sort of military manoeuvering and they are ill adapted to the leadership of an armed movement." Quoted from C. de la Jonquiere, *L'Expédition de l'Egypte 1798–1801*, V, 597, by Afaf Lutfi el-Sayed Marsot in "The Role of the *'ulamā'* in Egypt during the Early Nineteenth Century," p. 271.

[14] Gaston Wiet, ed. and trans., *Nicolas Turc, Chronique d'Egypte: 1798–1804* (Cairo, 1950), p. 78.

immediately following and their elevation to the highest councils formerly reserved for the members of the foreign elites inaugurates a period that has aptly been called by the Egyptian historian Abd al-Rahman al-Rafi'i the era of "popular leadership" (za'ama sha'biya).[15] They were in truth far more powerful than they had ever been, but they could not help the French establish a truly native government. In the hour of their triumph, when Napoleon offered them the highest positions in his government, they betrayed the signs of submission which centuries of foreign domination and training had taught them. They informed Napoleon that it was customary for them to have Turkish officials at the head of all bureaus and turned their backs on the most important and lucrative political offices in Egypt.[16] They could not conceive of a new form of government in which they would assume the positions previously held by the ruling elite, but desired only to advise, as was their custom, the government of others. Turks were therefore retained by Napoleon as Commander of the Pilgrimage, governor of Cairo, and chief of the army and police.[17]

The unwillingness of the ulama to accept the responsibilities of political decision-making and defense was not only a reflex of their centuries-long submission to political tyranny, it was in essence an admission of their own inability to perform these vital functions themselves. Their response, moreover, was in perfect harmony with their own concept of the basic division of functions among the various elements of Islamic government, for each element, the military, the bureaucratic, the commercial, and the religious, had developed particular spheres of competency. Just as the ulama would brook no intrusion by others in their special field of religious interpretation and instruction, so they in turn could not presume to encroach upon the functions of the scribes, the military, or the rulers. At the height of their determination to halt the destruction of their capital and villages after the French withdrawal they would ask another foreigner, Muhammad Ali, to rule them instead of assuming control themselves, despite the formation of popular resistance forces drawn from the population of the capital. Direct rule was too revolutionary an idea and certainly an impossibility in view of their inability to perform the most important governmental functions of defense and the maintenance of internal security.

The ulama never ceased to view the French occupation as more than

[15] al-Rāfi'i, *'Aṣr Muḥammad 'Ali* (Cairo, 1951), pp. 19, 24, 80.

[16] Jabarti, VI, 23.

[17] Antoine Galland, *Tableau de l'Egypte pendant le Séjour de l'Armée Française* (Paris, 1840), I, 74.

a political-military crisis. A religiously alien and morally inferior force was in temporary occupation of their land, so it was natural that their constant concern was for their liberation from the infidels. The ideas of liberty, equality, and fraternity for which Napoleon purported to stand had no effect upon the ulama. Neither did the scientific aspect of the occupation leave much of an immediate impact. Such representatives of the intellectual class as the historian al-Jabarti were neither impressed nor capable of understanding the implications of the modern scientific experiments performed for their benefit. It would be many decades before pressures upon the ulama would evoke an ideological readjustment. The earliest and most consistent responses to these challenges to their well-entrenched system of belief and practice were political in nature, for the challenge itself was viewed as political, not cultural or ideological. These earliest responses, moreover, have been characteristic of the ulama's response to modernization to the present. Even today, nonideological responses dominate the strategy and thinking of the ulama, for modernization still remains a political problem first and foremost in the eyes of the ulama. This question is dealt with at length below.

The withdrawal of the French in July–August 1801 left Egypt once more without an effective government. Rival Mamluk and Ottoman forces now renewed their struggle to organize a government, but their efforts were complicated by the loss of cohesion among the elements comprising their own forces. The ulama were to benefit from the instability of these frantic years in two basic ways. They were, first, to continue the extraordinary expansion of their wealth, and hence their social position, by acquiring control of revenues previously reserved for the foreign elites, and second, to increase their political influence. Just as the Ottoman-Mamluk elites had always interfered in the affairs of the religious elites by arbitrating disputes among the religious leaders, so now would the native ulama play the role of mediators in the quarrels among the various military factions. The native ulama, moreover, performed the indispensable legitimizing function in government. Only they could convince the populace to accept the government of a particular faction; only they could convince the Sultan that his own interests could best be served by recognizing a governor of their choice.

The struggle for preeminence among the various Mamluk factions, the Janissaries who remained under the nominal command only of the wali or governor, and the Albanians lasted from the time of the French withdrawal to 1806 when the Qapudan Pasha withdrew Ottoman forces from the shores of Egypt for the last time.[18] These years of constant warfare saw the people of Cairo suffer perhaps the worst depredations in their memories. Bedouin, Janissary, and Mamluk bands controlled the countryside, stopping all the normal transactions of economic and social life. Conditions in the capital were even worse as feuding military corps, Janissary, Mamluk, or Albanian, would engage in periodic acts of violence against the populace or one another. Tired of the long years of chaos, the ulama finally closed ranks behind a military leader who promised to restore order, security, and justice. Behind the charismatic Naqib al-Ashraf Umar Makram, their own popular leader, the ulama declared their wali deposed and offered the governorship to Muhammad Ali, who had a tenuous leadership of the Albanian corps. Umar Makram and Shaikh al-Azhar Abdallah al-Sharqawi by their own hands then conferred upon him the dignity and symbols of that office.[19] At this supreme moment in the long history of Islamic Egypt the people of Cairo had chosen their own ruler, or so it seemed. Upon closer examination the nature of the shaikhs' act seems less revolutionary than it might have first appeared.

The ulama had exerted their influence to designate their own ruler and had extracted from him a number of concessions,[20] but they had merely chosen one among a number of foreigners whom they wished to be their ruler. The opportunity to choose a native Egyptian ruler was missed, for, very simply, there was neither an Egyptian candidate nor a regular native military force to defend the people's choice. More importantly, the ulama held back in defying the will of the Sultan, just as the Mamluks themselves had always done. They simply designated Muhammad

[18] Though Muhammad Ali had been acknowledged wali of Egypt in 1805, the next year the Sultan sought to replace him with a wali of his own choosing. A new wali and an Ottoman force under the command of the Qapudan Pasha had been dispatched to Egypt, but Muhammad Ali used the power of his own forces and the determination of the ulama to successfully resist the Sultan's will. The withdrawal of the Qapudan Pasha's force in 1806 was the last departure of an Ottoman army from Egypt.

[19] Jabarti, VII, 372.

[20] It was only after Muhammad Ali subscribed to the demands put forward by the ulama that they proclaimed him their new Pasha. The following articles embodied their demands: (1) that the Albanian troops should be quartered in Giza, not in Cairo; (2) that no Albanian should be permitted to enter Cairo unless he belonged to the Guard; (3) that all canteens should be confined to the Island of Roda; (4) that no unlawful contribution should be levied upon the country; (5) that escorts should be provided for the caravan to Mecca; (6) that communication with Upper Egypt should be restored (Georges Douin, *L'Angleterre et l'Égypte: La Politique Mameluke (1803–1807)* [Cairo, 1930], II, 231).

Ali as a replacement for the deposed wali until the Porte named a new governor or confirmed their candidate. Having summoned the courage finally to assert a positive influence over the affairs of government, the ulama had chosen to support another foreigner and to oppose the Sultan's choice of wali without challenging Ottoman authority in Egypt. In short, the Sultan's representative was deemed undeserving, but the Sultan's authority was not challenged, for had the ulama designated Muhammad Ali their wali without reference to the Sultan it would have meant a challenge to Ottoman authority in Egypt as strong as that thrown to George III in the American Declaration of Independence. It would have constituted an Egyptian declaration of independence from the Ottoman Empire.

The ulama were an indispensable ally to Muhammad Ali in his rise to power, for they secured for him the one important element of authority which force alone could not command, legitimacy. They besieged their former wali in the citadel, wrote to the Sultan praising Muhammad Ali's justness and administrative skills, and organized popular defense forces to defend their capital against Mamluks, Ottomans, Bedouins, and a British expeditionary force which reentered Egypt in 1807.

The dramatic events of these chaotic years posed no problems of modernization for Egypt. The crises were viewed in a traditional manner and no thought was given to radically changing any element in the system of government. In this revolutionary age the ulama sought only to reestablish a former system of cooperative government in which their own supervisory and veto power would be maximized.[21] For a brief period they had indeed succeeded in putting together a coalition of military force tempered by their own participation. The early career of Muhammad Ali gave no indication of a dramatic departure from traditional forms or methods of government. It appeared as if the ulama had intervened once again to bring their system back to its historic equilibrium. They had successfully elevated a man of their own choice to rule them. The people had taken to the barricades to defend their choice against all his enemies. He invited shaikhly participation in decision-making, accepted their demands, and ap-

[21] In his incisive discussion on the aspirations and demands of the Pakistani ulama during the debate on the Islamic constitution which Pakistan hoped to create in the 1950s Leonard Binder discovered that the maximum goal of the ulama was to be elevated to the position of final authorities on all legislation passed by the legislature. They did not desire to rule directly, but to have a veto power on all legislation. This, he argued, was but the maximization of their traditional demands (*Religion and Politics in Pakistan* [Berkeley, California, 1961]).

peared to rule in their interests. "If I deviate from the straight path," he told them, "your duty is to counsel me and direct me."[22] If justice was not the result of this happy marriage it was largely the fault of their own shortcomings and their inability to maintain their influence in a stable political situation.

The ulama had certainly not meant to elevate a wali who would return to the arbitrary ways of his predecessors. In protecting him from his enemies they were but defending their own positions. They did not let him forget that he owed his position to their support and on numerous occasions criticized his harsh taxes. Umar Makram in particular was an obvious threat to the new Pasha's ambitions, for he argued that the people had the right to depose any unjust ruler, whether he be wali, caliph, or sultan. Several years later when the relations between the ulama and Muhammad Ali had become strained Umar Makram declared, "We will write to the Sublime Porte and the people will revolt against him and I shall depose him from his throne as I have sat him upon it."[23]

It was not simply for their increased political influence that this period has been called the "Golden Age" of the ulama, but also for the enormous expansion of their social influence and their rapid acquisition of extravagant wealth. As a social class the higher ulama came to share in the control of the vast revenues of the land and to emulate their former amirs in lavish expenditures. They had already begun to acquire iltizams in the late eighteenth century, but during the course of the Mamluk-Ottoman wars, the French occupation, and the rise of Muhammad Ali, the hold of the Mamluks over the land had been broken and they had gained control of many of the vacated iltizams. The great shaikhs, says Jabarti, even used their privileges to speculate in the purchase of iltizams.[24] Restraints on their open diversion of waqf revenues entrusted to their administration were also removed. These and other privileges, such as the right to maintain their holdings tax free, were expanded by Muhammad Ali until the last serious threat to his authority had vanished, at which time the "Golden Age" was brought to a sudden end.

With their newfound wealth the ulama purchased property, village lands, and slaves, gave extravagant parties, and built mansions that, as Jabarti decries, rivaled those of the former amirs.[25] In imitation of the amirs they set themselves above the people, mistreated their former subordinates, and, like the former multazims, beat or imprisoned their fallahin

[22] Jabarti, VIII, 213.
[23] Cited in al-Rāfi'i, *op. cit.*, p. 91.
[24] Jabarti, VIII, 149.
[25] *Ibid.*, p. 150.

for failure to meet the exorbitant taxes they imposed. "They neglected study and education and did not occupy themselves with that justice with which they preserved their privileges," said Jabarti.[26]

Muhammad Ali purposely exempted their holdings from taxes while increasing the burden on the peasants in the hope that the shaikhs' participation in his illegal programs would make it exceedingly difficult for them to effectively protest, in the name of the suffering masses, the exactions to which the people were being subjected. For their part, the ulama showed themselves eager to participate in the Pasha's government and thereby received the rewards which the Pasha offered for their support. The spirit that overcame the ulama was deeply lamented by Jabarti, who wrote:

At the time in which we live the importance of a man is the result of the grandeur of his house, the richness of his clothes, the great quantity of his income and the large number of his servants. And this importance is augmented when the person enjoys the advantages of which we are going to speak, and also possesses several qualities which interest other men, such as charity and hospitality. Likewise, if we suppose a man combines all these qualities of the soul and all the science of the world, this man, if he has no fortune, is discredited and he is not the object of one's attention.[27]

In the final analysis the ulama were an unequal match in the forthcoming struggle with the hostile government of Muhammad Ali, but the greed, personal rivalries, petty jealousies, and self-delusions of the ulama themselves severely weakened their position once the military threat of the British invasion of 1807 had passed. These must be viewed as a contributing factor in their sudden demise once Muhammad Ali sought to curtail their privileges, influence, and wealth.

It has been necessary to deal at length with the role of the ulama in traditional society and government to lay the foundation for the following discussion on the responses of the ulama to modernization. The native ulama had drawn exceedingly close to the foreign military-bureaucratic elites through their intimate contact over a wide range of social, economic, and political relations. It was largely through such intimate personal contact, and not as a consequence of the official government positions they held, that the ulama were able to exert their influence over their patrons and rulers.[28] Cooperation between the two groups was actually so close

[26] *Ibid.*, p. 149.

[27] *Ibid.*, IX, 42.

[28] Speaking of the close relationship that existed between the Mamluk Amir Muhammad Bey Abu Al-Dhahab and one Shaikh Ali, Jabarti comments that "The Amir never refused a request addressed by the Shaikh"(*ibid.*, III, 222).

that it must be argued that the ulama had become an important element of traditional government. Such cooperation had become rewarding to the ulama in many ways.

Despite the new situation created by the French occupation and the scattering and subsequent self-destruction of the Ottoman-Mamluk elites the ulama did not emerge at the head of a native Egyptian government. Their "Golden Age" points up both their ultimate strengths and inherent weaknesses as a corps, not the least of which was their own concept of cooperative government in which they would have no more than supervisory or veto powers. The incredibly chaotic period stretching from 1801 to 1807 offered them the opportunity to maximize their power and influence and to make the closest approximation to the model form of government which they long advocated. It should be apparent, however, that their ability to influence Muhammad Ali and the other contending parties during this period rested largely on the precarious positions of each of the parties and the availability of alternative candidates whom the ulama could choose to support rather than on the strength of any influence inherent in their own position. Once Muhammad Ali had disposed of all his rivals he quickly brought the ulama to heel.

The revolutionary aspect of Muhammad Ali's long reign lies in his willingness to depart from traditional patterns and concepts of government and to banish from the seats of power the representatives of Allah's sacred law. The most dramatic and far-reaching consequence of his new programs was the dissolution of the partnership between the ulama and the ruling elite. From first rejecting their criticism and intervention in his affairs the new Pasha gradually moved to a total rejection of their traditional attitudes and the ideas they continued to represent and propagate.

Expulsion from Olympus

Fundamental to the governmental concepts of the new Pasha was the complete centralization of all authority and power in his own hands. Institutions of traditional society such as the semiautonomous guilds, village administration, and the dervish orders were all brought under the firm control of the government. In the same manner that he extended his control over the land and commerce and their revenues, so too did he break the independent power of the religious establishment.

Once free of the military threat of the Mamluks and his other enemies, the Pasha turned on his partners in government, the ulama. Taking advantage of natural feuds and deep-rooted jealousies among the ulama, Muhammad Ali was able to divide their ranks with relative ease, and once their ranks were split, whatever power they had enjoyed was quickly dissipated. Even during the "Golden Age" the ranks of the ulama were never firm. In 1805 Shaikh al-Azhar Abdallah al-Sharqawi had been temporarily confined to his house when a serious challenge to his position had been mounted by a junta of shaikhs including the powerful Naqib al-Ashraf Umar Makram, Shaikh al-Sadat Abu al-Anwar al-Sadat, and the hopeful new candidate Muhammad al-Amir.[29] Such an internal quarrel demonstrated to Muhammad Ali the inherent divisions in the ranks of his allies and in 1809 he moved rapidly and without opposition to depose and banish the most serious threat to his rule, the charismatic Umar Makram. Those shaikhs who helped Muhammad Ali dispose of the Naqib were generously rewarded, while the Hanafi mufti, Shaikh Ahmad al-Tahtawi, who defended Umar was also deposed.[30] The deposition of Umar Makram marks the turning point in the relations between Muhammad Ali and the ulama, for with this most serious challenger to his rule banished the ulama had no leader and no longer posed a serious threat to the new regime. Jabarti sadly comments that the ulama deposed Umar without thinking of the consequences.[31] The historian al-Rafi'i insists that the ulama "did not preserve their former influence after the exile of al-Sayyid Umar."[32]

Through bribes, flattery, and applied discipline the Pasha turned the ulama from vociferous spokesmen of the masses into propagandists of his regime. Everyone went along with the Pasha's programs, says Jabarti, to preserve the high positions to which the Pasha had appointed them.[33] Muhammad Ali deposed those shaikhs who defied him and interfered actively in the nomination and selection of ulama to all the high religious offices. In these early years of his reign when an incumbent such as Umar Makram was deposed, his vast personal wealth was seized by the Pasha. Nothing was safe from Muhammad Ali's grasp. When Umar's successor died in 1813 the Pasha also confiscated all his wealth. These were frightening examples for the entire corps of higher ulama and effectively silenced those who might have taken a more vociferous stand against the Pasha.

Having broken the personal power of the ulama, Muhammad Ali moved against the wealth of the entire religious establishment. He abol-

29 *Ibid.*, VII, 411.
30 *Ibid.*, VIII, 223.
31 *Ibid.*, p. 213.
32 al-Rāfi'i, *op. cit.*, p. 645.
33 Jabarti, IX, 225.

ished the system of iltizam, thereby taking from the higher ulama an important source of personal wealth, and seized the revenues of the lucrative and extensive awqaf khairiya of the religious community, giving in its place a fixed stipend that was sufficient only to keep the largest mosques and schools from falling into total ruin.[34] By 1815 Jabarti claimed that the awqaf produced no wealth for the religious establishment and a large number of kuttabs, the primary school of the Muslim community, were in ruin.[35] Such a policy of financial starvation, continued throughout the century, had a devastating impact upon the Muslim institutions. By 1875 when Ali Mubarak made his famous survey of mosques and schools he reported that "the majority of the schools have become ruined and have become mosques."[36] He also noted that there were no more salaries for professors, except at al-Azhar.[37] Many mosques, deprived of their revenues, had in turn sunk to the level of a zawiya, that is, they could not support the imams, muezzins, khatibs, and janitors necessary to sustain public services and were turned into occasional meeting places for small groups of dervishes. The very function of the mosque was therefore lost. Many buildings constructed by the Mamluks only a century earlier were in almost total ruin, indicating the rapid decay of these noble edifices.[38] Even al-Azhar was in a pitiable state. Its walls and pillars were in such danger of falling that they required wooden supports.[39]

To conceive and supervise his modernizing programs the Pasha relied almost entirely upon foreigners. He generously rewarded those who offered him new skills or techniques or contributed new ideas for the establishment of a powerful military force, which in the final analysis was the purpose for the new schools, industries, agricultural and commercial programs he introduced into Egypt. Natives were used only as laborers, soldiers, or as the raw material for his experiments. Members of the former intellectual class who could not adapt to the new conditions imposed upon them were totally disregarded. Jabarti, for instance, was himself alienated from Muhammad Ali and complained that only people who could help the Pasha in his new projects could approach him. These were, he sadly noted, above all, the foreigners.[40]

[34] It should be noted, however, that he did not seize the numerous awqaf ahliya that were the basis of the personal wealth of the great ulama.

[35] Jabarti, IX, 119.

[36] Mubārak, *op. cit.*, I, 87.

[37] *Ibid.*

[38] See A. A. Paton, *A History of the Egyptian Revolution* (London, 1870), I, 343.

[39] Bayard Dodge, *Al-Azhar: A Millennium of Muslim Learning* (Washington, D. C., 1961), p. 106.

[40] Jabarti, IX, 225.

With no skills or ideas to contribute to Muhammad Ali's new regime, the ulama were virtually ignored by the Pasha, notwithstanding the students he selected from their ranks for training in his new schools or in Europe. Throughout his reign he showed an open disdain for the ulama. He no longer consulted them on matters of government and policy and if they opposed him he simply found a way around their opposition.[41] Though he abused them on occasion, Muhammad Ali did not seem to overwhelm them with fear as did his son and right hand, Ibrahim Pasha. This prince, who was said not to have had a single friend in Egypt,[42] made any approach to the ruler not only difficult but hazardous. The ulama were kept in constant fear of his anger and punishment by his total lack of respect for the laws of God and universal custom.[43] His position at the right hand of his father placed an obstacle between the ulama and government which the ulama were never able to circumvent.

Although their ability to influence the government in a positive manner had been largely chipped away, the ulama still exerted a negative influence over the policies of the regime by establishing limits beyond which reform dare not be pushed. By the threat of public opposition or a popular revolt the ulama were able to throw their mantle of protection over broad areas of Egyptian life by arguing that these were in the domain of the shari'a. Alienated as they were from the regime of their Pasha, however, they could not play a role similar to that of their counterparts in Istanbul, where the Ottoman ulama helped formulate and implement the reform programs of their Sultans.[44]

The unity between state and society, the influence of the ulama over the ruling elites, the well-being of the entire religious structure, and the

[41] When, for instance, the ulama refused to give Muhammad Ali a fatwa permitting medical students to dissect the human body, he simply disregarded them and his medical students dissected human bodies in secret (Clot Bey, *Memoires de A.-B Clot Bey* [Cairo, 1949], p. 72).

[42] Paton, *op. cit.*, II, 305.

[43] Jabarti related a story he heard from an unnamed source concerning one of Ibrahim's atrocities. Ibrahim had had a man in Upper Egypt tied to a grill and roasted like a lamb. Commenting upon the story, Jabarti said that this was not extraordinary for a young man of twenty with no education and who knew not the bounds of law. The historian once asked Ibrahim, "Who has given you authority? God?" Ibrahim replied, "God has given me nothing. My father gave me power." See Jabarti, IX, 36–37.

[44] The role of the Ottoman ulama in formulating and implementing the reform programs of their sultans is examined by Uriel Heyd, "The Ottoman 'Ulemā and Westernization in the Time of Selim III and Mahmud II," in *Scripta Hierosolymitana* (Jerusalem, Israel, 1961), IV, 63–96.

basic equilibrium of society itself had depended to a great extent upon the close and friendly relations the ulama had been able to maintain with their rulers. But this traditional system of cooperative government was rudely shattered as the basic premise that underlay it, the mutual respect and cooperation between the "men of the pen" and "men of the sword" was abruptly ended. Though the higher ulama and their "middle-class" compatriots in the corps were generally able to maintain their socio-economic positions throughout the nineteenth century, their political influence in government affairs had been put to a virtual end. Those ulama of the lower ranks who previously had subsisted upon the good graces of the once tolerant and charitable amirs were ruined and the institutions of the Muslim community condemned to a lengthy period of neglect and decay.[45]

The character of the new "realities" with which Muhammad Ali confronted the ulama have largely determined the ulama-state relationships to the present. His attacks upon their former position and influence, his seizure of the wealth of the religious institution, and his use of force in stifling shaikhly opposition to his innovations at the level of the state demoralized the entire religious corps in Egypt. Though the impact of the hated innovations was first felt and largely confined to the level of government, the eventual effect of the introduction of new patterns of economic and political organization and the acceptance of new concepts of learning and technology would have a fundamentally disruptive impact upon the equilibrium of society itself as groups beyond the government were affected.

The First Responses: Opposition and Withdrawal

Their descent from power and the dramatic changes their Pasha introduced into Egypt posed for the ulama the first challenge of modernization. To be sure, the long-term consequences of modernization, the steady advance of secularism, the gradual expansion of a modernizing elite bent upon remaking society in its own image, and the centralization in govern-

45 Despite the general economic decline that has overcome the religious structure since the rise of Muhammad Ali, individual ulama continued to do well in business and other private enterprises. The hundreds of awqaf they made throughout the nineteenth century attest to the economic well-being of these "middle-class" ulama by the extent and value of the properties they protected in waqf.

ment of authority and functions once widely diffused in society eventually undermined the foundations upon which traditional society and religious influence rested, but the immediate challenge of change was more a direct attack against the personal influence of the higher ulama and the economic well-being of the entire corps than a reasoned confrontation with the traditional system of thought and conduct which they represented and defended. It was natural, therefore, that the ulama first perceived modernization not as a body of foreign ideas, which, in fact, it was not, but as a set of hated new regulations, of odious and illegal seizures of their power and wealth, of frequent purges, of interference by new groups in areas once reserved exclusively for them, of unreasonable demands that placed constant pressure upon traditional institutions and social groups. In short, modernization has meant for the ulama an agonizing and constant retreat from political power and social preeminence.

The earliest and most consistent responses of the ulama to deviations from former patterns have appropriately been political, not ideological. They have tried against overwhelming odds and with only limited success to preserve or reconstruct the special relationship they once enjoyed with the ruling groups. They have to the present persisted in defending, mostly implicitly rather than through open debate, a system of political relationships which has been inconsistent with the views of the governing classes since the early nineteenth century. Where their participation in government has been rejected they have continued to assert the preeminent position of the shari'a in the ideal Islamic society, including the necessity of the government and the ruling classes to remain in harmony with its precepts, and have claimed for themselves the sole right to interpret its meaning for all groups and classes.

Their responses to the challenges of modernization have been predictably, instinctively defensive, characterized by a strong desire for self-preservation. While seeming to retreat before the superior power of the regime they have in fact been able to obstruct, delay, or undermine new programs and the acceptance of ideas considered reprehensible, but have never been able completely to turn back, halt, or deflect their progress. Unwilling or unable to direct change, or even to make an accommodation to it, they have in the end been overwhelmed by change which inexorably penetrated first the government and the ruling elites, then their own institutions and other social groups. Considering the objectives they hoped to achieve, their responses have been unsuccessful if not entirely self-defeating.

For his part, Muhammad Ali partly dictated the response of the ulama by never forcing modernization upon them or their institutions. He ignored or overcame their opposition to modernization at the level of government, which, according to the very theory of state they expounded and defended, was considered the special domain of the ruler, but made no effort to try to change the beliefs of native society, its way of life, or its religious attitudes. It was not the intention of the Pasha to destroy the institutions of the old order but rather to create a new order alongside the old. Unwilling to offend the religious prejudices of the ulama and the overwhelming majority of tradition-bound Egyptians or to tamper with a sacred revealed law, the Pasha made no attempt to impose reform upon religious institutions. Having eliminated the interference of the ulama in his government, Muhammad Ali left them virtually alone, to teach, think, write, or practice whatever they wanted so long as they did not undermine his programs within the sphere of government.

The ulama met the early challenge to their former influence and concepts with a series of responses characteristic of long centuries of submission to tyranny. Deprived by circumstances and training from supporting the programs of their Pasha, the entire corps of ulama maintained a staunch attitude of opposition to modernization, notwithstanding the handful of high ulama who have shown sympathy for reform.[46] Where opposition was impossible because of the determination of the state to reform its own institutions the ulama have turned their backs upon change and withdrawn around their own institutions in an effort to preserve them from contamination through contact with the modernizing elements in society. From the early nineteenth century to the present these two responses, opposition and withdrawal, have been most characteristic of the ulama's attitudes and reactions to the challenge of modernization.

Throughout the nineteenth century the corps of ulama as a whole remained openly hostile to bid'a (innovation) of any form. With the exception of a few courageous shaikhs such as Muhammad Abduh, who

[46] In view of the solid resistance the united corps of ulama made to modernization it should be kept in mind that there is a significant lapse in time between the emergence of an idea and its spread and/or acceptance. It is certainly worthwhile to uncover the possible antecedents of reform in the attitudes of mid-nineteenth century ulama, but the vaguely modernist "tendencies" of a handful of ulama should not be taken as any indication of a general mood that characterized the corps as a whole. See Afaf Lutfi al-Sayyid, "The Beginning of Modernization Among the Rectors of al-Azhar, 1798–1879," in W. Polk and R. Chambers, eds., *The Beginning of Modernization of the Middle East* (Chicago, 1968), pp. 267–280.

braved the wrath of almost the entire corps of ulama, few voices were heard calling for reform. It would be entertaining to ennumerate the cases of shaikhly opposition to even the most superficial forms of modernization, such as the switch to European clothes, the wearing of a hat, the study of arithmetic, the dissection of the human body, or the efficacy of quarantine, but is not necessary to substantiate the contention that the religious structure had undergone virtually no qualitative or substantive change by the turn of the twentieth century.

The strategy adopted by the ulama was in perfect harmony with that employed by the reformers and kept modernization from being the cause of immediate hostility between the two groups. The reformers hoped in the beginning only to introduce change to a restricted circle of institutions or social groups while the policy of the ulama became one of containment, of limiting the scope and effects of modernization to the level of the state and the highest social classes. For most of the nineteenth century the two groups were able to maintain a precarious truce, each respecting the special competence of the other within clearly defined limits. But as the century progressed and modernization became a vital force in Egyptian society, the truce was broken and the reformers began to criticize the medievalism of the ulama and to demand readjustment from them.

It should be remembered that the religious structure was composed of several levels or ranks, distinguished by position, influence, wealth, and learning. The overwhelming majority of the men of religion were not forced into any meaningful relationships with the modernizing segments of society until the twentieth century and were hence free to practice and teach an open hostility to any form of innovation. Their isolation from the modernizing groups had become both their chief defense and the main factor in their declining influence and decaying economic position.

The opposition of the higher ulama to innovation was only slightly less rabid than that of the lesser ulama, but their actions were tempered by the necessity for preserving formal relations with the government and the ruling elites. Too vigorous a public opposition would bring swift retribution from their rulers, so their opposition has taken a far more subtle and devious form which is discussed in the next sections. Despite their hatred for the new programs and their bewilderment and frustration at their continued loss of prestige and influence the higher ulama cooperated with the government out of concern for their positions, lack of unity, or fear of reprisal. They did not perceive the dangers of secularization and allowed piecemeal reform. Each compromise, however, was to bring them closer to the day when their own views would no longer represent the majority opinion. Commenting on the strategy of the Ottoman ulama in cooperating in the reform programs of the Sultans, Uriel Heyd wrote, "Retrospectively, the support given by the high 'ulemā to the policy of opening the Ottoman Empire to European secular ideas and institutions seems a suicidal policy from the point of view of their corps."[47]

The responses of opposition and withdrawal had the satisfying short-term effect, as long as modernization represented a weak force in Egyptian society, of retarding and quarantining modernization. In the long run, however, it was a self-defeating defense, for it would only delay, not halt, the penetration of modernization through all levels of society. The immediate effect of this strategy was to drive the ulama into a physical and intellectual isolation that became almost suffocating. By consciously isolating their own institutions from the reform movement they hoped to preserve their own influence within a restricted sphere of activity, but in actuality, this response is the chief factor in their subsequent and dramatic decline. The German traveler Alfred von Kremer noticed the changing fortunes of the ulama in the early 1860s. "The religious class which had the previous highest influence over the country," he remarked, "has now under the tolerant government lost all influence and exerts direct influence only in matters of legislation and adjudication."[48]

Herr von Kremer might also have added education, where the government had been slow to rebuild on the ruined foundations of Muhammad Ali's earlier experiments. The lack of attention that succeeding Khedivial and British governments gave to education would be attacked by Egyptian partisans of modernization, but their criticism of the conditions which crippled Egyptian education and their calls for reform met with virtually no response.[49] Lord Cromer's own annual reports are a solemn testimony

[47] Heyd, *op. cit.*, p. 76.

[48] Alfred von Kremer, *Aegypten* (Leipzig, 1863), Part II, pp. 94–95.

[49] In one of his last pieces of writing Muhammad Abduh gave his personal view on the state of education in Egypt under Cromer's administration. He accused the government of spending a trifling amount on public education, a mere £E 200,000 from a total budget of £E 12,000,000. He charged that the fee that was charged at the government schools, no matter how small, kept the majority of families from sending their children to these schools. The type of instruction, moreover, was of little worth. It "hardly enables a man to acquire the means for earning a living wage." That this was the policy of the British administration was appalling to Abduh. "To sum up, the line of conduct which the State has mapped out for itself and which it seems resolved to adhere to is this: (1) To encourage summary education in the small schools called Kouttab, where the child is taught to read and write, and learns the four rules of arithmetic. (2) To

to his own dereliction in this field.[50] At the turn of the twentieth century religious kuttab-mosque education was responsible for whatever instruction the majority of the sons of the nation received, yet this instruction had little value for the society that was emerging.[51] Egypt would not have a modern university until 1908 and real advances were not made in education until nationalists were able to use the powers of their newly created parliament to reshape the content and change the direction of Egyptian education.[52] It was just in this area so fundamental to the erection of a modern state and the emergence of a new society that the gap between the reformers and the ulama, each representing a completely different system of values, norms, and beliefs, was so painfully apparent.

---

spread education as little as possible amongst the people. (3) To reduce secondary and higher education to the smallest limit. Egyptians are persuaded that those who direct their public affairs are not doing all they can to raise the moral and intellectual level of the rising generation. This opinion is deplorable from every point of view; it will create, sooner or later, a current of discontent in public opinion. . . . In weakening, reducing and mentally impoverishing the natives, the English are acting against their own interests. It is to their advantage that the Egyptians should become powerful, free and rich; their own prosperity and their own wealth depend on ours" (A. B. De Geurville, *New Egypt* [New York, 1906], p. 159).

50 In his annual reports to the Home Office Cromer himself admitted the ineffective nature of educational reform under his administration. Azharis were still responsible for education in the villages, he wrote in 1888, where they also acted as public scribes (*British Sessional Papers*, CX [1888,], 203.) In 1893–94 he commented that the government secondary schools were almost all confined to Cairo. Only one small school in Alexandria was under the administration of the Education Department. Government primary schools throughout the country numbered only 33! (*ibid.*, CXI [1893–94], 1152, 1154). By 1899 the situation had not improved to any great extent. The total number of students in schools under the Director of Public Education was only 7,735. Cromer estimated that 91.2 percent of males and 99.4 percent of females in Egypt were illiterate. The government was trying to aid some kuttabs, but the total number of students in the 55 kuttabs under the Department of Public Instruction was only 2,973. Upon these schools the government was spending only £E 2,700 annually (*ibid.*, CXII [1899], 103, 1007).

51 Numerically speaking, traditional education as dispensed by the ulama virtually dominated Egyptian education. In 1899 Cromer estimated the number of kuttabs throughout Egypt at 9,000 and the number of students receiving instruction in them at 180,000 (*British Sessional Papers*, CXII [1899], 1007). In other words, at the turn of the century the government schools were educating approximately 4 percent of the total number of children receiving instruction, not including the students at the private minority or parochial schools. Clearly 95 percent were receiving nothing more than the fundamentals of reading and writing (and memorization) from the Qur'an.

52 Until the secular university was founded al-Azhar remained virtually the only place in Egypt where one could receive education beyond the secondary level. Bayard Dodge related the delight-

The resurgence of modernism during the reign of Ismail, the pressures of competition with the modernized segments of society, the necessity to adjust medieval concepts and institutions to new realities, the calls for reform from a concerned elite and a few progressive ulama such as Muhammad Abduh, and the decision of the Khedive to intervene, though gently, in religious affairs forced the ulama finally to come to grips with reform. But reform, even to the present, has been imposed upon the ulama against their constant criticism and opposition. It has not been an accepted ideology within shaikhly ranks, for it has not been admitted that a divinely ordained system can be in need of reform. It has rather taken the character of a strategy. Paradoxically, piecemeal reform has been accepted as a means of retrieving lost influence and prestige and to undercut the need for further reform or modernization. The issue of reform, which has been the center of attention of both modernists and traditionists since the period of the Khedive Ismail, has determined ulama-state relations to the present. The ulama have not abandoned their tactics of opposition and withdrawal, but have for a most devious purpose added that of reform.

Reform

Islamic reform in Egypt has generally been treated as a body of modernist concepts based on a reworking of traditional religious principles and concepts. This explains in part the attention given to the important work of al-Afghani, Abduh, and Rida in many well-documented and carefully analyzed studies, for this trio indeed helped lay the philosophical foundations for what may be called the ideology of Islamic Reform. But reform has been more than a body of philosophical arguments divorced from the politics of Egyptian realities. Modernization has applied pressures not only upon the ideological system which the ulama espoused and defended, but in other areas of far more immediate importance to them as well. It is one of the basic arguments of this study that the nonideological pressures have been more immediately and painfully felt by the ulama than the ideological, and it has therefore been the reality of their worsening political, social, and economic positions vis-à-vis other socio-economic

ful story of three Coptic boys who disguised themselves as Muslims to gain admittance to al-Azhar and further their education. In a moment of surprise they uttered the names of Christian rather than Muslim saints and were discovered (Dodge, *op. cit.*, p. 143). True or not, the story indicates the importance of al-Azhar in the scheme of Egyptian higher education until the secular university was founded.

groups which has determined to a far greater extent than ideological debate the attitude and responses of the ulama to modernization.

The ulama have to the present remained apprehensive of modernization and are the target of constant criticism from the socialist regime. Such an ingrained reluctance to accept modernization cannot be traced to their conservative attitudes or traditional training alone, nor even to the theory of Islam as an unchanging body of belief and practice. The ulama show little awareness of being threatened ideologically. They have rather viewed modernization as a disruptive, almost disastrous, force which has destroyed the political influence, social position, and economic well-being they quite recently enjoyed. They have therefore seen it as a hostile, fundamentally evil, force and have shaped their responses to modernization to preserve their remaining political, social, and economic position rather than to defend the belief system upon which their position was predicated. "Islamic" reform has thus more often been a response to social and economic pressures than an ideological commitment to change.

It has been the rule to view the year 1872 as the beginning of modernization for the ulama and for al-Azhar, which was the spiritual and administrative center of the corps and the bastion of Islamic conservatism, for in that year the government of the Khedive Ismail laid down the first modern law for al-Azhar, setting forth the procedure by which those who wished to teach at that institution had first to be examined. In an attempt to broaden the background of the students the law specified that the candidate had to pass an examination in eleven basic fields, but its effect was practically the opposite of what was intended, for in fact it limited the interest of the students to only those eleven areas which would be necessary to pass the examination and secure a position. Al-Azhar's curriculum actually contracted as interest in other areas declined. Acting in a manner that became all too characteristic of their response to virtually all succeeding reforms, students and shaikhs blocked this well-intentioned but timid attempt to introduce change into the Azhar system so that it had to be reconfirmed in a series of decrees promulgated for al-Azhar between 1880 and 1897.[53]

The failure of the Azharis to apply rigorously the law of 1872, coupled with the confusion generated by the Urabi revolution and the subsequent British occupation, led to another two decades of neglect of educational

[53] For a translation of these early laws see Pierre Arminjon, *L'Enseignement, la Doctrine et la Vie dans les Universités Musulmanes d'Egypte* (Paris, 1907), pp. 273–291.

reform. The law of 1872 must therefore be judged a false step in the long and tortuous course of reform and we must look to the decade of the 1890s for the true beginnings of reorganization and modernization at al-Azhar.

Meaningful structural reform at al-Azhar begins with the prodigious efforts of Shaikh Muhammad Abduh who, with the cooperation of Shaikh al-Azhar Hassunah al-Nawawi (1895–1899), worked against exceedingly difficult odds to create the skeleton of a formal bureaucracy for al-Azhar, to improve the pitiful conditions of its students and shaikhs, and to introduce a spirit of modernity into Islamic thought and practice through the reform of Islamic education. Though he was to fail in the third, and by far the most important area of his program, Abduh's success in the other areas created for al-Azhar the framework of a modern administration. His efforts in urging the government to disregard the opposition of the conservative majority of students and shaikhs and to decree reform in the area of Islamic education, especially regarding the organization of religious studies at al-Azhar, are therefore responsible for the first progress al-Azhar made toward modernizing its institutions.

Abduh's reforms are directly responsible for the emergence of the Shaikh al-Azhar as the recognized head of all ulama in Egypt and the positioning of al-Azhar at the center of all Islamic education in Egypt.[54] In 1895 he helped sponsor the first administrative law of importance for al-Azhar, a statute that created from among the most important shaikhs (Shaikh al-Azhar and the four muftis) an administrative council with advisory powers. The addition of two government nominees to the council began the process of direct government interference in al-Azhar's internal affairs and made the ulama suspicious of government intentions.[55] The Shaikh al-Azhar was recognized as the executive head of al-Azhar's educational system and given the chairmanship of this Majlis al-Idarah, or Ad-

[54] See my paper presented to the International Colloquium on the History of Cairo (Cairo, 1969), "The Emergence of the Shaykh al-Azhar as the Pre-Eminent Religious Leader in Egypt," soon to be published under the auspices of the Egyptian government.

[55] The availability of several studies on the reform movement at al-Azhar makes unnecessary the constant citation of information in footnotes. Besides the study by Arminjon, see Dodge, *op. cit.*, pp. 125–156; Crecelius, "The Ulama and the State in Modern Egypt," pp. 199–362; and 'Abd al-Muta'āl al-Ṣa'īdi, *Tārīkh al-Iṣlāḥ fī al-Azhar* (Cairo, 1950). Translations of the laws of the middle reform period can be found in Achille Sekaly, "La Reorganisation de l'Universite d'el-Azhar," *Revue des Études Islamiques*, 10 (1927), 95–118, 465–529; and "L'Universite d'el-Azhar et ses Transformations," *Revue des Études Islamiques*, 11 (1928), 47–163, 225–237, 401–472.

ministrativ Council. That same year the Ahmadi school at Tanta and the madrasas of Dassuq and Damyat were attached to al-Azhar, thereby beginning the process that maade al-Azhar the formal administrative center of Egypt's system of Islamic education.

Under Abduh's constant urging the Administrative Council quickly assumed responsibility for students, professors, courses, and finances, and tried, with but limited success, to introduce further change into the system. The council immediately turned its attention to the reform of the appalling conditions prevailing at al-Azhar and to the modernization of its curriculum. Its efforts, however, were met with fierce opposition from both students and ulama. Its decrees were usually ignored and therefore incapable of changing the character of instruction or the general operating procedures at al-Azhar. Despite the opposition to the substantive work of the Council, Abduh was able to improve salaries of shaikhs, some of whom were receiving only 16 piastres per month, to establish a system for the granting of robes of honor to shaikhs in recognition of their excellence, and to create a small library for the school by combining the separate holdings of some of the riwaqs (administrative-residential units into which students were divided). But all efforts to introduce a new spirit into the system by the introduction of new fields of study or new methods of interpretation met with utter failure. Abduh struggled with the problem of reform through 1905 when, dispirited by the constant agitation of his colleagues against him and frustrated by the political opposition of the Khedive to his well-intentioned programs, he resigned his powerful position as Grand (Hanafi) Mufti and withdrew from active participation in Azhar affairs. He died shortly thereafter.

Two important laws which became the foundation for al-Azhar's future development were imposed upon the ulama in 1908 and 1911. The law of 1908 was meant both to consolidate the gains made in the laws sponsored by Abduh and to introduce curricular changes by making courses of modern studies and annual examinations compulsory. It set up the governing body of al-Azhar, the Majlis al-A'la, or Supreme Council, which assumed responsibility for the Azhar budget and those of its appendages. It thus took its place beside the Administrative Council as the second major committee directing Azhar affairs.

Reactions to the reform measures of this law, particularly to the introduction of compulsory new studies, was violent. Student and shaikhly opposition to it obstructed the implementation of any reform measures and ultimately forced the suspension of the controversial law in 1909.

Though reformers would have the program contained in the hated law reaffirmed that same year, continued opposition by the majority of Azharis made it impossible to apply. Sections applying to strictly administrative matters were to stand, however.

Opposition to the substantive issues of the law of 1908 forced reformers to use the powers of government to impose upon al-Azhar the law of 1911. This law reiterated the main points of the law of 1908 and pushed for reform in areas still neglected. It reaffirmed al-Azhar's position as the superior institution of Islamic instruction in Egypt and pronounced the Shaikh al-Azhar the leading religious figure in the country. The Administrative Council and the Supreme Council were both reorganized to give the government more leverage in Azhar affairs, but the Shaikh al-Azhar retained his chairmanship of both bodies. A third council, usually rendered into English as the Council of Great Scholars (Hai'at Kibar al-Ulama), which was to assume some importance as a result of its activities in defense of conservatism, was also created.

Unlike previous laws, this one specified a wide range of disciplinary powers which the various councils could now employ. Students and ulama were not to engage in political activities and were now answerable for their conduct in and out of al-Azhar to the Supreme Council. Undignified acts or those disrespectful to Islam could be punished. Suspension, loss of salary or stipend, or demotion (in the case of ulama) could be applied against students and shaikhs. The Council of Great Scholars was also given the power to strip any alim of his title for acts against Islam, a power it was to employ in the famous cases of Ali Abd al-Raziq and Taha Husain.

The series of laws that reorganized al-Azhar and the system of Islamic education between 1895 and 1911 had created in a remarkably short period a modern administration for al-Azhar, had given this administration responsibility for the direction of affairs within the entire system of Islamic education, had established a trio of official governing bodies over which the Shaikh al-Azhar presided, and had put into his hands and those of the various councils broad powers to discipline ulama and students. But all substantive reform was undermined by the obstinate refusal of the ulama to permit or implement those parts of the laws dealing with changes of curriculum. It is terribly ironic that conservative shaikhs maintained a virtual monopoly over the mashyakha (shaikhship) of al-Azhar between 1899 and 1927 and used the considerable powers that the reformers had attached to the office to block attempts at further reform.

The Defense of Position

Far-reaching social and economic changes that swept Egypt between the reign of Ismail and the emergence of a quasi-independent state in 1922 gave to modernism the necessary momentum to overcome the centuries-long equilibrium of traditional society and posed new challenges for the ulama. The twin thrust of the modernist movement in Egypt has been generally defined as liberal reform and nationalism. Its proponents are therefore referred to as liberal-nationalists.[56] The increasing tempo of the liberal-nationalist movement was marked by the noticeable retreat of the ulama from the center of the political arena and their further isolation from the modernizing elites. The emergence of modernized professionals such as the lawyers, doctors, journalists, and teachers and their organization into political parties meant the entire nature of Egyptian society and politics had undergone dramatic change. Functions once the special prerogative of the ulama were now assumed by new groups and new institutions such as the emerging parliament. But the rise of new social groups and the creation of modern institutions does not in itself explain the dramatic decline of the influence of the ulama in the twentieth century. The very nature of the liberal-nationalist movement made it difficult for the ulama to cooperate with the new groups or to make their accommodation to the forces that were sweeping Egypt, for liberal-nationalism inherently threatened the very system of thought and conduct which the ulama had erected and continued to defend. And upon that system was predicated their remaining influence and importance.

The modernist movement was given impetus by the overriding political issue of the period, independence. Though the ulama were to maintain a staunch anti-British attitude and were to play an important role

[56] Nadav Safran discussed liberal-nationalism in the following way. "We do not use the term 'Liberalism' in the sense in which it was understood in the nineteenth century, with its limitation of the role of the state and its emphasis on individualism and the sancity of property. Liberalism in this sense could hardly have a place in Egypt given her still embryonic capitalism and her long tradition of state action, even though some political leaders and thinkers, notably Lutfi al-Sayyid, came at times near to it. We use the term to refer to a general commitment to the ideal of remolding society on the basis of an essentially secular conception of the state and rational-humanitarian values" (*Egypt in Search of Political Community* [Cambridge, Mass., 1961], p. 275 n. 1 to chap. vi).

in the Egyptian independence movement, they were nevertheless to withdraw from active participation in that movement after 1922. The revolution of 1919 was virtually the last in which the ulama played a key role, for with independence in 1922 the ulama withdrew from the center of the political arena to act out a minor supporting role in the wings. The answer to this dramatic withdrawal seems to lie in the nature of the nationalist movement itself, which was modernist and secular, and in the nature of nationalism as distinct from independence.

Nationalism seeks more than independence, which is but the first step toward true nationalism. Independent nationalist governments have been eager to employ the considerable coercive power of their modernizing regimes to organize society and its institutions for rapid social and economic change. Independence is but the necessary prerequisite for the reshaping of society itself by nationalist groups. Expressed politically, nationalism has generally meant the centralization of all authority in the institutions of the state. Islamic modernist regimes have thus sought to bring the independent power of traditional institutions, including those of the ulama, to an end as they have sought to extend their firm control over previously autonomous religious institutions such as the schools and religious courts.

The theoretical justification for the centralization of all authority in the state, where ideological justification has been felt necessary, has been found in the Western concept of sovereignty. Sovereignty has been seen residing either in the people who express their will through representative institutions or in the state itself, which is seen as the embodiment of the people. To this theory of sovereignty the ulama have remained steadfast opponents, but they have made only feeble efforts to refute it, attacking its manifestation, the centralization of authority, rather than the theory itself.

The twin goals of the liberal-nationalists, liberal reform and nationalism (as distinct from mere independence), were both anethema to the ulama, for both restricted their remaining functions and undermined their residual influence. It was ideologically impossible, therefore, for the ulama to join enthusiastically the liberal-nationalist movement since they were considered one of the prime targets for the criticism of the liberal-nationalists after independence.

A continuous battle was fought between the ulama and the liberal-nationalists over a myriad of fronts, but the major confrontations were centered on the question of the reform of Islamic institutions, namely education and the sacred law. Threatened directly by the attempt of the liberal-nationalists not only to impose reform upon their institutions but to subject them and the ulama to the will of the nationalist state, the ulama responded with more than vocal opposition as they periodically entered the political arena to thwart the attempts to modernize their institutions through legislation. In channeling their energies into the political defense of position they largely abandoned (or at least neglected) the necessary ideological defense of their position. They did not understand the basic incongruity of trying to defend a political position without defending the concepts upon which that position was predicated, for in failing to engage the liberal-nationalists in serious ideological debate the ulama conceded the fundamental contentions of their opponents.

Like other socio-economic groups, the ulama had since the late nineteenth century sought to secure and maintain the constant flow of Azhar graduates into the government bureaucracy. Ulama had three basic channels reserved exclusively for them, absorption within the religious structure as imams, muezzins, khatibs, and so forth, entrance into all the school systems as teachers of Arabic, or absorption into the shari'a court system as judges or clerks. The defense of position pivoted upon the attempt by the ulama not only to preserve their independence from government control, but to maintain these channels open (and restricted) for the graduates of their schools. But modernization tended to diminish the number of places available for religious graduates in the bureaucracy, first by creating rivals to their positions, then by demanding new skills. The creation of the Dar al-Ulum in 1872 and of the School for Qadis in 1908 was an attempt by the government to expose teachers and judges to a broader curriculum, but the ulama rightfully looked upon these institutions as serious rivals. Their suspicions were confirmed when the government began preferring graduates of these new institutions to those of al-Azhar. Such mundane economic considerations have moved the ulama toward an active defense of position far more effectively than any necessity for ideological debate. Their objections to shari'a reform, for instance, have not been that the shari'a is not in need of reform or that the state has not the right to decree legal reform, but that by changing the basis of legal interpretation the state was depriving ulama, who remained unfamiliar with the principles of modern legal interpretation, of one of the few remaining means for entrance into the state bureaucracy. Beginning with the opposition to the mixed courts of the nineteenth century and ending with their criticism of the absorption of all court systems into one modernized national system in 1956, the ulama have made their objections to change on economic, not ideological, grounds. Their anxiety over job security has risen after independence as society has less use for their traditional skills and as the liberal-nationalists have deliberately sought to block their entry into the bureaucracy. Yet even the specter of approaching doom has not forced the ulama to accept reform where it means submission to the nationalist state. It has rather elicited a more vigorous defense of remaining position.

The years immediately after the creation of an independent Egyptian state were among the most turbulent for the ulama in the twentieth century to date, for they were involved in simultaneous tests of strength between King Fuad and his Wafdist-dominated parliaments over the implementation of the constitution, the reform of native society, the modernization of education, the interpretation of Islam, and the control of al-Azhar itself. The conservatives of al-Azhar found themselves defending their autonomous position from attacks from without while simultaneously putting down reform-minded insurgents from within their own ranks. It was a period of intense stress from which the ulama emerged victorious, yet farther removed from the mainstream of contemporary Egyptian life and thought.

Two issues of absolutely critical importance provided the ulama in the early twenties the opportunity to impose a debate on the liberal-nationalists as to the very essence of their theories, yet the ulama withdrew in general confusion from such a debate and permitted the opportunity to pass. The emergence of an independent national state founded on the collective sovereignty of the people who express their will through elected parliaments employing the right to legislate was revolutionary in every sense of the term, yet the ulama raised no objection on the issue of man-made as opposed to God-given law. The ulama only insisted that all legislation had to be in conformity with (or at least not in opposition to) shari'a law. The war was over without a battle being fought. A secular legislature was thus created to assume responsibility for initiating new law and the ulama made no opposition on the solid argument that legislation must come from God. Nationalism had triumphed over Islam and a secular state had emerged under infinitely less strain than had accompanied the emergence of secular states in Europe.

The abolition of the caliphate by the Turks in 1924 provided the second opportunity for the ulama to seize the initiative and reassert their own theories of sovereignty and the state, but once again, though the issue received far more debate than that of sovereignty, the ulama showed themselves unable to act decisively. Several conferences were held, one of them under the patronage of King Fuad who hoped to transfer a revived caliphate to Cairo, but the ulama could not agree on some of the most pressing questions concerning the revival of this office and the theory that underlay it. The Sharif of Mecca unilaterally pronounced himself caliph but saw the holy cities added to the expanding state of Ibn Saud. With the defeat of the Sharif Husain the caliphate passed into history.

Within al-Azhar itself the conservative majority was successful in beating back the growing group of ulama calling for meaningful reform. With its authority to transfer shaikhs to various institutions, the Supreme Council banished the most outspoken leaders of reform to Upper Egypt. The cases of Ali Abd al-Raziq and Taha Husain in the 1920s also demonstrated the ability of the conservatives to limit discussion on matters of faith. Conservative ulama were also able to resist the attempts made by parliament to impose modernization upon their institutions through legislation. Using their influence with the king and conservatives in parliament to good advantage, they were able to insure that legislation that passed through parliament did not threaten their autonomy or, if it did, would be neutralized by the action of the king. For the ulama modernization had become above all a problem of political independence. Even the hesitant modernists among the ulama were unwilling to accept modernization if it meant the loss of their remaining administrative and political independence.

Political considerations appear to be a major influencing factor in shaping the ulama's attitudes toward modernization. To spare their institutions the agony of party strife and to protect them from outside interference the ulama sought to remain aloof from political battles that did not directly involve their own interests. They neither formed a party of their own nor joined the established political groupings in any significant number. The pressing issues of the day, nationalism, independence, and constitutionalism, interested them, but did not provoke them to instant and united action as did challenges, no matter how slight, to their own vested interests and remaining autonomy.

Two basic issues, the control of al-Azhar's administration, hence the autonomy of the entire corps, and the modernization of religious institutions, nevertheless drew the ulama into the political arena where their own special interests became entangled with the overriding political issues of the day. The struggle for the control of al-Azhar, and its rectorship in particular, was the more intense issue and poisoned Azhar-government relations since independence, but the question of modernization was far more important. Experience had shown, however, that modernization could not proceed until the ulama and al-Azhar were brought under the firm control of the state.

The constitution had given the king responsibility for al-Azhar's entire system, but in 1927 a Wafdist-controlled parliament rammed through the now famous Law No. 15. Henceforth, al-Azhar and all its institutes were to be administered by the king through "the intermediary of the Prime Minister." The Azhar budget was made the responsibility of parliament and the appointment of the Rector was to be made by royal decree upon nomination by the Prime Minister.[57]

The first test of the new law came when the conservative rector al-Jizawi died that same year. The struggle over the method of his successor's appointment was more important than the personalities or programs of the candidates and involved parliament, king, and ulama in a ten-month tug-of-war. Parliament ultimately succeeded in imposing the law and its candidate, Shaikh Mustafa al-Maraghi, upon the king and the ulama, but the latter considered Maraghi an outsider and refused to cooperate with him. His expansive programs for the regeneration of al-Azhar and Islam and his active membership in the Liberal Constitutionalist Party turned the shaikhs against him. Their unwillingness to cooperate with him, coupled with the king's anger over Law No. 15, kept him from introducing the promised reforms and forced him to resign in October 1929, whereupon his rival, Shaikh Muhammad al-Zawahiri, was appointed according to the conditions of Law No. 15.

That Zawahiri, too, was a reformer indicated to what extent the need and desire for reform had spread among students and shaikhs. But reform had come to be interpreted as the securing of economic advantages from parliament. His sweeping reform of 1930, which offered many advantages to the ulama without threatening their remaining autonomy, was therefore well received. His efforts to improve conditions for the ulama were undermined, however, by the hostility of the Wafd to the law, for King Fuad had used the absence of the Wafd from office to abrogate the sections on appointments of Law No. 15 of 1927 and to reserve to himself the sole right to make appointments in the Azhar system. Though this right was reconfirmed in Law No. 26 of 1936 the Wafd chose to renew its struggle with the king for the control of the rectorship in 1942 with the result that

[57] For a translation of this important law see *Revue des Études Islamiques*, n.v. (1928), 97–98.

the university was paralyzed for approximately two years until the Wafd was turned out of office in late 1944. This battle for the control of the rectorship had not run its course when the Nasir revolution decided the issue in favor of the government.

Zawahiri's law took primary and secondary education from the mosque and assigned them to the religious institutes. The higher studies were divided into three faculties resembling those of European universities. Each of the faculties, theology, law, and Arabic language, had a section of specialization and the responsibility for the administration of the university was transferred from the shaikhs of the four rites to the deans of the new faculties. The government's School for Qadis was entirely absorbed into the Faculty of Law and the preparatory schools for it and the Dar al-Ulum were abolished, thereby ending the competition both had given to Azharis as teachers and judges.[58] With but few modifications this law remained the fundamental law of al-Azhar until 1961. It had dramatically changed the organization of studies within al-Azhar and had destroyed competition in their fields from government schools, yet it had failed to modify the type of religious education offered within the religious institutes and the university and could thus not hope to affect the character of religious thought or the quality of the graduates. Conservatives were temporarily pleased with the new trappings of modernization such as classrooms, blackboards, desks, and titles, but liberals increased their demands for meaningful reform. There had been reform, but little modernization.

Partly to punish Azharis for their opposition to modernization, and Zawahiri in particular for his role in helping the king overcome Law No. 15, and partly to bar unqualified Azhar graduates from the bureaucracy, parliament withheld appropriations from al-Azhar and refused to recognize its certificates, thus barring its graduates from government positions.[59]

[58] Sylvia Haim has noted an article by Father J. Jomier that pointed out that the teaching of Arabic, even in Christian and nonreligious schools, remained an Azhar monopoly ("State and University in Egypt," *Universität und Moderne Gesellschaft*, Chauncy D. Harris and Max Korkheimer, eds. [Frankfurt am Main, 1959], pp. 99–118).

[59] By assuming responsibility for the Azhar budget parliament was able constantly to meddle in Azhar affairs and to punish Azharis for their opposition to parliament. Zaghlul had begun the practice of using parliamentary leverage to punish Azharis for their opposition to reform laws. The ministry of Muhammad Ziwar had legislated job equality and higher pay to the Azharis, but when Zaghlul returned to power after the fall of the Ziwar Ministry in 1926 he annulled these laws under the pretense that they had not been passed by both houses of parliament (Ṣa'īdi,

Zawahiri, who was above all concerned with preserving al-Azhar free of outside interference, disciplined shaikhs and students for any signs of cooperation with the forces arrayed against his institution. As discontent with his administration rose within religious ranks and gave rise to increasingly violent demonstrations in favor of positive reform, Zawahiri took repressive measures, punishing students, banishing many ulama to Upper Egypt and pensioning off many others at £E 3 per month. His resistance to parliament and to the parties, however, forced him into an ever closer embrace with King Fuad, who now opened his private treasury to grant al-Azhar funds withheld by parliament. As a result, al-Azhar became a royalist bastion, an unwilling partisan in the bitter struggle between parliament and king, and subsequently lost much of the independence it was so eager to defend. Zawahiri thus kept al-Azhar free of party or parliamentary control, but his inability to ameliorate the worsening economic condition of the shaikhs and students ultimately led to his resignation amid open revolt. He was succeeded in late 1935 by Shaikh Mustafa al-Maraghi.

It was only with difficulty that Maraghi maintained his position until death overcame him in 1945, for despite his attempts to introduce further reform and the strong backing of King Faruq, he, too, made no progress in assuaging the crisis of Islam or in solving the immediate economic problems confronting the ulama. Throughout his second rectorship problems concerning Islam in general were completely overshadowed by a seemingly endless series of political crises that centered on al-Azhar, many of them of Maraghi's own making. His relations with parliament were particularly hostile. Job security remained the most vexing problem to the ulama, for though the ministries of Education and Justice were required by law to grant positions to Azhar graduates, neither the rector nor the king could do more than protest when ministers periodically refused to admit more poorly trained ulama into their already overstaffed ministries.[60] So persistent was this problem that as late as 1951 Shaikh

---

op. cit., pp. 110–111). Zaghlul's discriminations against al-Azhar's graduates caused severe frustrations among the ulama. Their condition grew so serious that the press took to their defense and pleaded with the senators and representatives of parliament to grant job equality to religious graduates. On May 7, 1927, *al-Akhbār* complained that religious institutes were almost excluded from the nation and that religious students even found it hard to gain admission to Dar al-Ulum, the teacher training college. Cited by Ṣa'īdi, *op. cit.*, pp. 145–149.

[60] In 1938 Muhammad Husain Haykal, the Minister of Education, refused to admit Azhar teachers of low quality

al-Azhar Abd al-Majid Salim led the ulama in an unprecedented and widely publicized strike to draw attention to their plea for higher pay and equality with government school teachers. Their plight had grown so desperate and their salaries remained so abysmally low that even the daily press, which usually attacked them for their opposition to reform, took up their cause and called upon the government to improve their conditions.[61]

Zawahiri and Maraghi had been iron-willed shaikhs who had forged close relationships with the palace to keep their institutions free of parliamentary or party control. Zawahiri had used repressive measures to hold his own ranks in order, but Maraghi's inability to solve his inherited problems, despite his own attempts at repression, gave rise to protests and demonstrations of increasing frequency and violence which neither he nor his successors were able to control.

Beginning in the mid-thirties the students at al-Azhar became an increasingly disruptive force. Student dissatisfaction had driven al-Zawahiri from office, but student action was powerless to alleviate the depressing conditions within the religious structure and did nothing more than disrupt studies at the university. Political movements also penetrated al-Azhar during Maraghi's second rectorship and created cadres from among shaikhs and students at the university, so party conflicts were to disrupt al-Azhar further. The ulama, too, were seriously divided by personal rivalries and conflicting approaches to reform. This combination of political conflict, student riots, and shaikhly rivalries paralyzed the entire Azhar system from the mid-thirties into the early Nasir period, making even further organizational reform impossible. Chaos within the system can be deduced from the six changes of rector over the period 1945–1952.

King Faruq did little to reform this corrupted system, though he did make some efforts to improve its financial position. Like his father, he had found that al-Azhar was one of the few elements he could counterpose to the British and parliament and demanded its support in return for the favors he showed it. He protected the ulama against the designs of parliament, created five new religious institutes, and raised the religious budget from £E 324,000 to £E 900,700 during his reign, but his generosity actually

to his ministry despite a law that guaranteed such entrance. Azharis struck in protest but were unable to influence a change in Haykal's policy. The king was unable to intervene in the matter and Azharis were not to reenter the ministry until Haykal left his post in the summer of 1939 (Haim, *op. cit.*, pp. 104–105).

[61] See Egyptian dailies for the period January–February, 1951.

delayed modernization at al-Azhar by giving sustenance to a system that had petrified in the period before independence and was no longer capable of creative response to challenge.

Students and shaikhs truly desired reform, but the majority were afraid of the extent to which it might be carried, for each reform had brought more government interference in their affairs. They were unwilling to countenance reform at the expense of their remaining autonomy and correctly perceived that religion's submission to the state, not religious reform, was the goal of the liberal-nationalists. Each Shaikh al-Azhar therefore assumed an untenable position. He was expected to scrupulously defend al-Azhar's traditional autonomy and secure from parliament economic advantages for his corps, but he could not hope to achieve the latter without giving up the former. As the ulama did not cease to value their own autonomy above reform when the latter meant submission to the state, they and their institutions continued their drift into total isolation from the modernizing segment of society. This isolation had grown so complete by the time the monarchy was overthrown that only a radical change in the entire system and character of religious education was thought capable of retrieving the situation.

Obstructionism

Despite the progress of reform since 1895 al-Azhar and the corps of ulama have not been able to shed the oppressive burden of medievalism that has been responsible for the troubles of the corps, of al-Azhar, and of Islam in general. Writers, both European and Egyptian, have in the last few decades made constant reference to the lack of substantive change at al-Azhar, especially in its vital curriculum, claiming that its numerous reform laws created only a facade of progress behind which al-Azhar and the ulama remained unregenerated. In 1947 Professor Gibb noted in a classic study that continuous revisions in al-Azhar's governing laws affected "the organization of studies rather than their spirit or substance."[62] Gibb's observation has been corroborated by several others since then.

The reformist shaikh Abd al-Muta'al al-Sa'idi commented in 1950 that the reorganization had done nothing to change the type of instruction offered at al-Azhar. Despite the inclusion of new courses in the syllabus, the medieval religious sciences continued to reign supreme, stifling any progress in modern studies.[63] In 1951 Salama Musa remarked of al-Azhar,

[62] H. A. R. Gibb, *Modern Trends in Islam* (Chicago, 1947), p. 40.

[63] Ṣa'īdi, *op. cit.*, p. 126.

"It still continues its ancient studies which are medieval in subject and methods; it does not accept any student who is not a Mohammadan."[64] Al-Azhar was not shaken from its lethargy in the first few years of the Nasir revolution, for in 1956 Jörg Kraemer wrote that "the 'classical' subjects are still taught on the basis of certain famous and age-old commentaries and super-glosses of the 12th, 13th and later centuries A.D."[65] It was to put a final end to the problems of the ulama and to revitalize Islam that the government imposed upon al-Azhar the radical reform law of 1961.[66] The government's criticism of al-Azhar and the ulama was contained in the prolegomena to the reform. It attacked the isolation that had deprived the nation of religious-cultural harmony, blamed the useless medieval studies and the timidity of the ulama for the failure of Islam to make a proper defense of cherished beliefs and values, and called upon the ulama to close ranks with society. Al-Azhar had always held an important place at the center of the nation's life and had always acted as an impregnable bastion in the event of attacks upon it or Islam, but

> the fact that al-Azhar has for long years been compelled to stand in the face of all attempts at aggression has made it acquire a sort of reserve which is probably one of the characteristics of the defensive attitude it has adopted all through those centuries. When life revived around it, and the causes that led up to its reserved and rigid attitude no longer existed it failed to find proper means of renewed activity that would help it adapt itself to contemporary times while retaining its characteristics and assuming its duties of defending Religion and preserving the heritage of Islam.[67]

The failure to modernize their curriculum and their isolation had created serious economic and psychological problems which the nation could no longer tolerate. "A serious unemployment problem had also arisen among them which aggravated their isolation from society; a crisis which had profound effects on the minds of the Azharis and the people at large and did not fail to produce adverse effect on the power of the creed. . . ."[68]

[64] Salama Musa, "Intellectual Currents in Egypt," *Middle Eastern Affairs*, II (1951), 270. A good deal of conflict centered on the medieval texts that were still in use as virtually the only materials in many fields of study at al-Azhar. Muḥammad 'Abd al-Mun'im al-Khaffāji deplored the use of thirteenth-century texts in his history of al-Azhar (*al-Azhar fī Alf 'Ām* [Cairo, 1954], I, 137). Muḥammad 'Abdallāh 'Inān has included an entire list of medical books still in use at al-Azhar in 1958 (*Tārīkh al-Jāmi' al-Azhar* [Cairo, 1958], p. 262).

[65] "Tradition and Reform at al-Azhar," *Middle Eastern Affairs*, VII (March, 1956), 92.

[66] For an analysis of this law see my "al-Azhar in the Revolution," *Middle East Journal* (Winter, 1966), 31–49.

[67] *Arab Political Encyclopedia: Documents and Notes* (Cairo, Information Department, August, 1961), p. 79.

[68] *Ibid.*, p. 80.

Where all opposition and withdrawal had failed and the government at last successfully imposed (or at least decreed) reform on al-Azhar the ulama have employed the last weapon in their arsenal of defense, obstructionism. Obstructionism has always been evident in the dealings of the ulama with their rulers, but it has become far more apparent and more widely practiced as their own institutions were inevitably drawn into closer contact with government, with the result that their own hold over these institutions has been loosened. It has been a most successful response to the attempts to impose reform on the ulama, being largely responsible for the preservation of al-Azhar's autonomy and the independence which ulama continued to enjoy.

Obstructionism was often simple overt opposition to reform and the obstinate refusal to implement it, but as the ulama's political influence continued to worsen relative to other groups obstructionism took far more devious forms. Obstructionism goes beyond passive resistance. It has been the ulama's special ability seemingly to accept reform while working against it, to admit the necessity for change while restricting, isolating, and smothering it, to welcome outsiders into their institutions while preparing the means for their expulsion, to publicly countenance new ideas while privately preaching against them, to maintain cordial public relations with the government while privately struggling against its interference in religious affairs. It has been particularly effective in preserving for the ulama a sense of independence of thought and action in the face of constant encroachments on their institutions by parliament, king, and president. Several examples will suffice to demonstrate the tenacious tactics and effects of this obstructionism.

Despite their acceptance of the national state and their allegiance to such concepts as Arab nationalism, the ulama have not totally abandoned their traditional concept of the universal Islamic umma. Even the present regime finds it advantageous to make frequent reference to a unity larger than the Arab nation, so ideas and concepts of often vague compatibility are permitted to exist side by side. But this permits the ulama to retain not only the basic traditional concept of the universal umma, but the many ancillary concepts that it assumes. Psychologically speaking, the ulama have still not had to abandon their traditional belief system. The leading shaikhs have likewise been able to give halfhearted consent to the regime's birth control programs to save their positions while at the same time remaining firmly opposed to such programs in private.

The example of foreign language instruction, which was included in the Azhar curriculum as early as 1901, gives us some idea of the ability of the ulama to delay reform through obstructionism. Though included in the syllabus, foreign languages remained a dead letter, so in 1936 King Faruq *ordered* the *immediate* introduction of such languages as Persian, Hebrew, and English at al-Azhar.[69] Then, in 1958 the then Vice-Rector Shaikh Mahmud Shaltut announced that al-Azhar would immediately begin the teaching of English. Yet the teaching of this and other foreign languages has barely begun and al-Azhar remains with but few exceptions monolingual. I have not yet met a single Azhari who learned a foreign language within the Azhar system. The administrators and few professors who are familiar with a foreign language either are transfers from the secular universities or learned their language outside the Azhar system.

Practiced with great patience and finesse, obstructionism has worn down a long line of vigorous reformers. Included in the list of those who came off second best in their jousts with the ulama, despite the preponderance of political power or leverage they enjoined, are Muhammad Abduh, Sa'd Zaghlul, Taha Husain, Mustafa al-Maraghi, King Fuad, King Faruq, and, some would argue, President Abd al-Nasir.

The ulama continue to employ effectively the tactics of obstructionism, though within a constantly diminishing sphere as their remaining political influence is slowly dissipated. The law of 1961 which "nationalized" al-Azhar and subjected the university and the ulama to the revolution is the latest example of the ability of the ulama to thwart or deflect the good intentions of the government in a last desperate attempt to preserve what little independent influence remains to them. Obstructionism is largely responsible for the failure of this law to achieve its stated objectives.

The ulama have worked to isolate and ostracize government-appointed outsiders who have assumed positions of leadership on the Azhar faculty and in its administration. They have exasperated a series of United Arab Republic vice-presidents sent to administer al-Azhar while keeping these men at arm's length. Few have been able to endure the frustration of dealing with the ulama for long. This ill treatment of the outsiders, coupled with the feeling of frustration and exasperation which develops in them, generally combine to force the intruders out of the system. Many changes in personnel have therefore marked the attempt by the government to plant non-ulama in the system. In 1969 three professors on loan to traditional departments from other Egyptian universities requested transfers to other faculties, leaving their departments without a single outsider after their

[69] *Al-Azhar University*, no author (Cairo, 1950).

departure. The frustrations of daily dealings with the defiant ulama, they claimed privately, were injurious to their health and sanity. The traditional core of religious studies therefore remains virtually unchanged since 1961.

Obstructionism has been a most effective weapon as practiced with sophisticated finesse by the ulama. It is certainly responsible for whatever autonomy the shaikhs have been able to retain after 1961, but obstructionism and all the other tactics employed by the ulama seem completely ill-chosen, for they have all been negative and have therefore been successful only in delaying the final capitulation of the ulama to the state. They have been fashioned to defend what little prestige, influence, and position remained, not to retrieve what had been lost. As a result of their refusal to come to grips with the main issues of modernization, social and ideological change, they have forfeited any role they might have played in shaping modernization in an Islamic context. They themselves have therefore been most responsible for the economic straits in which they now find themselves.

Modernization has been successfully delayed in Egypt by the ulama, but at a terrible price for Islam and the ulama. The shaikhs have become completely isolated from the modernizing segment of society and their traditional views almost totally rejected. They have lost their once favored political and social positions and find themselves in desperate economic straits. The traditional institutions which they had sought to preserve have all disappeared or been transformed. Even their interpretations of Islam have been rejected in favor of those offered by secular theorists working though the Supreme Council for Islamic Affairs.[70] As Professor Afaf Lutfi al-Sayyid Marsot has written,

> Once education, law and justice were removed from the hands of the 'ulamā', their political influence waned. Once nationalism replaced the overall concept of the Muslim community as the focus of loyalties, the political influence of religion waned. When the modern Muslim relegated religion to the realm of the spiritual, and admitted that society could be ruled by a civil code of law, his dependence on the 'ulamā' as other than religious teachers disappeared, and their influence on him in matters other than religious disappeared likewise.[71]

[70] For the role that secular theorists writing in the Supreme Council for Islamic Affairs's *Minbar al-Islam* have played in shaping the concept of Islamic socialism see my "Die Religion im Dienste des islamischen Staatssozialismus in Ägypten," *Bustan*, 3 (1967), 13–20.

[71] Afaf Lutfi el-Sayed (Marsot), "The Role of the *'ulamā'* in Egypt during the Early Nineteenth Century," p. 280.

Given the disproportionate amount of power represented by the state, it is a marvel that the ulama have successfully retarded the acceptance of modernization so long and have remained semiautonomous in the face of such unequal force, for in reality, as Shaikh Abd al-Latif Diraz, a former Vice-Rector of al-Azhar has written, the ulama "have no weapon . . . except a tongue of refined eloquence and a pen of sharpened style."[72] Minor weapons indeed, but expertly, though futilely, employed against overwhelming odds.

[72] Quoted in Ibrāhīm Amīn 'Abduh and 'Abd al-Raḥmān Ḥilmi Darwīsh, *al-Azhar wa al-Nashāṭ al-Ijtimā'i* (Cairo, 1936), p. 4.

8 The Roots of the Ulama's Power in Modern Iran*

NIKKI R. KEDDIE

STUDENTS OF MODERN Iranian history and politics have often been struck by peculiar features that may conveniently be formulated as two questions: Why have the modern Iranian ulama exercised and retained so much more political power than the ulama of other Middle Eastern countries? And why, perhaps uniquely in world history, was the power of the leaders of the official, traditional religion, exercised in favor of a popular, modernizing constitutional revolution from 1905 to 1911? Having dealt elsewhere with the second question,[1] I concentrate here mainly on the related question of the ulama's power, especially in the period before the constitutional revolution—the more recent period having recently been well covered by Leonard Binder, Charles Gallagher, and A. K. S. Lambton.[2] Many of the factors discussed below continue to

* This chapter first appeared in *Studia Islamica*, 29 (1969), 31–53.

[1] See Nikki R. Keddie, "The Origins of the Religious-Radical Alliance in Iran," *Past and Present*, 34 (July, 1966), 70–80; "Iranian Politics 1900–1905: Background to Revolution," *Middle Eastern Studies*, V, 1, 2, 3 (1969), 3–31, 151–167, 234–250; *Religion and Rebellion in Iran: The Tobacco Protest of 1891–1892* (London, 1966); and "Religion and Irreligion in Early Iranian Nationalism," *Comparative Studies in Society and History*, IV, 3 (April, 1962), 265–295. The ulama's role in the revolution is also discussed in Hamid Algar, *Religion and State in Iran 1785–1906* (Berkeley and Los Angeles, 1969), and in several articles by A. K. S. Lambton, especially "Secret Societies and the Persian Revolution of 1905–6," *St. Antony's Papers*, Vol. IV (London, 1958), pp. 43–60.

[2] Leonard Binder, "The Proofs of Islam: Religion and Politics in Iran," *Arabic and Islamic Studies in Honor of Hamilton A. R. Gibb*, George Makdisi, ed. (Leiden, 1965), pp. 118–140; Charles F. Gallagher, "Contemporary Islam: The Plateau of Particularism, Problems of Religion and Nationalism in Iran," *American Universities Field Staff Reports* (New York, 1966); and A. K. S. Lambton, "A Reconsideration of the Position of the Marja' al-Taqlîd and the Religious Institution," *Studia Islamica*, XX (1964), 115–135. See also the papers by Gustav Thaiss and Hamid Algar in this volume and Hamid Algar, "The Ulama in Twentieth Century Iran: Some Considerations, Historical and Contemporary," delivered at the conference on The Structure of Power in Islamic Iran, University of California, Los Angeles, 1969.

operate in the more recent period. Owing to the immensity of the time period covered, there can here only be outlined some hypotheses about the bases of ulama power, with a small part of the evidence for them. The word "ulama" below usually refers to the articulate leaders of the ulama, who are the only ones whose words and acts can readily be studied.

Many scholars, including myself, have cited the Twelver Shi'i doctrine of the illegitimacy of any state, even a Twelver one, pending the return of the hidden imam, as a basis of the Iranian ulama's effective and growing hostility to Iran's Qajar dynasty in the nineteenth and early twentieth centuries. While still noting the political importance of this doctrine, I would now add that religious doctrines change with time and circumstance more than either their adherents or scholars like to admit. We should ask why the Iranian ulama increasingly stressed the illegitimacy of the state, finally comparing the Qajars with the execrated Umayyad killers of the Imam Husain,[3] while the Sunni ulama had for centuries usually been content to acquiesce in the rule of even the most oppressive and impious kings.

Early Sunni doctrine had nearly as much basis for insisting that rulers follow the dictates of the ulama as did Twelver doctrine, and the Sunni ulama could occasionally find religious reasons to limit or depose a ruler, as seen in several depositions of Ottoman Sultans. But in these cases the Ottoman ulama were usually acting as tools or minor allies of more powerful classes; never in modern times did they have the independent power of Qajar ulama. And, while the Ottoman ulama's power declined in the nineteenth century, that of the Qajar ulama increased. What must be compared is the growth in the independent power of the Shi'i ulama as contrasted with the nineteenth-century decline of independent ulama

[3] Algar, *Religion and State*, p. 252, says: "Ṭabāṭabā'ī in one of his sermons compared the tyranny of the Qajars with that of the Umayyads who had martyred the Imam Ḥusayn, and by many the comparison was taken literally. It was thought that the Qajars were directly descended from the Umayyads, and even that the dagger which had been used to behead the Imam Ḥusayn was in the possession of 'Alā ud-Daula. So firm was the conviction, that the blockade imposed on the Masjid-i Shāh had to be relaxed for fear of suggesting another point of comparison with the Umayyads—that of denying food and drink to the descendants of the Prophet." These points are made by a participant in the constitutional revolution, Nāẓim al-Islām Kirmānī, *Tārīkh-i bīdārī-yi Īrānīyān* (Tehran, 1332 s./1953–54), pp. 378–415. Algar also notes earlier associations by the ulama of the Qajars' ancestors with the Umayyads. Such charges clearly undermined the shahs' claims to be the "Shadow of God" on earth.

power in the Ottoman Empire, Egypt, and elsewhere. For this comparison the juxtaposition of disembodied doctrines is of limited use.

Once the question is posed in this comparative way, a knowledge of modern Middle Eastern history tells us that the ulama's power declined in those states, like Egypt and the Ottoman Empire, where the central government was able to strengthen itself significantly through the creation of a modernized army and central bureaucracy. These gave the government the coercive base necessary to enforce its will on the ulama in many spheres that had been largely or totally subject to ulama control, such as education, law, and administration of pious endowments. Not that the government's posture was always coercive rather than persuasive, nor were the ulama without triumphs; but the general trend toward greater government control in the ulama's spheres of power is unmistakable.[4] In Iran, however, there is a rise in ulama power, which is directly related to a governmental "power vacuum." Despite references in Qajar times and after to the absolutism of the Qajar shahs, careful study shows how limited their power really was. The autocratic mythology surrounding the shahs and their potent capriciousness in certain spheres have all too long been mistaken for absolute power within their country. The Qajars never established an effective central army or national bureaucracy, much less really modernized ones. Taxes were farmed, governorships put up to auction, and royal or state domains sold in the Qajar period; outside the Tehran area the central government did little beyond collecting revenue. The army became increasingly a paper organization whose appropriations were stolen by the courtiers lucky enough to have the right posts, and the government's chief military support consisted of unreliable tribal levies, whose pay was made up largely of booty. In this situation the ulama, who often had their own "private armies" and who were much more widely respected than was the unpopular Qajar government, could frequently impose their will on a government that had little coercive force behind

[4] On the declining power of the Egyptian ulama in the nineteenth century see Daniel Crecelius, "The Ulama and the State in Modern Egypt," unpublished Ph.D. dissertation (Princeton, 1967), and Afaf Loutfi el-Sayed, "The Role of the *'ulamā'* in Egypt in the Early Nineteenth Century," in P. M. Holt, ed., *Political and Social Change in Modern Egypt* (London, 1968). On the Ottoman ulama see Niyazi Berkes, *The Development of Secularism in Turkey* (Montreal, 1964), and Uriel Heyd, "The Ottoman 'Ulamā and Westernization in the Time of Selīm III and Maḥmūd II," *Studies in Islamic History and Civilization*, Uriel Heyd, ed. (Jerusalem, 1961). See also the papers on Egypt and the Ottoman Empire in this volume.

it. Among the numerous ulama victories in the Qajar period, with the government having no recourse against the combination of ulama leadership and popular following were: the call for a jihad against Russia in 1826, the demand for the repeal of the all-embracing Reuter concession in 1873, the struggle for the repeal of the British tobacco monopoly concession in 1891–92, and the constitutional revolution itself.[5]

Having found one reason for the ulama's power in the government's relative impotence, we are led to new questions: What caused that impotence, and why did not the Iranian government modernize and centralize the instruments of power as did other Middle Eastern governments? I am presently incapable of answering these questions satisfactorily, and can only make a few suggestions.

1. Some weight must be given to the personalities of the Qajar shahs: Crown Prince 'Abbas Mirza, who early in the century began work on a modernized army and bureaucracy, unfortunately was killed before he came to the throne, and none of the other Qajar rulers was seriously concerned with modernization. The long rule of Nasir ad-Din Shah, from 1848 to 1896, was crucial in maintaining Iranian backwardness. This Shah, after a few ineffective attempts at reform which were countered by the ulama and other vested interests, relapsed into unconcern. His fear of rebellion or assassination made him discourage the extension of Western education among his subjects, which might have formed a base for modernizing reforms.

2. The role of Russia and Great Britain counted for something in Qajar conservatism. Either formally or informally Britain and Russia had, for their own reasons, guaranteed the continuity of the dynasty and the territorial integrity of Iran on several occasions after the early nineteenth-century losses of territory to Russia. The dynasty felt it could count on foreign arms in case of dynastic revolt or territorial breakoffs, and hence felt no urgency about building its own army. Also, Anglo-Russian rivalry

[5] On these victories see especially Algar, *Religion and State*; Keddie, *Religion and Rebellion*, and "La rivoluzione costituzionale iraniana del 1905–1911," *Rivista Storica Italiana*, LXXX, 1 (1968), 61–70; Firuz Kazemzadeh, *Anglo-Russian Relations in Iran* (New Haven, 1968); A. K. S. Lambton, "Secret Societies," "The Tobacco Regie: Prelude to Revolution," *Studia Islamica*, XXII (1965), 119–157, and XXIII (1965), 71–90, and "Dustūr: iv-Iran," *EI*², and the sources cited in them, especially the Persian books by Amīn ad-Dauleh, Shaikh Hasan Karbalā'ī, Ahmad Kasravī, Nāẓim al-Islām Kirmānī, Mahdī Malikzādeh, Ibrāhīm Taimūrī, Sayyid Ḥasan Taqīzādeh, and 'Abbās Mīrzā Mulk Ārā.

was a force discouraging modernization: dominant opinion in both the British and Russian governments, for example, opposed the construction of railroads in Iran, and this is one reason why railroads, which would have enhanced governmental power in the provinces, were not built until the 1920s. Also, concessions for economic enterprise to any country often brought forth complaints from England, Russia, or both, and these complaints might be effectively echoed by the ulama or other powerful forces in Iran, so that Nasir ad-Din Shah became increasingly frightened at the foreign policy consequences of economic modernization.[6]

3. Centralization in Iran was more difficult than in Egypt or the central districts of the Ottoman Empire because of Iran's mountainous topography, the long and difficult distances between population centers, and the independent military and political power of the nomadic tribes. Without expanding on the geographic part of this statement, one can note that the historic role of the tribes in Iran and the Middle East cries out for serious study. Middle Eastern scholarship has no work comparable with Owen Lattimore's *Inner Asian Frontiers of China,* even though the role of nomadic tribes is much greater in Middle Eastern history than in Chinese. In the absence of such a study, one can only state that the tribes controlled much, and probably most, of the armed force within Iran, that the government often had to conciliate them, and that they formed a serious obstacle to centralization and modernization.

4. Finally, there were other powerful men who effectively opposed what efforts at modernization were made—notably the reforms of the chief ministers Amir Kabir in the mid-nineteenth century, Sipahsalar-i A'zam in the 1860s and 70s, and Amin ad-Dauleh in the 1890s. All these attempts ended in the resignation, forced exile, and sometimes death of the minister involved and the subsequent reversal of many of his reforms.[7] Among the opponents of reform were vested interests at court whose own prerogatives were adversely affected, and also leaders of the ulama who feared both the growth of Western, infidel influence and a threat to their own

[6] This is shown especially in the British Foreign Office documents on Iran, which include direct reports of the Shah's words. On Anglo-Russian rivalry in Iran, see especially Kazemzadeh, *op. cit.*

[7] On these men, in addition to the standard historical accounts, see Algar, *Religion and State,* Kazemzadeh, *op. cit.,* and, in Persian, Farīdūn Ādamiyyat, *Amīr Kabīr va Irān* (Tehran, 1334 s./1955–56); Khān Malik Sāsānī, *Siyāsatgarān-i Daureh-yi Qājār* (Tehran, 1338 s./1959–60); and Mīrzā 'Alī Khān Amīn ad-Dauleh, *Khāṭirāt-i Siyāsī,* H. Farmānfarmāiyān, ed. (Tehran, 1341 s./1962–63).

position. We are thus led by a partially circular argument back to the power of the ulama: granted that the continued weakness of the Qajar state was one factor in ulama power, this ulama power, which itself helped cause the continued weakness of the Qajar state, must also have had other roots.

There were historical and doctrinal reasons why the Twelver Shi'i ulama of Iran should both have and claim greater power than the ulama of Sunni countries. Here I will not attempt the somewhat artificial task, dear to some Iranian nationalists and a few Orientalists, of separating out those features which are specifically "Iranian" from those which are not, except to make two generalizations: (1) Where "Iranian" features that deviate significantly from non-Iranian Twelver Shi'ism have been found, these have usually been not in ideas held by the leading ulama but in the deviant movements that have hitherto attracted most of the attention of scholars, such as the Babis, the philosophers, the Sufis, and in popular sects like the Nusairis and the Ahl-i Haqq or 'Ali-Ilahis. Here I am concerned not with these movements but with the role and doctrines of recognized leaders of the ulama. (2) In the absence of a clear influence from the non-Shi'i Iranian past, it is almost impossible to prove that the doctrines or power of the ulama developed in a certain way because they were Iranians, especially since there exists no modern non-Iranian Twelver Shi'i state with which to make a comparison. Since both the Safavids and the Qajars spoke Turkish, and since the earliest leaders of the Safavid ulama had to be imported from Arabic-speaking lands, it seems improbable that the Persian national character was the crucial factor in the developments discussed here.

To return to the bases of ulama power: First, the development of Twelver Shi'i doctrine and legal theory preceded by many centuries the formation of a Twelver Shi'i state in Iran; the Buyids (A.D. 945–1055) were Twelver Shi'ites, but they protected the Sunni caliph and did not try to enforce Shi'ism, and so do not form a real exception to this statement. In contrast with the Sunni ulama, who had to work out their doctrine under the rule of a government that claimed political sovereignty, the Shi'is lacked political protectors, which for centuries weakened their real power, but also enabled them in theory to deny the sovereign claims of any state.

No reconciliation was found or felt necessary between the claims of the ulama and those of the state; after the "Greater occultation" of the Twelfth Imam there is no really legitimate power pending his return. It is often said that the mujtahids exercise power by interpreting the Imam's will, but this doctrine is apparently a late one that has no basis in early Twelver theory. It was a natural doctrine for the mujtahids and other leading ulama, and was apparently partially developed before the Safavids came to power at the beginning of the sixteenth century. But, as is too seldom noticed, it became widespread only in the period of Safavid decline and during the eighteenth century, when there was no powerful government in Iran.

The leaders of the early Safavid ulama were imported by the Safavids from abroad and were dependent on official posts and other backing from the government for their power. They had no base among the largely Turkish-speaking tribesmen who made up the religious and military forces which had brought the Safavids to power. Indeed, there is overwhelming evidence that the religion of these tribal backers of the Safavids, as described by contemporary witnesses and by the poetry of Isma'il, the first Safavid Shah, was strikingly different from the learned Twelver Shi'ism of the official ulama.

By putting together the evidence from a variety of sources, one sees that behind the Safavid rise were some of the closely related popular religious groups in Anatolia, Syria, Kurdistan, and western Iran, whose views were reflected in the fifteenth-century Safavid movement. Although such popular religions often leave little in the way of scriptural and other written documents, an idea of their beliefs can be obtained by combining evidence from the early Safavid movement with later information about the doctrines of these groups. Among these closely related popular groups were the Hurufis; the Hurufi-influenced Bektashi dervish order; the Syrian Nusairis or 'Alavis and related groups; the forerunners of the Ahl-i Haqq or " 'Ali-Ilahis"; various Anatolian Turkish heresies; and the fifteenth-century Safavid-formed Qizil-bash, all of whom have descendants who can be studied even today. The desire of outsiders to separate and classify has made these groups seem more separate than they really are; even today the Iranian Ahl-i Haqq are often known as 'Ali-Ilahis, 'Alavis, or Nusairis, and recognize their ties with these other groups, and similar terminological looseness and recognition of kinship exists among others of these groups.[8]

[8] On the interrelationships of these sects see especially John K. Birge, *The Bektashi Order of Dervishes* (London, 1937); Michel M. Mazzaoui, "Shi'ism and the Rise of the Safavids," (unpublished Ph.D. dissertation, Princeton, 1966); V. Minorsky, *Notes sur la Secte des Ahlé-Haqq* (Paris, 1921); C. Huart, *Textes persans relatifs à la secte des Houroûfîs* (Leiden, 1909); and the relevant sources they cite.

Particularly significant of their ties to the Safavids is the use by many of these groups of Shah Isma'il's poetry and his religious-poetical name of Khata'i.[9] When one looks carefully at the evidence, it becomes clear that the religion that the Safavids followed while they were winning territory was quite different from the learned official Twelver Shi'ism that they began to enforce once they came to power. It would appear that the learned version of Twelver Shi'ism was almost unknown in the territories from which the Safavids drew their original military support, and it may be that Shah Isma'il did not know that the religious views he was propounding, which already had a wide base in eastern Anatolia and western Iran, were different from those of a learned tradition not well known in that area.

Judging both from contemporary reports and from the later views of these popular religious groups, one can see that their main point of similarity with learned Twelver Shi'ism was in their shared veneration for the Twelve Imams. On other points, however, they combined, according to the groups to which they appealed, ancient Iranian, Near Eastern, Turkish, and Christian elements with an intense popular religiosity and belief in the earthly presence of divinity. Such beliefs had earlier been found more among Isma'ilis than among the Twelvers. It is possible that when the Isma'ilis were dispersed and persecuted after the Mongol conquest of Iran they began to spread some of their ideas sub rosa among non-Isma'ili groups to which they migrated.[10]

Among the common features of these religious groups were: belief in divine incarnations, including 'Ali, the later Imams, and often the local sectarian leader; remnants of solar and lunar beliefs; reincarnation; and a strong and activist messianism. Leaders claiming to be mahdis or divine incarnations had arisen among the Turks of Anatolia before the Safavids, and the Ottoman state had tried to suppress them even before Safavid power added to the menace.[11] In the fourteenth and fifteenth centuries

[9] Birge, *op. cit.*, pp. 66–69; V. Minorsky, "The Poetry of Shāh Ismā'īl I," *BSOAS*, X, 4 (1942), 1006*a*–1053*a*.

[10] The theory of Ismā'īlī influence is put forth especially by W. Ivanow, *The Truth-Worshippers of Kurdistan: Ahl-i Haqq Texts* (Leiden, 1953); Turkish and Mongol influences are discussed in M. F. Köprülüzade, *Influence du chamanisme Turco-Mongol sur les ordres mystiques musulmans* (Istanbul, 1929); while ancient Iranian and Christian influences are discussed by numerous Persian and Western authors.

[11] See Mazzaoui, *op. cit.*; the articles "Bābā'ī," and "Badr al-Dīn," in *EI*², and the sources cited therein. Hanna Sohrweide, "Der Sieg der Ṣafaviden in Persien und seine Rückwirkungen auf die Schiiten Anatoliens im 16. Jahrhundert," *Der Islam*, 41 (1965), 95–223, also discusses the heterodox movements in Anatolia and their ties with the Safavids.

'Alid and Twelver Shi'i elements spread even among Sunni writers and Sufi orders in Anatolia and Iran.

When looked at in the light of these widespread religious movements in Anatolia and nearby areas, the religious history of the Safavids before they took power does not appear strange. The originally Sunni Sufi order of the Safavids may have been affected by the rise in 'Alid and heterodox sentiments that affected the Turkish speaking population of western Iran as well as Anatolia in the period following the Mongol invasions. Minorsky's view that Junaid, the Safavi leader who in the mid-fifteenth century converted the order both to militancy and to Twelver views, was encouraged in these changes by his travels among the tribesmen of Anatolia, seems confirmed.[12] Minorsky, however, does not particularly trace the origins of the unorthodox views expressed by Junaid's grandson, Isma'il, in his poetry. The religious views expressed in Isma'il's poetry, which seem also to be those of Isma'il's father and grandfather, were not personal peculiarities, but rather show many of the elements of the interconnected popular sects mentioned above, including deification of 'Ali, solar and lunar worship, a belief in the passage of the divine spirit from one leader to the next over time, metempsychosis, and messianism.[13] The fifteenth-century Safavid leaders differed from some of the other sects primarily in their claim to be themselves divine incarnations, but similar claims had been put forward by many Muslim messianic leaders, including some among the Anatolian Turks in the centuries right before the Safavids. It may be surmised that one reason for the popularity of Junaid, Haidar, and Isma'il among Turkish tribesmen lay in their reaction against the centralizing and orthodox tendency of the Ottomans, which interfered with the tribesmen's freedom.

An early source tells us that when Isma'il came to power it was difficult to find a work explaining Twelver Shi'i doctrine, and only one such work was found in a private library.[14] Whether or not this report is literally

[12] V. Minorsky, "Shaykh Bālī-Efendi on the Ṣafavids," *BSOAS*, XX (1957), 437–450, esp. pp. 439–440. More detailed evidence is in Sohrweide, "Der Sieg," pp. 118–122.

[13] Minorsky, "The Poetry of Shāh Ismā'īl I." See, in addition to the works cited in nn. 7–11 above, the articles "Kizil-Bāsh," in *EI*[1], and "Nuṣairī," in the *Shorter Encyclopaedia of Islam* (Leiden, 1953); Jean Aubin, "Études safavides: I, Šāh Ismā'īl et les notables de l'Iraq persan," *JESHO*, II, 1 (1959), 37–81; M. Molé, "Les Kubrawiya entre Sunnisme et Shiisme aux huitième et neuvième siècles de l'hégire," *REI*, XXIX, 1 (1961), 61–142. The dīvān of Shāh Ismā'īl has been published in the original Turkish by Tourkhan Gandjei, *Il canzoniere di Šāh Ismā'īl Ḫatā'ī* (Naples, 1959).

[14] Hasan-i-Rūmlū, *Aḥsanu't-Tawār-*

true, it does indicate that Isma'il probably came to power without a knowledge of the learned traditions of Twelver Islam. It is known that Isma'il and his successors had to import theologians and jurists from the Arabic-speaking lands to the southwest of their domains. Isma'il and those around him may well have been unaware of the discrepancies between their own views and those of learned Shi'ism until they began to bring in learned ulāma and their texts. Like other dynasties that had arisen from heretical and popular religious movements, however, the Safavids soon realized the unsuitability of such popular religions to the functioning of a stable government based on the cooperation of the conservative and property-owning classes. Thus, out of their fifteenth-century "heretical" beliefs the Safavid shahs retained only that element that was useful to their own power—a claim of their own divine or semi-divine role.

The leaders of the early Safavid ulama were dependent on the Safavids for their positions, which were often official ones. The religious troubles of the early Safavids came not from these state-connected ulama, but from their own former extremist, or "Sufi," followers, and from the Sunnis. In early Safavid times we do not hear particularly of the ulama's superior claims to sovereignty. The ulama seem then to have cooperated with the state, probably because they depended on the state for their position, and they may even have accepted the claims of some of the Safavid monarchs to leadership based on supposed descent from the imams. This claim by the Safavid rulers looks aberrant to us today partly because we are accustomed to a Twelver practice that accords only the mujtahids, and not any temporal ruler, some of the charisma of the imams. If we recognize the triumph of the mujtahids as a late development, however, the claim of the Safavid shahs no longer seems so strange: In the absence of any universally recognized claimant to the legitimacy and charisma of the imams, the shahs might have as good a claim as the mujtahids. The claims of the first Safavid leaders to be imams or divine incarnations could hardly be accepted by the orthodox, but a satisfactory compromise between the claims of the rulers and those of the ulama seems to have been found in a theory of the divine rights of kings, based on the concept that the Shah

īkh, C. N. Seddon, trans. (Baroda, 1934), p. 27: "In those days men knew not of the Ja'farī faith and of the rules of the twelve Imāms. For of books on this matter there were none. Yet Qāẓī Naṣrullāh Zaytūnī had the first volume of the Qawā'id-i-Islām of Shēkh Jamālu'd-dīn Muṭahhar of Ḥilla, and therefrom he gave religious teaching, till, day by day, the sun of the Shī'a faith rose higher and lightened the dark places of the earth." Mazzaoui, *op. cit.*, discusses the question of what book is probably referred to here.

was the shadow of God (zill-allah) on earth. This theory, which appears not to have been based on Twelver Shi'i doctrine, was nonetheless developed and endorsed by some of the leading Shi'i theorists in Safavid times.[15] From Safavid times onward the theory has sometimes been considered a Shi'i one, but it has often been rejected by leaders of the Shi'i ulama, and seems to be connected more to earlier Persian royal theories, including those from Sunni periods, than to earlier Shi'i doctrines.[16]

The patronage of the orthodox ulama by the Safavids included contributions to the ulama's economic power through donations of waqf property, endorsement of ulama control over religious taxes, and payment for their official and religious functions. The economic and ideological power thus granted to the ulama by the shahs worked in the shahs' favor as long as the latter had independent sources of strength. As Safavid power declined in the seventeenth century, however, some of the ulama began to deny the religious legitimacy of the shahs' power, and to claim that the mujtahids had a better right to rule.[17] To quote Jean Chardin, the perceptive late seventeenth-century resident of the Safavid capital of Isfahan:

> The Persians are divided among themselves regarding who has the right to take [the Twelfth Imam's] place, and to be sovereign in both spiritual and temporal matters. The Men of the Church, and with them all devout persons, and all those who profess the strict observance of religion, hold that in the absence of the Imam, the royal seat should be filled by a mujtahid masum, terms that signify a man pure in manners who has acquired all the sciences to such a perfect degree that he can respond immediately and without prompting to all questions that are posed to

[15] On this point see especially the excellent paper by Amin Banani, "The Social and Economic Structure of the Persian Empire in Its Heyday," which will be published among the papers of the Middle East Colloquium at Harvard University, 1967–68.

[16] Joseph Eliash, "The Ithnā'asharī Juristic Theory of Political and Legal Authority," *Studia Islamica*, XXIX (1969), 17–30, insists on the illegitimacy in strict Twelver theory of any idea that the ruler can be the representative of the sharī'a or the shadow of God on earth. Nonetheless such a theory, with roots in the Iranian past, was propagated even by members of the ulama in Safavid times. See A. K. S. Lambton, "Quis custodiet custodes? Some Reflections on the Persian Theory of Government," *Studia Islamica*, V–VI (1956), 125–148 and 125–146.

[17] On the growth of the power of the mujtahids in Safavid times see Banani, *op. cit.*, and R. M. Savory, "The Principal Offices of the Ṣafawid State during the Reign of Ṭahmasp I," *BSOAS*, XXIV, 1 (1961), esp. p. 81. The shifting position of the Safavid ulama is also discussed in the second part of Lambton, "Quis custodiet custodes?" and in V. Minorsky, trans. and ed., *Tadhkirat al-Mulūk: A Manual of Safavid Administration* (London, 1943), which includes much information on Safavid religious history in the introduction and appendixes.

him on religion and civil law. But the most accepted opinion, which has prevailed, is that in truth this right belongs to a direct descendant of the Imams, but that it is not absolutely necessary that this descendant be either pure or learned to such a great degree of perfection. . . . This is, as I have just said, the dominant opinion, because it is the one that establishes and affirms the right of the reigning king. . . . [The Persians] thus commonly regard their king as the Lieutenant of Muhammad, the successor of the Imams . . . and the Vicar of the Twelfth Imam during his absence. They give him all these titles, and in addition that of Caliph, by which they again mean the Successor and Lieutenant of the Prophet, to whom belongs by right the universal government of the world, both spiritual and temporal, during the absence of the Imam. . . . although it must be important to the government that this opinion be universal, they nevertheless allow the Men of the Church to teach rather openly the contrary opinion, which is that the Vicar of the Imam must be not only of his descent; but that he must also be without blemish and learned to the highest degree. "How could it be possible," say these men of the Church, "that these . . . impious Kings, drinkers of wine and carried off by passion, be the Vicars of God, and that they have communication with Heaven, in order to receive thence the light necessary for the guidance of the faithful People? How can they resolve the cases of conscience and the doubts of Faith, in the way in which a Lieutenant of God must, they who sometimes scarcely know how to read? Our Kings being iniquitous and unjust men, their domination is a tyranny to which God has subjected us to punish us, after having withdrawn from the world the legitimate Successor of His Prophet. The supreme Throne of the Universe belongs only to a Mujtahid, or man who possesses sanctity and science above ordinary men. It is true that since the Mujtahid is holy, and consequently a peaceful man, there must be a King who carries a sword for the exercise of justice; but he must only be like his Minister, and dependent upon him.[18]

This claim that legitimate power belonged to a mujtahid had some support in prior Shi'i theory, and was further helped by the continued decline of the central state until the nineteenth century. (The power and pretensions of religious leaders generally flourish most in periods of political weakness and decentralization—witness medieval Europe and the decentralized periods in Japan and China when the Buddhist church and monasteries flourished—and the Iranian ulama fit into this general pattern).

It is perhaps against this background that we can understand the eighteenth-century victory of one school of Twelver thought—the Usulis, or mujtahidis—over the other main school, the Akhbaris, or followers of

[18] *Voyages de Monsieur le Chevalier Chardin en Perse*, Vol. II (Amsterdam, 1711), pp. 206–208. I have omitted some of Chardin's italics. On the mujtahids' claims to succession to the imams, see also *ibid.*, pp. 337–338.

Traditions. Although the latter are usually presented as innovators who first appear in the seventeenth century, Scarcia has justly noted that both schools developed out of a common background.[19] The triumphant Usulis were those who claimed the key role for the mujtahids in the interpretation of law and doctrine; all believers were supposed to pick a living mujtahid to follow and to abide by his judgments. This doctrine gave the living mujtahids a power beyond anything claimed by the Sunni ulama, and gave to their rulings a sanction beyond anything merely decreed by the state. The Akhbaris, who claimed that the Traditions of the Prophet and the Imams provided sufficient guidance, without need for rulings by a mujtahid, were largely defeated in the course of the eighteenth century. If Gobineau is to be trusted, Akhbari views, because of their laxness about which Traditions to accept and follow, retained their popularity with the bourgeoisie in the nineteenth century, but there is no question that Usuli or mujtahidi views, with their glorification of the power of the living mujtahids, were followed by the great majority of the ulama.[20]

This series of doctrinal developments with clear implications for ulama power bears comparison with developments in early Abbasid times: there are some similarities, but the different outcomes of the two cases is most significant for the discussion of ulama power. Both Abbasids and Safavids came to power with the support of popular religious movements with a strong Shi'i-messianic tinge; both turned against their more extreme followers and patronized an ulama class that, perhaps coincidentally, had a largely Mu'tazilite, that is, moderately rationalist, theological outlook. In both cases the claim of the jurists among the ulama to apply reason and educated judgment to questions of law and doctrine was challenged by professional Traditionists and others who wanted to rely instead on literal acceptance of hadiths (or akhbar, another term for Traditions) coming from the infallible leader or leaders of the past. In Abbasid times victory went ultimately to those who wanted to limit rationalism in the theological field and both reason and individual judgment in the legal field: Mu'tazilite theology was rejected and reason given a much smaller role in later theological schools, while individual judgment was early banished from legal theory and the door of ijtihad, or interpretation of law and doctrine, was closed shortly thereafter. In modern Iran, however,

[19] Gianroberto Scarcia, "Intorno alle controversie tra Aḫbārī e uṣūlī presso gli imāmiti di Persia," *Rivista degli studi orientali*, XXXIII (1958), 211–250.

[20] Cf. Comte de Gobineau, *Religions et philosophies dans l'Asie Centrale* (10th ed., Paris, 1957), pp. 35–39.

the outcome was quite different. First, it should be noted that the very need of dealing for the first time in practice with questions arising from relations with a Shi'i state helped give to the discussions among the Iranian ulama an intellectual vitality that had been largely lacking among the Sunni ulama since early Abbasid times. This relative vitality helps explain the successful adaptation of the ulama to new conditions in the nineteenth century. Second, the actual outcome of the seventeenth- and eighteenth-century quarrels favored both power and flexibility for the mujtahids, whereas the outcome of Abbasid discussions tended to limit the power and flexibility of members of the ulama class. The closing of the door of ijtihad in Abbasid times may have been a defense of ulama-evolved legal doctrines against the encroachment of the state; but even this interpretation implies that what was needed was a defense; there was no question of taking the offensive against an impotent state. Such an aggressive posture is just what is implied by the Usuli doctrine of ijtihad; the legal, and even political, rulings of a mujtahid have a validity superior to any merely temporal ruling by the state. This doctrine was vindicated in practice in 1891 by the universally observed fatwa outlawing smoking as long as the British tobacco monopoly remained, and on several other occasions. Also, the Usuli doctrine puts a special stress on the role of the living mujtahid. The ijtihad of an individual mujtahid is always merely probable; although it must be followed by his own supporters, it establishes no precedent and believers are forbidden to follow the rulings of a deceased mujtahid in place of a living one. Although doctrinal reasons relating to the unknowability of the will of the hidden imam may be found for this emphasis in Twelver ijtihad, we may surmise that an equally important reason for Usuli insistence on this doctrine was the power it put into the hands of the living mujtahids of any period. Scarcia has noted that the Usuli mujtahid acts really as a legislator for his followers.[21] We may add that the mujtahid's direct power over his followers' conduct, political as well as personal, is, partly because of this doctrine, much greater than is that of the Sunni alim. Finally, this doctrine of continuous reinterpretation of the will of the imam, though it may have started for quite other reasons, institutionalized a flexibility regarding legal, and especially political, questions which was impossible according to Sunni doctrine. It usually evokes laughter in an audience knowing Sunni ways to quote the fatwa saying that smoking was, in a certain period, against the will of the Hidden Imam, or to quote the article in

[21] Scarcia, *op. cit.*, p. 237.

the Iranian constitution saying that the parliament had been formed with the blessing of this Imam. Yet this was simply expansion of standard Usuli practice into new political spheres, where such expansion was favored by recently evolved tenets of Twelver theory, by the relative impotence and unpopularity of the state, and by the growing influence and popular ties of the ulama. The Mu'tazilite rationalism of Twelver theology may have further encouraged the application of educated reason to new problems.[22]

Another base of ulama power was their financial position, which appears to have been stronger than that of the Sunni ulama even in the early nineteenth century, and certainly later in the century. In the absence of serious studies I can say little about this most important point, but will mention simply that the high and assured income of the ulama seems to have had its roots both in a doctrine that assured the ulama administration of the Islamic *khums* tax, and in Safavid practices. In establishing officially favored ulama, whom they saw as key supporters and not as potential rivals, the Safavids stressed the obligatory nature of large alms to be administered by the ulama, which the Qajars had to follow in order to get any cooperation from them.

Even the widespread confiscation of waqfs by the anti-ulama Nadir Shah in the eighteenth century did not break their financial power, which was increasingly restored largely on the old bases under subsequent rulers, including the Qajars. What had been a pillar of state policy in early Safavid times later turned into a financial base for antigovernment action.[23]

[22] Western scholars sometimes note, but rarely stress the implications of, the Mu'tazilite basis of Twelver theology. It can be appreciated from the translation by W. M. Miller of a major Twelver Creed, *al-Bâbu'l-Ḥâdî 'Ashar* (2d printing; London, 1958). In it not only are the Ash'arites time and again stated to be wrong and the Mu'tazilites right on doctrinal points, but the stress is on the rationality and comprehensible justice of God; certain things are incumbent (*wājib*) on God because of justice and rationality (which implies natural law); and men have free will. While Orientalists have long discussed the significance of Abbasid Mu'tazilism, the question has scarcely been raised for the much longer-lived Twelver Mu'tazilism.

[23] Regarding the special economic strength of the Shī'ī ulama, Eliash notes: "In the absence of the Hidden Imam, the legitimacy of any Muslim political regime, even that of a Twelver-Shī'ī government, was denied. A significant development with far-reaching political consequences follows from this, namely, the duty of the Twelver-Shī'ī believer to pay a tenth of his yearly income directly to the mujtahids and not to the Twelver-Shī'ī government, and another tenth to the poor among the descendants of 'Alī who practise Twelver-Shī'ism, which also may be paid through the mujtahids. In modern Persia, the payment of *Khums* gives the Twelver-Shī'ī divines economic in-

A base of ulama power that I and others have noted elsewhere was the location of the Shi'i leadership outside the borders of Iran, in the shrine cities of Ottoman Iraq. Here it may be added that this was partly a question of conscious ulama choice; under the Safavids the Shi'i leaders had resided in the Safavid capital, Isfahan, and their movement abroad was in part a sign of their growing independence in the post-Safavid period. This location of religious leadership outside the state's borders plus the tendency to pick a single shrine mujtahid as the source of the most authoritative rulings, created in nineteenth-century Iran some surprising similarities to medieval European Catholic states. Unlike other Muslim countries, but like the medieval West, nineteenth-century Iran exhibited a kind of separation of church and state—not the modern type of separation, but rather one in which the religious organization asserted, and could often support, claims superior to those of the merely secular government. Government in both Iran and medieval Europe not only lacked impressive ideological underpinnings unless the religious leaders wished to bestow them, but also lacked an effective monopoly of military force. The religious institution had coercive powers of its own, while the government had to rely on feudal or tribal levies, who would often move only when it was in their own interest to do so. Finally, the heads of the religious institution, to whom its members looked for doctrinal and practical leadership, resided abroad and were beyond the political or financial control of the merely secular ruler. To pursue the comparative remarks further, without claiming total equivalence, one might say that Sunni states like Egypt or the Ottoman Empire, where the leaders of the religious institution resided in the capital and were vulnerable to government influence, and where the ruler was generally stronger than he was in Iran or the feudal West, exhibited some of the features of the so-called Caesaro-papism of the Byzantine and Russian empires.

One remark may be added regarding the ulama's role in leading the

---

dependence from the political ruler and thus enables them to exercise political power in addition to their direct religious influence among the masses" (Joseph Eliash, " 'Alī b. Abī Ṭālib in Ithna-'Asharī Shī'ī Belief," unpublished Ph.D. dissertation [London, 1966], p. 196). On the economic and general position of the ulama through the early nineteenth century, see John Malcolm, *The History of Persia*, Vol. II (London, 1815), chap. xxii. The ulama accumulated wealth through trade, landownership, fees, and bribes, and mujtahids seem to have grown wealthier in the 19th century. See especially Algar, *Religion and State, passim.*

constitutional revolution. None of what was said above regarding ulama power points automatically to a revolutionary role for the ulama. Indeed, the partial comparison with the medieval Catholic Church might make such a role seem particularly strange. It appears that the threat of Western conquest or Western-inspired secularization is the key to explaining this surprising "radical" role for a traditional religious class. Upon a preexistent power conflict between "Church" and state there was superimposed a Western infidel threat to the power of the religious classes in two forms: first, the proposed secularization of institutions traditionally controlled by the ulama, and second, the increased control of Iran and its resources by Western governments and their subjects, which might culminate in foreign, infidel rule. The ulama, given their strength and relative popularity, were able to react effectively to both threats. Their reaction appeared "reactionary" when it was directed against modernization and centralization, and "progressive" when directed against imperialist controls, but in both cases the ulama were acting consistently with the preservation of their own power. During the constitutional revolution the ulama were led to support a modern constitution partly by their belief that it would further enhance their power. When this turned out not to be the case, the ulama returned to their policy of fighting secularization and government encroachment on their prerogatives. There is thus broad continuity between the policies of the ulama before and after the constitutional revolution, however much they may appear as largely "progressive" in the years before the revolution and largely "reactionary" in later years.

To summarize very briefly the period since the revolution and World War I: The creation for the first time in Iran of a centralized national state backed by a modern army beginning under Reza Shah in the 1920s necessarily resulted in curbs on the independent power of the ulama. The centralization of power under the Shah, his army, and bureaucracy, plus the growth of a modern educational and judicial system, curbed the ulama's power and intellectual influence. As in many Islamic countries there developed a split between the higher classes having a modern education and generally hostile to the ulama, and the lower classes who were still largely subject to the ulama's influence. Many in the government and upper classes, however, continue to think that the influence of the ulama on the lower classes is a good thing, since it helps keep these classes from getting dangerous and revolutionary ideas. Also, the government often fears to alienate the leaders of the ulama completely, and so has given in to ulama pressure on some issues that do not directly challenge the government's power and main programs.

Since World War II there have been partial revivals of earlier alliances, with some of the ulama uniting with nationalists against government policies that these ulama saw both as contrary to Islam and as subservient to infidel foreign powers. These revivals of the religious-nationalist alliance appeared both in the movement centering on oil nationalization in the early 1950s and in the opposition to the government's policies in the 1960s. During demonstrations against the government in 1963 the terminology used against the Qajars was revived to some effect, but by now the government had the power and arms to deal far more summarily with its opponents than the Qajars had been able to do. Professor Lambton described the causes of 1963 demonstrations as follows:

> These disturbances were the culmination of a movement of resistance to the exercise of arbitrary power by the government, which by the summer of 1963 was felt by some to be intolerable. Fundamentally the movement was a protest by the religious classes against what they believed, rightly or wrongly, to be injustice (*ẓulm*). This was not the only issue: the flames were no doubt fanned by all, or many, of the discontented elements of society, including those who opposed the government because of its land reform programme or its intention to enfranchise women, obscurantist *mullās* who believed that their power over the people would be weakened by the spread of education, and those who opposed the government because of its alignment with the western powers. The movement was led by members of the religious classes, who made forthright attacks on the government in the mosques and in broadsheets. When finally a *mujtahid*, Āyatullāh Khumaynī, the most prominent critic of the government, compared the shah to Yazīd, the Umayyad governor who is still execrated by the Shī'a for the death of Ḥusayn at Karbalā, the government had no choice but action. Khumaynī and others were arrested. Demonstrations in their favour were put down ruthlessly with heavy loss of life. The disturbances were subsequently alleged to have been stirred up by the opponents of land reform and women's suffrage. They no doubt had a finger in the pie, but action. Khumaynī and othere were arrested. Demonstrations in their turbances solely, or indeed mainly, to them.[24]

Nationalists who backed the 1963 movement claim that the main thrust of Khumayni and his associates was not against reform but against the government's autocratic ways and its subservience to Western Powers, especially the United States, from whom it accepted a new and unpopular

[24] Lambton, "A Reconsideration," pp. 120–121.

Status of Forces agreement. They challenge the government to produce authentic copies of the fatwas that pro-government sources allege were issued against land reform and women's suffrage. Whatever the truth regarding the relative weight of specific issues among the religious opponents of the government, it appears clear that many of them opposed both the government's proposed reforms and its complaisance toward United States policy, both of which could be seen as a threat to their own beliefs and position.

Given the continued growth of government power, and the expansion of the army, the bureaucracy, and of secular education, even in the villages, it appears probable that the political power of the ulama will continue to decline as it has in the past half century. Although leaders of the ulama in Iran retain more independent influence on political questions than those in most other Muslim countries, they now appear at most able to modify or delay certain government policies and not strongly to influence their basic thrust and direction. Despite the ulama's economic and social conservatism, however, the issues they raise continue to strike a responsive chord among many Iranians.

9 The Oppositional Role of the Ulama in Twentieth-Century Iran*

HAMID ALGAR

THE PARTICIPATION of a large and influential number of the Iranian ulama in the Constitutional Revolution (1905–1911) has of late been the subject of several essays in analysis and explanation.[1] The interpretations offered have largely centered upon the historical situation of nineteenth-century Iran, implicitly regarding the support extended by the ulama to the liberal cause of constitutional government as the outcome of a certain conjunction of circumstances and almost as an anomaly. Doctrinal and ideological motives for opposition to tyranny have been regarded as secondary, and the ulama's support for the constitution is thought indeed to have proceeded from confusion and shortsightedness. There are, however, grounds for discerning a stance of opposition to tyranny as one of the fundamental and most pervasive characteristics of Ithnāʿasharī Shiʿi Islam, and this stance was not inspired exclusively by the defects of Qajar rule. Furthermore, an almost unbroken line of descent connects the oppositional role of the ulama in Qajar Iran with the present struggle of an important group of the Iranian ulama against the Pahlavi regime. Despite far-reaching changes in the intellectual, cultural, social, and political countenance of Iran, the voice of the ulama is still heard demanding an end to what it identifies as tyrannical and arbi-

* This article is the abbreviated and revised form of a paper first presented at the Conference on the Structure of Power in Islamic Iran at the University of California, Los Angeles, in June 1969. A full version is to be published elsewhere.

[1] Nikki R. Keddie, "The Origins of the Religious-Radical Alliance in Iran," *Past and Present*, 34 (July, 1966), 70–80; Hamid Algar, *Religion and State in Iran, 1785–1906: The Role of the Ulama in the Qajar Period* (Berkeley and Los Angeles, 1969); and A. K. S. Lambton, "The Persian 'Ulama and Constitutional Reform," in *Le Shiʿisme Imamite: Colloque de Strasbourg, 6–9 mai 1968* (Paris, 1970), pp. 245–269. The present article should be seen as partially amending the conclusion reached in my book (p. 259) that "the ulama failed to perceive the nature of what was being demanded [in the Constitutional Revolution] and its implications for Iran and themselves."

trary rule. It is the dual purpose of this paper to delineate the chief religious and doctrinal considerations that have inspired the persistent opposition of the ulama to monarchical absolutism, and to examine the expression of that opposition in the present century, particularly in the last decade.

The political theory of Ithnāʻasharī Shiʻi Islam is, in the first place, part of its overall definition of the Imamate: to the Imam alone, divinely protected against sin and error, belongs all legitimate rule. The political vocation of the Imams was continuously frustrated; and with the occultation of the Twelfth Imam, Muḥammad al-Mahdī, in 874, even the possibility of the legitimate exercise of power disappeared from the world. Hence all states are inalienably usurpatory, even those of formal Shiʻi affiliation. This usurpatory nature of the state was to a degree obscured by Safavid claims of Imamite descent, but emerged with great clarity in the Qajar period, inspiring a pervasive attitude of repugnance to the state and its representatives. The curbing and limitation of this illegitimate organ, implied in the constitutional concept, were therefore attractive to ulama nurtured in a traditional perspective of distrust of temporal power.

Other political attitudes may also be seen to derive from the occultation of the Imam. It is related that the Twelfth Imam, immediately upon his birth, uttered the confession of faith and prostrated in the direction of the *qibla*. His father, Imam Ḥasan al-ʻAskarī, then commanded him to speak, whereupon he recited the Qur'anic verse (28:4): "We desired to be gracious to those that were abased in the land, and to make of them leaders and the inheritors."[2] This anecdote indicates the messianic dimension of the Twelfth Imam: his return is to bring about the redemption and elevation of the oppressed. The aspiration for the return of the Twelfth Imam from the plane of occultation to that of manifestation, a vital part of Ithnāʻasharī spiritual and devotional life, is therefore also an aspiration for social justice and the relief of the downtrodden. While such justice and relief are, in their plenitude, to be expected only from the renewed manifestation of the Imam, they may be partially achieved by those who desire his coming and wish, as it were, to prepare the way by anticipating the characteristics of his dominion.[3]

[2] Quoted in Fakhr ad-Dīn ʻAlī Ṣafī, *Laṭā'if aṭ-Ṭavā'if*, Aḥmad Gulchīn-i Maʻānī, ed. (Tehran, 1336 Sh/1957), p. 61.

[3] This sentence is a summary of thoughts expressed to me in May 1970 by a group of Shiʻi friends in Mashhad. It is of course true that from a differ-

It is not only with the Twelfth Imam that aspirations for justice and abhorrence of tyranny are connected. At the level of popular emotional expression, one of the chief themes of Ithnā'asharī Shi'i Islam is without doubt the martyrdom of Imam Ḥusayn at Karbala after his abortive uprising against the Caliph Yazīd. His death at the hands of the Umayyads is ever present in the Shi'i consciousness, not simply as a historical fact, nor yet as a cause for pious commemoration, but as a living reality of universal significance. In his person, the aspiration to justice is seen to have confronted the tyranny of an impious regime, and those who weep in memory of his martyrdom are lamenting too the recurrent temporal defeat of this aspiration. Insofar as they not only mourn his martyrdom, but seek to prove worthy of his sacrifice, they emulate his example and battle against contemporary manifestations of tyranny. Imam Ḥusayn's struggle against the Umayyads is thus transfigured into an archetype of the conflict between justice and tyranny. All autocratic regimes are held to be similar to and reminiscent of the Umayyads, and on occasion even to be descended from that dynasty.

This tendency, still to be observed in contemporary Iran where the Shah has been designated "the Yazīd of the age," was marked in the Qajar period. It made its first recorded appearance in the reign of Muḥammad Shāh (1834–1848), when it was rumored that the Qajars had been present in the Umayyad army at Karbala.[4] Such rumors gained particular currency and vigor in the period of the Constitutional Revolution. The descent of the Qajaars from the Umayyads was thought to be attested by the supposition that the dagger that had been used to behead the Imam was in the possession of 'Alā ad-Daula, governor of Tehran.[5] Similarly, when the royalist forces were besieging Tabriz in 1909, the *mujtahids* of Najaf declared that the blockade of the city was "tantamount to denying the water of the Euphrates to the companions of the Lord of Martyrs [Imam Ḥusayn]."[6] In like manner, many of the early constitutionalists tended to equate themselves with the martyred Imam: thus in order to establish the legitimacy of the *anjumans*, the semisecret societies established for the

ent, possibly more traditional, perspective, the profusion of tyranny is a sign of the imminence of the return of the Twelfth Imam, and thus a "preparation" for his coming.

[4] A. Sepsis, "Quelques mots sur l'état religieux actual de la Perse," *Revue de l'Orient*, III (1844), 106.

[5] Nāẓim al-Islām Kirmānī, *Tārīkh-i Bīdārī-yi Īrānīān* (new ed.; Tehran, 1332 Sh/1953), p. 415.

[6] Aḥmad Kasravī, *Tārīkh-i Mashrūṭa-yi Īrān* (5th imp.; Tehran, 1340 Sh/1961), p. 729.

support of the constitutionalist cause, it was claimed that the first such *anjuman* had been founded by Imam Ḥusayn.[7]

This acute consciousness of the tragedy at Karbala as a living piece of metahistory was fostered throughout the nineteenth century by the practices known as *ta'zīya* and *rauḍakhᵛānī,* commemoration of the martyrdom of the Imam by dramatic performances and the recitation of verse. Although neither practice had its origin in the Qajar period, it was then that both reached a climax of development. In the present century both continue to be cultivated, probably on a socially more restricted scale, but with undiminished passion and devotion. Although certain legendary and superstitious elements are to be found in the material performed and recited, both practices operate as a means of expressing often intense religious emotion and loyalty. This is particularly true of the *ta'zīya,* where the violent self-flagellation of some participants should be seen primarily as a result of the desire to share in the Imam's martyrdom. Through revolt against an existing tyranny, this desire may be more realistically fulfilled. It is hardly an exaggeration to say that the emotions generally displayed in the *ta'zīya* can, in the course of political agitation, leave their representational framework of expression to make of the contemporary struggle a reenactment of Karbala.[8] This potentiality of the *ta'zīya* for the inspiration of revolt has moved several Iranian statesmen and governments to work for its abolition; concern for its possible illegitimacy in terms of religious law and precedent has been secondary.[9]

Powerful emotional attitudes deriving from the occultation of the Twelfth Imam and the martyrdom of Imam Ḥusayn serve, then, to inspire a desire for social justice and hostility to tyranny. In addition, the structure of religious authority in Ithnā'asharī Shi'i Islam predisposes the community and the scholars who lead it to a stance of practical hostility to the state. Authority in religious matters belongs, strictly speaking, to the Twelfth (or Hidden) Imam, whose withdrawal from human affairs is only apparent, and who is, indeed, frequently referred to as *Ṣāḥib-i Zamān,* the Lord of the Age. During his occultation, however, there exists the need for some practical manner of guiding the community. This need is fulfilled by the practice known as *taqlīd,* that is, submission to

[7] Kirmānī, *op. cit.,* p. 206.

[8] On the social and political significance of *ta'zīya* see too the article by Gustav Thaiss, "Religious Symbolism and Social Change: The Drama of Hussain," in the present volume.

[9] Concerning such attempts by Amīr Kabīr, chief minister from 1848 to 1851, see Algar, *op. cit.,* pp. 135–136. More recently, Riḍā Shāh vainly tried to suppress the performance of *ta'zīya.*

the authoritative direction of a religious scholar in matters touching on the enactment of religious ordinances. The scholar who dispenses such guidance is the *mujtahid,* that is, he who is capable of exercising personal judgment on the matters concerning which guidance is sought. From among those who have fulfilled the technical requirements for the function of *mujtahid,* the believer will select one whose guidance he will follow, and the *mujtahid* thus chosen is known as the *marja'-i taqlīd* (pl., *marāji'-i taqlīd*), the source of imitation. The criteria to be observed in the choice of a *marja'* are above all learning and piety. On occasion, certain outstanding *mujtahids* have been able to establish themselves as sole *marja'* for the entire community, but more commonly a number of *mujtahids* serve as "sources of imitation," each with his own following.[10]

Since the political sphere, no less than other areas of human activity, should be subordinated to religious precept, the practice of *taqlīd* has important political consequences. The *mujtahid,* in his capacity as *marja',* is liable to dispense guidance on political matters in a sense opposed to the will of the state and ipso facto to become a leader of opposition. Definitive exposition of the concepts of *taqlīd* and *mujtahid* (in their distinctive Shi'i senses) was the achievement of Āqā Muḥammad Bāqir Bihbihānī (1705–1803), who is connected by a direct line of intellectual and spiritual descent with the ulama of the present age.[11] The theoretical clarification of the position of *mujtahid* as *marja'-i taqlīd* took place on the eve of the establishment of Qajar rule, and its political implications became progressively clearer throughout the nineteenth century. The monarch was theoretically bound, no less than his subjects, to submit to the authoritative guidance of a *mujtahid* and in effect to make the state the executive branch of ulama authority. Throughout the Qajar period the ideal remained far from fulfillment, and there was therefore a certain tension inherent in relations between the ulama and the monarchy. The participation of the ulama in the Constitutional Revolution may in part be regarded as a sign that this tension had given way to open rupture.

These religious and doctrinal motives for hostility to the state were powerfully reinforced throughout the century by the course of political events. The Qajars became associated with aggressive non-Muslim powers that threatened to achieve total control of Iran and destroy its nature as an Islamic community. Calls for resistance to the foreigners that were

[10] For a fuller account of the principles and practice of *taqlīd,* see Algar, *op. cit.,* pp. 5–11.

[11] Concerning Bihbihānī, see *ibid.,* pp. 34–36 and the sources cited there.

encroaching on Iran were also directed against the state whose weakness made such misfortunes possible. When attempts were made to remedy the debility of the state through certain measures of reform and westernization, the hostility of the ulama only increased, for their prerogatives—particularly in the sphere of law—were progressively restricted. The reforming minister Mīrzā Ḥusayn Khān Sipahsālār, with a kind of implicit secularism, flatly declared his opposition to the "interference" of the ulama in affairs of state.[12] There was, then, a dual target for ulama opposition—foreign domination and domestic tyranny; and the ulama bequeathed this duality of concern to the constitutionalists.

In their hostility to the state, the ulama found themselves in frequent alliance with the urban mercantile classes. The ulama and the merchants each represented powers largely independent of the state, and religious direction and economic enterprise tended to complement each other. Commercial practice was regulated by ordinances of the *sharīʿa,* which were formulated and interpreted by the *mujtahids,* and much of the business of the courts that administered religious law comprised commercial matters. Donations and religiously sanctioned taxes (*zakāt, khums*) paid by the merchants formed the second most important source of ulama income after the endowments (*auqāf*) attached to mosques and institutes of religious learning. Such payments, although not enforced by any regular system of collection, appear to have been considerable throughout the nineteenth century. Both ulama and merchants were disposed to hostility to the state: a strong, self-assertive state threatened the judicial and other prerogatives of the ulama, and was liable to visit extortionate taxation on the merchants. Both classes, too, feared European penetration of Iran as inimical to their interests. In the face of the dangers presented by a tyrannical state in league with foreign powers, the ulama and the merchants offered each other aid and refuge: the sanctuary provided by mosques was an ultimate refuge for the tyranny of the state, while the closure of the bazaar gave the ulama a powerful instrument of pressure on the government. The alliance of mosque and bazaar, still strong and operative in Iran, is thus ancient and well founded.

The considerations enumerated thus far—religious, historical, and social—explain why the ulama were predisposed to participation in the constitutional movement insofar as it represented a continuation of their traditional opposition to the state. The call for a constitution, however, went beyond the traditional denial of legitimacy to expound and demand

[12] *Ibid.*, p. 171.

a system of government preferable to the existing tyranny. It is important therefore to determine the degree of conscious and deliberate ulama involvement in this innovative call, and to distinguish it from various circumstantial pressures brought to bear on them.

Most important among these was the desire of reformers of secular and westernizing bent to present their plans of governmental change as sanctioned or even enjoined by Islam. Despite the frequent absence of substantial religious belief in these reformers, such a strategy was considered necessary because of the emotional loyalty of the mass of the people to Islam and the directive position occupied by the ulama. The facile and tactical identification of Europeanizing reform—including the establishment of constitutional government—with the essential dictates of religion was expounded primarily by Mīrzā Malkum Khān (1834–1908), a freethinker of Armenian origin who variously styled himself Muslim and Christian as occasion demanded.[13] His policy was followed by certain of the *anjumans* that were established to support the constitution.

Islamic law was pronounced to be identical with Western concepts of government, but only by way of assertion, never by proof: "*mashrū'īyat* and *mashrūṭīyat* are one and the same: government according to the law of Islam, justice and equality, or according to science and civilization."[14] Ulama who had accepted this equation might reasonably have expected, after the attainment of a constitution, that the *sharī'a* would be consistently implemented as the law of the state. Such expectations were disappointed, and a number of *mujtahids*, headed by Shaykh Faḍlullāh Nūrī, passed into active opposition to the constitution.[15]

There was, however, an important group among the ulama which remained uninterruptedly loyal to the constitutionalist cause until Muḥammad 'Alī Shāh's second coup d'etat in 1911, though not without certain reservations. Their persistence in support of the constitution is an important indication that ulama participation in the movement had not been the result simply of circumstantial pressure and confusion induced by secularist stratagems. From 1907 onward, the essential difference between constitution and *sharī'a* appears to have been generally recognized by both supporters and opponents of the constitution among the ulama. While Shaykh Faḍlullāh Nūrī and his followers deduced from this difference an

[13] For a detailed analysis of the life and thought of Malkum, see my forthcoming monograph on him.

[14] Quoted in Kirmānī, *op. cit.*, p. 214.

[15] See Kasravī, *op. cit.*, pp. 238, 287, 294; Mahdī Malikzāda, *Tārīkh-i Inqilāb-i Mashrūṭīyat-i Īrān* (Tehran, 1327 Sh/1948–1949), II, 29–31.

incompatibility of constitutionalism with Islam, other ulama—untouched by secularist influence—concluded that constitutional government was not only innocuous from the standpoint of religion, but indeed enjoined by it. It may be said that this view of the matter has established itself as the dominant one among the Iranian ulama, and continues to inform their political attitudes in contemporary Iran.

It was in particular three *mujtahids* resident in Najaf that lent powerful and determined support to the constitutionalist cause after the defection of Shaykh Faḍlullāh Nūrī: Mullā Muḥammad Kāẓim Khurāsānī, Mullā 'Abdullāh Māzandarānī, and Ḥājjī Mīrzā Ḥusayn Khalīlī Ṭihrānī. While Nūrī and his followers demanded that the Majlis act unequivocally to make the *sharī'a* the law of the state, the prevalent opinion in Najaf was that consistent implementation of the *sharī'a* was impossible during the continued occultation of the Imam, one of the signs of whose advent will, in fact, be the perfect application of the law. Pending his renewed manifestation, it was nonetheless deemed preferable to limit the oppressive acts engaged in by the inescapably usurpatory state. Such limitation was to be conveniently achieved by laws regulating the operation of the state and supervision of their enforcement by a consultative assembly. The question of whether the constitution was equivalent to the *sharī'a* was, then, misconceived and irrelevant to the true concerns of the ulama and the community under the conditions of the occultation.[16]

From this circle of constitutionalist ulama in Najaf emerged the most detailed and coherent justification of constitutional government from the standpoint of Shi'i Islam to have been composed up to the present. The work, entitled *Tanbīh al-Umma va Tanzīh al-Milla dar Asās va Uṣūl-i Mashrūṭīyat* (An Admonishment to the Nation and an Exposition to the People concerning the Foundations and Principles of Constitutional Government), by Shaykh Muḥammad Ḥusayn Nā'īnī (1860–1936), is a rare document of modern Shi'i political theory, one that seeks to reconcile continued awareness of the occultation of the Imam, together with the resultant impossibility of legitimacy, with the practical need for a form of government that does not grossly offend the dictates of religion. The book continues to be of relevance to relations between state and ulama in Iran, and has recently been reprinted with an introduction and notes by one of the most active opponents of the Shah's regime among the ulama, Āyatullāh Sayyid Maḥmūd Ṭāliqānī.[17]

[16] Kasravī, *op. cit.*, p. 286.
[17] Ṭāliqānī's edition of the work was published in Tehran in 1955.

Nā'īnī begins his treatise with a definition of the fundamental duties of the state, external and internal, and proclaims that the only power to which the state is entitled is that needed for the fulfillment of these duties. When rulers pervert government for selfish purposes and establish a tyrannical and absolute power, they are deviating from a God-given norm. The head of such a perverted government tends to usurp the divine attributes, and the most extreme form of tyranny consists in the explicit deification of the ruler, as was the case with the Pharaohs. The mission of the Prophet Moses, as of all the messengers of God, was to destroy the *shirk* engendered by tyranny and establish the limits of human rule, exercised as a divine trust.

The perversion of the state into tyranny is best avoided by the *'iṣmat* of the ruler, that is, by his freedom from sin and error and unfailing inclination to do the will of God. In the absence of the Imam, some other means must be found. These are essentially two: a constitution defining the rights and duties of the state and its subjects; and an assembly of "the intelligent and wise ones of the land and the well-wishers of the people" to supervise enactment of the constitution and watch over the workings of the state. The constitution must contain no provisions contrary to Islam; and the assembly, to secure its religious permissibility, must include among its members "a number of just *mujtahid*s or of those delegated by them, who amend, approve, and agree to the decisions taken by it." The assembly as a legislative body should concern itself with *'urfīyāt*, that is, matters pertaining to spatially and temporally determined circumstances of no interest to, and therefore not legislated by, the *sharī'a*. The presence of *mujtahid*s in the Majlis would ensure the religious innocuity of all legislation enacted concerning these matters.

This prevention of absolutism, through the establishment of a constitution and a popular assembly, is a religious duty despite the occultation of the Imam and the concomitant withdrawal of legitimacy from the earthly plane. The duty of "enjoining the good and forbidding the evil" remains with the community at all times, and the impossibility of its perfect fulfillment does not release the believers from the obligation to strive to perform it as fully as possible. Manifestations of evil should always be combatted, and the political conclusion to be drawn from this is the necessity of a constitution. The unfettered rule of a tyrant is productive of limitless evil, while to restrict the powers of a ruler through the institution of laws and the exercise of supervision by a popular assembly will result in a restriction of the evil that flows from his rule. Unrestricted tyranny is a usurpation of the attributes of God, as well as a false claim to the right to rule. It moreover robs its subjects of their God-given liberty and is therefore triply reprehensible. Constitutionally limited rule, by contrast, does not offend God by unlawfully holding absolute power, nor does it usurp men's freedom; it stands as usurper only with respect to the Imam and is therefore to be preferred.

This theme of reducing the illegitimacy of the state to the minimum that is inevitable under the conditions of occultation is illustrated by Nā'īnī with a number of analogies, one of them related in the framework of a dream and emanating from the Hidden Imam himself.

After expounding the central theme of constitutionalism, its religious sanction, and the total illegitimacy of tyranny, Nā'īnī adduces additional arguments drawn from the circumstances of the day, above all the alliance of the incumbent tyrant, Muḥammad 'Alī Shāh, with the infidel power of Russia, and proceeds to refute various objections raised by the enemies of the constitution among the ulama. Despite certain weaknesses, Nā'īnī's discussion of the constitutional principle is a valuable document that has not been done full justice by the above summary.[18] It permits greater understanding of the role played by an important segment of the ulama in the Constitutional Revolution, and is indicative of the manner in which, later in the twentieth century, the ulama have been able to appeal to the Qur'an and the constitution as twin sources of authority.

Muḥammad 'Alī Shāh's attempts at reimposing absolute rule on Iran were militarily defeated, but the years following his abdication brought frustration for the constitutional movement. The Majlis was dissolved in December 1911 and not reconvened until November 1914. World War I saw the progressive emigration of many supporters of the constitution to Istanbul and beyond, and all semblance of independent political life was at an end. When the Qajar dynasty was overthrown and Riḍā Shāh recreated an autonomous Iranian state, constitutionalism was not a guiding ideal, and the Majlis had an almost exclusively decorative function. Among the few opponents of Riḍā Shāh in the Majlis before his assumption of absolute power should be mentioned one member of the ulama, Āyatullāh Mudarris.[19] After Mudarris had been removed from the scene, the political activity of the ulama was restricted to intermittent protest against Riḍā Shāh's autocratic imposition of repugnant measures of

[18] A more complete account of the work will be given in the fuller version of this paper.

[19] See Ḥusayn Makkī, *Tārīkh-i Bīstsāla-yi Īrān* (Tehran, 1324–1326 Sh/1945–1947), II, 191; and Yaḥyā Daulatābādī, *Tārīkh-i Mu'āṣir yā Ḥayāt-i Yaḥyā* (Tehran, n.d.), IV, 288.

change, and to such protest the response was violation of the shrines at Qum (in 1928) and Mashhad (in 1935).

It is not until the succession to the throne of the present Shah and the beginning of the postwar period that we find the interest of the ulama in political activity reawakening. The Majlis displayed signs of life and a certain freedom of expression and controversy sprang up, of which a segment of the ulama made use.

The political activities of the ulama in the period that ended with the royalist coup d'etat of Murdād 28, 1332/August 19, 1953, are associated primarily with the name of Āyatullāh Abūl Qāsim Kāshānī, a figure of much disputed character. Born in the late nineteenth century, he was taken to Najaf by his father at an early age, and spent the first part of his life in Iraq. He studied under two of the great constitutionalist *mujtahids* of Najaf, Muḥammad Kāẓim Khurāsānī and Mīrzā Ḥusayn Khalīlī Ṭihrānī, eventually coming to act as secretary of the former. In 1919 Kāshānī was sentenced to death in absentia by the British for opposing the mandate in Iraq, but escaping he took refuge in Iran. Throughout the reign of Riḍā Shāh he abstained from political activity, but in June 1942, after the Anglo-Russian invasion of Iran, he was arrested by the British for alleged contacts with German agents, and he spent the rest of the war years in exile.[20]

His postwar political career began in 1948 when he organized demonstrations against the erection of a Jewish state in Palestine, collected financial aid for the Arab cause, and attempted even to provide for the dispatch of volunteers to Palestine. With the beginning of the campaign for the nationalization of the oil industry, Kāshānī's importance increased as he came to be one of the most prominent organizers of mass support for Dr. Muḥammad Muṣaddiq's National Front. In the Majlis, he had a number of representatives, forming a group known as the Mujāhidīn-i Islām under the leadership of Shams Qanātābādī, while outside he temporarily cooperated with the celebrated activist organization, the Fidā'īyān-i Islām.

Kāshānī's proclamations issued in 1951 and 1952 express the same duality of concern that the constitutionalist movement had inherited from the ulama of the nineteenth century: opposition to absolutism (thought to be manifested in certain proposed modifications of the constitution) and to foreign domination (represented by the Anglo-Iranian Oil Company).

[20] Āghā Buzurg at-Ṭihrānī, *Ṭabaqāt A'lām ash-Shī'a* (Najaf, 1375 Q/1956), I:1, 75–76; L. P. Elwell-Sutton, *Persian Oil: A Study in Power Politics* (London, 1955), pp. 195–196.

In his protests against these targets Kāshānī appealed to both the *sharī'a* and the constitution as sources of authority.[21]

In 1953, Kāshānī's relations with Muṣaddiq deteriorated, probably because of his attempts to subvert government authority with the writing of letters of recommendation to various ministries on behalf of his followers. These Muṣaddiq refused to honor. When the royalist coup d'etat occurred in August 1953, Kāshānī lent it his support and thus avenged himself. It should, however, be said that personal motives alone were not decisive in this transference of loyalties: many ulama had been alarmed by the militant irreligiosity that had increasingly shown itself during the last days of Muṣaddiq's rule. After August 1953, Kāshānī receded into the background of Iranian life, and his death in 1962 was largely unnoticed.[22]

Kāshānī was politically the most active of the ulama of his day, but was surpassed in learning and piety—the prerequisites for clerical eminence—by the late Āyatullāh Sayyid Āqā Ḥusayn Burūjirdī, who by the time of his death in 1961 was the sole *marja'-i taqlīd* of the Shi'i world.

Burūjirdī was a descendant of Sayyid Muḥammad Baḥr al-'Ulūm, one of the most prominent *mujtahid*s of the early nineteenth century, and came of a family traditionally celebrated for religious learning. Born in Burujird, a small town near Arak in western Iran, in 1292 Q/1875, Burūjirdī studied first in Isfahan and then in Najaf, under Shaykh Muḥammad Kāẓim Khurāsānī and Shaykh ash-Sharī'a Iṣfahānī. After seven years in Najaf during which he acquired an unparalleled knowledge of *fiqh* and *ḥadīth*, he returned to his birthplace in 1327 Q/1909, staying there with brief interruptions for a period of thirty-seven years. Throughout this long residence in Burujird, a relatively unimportant town, he contented himself with the further study of *ḥadīth* and teaching at the local madrasa. This lack of worldly ambition which characterized his career had quietism as its political expression.

In 1364 Q/1945, Burūjirdī came to Tehran for medical treatment, and instead of returning to Burujird he was prevailed upon to take up residence in Qum. The most prominent teacher among the ulama of the city, Shaykh 'Abd al-Karīm Ḥā'irī Yazdī, had recently died, and shortly after-

[21] See his letters to Dr. Muṣaddiq quoted in the collection of Muṣaddiq's speeches, *Nuṭqhā-yi Duktur Muṣaddiq dar Daura-yi Shānzdahum-i Majlis-i Shaurā-yi Millī* (New York [?], n.d.), pp. 35, 50, 91.

[22] On Kāshānī's relations with Muṣaddiq see R. W. Cottam, *Nationalism in Iran* (Pittsburgh, 1964), pp. 152–156.

ward he was followed by the chief *marja'-i taqlīd,* Sayyid Abūl Ḥasan Iṣfahānī, also resident in Qum. A dual vacuum thus arose which Burūjirdī came to fill. In the course of two years, he emerged as sole *marja'*, gathering to him the following of a number of *mujtahids*, most of them living in Najaf, who had also functioned as sources of guidance.[23]

The position of sole *marja'* had first been attained in the 1860s by Shaykh Murtaḍā Anṣārī,[24] and a certain parallel may be drawn between the careers of the two men. Both were lacking in worldly ambition, and both were averse to making political use of the obedient following they commanded as sole *marja'*. Yet both prepared the way for other *mujtahids* who convincingly demonstrated the political power inherent in the institution of *taqlīd*. After an interval, Anṣārī was succeeded as sole *marja'* by Mīrzā Ḥasan Shīrāzī whose *fatvā* was the primary factor in bringing the celebrated tobacco boycott of 1891–1892 to a successful conclusion.[25] No single successor emerged to Burūjirdī, but his religious and educational achievements in Qum made of that city a vital center of spiritual direction and thereby laid the foundations for its political role in the 1960s. The exercise of that role has been associated with Āyatullāh Khumaynī, the most eminent representative of the religious opposition to the present regime in Iran.

Several achievements of Burūjirdī deserve specific mention. In the field of *ḥadīth,* he is remarkable for having revived the practice of independent investigation, and for instigating a critical revision of the fundamental work, *Wasā'il ash-Shī'a ilā Taḥqīq Masā'il ash-Sharī'a* by Muḥammad b. Ḥasan al-Ḥurr al-'Āmulī (d. 1688). He displayed a lively concern for a Sunni-Shi'i *rapprochement*—a concern perpetuated by Khumaynī—and to this end he corresponded and cooperated with successive rectors of the Azhar. He also dispatched emissaries to Europe to work among Iranians resident abroad and propagate Shi'i Islam among interested Europeans. Possibly most important was his organization of the affairs of the *marja'* on a more efficient basis: bookkeeping was introduced to record the sums of money received and dispensed as *sahm-i imām,* and a register was established of local agents authorized to collect money and forward it to Qum. This network of communication, set up by Burūjirdī, has survived his

[23] Biographical information drawn from aṭ-Ṭihrānī, *op. cit.*, II:1, 605–609.

[24] See concerning Shaykh Murtaḍā Anṣārī, Algar, *op. cit.*, pp. 162–165, and aṭ-Ṭihrānī, *op. cit.*, III, 429.

[25] See N. R. Keddie, *Religion and Rebellion in Iran: The Tobacco Protest of 1891–1892* (London, 1966).

death and serves to disseminate guidance in political as well as narrowly religious matters.[26]

After his coup d'etat of August 1953, the present Shah has intermittently attempted to cultivate something of an Islamic exterior for himself and his regime, although such efforts have notably declined in recent years. This is done in part by much publicized visits to shrines within Iran—particularly Mashhad—and in part by the patronage of a small group of ulama, headed by Āyatullāh Bihbihānī and Dr. Ḥasan Imāmī, the *imām jum'a* of Tehran, who do not shun association with the state. The elements of this policy are familiar from the Qajar period, when similar attempts were made to lessen the inherent illegitimacy of the state by assuming attitudes of piety. It has, however, always been doomed to failure. Its fruitlessness has been particularly apparent during the last decade in Iran, for there has taken place a remarkable resurgence in the role of the ulama as leaders of popular opposition to the regime.

We have noted the support accorded by Kāshānī to the royalist coup d'etat, and the quietism practiced by Āyatullāh Burūjirdī. The first few years after 1953 also witnessed no significant ulama hostility to the regime. It was widely felt that in the last days of Muṣaddiq's regime a genuine communist threat had existed, which was averted by the Shah's return. Burūjirdī, in his capacity of sole *marja'*, communicated an attitude of quietism to his vast following, and indeed on occasion went beyond such neutrality to certain demonstrations of friendliness to the regime: royal visits to his residence were not repelled.[27]

On the death of Burūjirdī, the Shah sent a telegram of commiseration to Āyatullāh Shaykh Muḥsin al-Ḥakīm, an Arab *mujtahid* resident in Najaf, thereby intimating the desirability of his succession to Burūjirdī as sole *marja'*. Doubtless it was hoped to lessen the importance of Qum and prevent the emergence of a center of clerical power within Iran. A *mujtahid* resident in Najaf—one moreover of Arab birth—might be thought unlikely to be intimately aware of and concerned with the affairs of Iran. The process whereby *mujtahids* emerge as *marja'* is, however, for all its

26 Concerning these achievements, see Murtaḍā Muṭahharī, "Mazāyā va Khadamāt-i Marḥūm Āyatullāh Burūjirdī," printed at the end of the collective work entitled *Baḥthī dar bāra-yi Marja'īyat va Rūḥānīyat* (2d ed., Tehran, n.d.), pp. 233–249.

27 Certain opponents of the regime hold that the significance of these contacts between Burūjirdī and the Shah has been exaggerated, since the late Āyatullāh toward the end of his life had many of his faculties impaired and was imperfectly informed of the political realities around him.

informality, one that excludes appointment by the state, and by the time of his death on June 1, 1970, Āyatullāh Ḥakīm had been able to gather only a limited following within Iran.

It is rather three Iranian *mujtahids* that have emerged as joint heirs to Burūjirdī's position: Āyatullāh Rūḥullāh Khumaynī, now in exile in Najaf, Āyatullāh Muḥammad Hādī Mīlānī, resident in Mashhad, and an Azerbayjani, Āyatullāh Kāẓim Sharī'atmadārī of Qum.[28] Of the three, Khumaynī is the most important and influential, and it is primarily with his name that the latest exercise of the traditional political role of the ulama—opposition to absolutism and foreign domination—is associated. Little is known of his early life. He was born in 1320 Q/1902–1903 into a traditionally religious family. He studied the religious sciences in Qum, chiefly under Shaykh 'Abd al-Karīm Ḥā'irī Yazdī, and though not a prolific writer has written a work in Arabic entitled *Sirr as-Ṣalāt* (The Inner Significance of Prayer).[29] His fame and popularity rest, however, not so much upon his learning—in which Sharī'atmadārī and others are acknowledged to excel him—as upon his forthright and uncompromising hostility to the Shah's regime.

This hostility began to be openly expressed in 1963, when the autocracy of the regime reached a point many of the religious classes, in common with other segments of society, found intolerable. Khumaynī began preaching against the Shah's rule from the pulpit of the Fayḍīya madrasa in Qum. He is related on one occasion to have taken a copy of the Qur'an in one hand, and of the constitution in the other, and accused the Shah of violating his oath to defend Islam and the constitution. On Shavvāl 25, 1382 Q/March 22, 1963, the madrasa was attacked by paratroopers and members of the security police; a number of students were killed and Khumaynī was arrested.

The day chosen for the attack was the anniversary of the martyrdom of the sixth Imam, Ja'far aṣ-Ṣādiq, and the effect of such timing could only

[28] There are a number of other *mujtahids* each of whom has a certain following relying on his guidance, such as Āyatullāh Shāhrūdī and Āyatullāh Khū'ī of Najaf, and Āyatullāh Khūnsārī of Tehran. Burūjirdī may well have been the last *mujtahid* to hold the position of sole *marja'*. Soon after his death, the institution of *marja'* was reconsidered by a number of Shi'i thinkers, some of whom concluded that a collective *marja'* was more appropriate to the needs of the age than an individual one. See *Baḥthī dar bāra-yi Rūḥānīyat va Marja'īyat*; and an analysis of its contents by A. K. S. Lambton, "A Reconsideration of the Position of the *Marja' Al-Taqlīd* and the Religious Institution," *Studia Islamica*, XX (1964), 115–135.

[29] aṭ-Ṭihrānī, *op. cit.*, I:2, 759.

have been to identify the regime with persecutors of the Imams. Such identification became infinitely clearer and stronger two and a half months later, when the drama of Muḥarram was played out not simply in the *ta'zīya* but in the streets of Tehran and other Iranian cities.

Between Shavvāl and Muḥarrām, March and June, Khumaynī, released after a temporary detention, resumed his denunciation of the government and its policies. It was later officially asserted that his agitation was directed against the government's program of land reform and its plan to enfranchise women. These assertions, which received almost universal credence in the world press,[30] do not stand the test of scrutiny. Khumaynī explicitly denies harboring any objection to the principle of land reform and has himself no holdings in Iran which might be endangered by its application. Sharī'atmadārī and Mīlānī, both associated with the events of June 1963, have similarly disclaimed opposition to land reform.[31] The regime has failed to produce *fatvās* delivered by any of the three *mujtahids* condemning land reform: all that can be pointed to is a statement by Burūjirdī delivered in 1960, denouncing the limitation of the size of land holdings as contrary to religious law.[32] As for female enfranchisement, the issue would seem to be an artificial one until Iranian elections have more substantial content and effect.

The real targets of Khumaynī's criticism of the regime in 1963 appear to have been the following: autocratic rule and violation of the constitution; the proposal to grant capitulatory rights to American advisors and military personnel in Iran and their dependents; the contracting of a $200 million loan from the United States for the purchase of military equipment; and the maintenance of diplomatic, commercial, and other relations with Israel, a state hostile to the Muslims and Islam.

These criticisms were made in a number of declarations couched in forthright language. In one such declaration, the agreement granting capitulatory rights to American personnel was termed "a document for the enslavement of Iran." Henceforth no one would be safe from the arbitrary behavior of Americans in the country. That matters have come to such a pass is the result of the existing tyranny. "If the ulama say that the

30 *Izvestiya* (Moscow), June 6, 1963, found itself in agreement with the Shah's regime on the definition of a reactionary.

31 See statement by Sharī'atmadārī to *Le Monde* (Paris), June 12, 1963.

32 Professor Lambton, in her *Persian Land Reform, 1962–1966* (Oxford, 1969), p. 112, concedes that Khumaynī did not attack the Shah "on grounds of land reform," but claims that "many of the religious classes continued to have reservations [against land reform]." No supporting evidence is offered.

power of the bayonet must cease interfering with the destinies of the country . . . and that this Muslim nation must no longer be robbed of its freedom, it is so that disgrace such as this no longer be visited upon us." Since the Majlis is not popularly elected, its vote is "illegitimate and contrary to the Qur'an."[33]

The declaration then proceeds to denounce America as an enemy of Islam in all its policies, this hostility being particularly apparent in its limitless support for Israel and the nature and extent of its influence in Iran. Khumaynī concludes with what is in effect a call for a popular uprising to overthrow the regime. "The Iranian army must not permit such scandalous events to happen in Iran. . . . *It must cause this government to fall* [emphasis supplied]. . . . The people must demand of the ulama that they not remain silent on this matter; and the ulama in turn must demand of the *marāji'* that they do not overlook it. . . . The Muslim people must demand of its preachers that they inform all those who are unaware of this great disaster; the preachers must firmly and fearlessly protest against this disgrace and awaken the people."

On Khurdād 13, 1342 Sh/June 3, 1963, two policemen in plain clothes were attempting to remove a copy of one of Khumaynī's proclamations from a wall adjacent to the entrance to Gauhar Shād mosque in Mashhad when they were surrounded by a hostile crowd. Since they persisted in their undertaking, an onlooker rushed forward and stabbed one of them to death.[34] On the same day, Khumaynī made a particularly violent attack on the Shah in a speech delivered in Qum. He began by affirming that "the constitution has been bought with the blood of our fathers, and we will not permit it to be violated. Our sole demand is the execution of law." He then replied to a reported denunciation of the ulama by the Shah as parasites: "Am I a parasite, and men like me such as Burūjirdī, who was sixty thousand tumans in debt when he died, or these students who survive on a stipend of thirty tumans a month? Or are you, O Shah, the parasite, who have erected towering palaces and filled foreign banks with your untold wealth?"[35]

[33] Quotations from this and other pronouncements of Khumaynī are taken directly from copies of his declarations.

[34] *Iṭṭilā'āt* (Tehran), Khurdād 14, 1342/ June 4, 1963.

[35] Quoted from an anonymous pamphlet, *Rūḥānīyat va 15 Khurdād*, published in 1349 Sh/1970 by the Confederation of Iranian Muslim Students in the United States and Canada. This booklet, fifty-seven pages in length, contains the fullest account available of the events of June 1963, and reproduces numerous declarations by Khumaynī.

These developments in Mashhad and Qum brought events to a climax. The following day, which was the tenth of Muḥarram and thus the anniversary of the martyrdom of the Imam Ḥusayn, Āyatullāh Khumaynī was arrested shortly before dawn by a detachment of security officers, hastily transported to Tehran, and immediately sent into exile in Turkey. When news of his arrest became known in the capital, the *ta'zīya* processions being held that day naturally and inevitably turned into antigovernment demonstrations. Clashes took place with police and troops in the Tūpkhāna square and the vicinity of the bazaar. The disturbances continued with added intensity on the following day, spreading to the university, while simultaneously outbreaks were reported from Shiraz, Varamin, Kashan, and Mashhad. June 7 was a Friday, and congregational mosques in the capital, especially the Masjid-i Shāh on the edge of the bazaar, were surrounded by tanks and heavy detachments of troops, to prevent worshippers from gathering for fear that a renewal of the rioting might occur.[36] The uprising continued however with undiminished force: on the same day a pamphlet was issued in Tehran calling for *jihād* against the Shah's regime and on June 8 a similar summons appeared in Qum.[37] A number of demonstrators were observed to be wearing shrouds as a sign of their positive response to the call. As early as June 5, orders had been given to the police, army, and security forces to shoot to kill,[38] but it was not until six days later that the disturbances had been finally repressed, with extremely heavy loss of life.

The role of the ulama in the episode was striking. Not only was the arrest of Khumaynī the immediate cause of the disturbances in Tehran, but in the provinces too—above all in Qum and Shiraz—leading ulama conducted demonstrations and were arrested. The slogans shouted by demonstrators expressed loyalty to Khumaynī and attacked the same targets of criticism that had been emphasized in his declarations.

Faced with this conjunction of religious leadership and popular discontent, the government accused the ulama of gross misuse of their religious influence and collusion with sundry elements whose interests they sought to serve: the landowning classes, tribal rebels in Fars, and a foreign government left unnamed but strongly hinted to be the United Arab Republic.[39] This foreign state had allegedly supplied Khumaynī with

36 *al-Ahrām* (Cairo), June 8, 1963.

37 *Iṭṭilā'āt*, Khurdād 19, 1342/June 9, 1963.

38 *Kayhan International* (Tehran), June 5, 1963.

39 *Iṭṭilā'āt*, Khurdād 16, 1342/June 6, 1963.

large sums of money to foment an uprising, and the Shah claimed in a speech delivered at Hamadan on June 8 that the demonstrators had received twenty-five rials per head to rebel against the government—a modest fee for risking one's life against overwhelming odds.[40] The charge was never substantiated.

Prime Minister 'Alam spoke of an "antiprogressive conspiracy," and later the term "black reaction" came to be the officially approved designation for Khumaynī and his followers. The imputation to Khumaynī of enmity to land reform and female enfranchisement is, we have already remarked, unconvincing: his declarations issued before the events of June 5 to June 11 mention entirely different matters as cogent reasons for opposition to the regime. Since going into exile in June 1963, Khumaynī has, moreover, by no means remained silent or inactive, and the motives for his opposition to the Shah's regime may be further clarified by an examination of his declarations and pronouncements in exile.

Khumaynī's initial place of banishment was Turkey, where he spent about a year, first in Ankara and then in Bursa, under close surveillance and in the company of an agent from the Iranian security police. In October 1965 Khumaynī was permitted to leave Turkey for Iraq, a clearly preferable place of exile, for the shrine cities furnish a suitable sphere of religious activity and contain many Iranian residents. Pilgrims coming from Iran to visit the shrines moreover provide a means of communication with Iran. On arriving in Iraq, Khumaynī visited each of the shrine cities in turn, going to Samarra, Kaẓimayn, and Karbala. He then settled in Najaf, his present place of residence, and with his arrival there, Najaf resumed the role of inviolable center of opposition to autocratic rule in Iran that it had played in the period of the Constitutional Revolution.

Khumaynī delivered his first public address since leaving Iran at the Shaykh Anṣārī mosque in Najaf on Rajab 20, 1385 Q/November 14, 1965. His *khuṭba* was general in scope and did not refer specifically to Iran. He began by asserting the supreme relevance of Islam to political and social life. "Islam has a system and a program for all the different affairs of society: the form of government and administration, the regulation of people's dealings with each other, the relations of state and people, relations with foreign states and all other political and economic matters. . . . The mosque has always been a center of leadership and command, of

[40] *Kayhan International*, June 9, 1963. This pecuniary line of argument may well have been suggested to the Shah by the circumstances of his own return to power in August 1953.

examination and analysis of social problems." He then called for Islamic unity and cooperation in the solution of such problems as those of Palestine and Kashmir, and in conclusion urged the ulama of the entire Muslim world to turn their attention more effectively to political matters.[41]

In April 1967, Khumaynī again addressed himself to the affairs of Iran, this time in an open letter to the prime minister, Huvaydā. The letter is written in a powerful and assured tone. "Throughout this long period in which I have been exiled for the crime of opposing the legal immunity of the Americans—something that strikes at the very roots of our independence—and have been banished from Iran in a manner contrary both to the *sharī'a* and the constitution, I have been observing the disasters that descend upon our oppressed and defenceless people." There follows a comprehensive critique of the state of the country, in which are repeated the essential points of the declarations issued by Khumaynī before June 1963. The letter contains, however, no mention of land reform or female enfranchisement, beyond a passing reference to the entire reform program as fraudulent.

The extent to which this and similar documents have been circulated in Iran since the exiling of Khumaynī is of course uncertain, nor can the degree of their influence be reliably estimated. While there has been no repetition of the events of June 1963, it nonetheless seems certain that there is a persistent current of religiously inspired and led opposition to the regime which is sustained by continued allegiance to the figure of Āyatullāh Khumaynī. The existence of this opposition, which obstinately disturbs the Shah's assiduously cultivated image of contented stability, became apparent once again in a series of events in the summer of 1970.

In May 1970, a consortium of thirty-five American investors met in Tehran to discuss further investment in the Iranian market. The fields under consideration for investment were extensive—industry, agriculture, mines, tourism, and the distribution of consumer goods. Hostile reactions were aroused in certain quarters by the meeting, and among the most important protests against further American penetration of the economy was one formulated by a Tehran *mujtahid*, Āyatullāh Sayyid Muḥammad Riḍā Sa'īdī. In a declaration circulated among the ulama of the capital, he denounced the expansion of American investment as "a catastrophe and an annihilating blow for the people of Iran." The regime that had

[41] See the document entitled *Jarayān-i Mashrūḥ-i Tauqīf va Tab'īd-i Haḍrat Āyatullāh Khumaynī az Zabān-i Farzand-i Īshān* drawn up by his son, Sayyid Muṣṭafā Khumaynī.

invited the investors to Tehran was "a tyrannical agent of imperialism." It was the duty of the ulama to imitate their forebears like Mīrzā Ḥasan Shīrāzī by rising up in protest against the usurpation of the economic resources of the country.[42]

This proclamation soon led to the arrest of Sa'īdī by the security police. He is reliably reported to have been tortured to death in Qizil Qal'a jail, and hastily buried in an unmarked grave in Qum.[43] News of his death quickly spread, and there took place in Qum a demonstration attended by about a thousand students from the madrasas of the city. Commemorative ceremonies due to be held in a number of Tehran mosques were banned. At the Ghiyāthī mosque where Sa'īdī had functioned as *imām*, a large crowd nonetheless gathered to honor his memory, and was addressed by Āyatullāh Sayyid Maḥmūd Ṭāliqānī, a prominent *mujtahid*, and Dr. 'Abbās Shaybānī, both members of the "Freedom Movement," concerning which something is said below. The two men were arrested by the security police. Ṭāliqānī was released a week later, but Shaybānī condemned by a closed military court, on October 18, 1970, to fifteen years' imprisonment.[44]

In reply to a letter from the religious scholars and students of Qum, offering their sympathies on the death of Sa'īdī, Khumaynī denounced the financiers' conference in terms reminiscent of those which had been used a century before in condemnation of the Reuter Concession. The alienation of all the resources of the country was to be feared if matters continued on their course. "Any agreement that is concluded with the American capitalists and other imperialists is contrary to the will of the people and the ordinances of Islam. Since the members of the Majlis are not elected by the people, their decisions are illegal and contrary to the constitution and the will of the people."[45]

At the same time that open hostility between ulama and state thus

[42] The full text of Sa'īdī's declaration is given in *Khabarnāma*, organ of the National Front in America, Mihr, 1349/Oct., 1970, pp. 2–4.

[43] Sa'īdī was tortured by the gradual crushing of his skull, and the introduction of boiling water into his intestines. A student at Tehran Polytechnic, Nīkdā'ūdī, who had also protested against the investors' conference, was tortured to death at the same time. See the report dated November 2, 1970, by Dr. Hans Heldmann, professor of criminology at Frankfurt University, concerning a journey to Iran undertaken in behalf of Amnesty International.

[44] On these events see *Khabarnāma*, Shahrīvar, 1349/ Sept., 1970; and declaration by Freedom Movement in Exile, dated November 1, 1970. The latter reproduces the text of the indictment against Dr. Shaybānī.

[45] *Khabarnāma*, Shahrīvar, 1349/ Sept., 1970.

reemerged, the Shah's favored *mujtahid* for the position of *marja'*, Shaykh Muḥsin al-Ḥakīm, died in Najaf. The question of *marja'īyat* again came to the fore, and with it too the influence and standing of Khumaynī in Iran once more became apparent. In accordance with precedent, the Shah sought, through messages of commiseration, to influence the choice of a new *marja'*, who might not only succeed to the somewhat restricted following of the late al-Ḥakīm but also eclipse Khumaynī. To this end he sent telegrams to Sharī'atmadārī in Qum and Āyatullāh Khūnsārī in Tehran. Khūnsārī sent a polite but reserved answer, while Sharī'atmadārī responded in an effusive and loyalistic tone that earned him widespread disapproval.[46] Demonstrations took place in Qum in front of his residence, with the participants reproaching him for abandoning the hostility he had shown to the regime in June 1963, and reaffirming their loyalty to Khumaynī as *marja'*. A telegram was sent by forty-eight ulama of the city to Khumaynī, offering their condolences on the death of al-Ḥakīm and pledging him their continued allegiance. A number of the signatories, as well as some of those who had demonstrated against Sharī'atmadārī, were arrested and banished to Zabul. Similar incidents took place in Tehran, where Āyatullāh Marvārīd spoke at the mosque of Ḥājj 'Azīzullāh concerning the qualifications of Khumaynī as *marja'*, and in Shiraz, where a meeting at the Masjid-i Vakīl was dispersed by troops.[47]

After these events of June 1970, there have been other manifestations of discontent and opposition in Iran which have furnished further evidence of Khumaynī's influence. Among the slogans raised during the strike at Tehran University in December 1970 was the cry "Long live Khumaynī!"[48]

It seems reasonable to connect with the continuing problem posed to the regime by the figure of Khumaynī certain remarks made by the Shah concerning the possible creation of a Sipāh-i Dīn, a Religion Corps. In the course of a lengthy and wide-ranging press conference held in January 1971, he said the following: "It is not improbable that we may create a Religion Corps in the future, so that if some of the students of the religious sciences have to perform their military service, they can do it [within the framework of this corps]. We should prefer to send them to such a corps, if we formed it. Because just as we say that religion must be separated from politics (and a few years ago we saw the results of mixing the two) and just as we are insistent in that respect . . . so too we encourage

[46] Report in *The Times* (London), June 24, 1970.

[47] *Khabarnāma*, Shahrivar, 1349/Sept., 1970.

[48] *Le Monde*, Dec. 20, 1970.

the people to piety and religion. No society has true stability without religion. . . ."[49]

A twofold purpose for the proposed Sipāh-i Dīn may be deduced from these somewhat confused statements. First, enlistment into the corps might serve as a punitive measure directed against clerical opponents of the regime, and as a cover for banishing them from their areas of activity and support. Recently a number of religious students arrested for their part in demonstrations have been punitively drafted into the army.[50] Particularly indicative in this respect is the Shah's reference to those "students of the religious sciences [that] *have to* perform their military service."

Second, the corps is probably conceived of as a means for extending the influence of the state into the heart of the countryside—parallel to the Literacy Corps—and for propagating a notion of Islam innocuous to the regime. The influence of men such as Khumaynī is to be uprooted, and religion confined to the narrow sphere of worship, ritual, and private morality, with the state's omnicompetence in the political realm undisputed.[51]

An indirect response to these remarks of the Shah is contained in a declaration by Āyatullāh Khumaynī circulated among the pilgrims at Mecca in Dhūl Ḥijja 1390/February 1971. He complains that "the poisonous culture of imperialism is penetrating to the depths of towns and villages throughout the Muslim world, displacing the culture of the Qur'an." Iran is under the domination of America, the enemy of Islam. "Invoking Islam and pretending to be Muslims, they [the regime] strive to annihilate Islam, and they abolish and obliterate the sacred commands of the Qur'an one after the other." Khumaynī concludes his condemnation of the regime with a bitter attack on the forthcoming celebration of the two thousand five hundredth anniversary of monarchy in Iran, as "a means of extortion and plunder for the agents of imperialism. . . . Anyone who organizes or participates in these festivals is a traitor to Islam and the Iranian nation."[52]

Whatever outcome may be predicted for this contest between religious

[49] *Iṭṭilā'āt-i Ḥavā'ī*, no. 7358, Bahman 5, 1349/Jan. 25, 1971.

[50] *Khabarnāma*, Mihr, 1349/Oct., 1970, p. 5.

[51] It might be noticed in passing that the Shah's insistence on total separation of religion and state is contrary to that article of the Iranian constitution which states that Ithnā'asharī Shi'i Islam is the religion of the state.

[52] This declaration was printed in Najaf. It is reported that some of those engaged in its distribution in Mecca were arrested by the Saudi government and delivered to the Iranian authorities.

and royal authority, it is certain that the issue is by no means settled, and that the Shah's desire to abolish religious comment on affairs of state is liable to continuing frustration. It has been said that since the events of 1963 the regime has been able extensively to undercut the opposition of the ulama to its policies.[53] Insofar as there has been no repetition of massive urban violence, this estimate appears to be true. Yet given the repressive nature of the political climate in Iran, it is impossible to judge with any accuracy the extent of Khumaynī's following, and of persistent religious opposition to the regime. The evidence cited above suggests that both are still considerable. It should moreover be remarked that in the view of certain elements in the religious opposition the time for massive demonstrations has passed, and attention should be turned instead to quiet preparation for guerilla warfare and isolated, small-scale uprisings. This view of affairs motivated the group known as the Ḥizb-i Milal-i Islāmī (Islamic Nations Party), led by Muḥammad Kāẓim Bujnurdī, which was broken up by the security police in 1965. Bujnurdī's father is a *mujtahid* in Najaf, and a follower and supporter of Khumaynī.[54]

It is furthermore certain that Khumaynī is highly regarded not only by those who owe him loyalty as *marja'*, but also by secular and even leftist segments of the opposition. After the ambiguities of Kāshānī and the quietism of Burūjirdī, the clear stance of Khumaynī and his followers has been able to win the confidence of many intellectuals in the ulama as a popular and even revolutionary force. The statement of Āyatullāh Mīlānī that in June 1963 "the clergy emerged from its corner of silence and stagnation to join the moving ranks of society" is often quoted with approval.[55] The ability of the ulama to organize the urban and rural masses for political action is clearly recognized, and positive mention of Khumaynī is a frequent feature of the leftist press in exile.

There has been operating within Iran a group the special concern of which is to create and maintain links between the ulama and other elements opposed to the regime. This is the Nihḍat-i Āzādī, or Freedom Movement, one of the constituent groups of the National Front, founded in 1961 with the good wishes of Dr. Muṣaddiq. The leading figures of the movement are two religiously inclined laymen, Muhandis Mahdī Bāzargān, a prolific

[53] See Nikki R. Keddie, "The Iranian Power Structure and Social Change, 1800–1969: An Overview," *International Journal of Middle East Studies*, II (1971), 17.

[54] This should not be taken to imply that Bujnurdī's group acted under the direction, or even with the support, of Khumaynī.

[55] *Īrān-i Āzād*, organ of the National Front in Europe, II:33 (Khurdād, 1344/June, 1966), 6.

and skillful writer on religious themes, and Dr. Yadullāh Saḥābī, both formerly professors at Tehran University, and one representative of the ulama, Āyatullāh Sayyid Maḥmūd Ṭāliqānī. All three of them—in particular Ṭāliqānī—have been subjected to repeated and prolonged imprisonment. Its support appears to be drawn largely from university students, both at home and abroad, and from the younger ulama, especially in Qum.[56]

There exists, then, a remarkable continuity in the political role of the ulama in Iran, a tradition of opposition to autocratic power that links the nineteenth century with the present. In the events of June 1963, many themes and motifs found in the Constitutional Revolution and even earlier episodes of Qajar history are apparent: the call for *jihād*, the blockading of mosques, the eruption of anger on the removal of religious leaders, the exiling of ulama to Iraq—all these are familiar to the student of nineteenth-century Iran. The recent political role of the ulama cannot however be regarded as an anachronistic curiosity. It must be recognized that in the present age as in the years of the Constitutional Revolution the state is held in certain quarters to be tyrannical and irreligious, and subservient to foreign and infidel powers. It is true that the state has now a more effective apparatus of repression at its disposal than was the case in the nineteenth century, and also that there are certain powerful ideological currents in the opposition to the regime that to an extent run counter to the influence of Khumaynī and his followers. Yet it would be rash to predict the progressive disintegration of the political role of the ulama. Despite all the inroads of the modern age, the Iranian national consciousness still remains wedded to Shi'i Islam, and when the integrity of the nation is held to be threatened by internal autocracy and foreign hegemony, protests in religious terms will continue to be voiced, and the appeals of men such as Āyatullah Khumaynī to be widely heeded.

[56] On the aims and ideology of the movement, see the text of Bāzargān's statements to the military review tribunal that tried him in 1963, *Difā' az Tez-i Nihḍat-i Āzādī-yi Īrān*, pt. 1 (n.p., Khurdād, 1343/June, 1964).

10 Activism of the Ulama in Pakistan

AZIZ AHMAD

THE ACTIVE ROLE of the ulama in Pakistan can best be studied in viewing their activities in chronological historical context. It will show that though the majority of them were at the outset against the establishment of Pakistan, the minority that supported the concept of the new Muslim state as well as some of the former opponents immigrated to Pakistan and soon busied themselves with the processes of politics and of constitution-making in the country in various ways which are outlined in some detail in this survey.

Before the 1947 partition of India, the majority of the Muslim ulama of the subcontinent opposed the creation of a separate state of Pakistan. This opposition of the consensus of the ulama of India to the Pakistan movement was the logical consequence of the opposition of these ulama to the Muslim League[1] which they accused, rather unjustly, of consistent loyalism to the British. Such loyalism had ceased to exist since the British annulment of the Muslim League–supported partition of Bengal in 1911, and more especially since the Indian National Congress–Muslim League axis was formed after the so-called Lucknow Pact of 1916.[2] Distrust of League leaders as "henchmen of the British" continued among the nationalist Muslim leaders and was shared by most of the ulama, notwithstanding the tribute they grudgingly paid, in the wake of the Congress leaders to the integrity and incorruptibility of Muhammad 'Ali Jinnah, the chief founder of Pakistan.

Before 1860 there was a stream of anti-British hostility among the ulama, and to a degree this hostility was transposed against the "pro-British" Aligarh movement led by Sayyid Aḥmad Khan, and then to the Muslim League and to the Pakistan movement. The strength of anti-

[1] As summarized rather tendentiously by Ziya-ul Hasan Faruqi, *The Deoband School and the Demand for Pakistan* (Bombay and London, 1963).

[2] Text in *Report of the 31st Indian National Congress* (Bombay, 1916), pp. 77–81; C. H. Philips, ed., *The Evolution of India and Pakistan 1858–1947* (London, 1962), pp. 171–173.

British sentiment among the ulama before 1860 has, however, been very much exaggerated, as established by the recent researches of Mushir al-Haqq who has demonstrated that Shah 'Abd al-'Aziz, whose famous anti-British *fatwa* is usually quoted as typical, was actually an attitude toward the British, which, to say the least, was ambivalent.[3] The story of the participation of the ulama in the Mutiny of 1857[4] is also to a very considerable extent imaginative hagiography projecting the present on the past.

All the same, one of the founders of Deoband, the Muslim college that opened in 1867, who had also been involved in the Mutiny earlier, Rashid Ahmad Gangohi, disliked Sayyid Ahmad Khan's "heretical" movement to the extent of extending his opposition to the Aligarh leader's politics. He even supported the Indian National Congress in opposition to Sayyid Ahmad Khan, provided it did not lead to any infringement of the *shari'a* or to the "humiliation of the Muslim community."[5] This attitude was actually reversed in the next generation at Deoband by Mahmud al-Hasan who strove with some success toward closer cooperation between Deoband and Aligarh.

One of the founders and the force behind the other Indo-Muslim center and college of ulama in the early twentieth century, the Nadwat al-'ulama, was Shibli Nu'mani who had parted company with Sayyid Ahmad Khan, and was, in his political poems, derisive of the Muslim League.

The leaders of both the Deoband school and the Nadwat al-'ulama in the 1930s and 1940s, decades of the Pakistan movement's incubation and momentum, namely Husayn Ahmad Madani and Sayyid Sulayman Nadwi, respectively, identified themselves with the Jam'iyyat al-'ulama'-i Hind, allied to the Indian National Congress, and generally suspicious of and, in the case of Deoband ulama, hostile to the Muslim League and therefore to the Pakistan movement.[6]

The Westernized elite led by Muhammad 'Ali Jinnah, which succeeded in winning over the Muslim masses, as exemplified by the Muslim

[3] Mushir al-Haqq, "Indian Muslim Attitude to the British in the Early Nineteenth Century: A Case Story of Shâh Abdul Aziz," unpublished M.A. thesis submitted to McGill University, 1964.

[4] Husayn Abmad Madani, *Naqsh-i hayat* (Delhi, 1953), ii, 42–43; Muhammad Miyan, *Ulama-i Hind ka shandar madi* (Delhi, 1957–1960), IV, 275–307.

[5] Muhammad Miyan, *Ulama-i Haqq awr unke mujahidana karname* (Delhi, 1946), pp. 98–100; Hafeez Malik, *Moslem Nationalism in India and Pakistan* (Washington, 1963), p. 196.

[6] Husayn Ahmad Madani, *Muttahida qawmiyyat awr Islam* (Delhi, n.d. [1938–39?]), *passim.*

League victories in the elections to the Viceroy's Legislative Assembly and to the Provincial Assemblies in 1945,[7] were grateful when two religious leaders, Shabbir Ahmad 'Uthmani and the Pir of Manki Sharif, emerged as supporters of the demand for Pakistan. Pir of Manki Sharif was a *pir* of the Northwest Frontier Province where the Congress was still strong. Shabbir Ahmad 'Uthmani was an eminent alim of Deoband, in his own right a figure as respected and as learned as the pro-Congress Husayn Ahmad Madani of whom he soon became the religio-political antagonist by founding the Jam'iyyat al-'ulam-i Islam, a pro-League party of the ulama which, though it did not attract as much a following as its old rival the Jam'iyyat al-'ulama-i Hind among the ulama, was held in veneration by the vast majority of Muslims who supported the Pakistan movement, as a symbol of religious support for the movement.

When Pakistan at last came into existence in 1947, the Jam'iyyat al-'ulama-i Islam was supplemented by another organization, the Jam'iyyat al-'ulama-i Pakistan. Shabbir Ahmad 'Uthmani rose to the high-sounding, but actually purely decorative office of Pakistan's first—and the last—*shaykh al-Islam.*

In the wave of migrations which followed the partition of the subcontinent, a substantial number of ulama soon immigrated to Pakistan from India, especially those who had not been active in the support of the Indian National Congress. Historically most active among these immigrant ulama was the Deobandi Ihtisham al-Haqq Thanawi who later became the chief orthodox critic of the modernist reforms in Pakistan. Old rivalry between Deobandi and the even more fanatical and self-centered Barelwi ulama was also transplanted to Pakistan.[8] Lastly, an especially revered Indian alim, Sayyid Sulayman Nadwi, was prevailed upon to visit, if not to immigrate to, Pakistan, to be one of the principal leaders of the ulama in 1948 in the great and interminable constitutional debate in Pakistan which at that stage, for a few months, took the form of a dialogue between the ulama and the secularized parliamentary agencies of Pakistan's first Constituent Assembly.[9]

[7] Ishtiaq Husain Qureshi, *The Struggle for Pakistan* (Karachi 1965), pp. 240–243.

[8] For a brief account of the divergent religio-political attitudes of these two rival theological groups see Leonard Binder, *Religion and Politics in Pakistan* (Berkeley and Los Angeles, 1961), pp. 31–33.

[9] There developed even an apologetics of the ulama of Pakistan emphasizing the role of ulama in the creation of Pakistan, and belittling the opposition of their vast majority to the Pakistan movement in India. This apologetics has generally taken the form of such tracts as *Tahrik-i Pakistan awr Ulama-i Rabbani* (Karachi, n.d.).

In the quest for a constitution the Constituent Assembly of Pakistan appointed a Basic Principles Committee which in turn appointed a Board of Islamic Learning (Ta'limat-i Islamiyya) in 1949. It is significant that Sayyid Sulayman Nadwi was invited to chair it instead of Pakistan's own Shaykh al-Islam Shabbir Ahmad 'Uthmani who was still alive though he died soon after (on December 13, 1949), and was on the committee that selected the members of the Board. It cannot be ruled out that 'Uthmani's inclusion in the Board as a mere member rather than as chairman may have been influenced by his failing health; but a more cogent reason seems to be that he had already emerged, as early as February 1949, a critic of the Government's policy of dealing sternly with the fundamentalist Abu'l A'la Mawdudi who had pronounced that the first Kashmir War (1947–48) between Pakistan and India could not be termed *jihad*, as Pakistan had not openly declared war against India, a statement that was exploited for propaganda purposes by India and Afghanistan. 'Uthmani had also emerged as a defender of the *mullas* against the attacks of Pakistan's secular-minded ruling elite.[10] Sulayman Nadwi, although included in India among the ulama called "Nehruwani" (Nehru's progeny), was credited with moderation in any dialogue between the ulama and the Westernized elite, in the liberal, moderate tradition of his great predecessor and preceptor Shibli Nu'mani (d. 1914); his school, the Nadwat al-'ulama was less conservative than 'Uthmani's, and, though orthodox, more perceptive of and responsive to the modernist trends. Almost all the writing of Sulayman Nadwi had been historical, and a historical perspective was expected of him, whereas all the writing of Shabbir Ahmad 'Uthmani had been rigidly theological. Even the Indian nationality of Sulayman Nadwi was probably considered a source of objectivity as he was not involved, at least at that stage, in the Pakistani politics as 'Uthmani was; and it was assumed that, being an alim, Sulayman Nadwi would not betray the interests of a Muslim state even though he was and remained a citizen of hostile India.

The "Views"[11] presented by the Board of Ta'limat-i Islamiyya is the first instance of a dialogue between the ulama of various shades of opinion

[10] *The Pakistan Observer* (Dacca), Feb. 10, 1949.

[11] "Views of the Board of Ta'limat-i Islamiyya on Certain Items Referred to Them by the Sub-Committee on Federal and Provincial Constitutions and Distribution of Powers," Appendix I, in *Report of the Sub-Committee on Federal and Provincial Constitutions and Distribution of Powers* (Karachi 1950).

and the secular-minded constitution-making machinery of the Government and people of Pakistan, which was making a genuine attempt at that stage to understand and digest the inspiration as well as the challenge of Islam to its task of evolving a constitution that could be modern and Islamic at the same time.

The Board of the Ta'limat-i Islamiyya also tried on its part to translate the concept of the classical caliphate as expostulated by al-Mawardi and the classical jurists into the theoretical structure of a modern national state. It therefore recommended a presidential system of government (as approximating to the classical position of the Caliph), but echoed Shabbir Ahmad 'Uthmani's assertion made as early as March 9, 1949, in the Constituent Assembly that the power to elect the Head of the State vested solely "in the learned and pious representatives of the People," that is, the ulama. It recommended the formation of a Committee of Experts on Shari'a to advise the president and the federal and provincial legislatures. The lower house of parliament (House of the People) was considered by the Board to be a modern version of the classical concept of *majlis al-hall wa'l 'aqd,* with powers to elect and depose the President of the State, to deal with differences of opinion between the President and itself, and to keep a watch over the activities of the executive. It also was to have the powers of declaring war, concluding peace and passing the national budget.

Most of the recommendations of the Board were, of course, rejected by the relevant Sub-Committee of the Constituent Assembly and by the Constituent Assembly itself; except for its persistent demand that the head of the State should be a Muslim. But the letter and spirit of the "Views" show that the purpose of the ulama was nothing less than appropriating all effective power in the State to themselves, as the theocratic advisers of the President who, indeed, was to hold office during their pleasure.

In this respect the role of the traditionalist ulama is paralleled by that of the fundamentalist Abu'l A'la Mawdudi who, after he immigrated to Pakistan, set himself to the task of forging a well-knit, well-organized, and well-disciplined political party, the Jama'at-i Islami. The ulama did not have the political experience or the political discipline of organizing a party with grass roots among the common people. According to orthodox ulama Mawdudi cannot be called an alim as he preached a return to the Qur'an and the Sunna, sidestepping but not denouncing the *fiqh;* and used comparatively a much more pseudo-modern idiom in his exposition of doctrine and as his instrument of religio-political propaganda than did the true ulama.[12] But he took every possible care not to annoy the ulama, and in fact, wherever possible to work in coordination with them.

After their work as a pressure group in the Board of Ta'limat-i Islamiyya, the next activist adventure of the ulama was aggressive politics. The occasion was the anti-Ahmadi agitation of 1952–53.[13] The agitation had been nursed by the Ahrar party which had earlier opposed the demand for Pakistan, then reached a nonpolitical modus vivendi with the Government of Pakistan; but from 1949 onward directed its overflowing energy against the Qadiyani group of Ahmadis who believed the founder of their sect Mirza Ghulam Ahmad of Qadiyan (1839–1908) was a minor prophet, asserted that they were Muslims, but had their own mosques in which they offered prayers separately. The Ahrar criticism was that by acknowledging the prophethood of Ghulam Ahmad, the Ahmadis denied the finality of the prophethood of Muhammad, placing themselves outside the pale of Islam; and as such could only have the status of a non-Muslim minority in Pakistan.

The theoretical orthodox position regarding the Ahmadis had been clear from the outset. Even before the foundation of Pakistan the outstanding Muslim intellectual Muhammad Iqbal,[14] Shabbir Ahmad 'Uthmani,[15] and Mawdudi[16] had denounced them as heretics or apostates.

In 1952 matters came to a head when, in a reaction to an aggressive protest speech by Pakistan's Ahmadi foreign minister, Zafrullah Khan, the ulama entered the arena of active agitation. An All Pakistan Muslim Parties Convention was convened in Karachi on June 2, 1952, on the invitation of a number of ulama. The demands of the Convention were that the Ahmadis be declared a non-Muslim community, that Zafrullah Khan be removed from the office of Foreign Minister and Ahmadis be generally

12 On Mawdudi see Freeland Abbott, "Maulana Maududi on Quranic Interpretation," *The Muslim World*, XVIII/1 (Jan., 1958), 6–19; *idem*, "The Jama'at-i Islami of Pakistan," *Middle East Journal*, II/2 (Winter, 1957), 37–51; *idem*, *Islam and Pakistan* (Ithaca and New York, 1968), pp. 171–182 and *passim*; Charles J. Adams, "The Ideology of Mawlana Mawdudi," in D. E. Smith, ed., *South Asian Politics and Religion* (Princeton, 1966), pp. 371–397; Aziz Ahmad, *Islamic Modernism in India and Pakistan* (London, 1967), pp. 208–223.

13 Government of the Punjab, *Report of the Court of Inquiry Constituted under Punjab Act II of 1954 To Enquire into the Punjab Disturbances of 1953* (Munir Report) (Lahore, 1954).

14 Muhammad Iqbal, *Islam and Ahmadism* (Lahore, 1936).

15 Shabbir Ahmad 'Uthmani, *al-Shihab* (1924; 2d. ed., Lahore, 1950).

16 Mawdudi, *The Qadiani Problem* (Pathankot, n.d.).

removed from all key posts in the Government.[17] From the list of the components of the Convention one gathers the names of a number of large and small religious parties at this time.[18]

The Convention appointed a Council of Action consisting of the most prominent ulama to issue an ultimatum to the Government to accept anti-Ahmadi demands. They demanded the resignation of the Prime Minister (Khwaja Nazim al-din) who had refused to dismiss Zafrullah Khan and picketed his residence. Other economic and political grievances such as food shortages, corruption in the civil administration, and frustration over the Kashmir problem became telescoped with this anti-Government movement.[19] Mawdudi and the Jama'at-i Islami joined the agitation but their stand was to keep it within constitutional channels, and to give it only a secondary emphasis, concentrating meanwhile on their principal objective, namely the "Islamization" of the society and the theocratization of the state. The ultimatum of the ulama was rejected, some of the ulama were arrested, and in Lahore, where the Provincial Government of the Punjab led by Mumtaz Muhammad Daulatana had connived at the religious disturbances and tried to channel them against the Central Government, Martial Law was imposed. The anti-Ahmadi agitation was thoroughly crushed by the initiative of the secular-minded civil service in cooperation with the Army.

The Court of Inquiry submitted to the Government of the Punjab a classical analysis of the agitation including the role in it of the ulama. The Commission found the ulama in disagreement even on such simple and basic questions as to "What is Islam and who is a . . . Muslim."[20] On the other hand this very obscurantism exaggerated the use of Islam as a slogan in Pakistan: "If there is one thing which has been conclusively demonstrated in this inquiry, it is that provided you can persuade the masses to believe that something they are asked to do is religiously right or enjoined by religion, you can set them to any course of action, regardless of all considerations of discipline, loyalty, decency, morality or civic sense."[21]

In 1953 the pendulum swung in the other direction, especially after the dismissal of the pious Prime Minister Nazim al-Din by the Governor-General Ghulam Muhammad who was a thinly disguised secularist. The new Prime Minister Muhammad Ali 'Bogra' was instrumental in the ab-

[17] *Munir Report*, p. 77.

[18] *Ibid.*, p. 78.

[19] Saleem M. M. Qureshi, "Religion and Party Politics in Pakistan," in Aziz Ahmad, ed., *Society and Religion in Pakistan* (Leiden, 1972).

[20] *Munir Report*, p. 205, also p. 219.

[21] *Ibid.*, p. 231.

olition of the Board of Ta'limat-i Islamiyya.[22] The new Law Minister A. K. Brohi asserted that a theocratic, even an Islamic government was nowhere enjoined in the Qur'an. Chawdhari Khaliq al-zaman a political chameleon, and at that time governor of East Pakistan, placed the ulama and the Communists into a single category of subversionists and advocated the separation of religion and politics, while Sardar Abd al-Rashid Khan, the governor of North-West Frontier Province, hinted at the desirability of evolving Pakistan as a secular state.[23]

The traditionalist ulama withdrew during the years 1954–1968 from active political confrontation to the position of a pressure group functioning not so much collectively as individually and leading not a theocratic or theological movement, but fighting pitched battles of propaganda and dissent on individual points of constitution-framing or lawmaking. In religio-politics their role became quite secondary to that of Mawdudi and his Jama'at-i Islamī which continued to maintain and develop its organization in the face of antagonism by the various successive governments.

Between 1954 and 1958 when the Martial Law was declared and Ayub Khan came into power, the tactics of the ulama were to take strong stands on individual issues, whereas the Government policy was to befriend or "buy" outstanding ulama through personal contacts and patronage. On religious issues of constitution-making the role of the ulama was not distinguishable from, and was quite secondary to, that of Mawdudi and his party.

Like all modern Muslim states Pakistan had to face up to problems of modernization of Family Law. A Commission was appointed in 1954, the "brain" of which was the modernist philosopher Khalifa Abd al-Hakim; it also included a retired judge of the High Court, as well as the eminent alim Ihtisham al-Haqq Thanawi who had a very conservative Deoband background. The liberal members of the Commission recommended reforms to curb polygamy and to make the process of divorce less easy and more humane.[24] Thanawi strongly dissented and the Government had to take cognizance of, and release to the public, his note of dissent,[25] in which he gave a more conservative interpretation than even

22 *Civil and Military Gazette* (Lahore), April 25, 1953.

23 *Ibid.*, June 25 and July 3, 1953.

24 Report of the Commission on Marriage and Family Laws in the *Gazette of Pakistan Extraordinary*, June 20, 1956.

25 *Gazette of Pakistan Extraordinary*, Aug. 30, 1956, containing the Note of Dissent by Maulana Ihtisham-ul-Haq.

Mawdudi[26] to the famous, and in modern times controversial Qur'anic verse dealing with polygamy[27] and cited the example of the Prophet and his Companions who had married more than one wife.

When the Martial Law Regime of President Ayub Khan finally decided to implement the Family Law reforms it chose a *via media* between the drastic reforms recommended by the Marriage and Family Law Commission and the classical and orthodox view stressed by Thanawi and echoed by other ulama.[28]

The Martial Law Regime was strong enough, unlike its parliamentary predecessor, to ignore the protest of ulama,[29] and to place the *waqf*s (pious bequests) under the control of a newly created Government department, that of Awqaf, in 1959. A much bolder step was the change in the name of the State which, unlike in the 1956 Constitution where it was "The Islamic Republic of Pakistan," was the "Republic of Pakistan" under the Martial Law Regime and in the Constitution of 1962 until its Amendment in 1963.

When, under pressure from elite groups within the country and of public opinion abroad, Ayub Khan decided to appoint a Constitution Commission to frame a constitution that could help to rehabilitate democracy in a strong presidential form, views were invited by the Commismission from various elements of public life and intelligentsia in the form of a questionnaire distributed in 1960. The ulama also answered the questionnaire.[30] The Constitutional Commission in its Report sided with the modernists, citing Amir Ali (Ameer Ali) profusely in its argument for absolute judicial equality and equality in human rights between Muslims and non-Muslims; refusing to treat them as mere *dhimmis* (protected but unequal subjects) of the classical concept on which the ulama and Mawdudi had insisted.[31] In answer to the crucial question regarding the Islamic provisions (also known as the "repugnancy clause") contained in Article

[26] For Mawdudi's and his party's view on the Marriage and Family Law Report see Khurshid Ahmad, ed., *Studies on the Family Law of Islam* (Karachi, 1959, 1961).

[27] "If you fear that you will not act justly towards the orphans, marry such woman as seem good to you, two, three, four; but if you fear you will not be equitable, then only one, or what your right hand owns; so it is likelier you will not be partial" (Qur'an 4:2–2 [Arberry's rendering]).

[28] *Muslim Family Laws Ordinance* (Ordinance VIII of 1961). For the summary of discussion on Family Law see Abbott, *Islam and Pakistan*, pp. 198–204, Aziz Ahmad, *op. cit.*, pp. 244–245.

[29] E. I. J. Rosenthal, *Islam in the Modern National State* (Cambridge, 1965), p. 278.

[30] *Answers to the Questionnaire of the Constitution Commission by Prominent Ulama* (Lahore, 1960).

[31] Government of Pakistan, *Report of the Constitution Commission of Pakistan* (Karachi, 1961), pp. 115–120.

198 of the Constitution of 1956, namely that no law should be enacted which was repugnant to the Qur'an and the Sunna, the breakdown of the answers is interesting. Ninety-seven percent favored the adoption of the repugnancy clause; 1.63 percent favored absolute secularism; and 1.14 percent considered that the law should be brought in conformity only with the Qur'an, deleting the reference to *Sunna*. In spite of the overwhelming support for the slogan of an Islamic State, the Commission debated at some length the question of the historical reliability and relativity of the given data of *sunna*, and recommended the formation of another commission to study the Islamization of general law, in consultation with similar commissions in other Muslim countries.[32] In internationalizing the entire question of the change of law in Pakistan, in accordance with the "repugnancy clause," the intention of the Constitutional Commission seems to have been to put the problem, which was also the basic pressure point of the ulama, in cold storage, as many Islamic countries would either not participate in such discussions or would give very varying and often liberal answers to the question.[33]

The Second Constitution of Pakistan (1962) defined Pakistan in its Preamble as "a democratic state based on Islamic principles of social justice." It laid down also that "the Muslims of Pakistan should be enabled, individually and collectively, to order their lives in accordance with the teachings and requirements of Islam."[34] This phraseology was much more vague and diluted than the clear reference to the Qur'an and the *Sunna* in the Constitution of 1956. However, the strong view of the ulama that the President must be a Muslim was accommodated. On the sensitive question of the "Islamization" of the general law the Constitution envisaged the creation of an Advisory Council of Islamic Ideology with a membership of five to twelve persons to be nominated by the President, who was to take into account the nominee's understanding and appreciation of Islam and of the economic, political, legal, and administrative problems of Pakistan."[35] The function of the Council was to be purely advisory, to advise the President, the provincial governors, and the National and Provincial Assemblies on a point referred to them. The Constitution also recommended the formation of an Institute of Islamic Research.

Both these bodies were created as the Constitution came into force at the inception of the Second Republic of Pakistan in 1962. The President,

[32] *Ibid.*, pp. 123–124.
[33] Aziz Ahmad, *op. cit.*, p. 247.
[34] Government of Pakistan, *The Constitution of the Republic of Pakistan* (1962), p. 1.
[35] *Ibid.*, pp. 95–96.

Ayub Khan, throughout his rule as the President of the Republic from 1962 to 1969 tried to balance the personnel of both these bodies giving greater weight to the modernists. The effort of the ulama was to "capture" both these organizations—a move in which they did not succeed; but they did succeed in exerting effective pressure on the Advisory Council of Islamic Ideology on such points as leading to its recommendation that bank interest fall into the category of *riba* (usury), forbidden in the classical law and the Qur'an, and as such was to be forbidden. The advice was not followed by the National Assembly, the executive, or the President. They also succeeded in ousting the moderately modernist director of the Institute of Islamic Research, Fazlur Rahman.

But by far the most solid victory of the ulama was achieved through the politicians and political parties including the ruling (Conventionist) Muslim League in the form of the First Amendment (1963) to the Constitution which restored the adjective "Islamic" in the name of the Republic of Pakistan, and reintroduced the "repugnancy clause" that existing laws should be brought in conformity with the Qur'an and the Sunna.[36]

Ayub Khan had to face continued opposition from the ulama in keeping the state and its development on the course of modernization. He did not clearly distinguish between the ulama and the Mawdudi group in describing their demands regarding the "Islamization" of all law in Pakistan, which meant equally a surrender of power by himself and by the elite that was assisting him in the civil services, the army, and the liberal professions in ruling the country. He accused the ulama of opposing Pakistan essentially and of their involvement in Pakistani politics later: "If they had not been able to save the Muslims from Pakistan they must now save Pakistan from the Muslims."[37] He accepted the fact of a certain measure of the popularity of their agitation and explained it: "Since no leadership could provide an immediate solution to all the problems of the community, the *ulama* were able to build up a large following for their point of view."[38] On the other hand, the ulama accused him of trying to rewrite "certain sections of the Qur'an."[39]

To counterbalance the growing influence of the traditionalist ulama

[36] *Constitution of Pakistan* (First Amendment), 1963, text in G. W. Choudhury, ed., *Documents and Speeches on the Constitution of Pakistan* (Dacca and Vancouver, 1967), pp. 862–871; for parliamentary discussions on the First Amendment see *ibid.*, pp. 830–861.

[37] Mohammad Ayub Khan, *Friends not Masters* (London, 1967), pp. 202–203.

[38] *Ibid.*, p. 203.

[39] *Ibid.*, p. 107.

and the fundamentalist Mawdudi, Ayub Khan tried to enter into a political alliance with the *pirs*, semieducated preceptors and holy men among an illiterate population, on whom had fallen the mantle of both popular Sufism of a near-heterodox variety as well as of orthodox Sufism which had decayed and thoroughly degenerated since the eighteenth century. Although Ayub Khan complains: "How can you run a parliamentary democracy when you have *pirs and faqirs* who can influence the people indirectly?"[40] he chose their alliance precisely because they could be useful instruments in the elections to the "Basic Democracies" he had created.[41] This alliance, no doubt, helped in the immediate objective of winning the elections in 1964–65; but it neither checked nor balanced the pressure of the ulama and their growing influence on the literate urban lower middle classes.

As the student agitation ignited political agitation against Ayub Khan during November 1968–March 1969, the traditionalist ulama joined in it late in December, 1968 when it had already gained great momentum. On December 27 a procession was organized in Lahore by the Jam'iyyat al-'ulama-i Islam, joined by the workers of Bhutto's Pakistan People's Party (socialist and based in West Pakistan), the National Awami Party (Qusuri's group, West Pakistan branch, socialistic), and the Pakistan Democratic Movement (PDM) (a conglomeration of right-wing parties with their base of power in West Pakistan). The demands voiced by the ulama were that laws of the land, should be Islamized, restrictions [*sic*] on the ulama removed, civil liberties reintroduced, and all-political detenus released. The last two demands were presumably under the influence of, and to retain the support of, the workers of other political parties. It was during this procession that a banner inscribed with the *shahada* (Muslim attestation of faith) fell down and was trampled by the police force trying to disperse the mob. This was regarded as a gross act of sacrilege and the agitation was fanned.[42] In his first-of-the-month broadcast on January 1, 1969, President Ayub Khan apologized for the incident that "had hurt the feelings of the ulama," and assured that the "Government holds every religious scholar in esteem and respects his sentiments. . . . The traditional relations, based on mutual respect will be re-established between the Government and the ulama."[43]

[40] *Ibid.*, p. 206.

[41] Khalid B. Sayeed, *The Political System of Pakistan* (Boston, 1967), pp. 174–176.

[42] *Dawn* (Karachi), Dec. 28, 1968; Jan. 5, 1969.

[43] *Ibid.*, Jan. 2, 1969.

At this stage the ulama were acting in collaboration with other political parties including the socialists whom they later denounced as also did Mawdudi. On January 4, Jami'yyat al-'ulama-i Islam joined in force (500 ulama participating) with Bhutto's socialist Pakistan People's Party at Sukkur in Sind in a demonstration demanding full restoration of democracy.[44] Another procession by the same organization of the ulama was led at Manshera in northwest Pakistan.

The other organization of the ulama, the Jam'iyyat al-ulama-i Pakistan, entered the arena of political agitation in the first week of January 1969. Its Executive Committee removed its President, 'Abd al-Hamid Bada'uni, from his office, as he was suspected of being sympathetic to Ayub Khan's regime.[45] On January 10, the Jam'iyyat al-ulama-i Pakistan observed a Demands Day. During the Friday sermons the ulama in various cities of West Pakistan demanded the introduction of Islamic laws, the repeal of un-Islamic ones, and the winding up of the Awqaf Department.[46]

On January 19, the Jam'iyyat al-ulama-i Islam denounced the police "brutalities" against students in East Pakistan,[47] presumably in an effort to gain a political foothold in that province. Jam'iyyat al-ulama-i Pakistan and Jam'iyyat-i ahl-i hadith both joined in the highly successful Demands Day agitation of the political parties of both East and West Pakistan, in which, supporting the demands of other political parties, the rallies of the ulama raised two additional slogans: enforcement of the shari'a law and the repeal of the Pakistan Family Laws Ordinance.[48]

By the first week of February 1969 the ulama coordinated their policy with that of Mawdudi in denouncing socialism and the two socialist parties. Bhutto's Pakistan People's Party in West Pakistan and Bhashani's National Awami Party (pro-Peking, preaching "Islamic socialism") in East Pakistan. The ulama of West Pakistan issued a statement that Islam was opposed as much to socialism and communism as it was to capitalism and feudalism, and that it was "inadvisable for the Muslims in general and the ulama in particular to associate themselves with these secular ideologies.[49]

As various parties joined to form the Democratic Action Committee (DAC) to forge a common front against Ayub Khan and his government, Jam'iyyat al-'ulama-i Islam became one of its members and was represented in the Round Table Conference between Ayub Khan and the DAC by

[44] *Ibid.*, Jan. 5, 1969.
[45] *Ibid.*, Jan. 6, 1969.
[46] *Ibid.*, Jan. 10, 1969.
[47] *Ibid.*, Jan. 20, 1969.
[48] *Ibid.*, Jan. 18, 1969.
[49] *Ibid.*, Feb. 10, 1969.

two representatives, one from each wing of Pakistan. On the eve of the Conference Mufti Mahmud, General Secretary of the Jam'iyyat al-'ulama-i Islam, declared that a number of ulama including himself were preparing a "manual of Islamic economics."[50] The most respected of the ulama, Ihtisham al-Haqq Thanawi, did not actively participate in the agitation but issued statements from time to time including one on February 24 in which he accused the Government of unethical conduct in such matters as trumping up the Agartala Conspiracy Case involving the leader of East Pakistan Awami League, Mujib al-Rahman, and accusing him of collusion with India in a plot to bring about the secession of East Pakistan.[51]

On March 6, 1969, the Jam'iyyat al-'ulama-i Islam issued its manifesto consisting of fourteen points, though some of these points consisted of more than one item. The fourteen points included the demands for the enforcement of an Islamic constitution; enforcement of shari'a laws; abrogation of un-Islamic laws including the Family Law; reorganization of the Awqaf Department under the direction of the ulama; formation of an Islamic Commission consisting of the ulama to advise Federal and Provincial Assemblies; dissolution of the Advisory Council of Islamic Ideology and reconstitution of the Islamic Research Institute so that its membership would be confined only to the ulama; introduction of the Islamic system of education; Radio Pakistan to be made the mouthpiece of Islamic propaganda; freedom of the press; substitution of the present economic system by the classical Islamic pattern; land reforms in accordance with the principles of Islam; industrial workers to be made shareholders in industries with free medical aid and free education; and the capital of the industry itself to be so redistributed that 75 percent of the total shares be offered to the common people; and that all medical graduates be given Class 1 physician's and surgeon's status in a newly formed Pakistan Health Service.[52] It is clear that the last few demands were a gesture toward other agitating groups including journalists, factory workers, teachers, and doctors to gain popularity among them.

I have outlined the exact extent of the involvement of the ulama in the agitation that overthrew Ayub Khan in March 1969. But, in comparison with the other components of that agitation—student unrest; frustration of West Pakistan intelligentsia over the 1966 Tashkent Declaration of a compromise settlement of the India-Pakistan warfare; East Pakistani economic grievances leading to a demand for autonomy, if not

[50] *Ibid.*, Feb. 26, 1969.
[51] *Ibid.*, Feb. 26, 1969.
[52] *Ibid.*, March 6, 1969.

actual secession; regionalism in former smaller provinces of West Pakistan; frustration of professional groups like lawyers, journalists, teachers, and doctors; strikes and the use of force by the industrial workers; rural upheaval in East Pakistan; a general urban frustration owing to the corruption of the administration and a general longing for the revival of civil liberties lost for a decade—in comparison with all these the role of the ulama in the agitation was insignificant and their influence minimal.

It will be seen therefore, that those ulama who were not opposed to Pakistan's coming into being or who supported its concept, men like Shabbir Ahmad Uthmani, soon after the creation of Pakistan demanded, as the price of their support, great say in the processes of constitution-making as well as in Islamization of the law. These ulama were joined by some others who were either earlier opposed to the concept of the new state or had remained neutral.

The pressure of the ulama was exerted on the Government through public statements, speeches in proreligious movements and through public relations with the highest functionaries of the Government. The ulama received valuable support from Mawdudi and his Jama'at-i Islami, who, however, kept his programs and organization quite separate from that of the ulama. The main adversary of the ulama was and has been the Westernized upper middle class elite which has governed Pakistan through politicians, the civil services, and the armed forces. The first "dialogue" between the ulama and the Westernized elite took place through the Board of Ta'limat-i Islamiyya in which the ulama scored one point at least, that the head of the state should be a Muslim. In the first and the second constitutions of Pakistan whatever religious concessions the ulama gained was through "public relations" with the politicians, with the Constitution Commission, and with the former President Muhammad Ayub Khan. On the whole they laid low during Ayub Khan's Martial Law Regime and the Second Republic. But they kept on pressing to capture the Council of Islamic Ideology and Institute of Islamic Research, in both cases with partial success. Before 1969 their one public agitation was on a point as trivial as the procedure of ascertaining the appearance of *'Id* moon which marks the end of Ramadan, the month of fasting. But, as I have outlined, they seized the opportunity of joining the agitation against President Ayub Khan which the students had started and which had assumed massive mass scale. In this agitation the role of the ulama was on the whole inconsiderable; but it shows their aptitude to try to seize a possible opportunity.

During 1969 and 1970 the ulama chose to play a direct role in active politics for the first time by contesting the elections. In the elections their candidates did not meet with much success. But at least in West Pakistan, where Zulfiqar 'Ali Bhutto's socialist People's Party triumphed in most of the Provinces, they were able to capture half a dozen seats. It is significant that in this direct political activity they tried to keep their identity separate from that of Jama'at-i Islami.

Insofar as the elections of 1970 show, the ulama have suffered a setback. In East Pakistan regionalism has triumphed against Islamic solidarity while in West Pakistan Islamic Socialism—in which the adjective "Islamic" is largely decorative and diplomatic—has for the time being at least gained a complete victory over the religious parties.

Part II

Saints and Sufis: Popular Religious Institutions

11 A Short History of the Khalwati Order of Dervishes

B. G. MARTIN

I

ONE OF THE MOST WIDESPREAD and ramified orders of dervishes or Sufis is that of the Khalwatiya (or Helvetiye in Turkish).[1] The order takes its name from the Arabic word *khalwa*, a method of withdrawal or isolation from the world for mystical purposes. Self-imposed solitude of this sort may well be of Christian origin; it is certain that it was being generally practiced by Muslim mystics at least by the end of the eleventh century, and its origins go back much before that time.[2]

The historical development of the Khalwati order may be conveniently divided into two periods, the first dating from the time of its origins and

[1] Indispensable sources for the history of the Khalwatiya order are Ahmad Tashköprüzade, *Al-Shaqā'iq al-Nu'mānīya fī 'ulamā al-dawlat al-'Uthmānīya*, printed on the margin of Ibn Khallikān, *Wafayāt al-a'yān . . .*, (2 vols.; Bulaq, 1299/1881–82), and its continuation by 'Ali Miniq, *Al-'Iqd al-manzūm fi dhikr afāḍil al-Rūm*, also printed on the margin of Ibn Khallikān. A third continuation of these two works is Nev'izāde 'Atā'ī, *Ḥadā'iq al-ḥaqā'iq fi takmilat al-shaqa'iq* (Istanbul, 1268/1851–52). Also H. J. Kissling, "Aus der Geschichte des Chalwetijje-Ordens," *ZDMG*, CII (1953), 233–289, which exploits otherwise inaccessible Turkish materials, such as Shaykh Yusuf Sinan Efendi's *Manāqib-i-sharīf ve ṭarīqatnāmeh-i-pīrān ve mashāyikh-i-ṭarīqat-i-'alīye-i-Khalwatīye* (Istanbul, 1290/1873). Kissling has also written in *Südostforschungen*, XV (1956), 237–268, an article entitled "Zur Geschichte des Derwischhordens der Bajrâmijje." For the Khalwatiya in Egypt, see Ernst Bannerth, "La Khalwatiyya en Egypte, quelques aspects de la vie d'une confrérie," *MIDEO* (Cairo), VIII (1964–1966), 1–74; also A. le Chatelier, *Les confréries musulmanes du Hedjaz* (Paris, 1887), esp. pp. 47–77, on the Khalwatiya; and E. W. Lane, *The Modern Egyptians* (3d ed.; London: Ward, Lock, n.d.). Also useful is 'Abd al-Rahman Jabarti, *'Ajā'ib al-athār fi'l-tarājim wa'l-akhbār* (Bulaq, n.d.); and 'Alī Pāshā Mubārak, *Al-Khitat al-Tawfīqīya al-jadīda* (20 parts in 10 vol-vols.; Bulaq, 1306/1887); and Muḥammad Khalīl b. 'Alī al-Murādī, *Silk al-durar fi a'yān al-qarn al-thanī 'ashar* (n.p., 1301/1883–84).

[2] Le Chatelier, *Confréries*, p. 49; see also Abū'l-Qāsim al-Qushayrī (d. 1072), *Risāla* (Cairo, 1949), pp. 54–56, a section on the *khalwa* and *'uzla*. Al-Qushayrī quotes in this connection the famous Egyptian mystic Dhū'l-Nūn al-Miṣrī (d. A.D. 860), and the use of the *khalwa* in this sense was surely in widespread use before the time of Dhū'l-Nūn.

diffusion in the Caucasus, Anatolia, and Azarbaijan from the late fourteenth century to the end of the seventeenth century, the second from the late fifteenth century to the mid-nineteenth century in Egypt and Muslim Africa. By 1865, it had again lost its momentum, but not before a number of its ablest leaders had founded branches which helped to spread Islam in many parts of Africa, both north and south of the Sahara.

Roughly, a *tariqa* or brotherhood may be defined as a hierarchical Muslim institution with a multiplicity of functional levels. Its leaders may use it at different times and places for varying purposes; its adherents use it for other ends. In some cases, the brotherhood may be the only Islamic institution that exists. Here it can assume many roles, often becoming an all-purpose organization. It has a useful social role to play besides its purely spiritual or quietistic mystical functions. An order may become involved in politics; it may provide medical or psychiatric help for its members, or it may become concerned with magic or astrology. For these purposes, it may include within its ranks remarkable magic-makers or miracle-mongers. The order is often directed by a highly charismatic personality (the Khalwatiya has had a long line of them), whose personal attraction for the common man, or for persons in other parts of society, contributes to the fluctuations of the popularity of the order and to the size of its membership. Then too, a *tariqa* may embrace different doctrines at different times. Thus, the Khalwatiya has experienced a number of oscillations, at one time approaching Shi'ism, at another achieving a stage of nearly unimpeachable Sunni orthodoxy. In some phases of its history, the Khalwatiya was financially independent. This enabled it to act as a built-in social mechanism of opposition to tyranny, or a sanctuary for those in flight from some despot. Throughout its history the Khalwatiya has been largely an urban, or big-town organization.

On the political and organizational plane, the origins of the Khalwatiya exhibit a number of interesting features. One of these is that the traditional founder of the order, the "first *pir*," Abū 'Abdallāh Siraj al-Dīn 'Umar b. Ikmal al-Dīn al-Ahji, or 'Umar al-Khalwati, was probably the founder in only a restricted sense.[3] If he inspired many Sufis, who followed his favorite style of meditation in a hollow tree (not every *khalwa* needs to be in a building) and revered him greatly, he was not the man to propel an organization very far in the institutional sense. This task was reserved to the "second *pir*," Shaykh Yahya Shirvani, from Shamakhi in

[3] Enver Behnan Şapolyo, *Mezhepler ve tarikatlar tarihi* (Istanbul, 1964), p. 172; Kissling, *Chalwetijje*, p. 237.

the Caucasus. In contrast with 'Umar al-Khalwati, a rather shadowy figure who is said to have died about 800/1397 in Tabrīz or Harat, Shaykh Yahya Shirvani is a well-attested historical personality, who died about 1463.[4] In his time, the Caucasus, Azarbaijan, and Anatolia were regions of great religious ferment and movement, areas of much political instability. A number of factors obtaining in those regions at the time are worth brief consideration.

In the wake of the depredations of the Mongols and then of Timur, the settled elements of the population in these places had taken second place before an influx of Turkish-speaking nomads. They circulated in and among the big towns, such as Ardabil and Tabriz in Azarbaijan and Shamakhi and Baku in Shirvan. Migrants from the east, the nomads had brought with them a Turkish folk Islam, a simplistic set of beliefs which had little in common with the Sunni orthodoxy of the period, whether of the Anatolian Saljuq type or the standard Shafi'i variety of Persia itself. In an unsettled, nomad-dominated society which was free to move east and west anywhere north of the boundaries of the Mamluk domains, the nomad, the learned man (*'ālim*), or the Sufi shaykh could go almost where he liked. As they moved, religious and social ideas also moved. The towns and cities of this vast region all had their competing "holy men," Sufi *shaykh*s who made miracles before the eyes of the astonished nomads. These minor religious leaders did not trouble their public with the complicated intellectual problems of "high Islam." Yet, their meetings, gatherings for the *dhikr* or for singing, enabled the local *shaykh*s to win many adherents by their promises of ecstasy or unity with God. At least they offered the hope of some peace of mind in an uncertain situation, or might even provide some rudimentary learning, some study of the Qur'an, some pastoral interest in their followers' cares. The *shaykh* had no objection to the 'Ali worship of his adherents, and he could accept the activities of the *fityan* or *ikhwan* organizations whom he met in the towns, with their stress on morals and ethics.[5]

It was in a situation much like this that the activities of Shaykh Yahya Shirvani were taking place. Like the religious and social spheres, the political scene too was fluid. Safavid *ghazi*s or march warriors from Ardabil were periodically raiding and slaving along the northern confines of Shirvan under their leaders Shaykhs Junayd and Haydar, much as the

[4] Kissling, *Chalwetijje*, p. 240.

[5] M. M. Mazzaoui, "Shi'ism and the Rise of the Safavids," unpublished Ph.D. dissertation (Princeton, 1965), pp. 32–33, 109–110.

Ottomans were doing further west. These two *shaykhs* were helped along politically by their family ties to the White Sheep Turkoman dynasty. With the decay of the White Sheep, the Safavids under Isma'il were able, by 1500, to mold their brotherhood into a state, a state that quickly took on a strong Twelver Shi'i coloration.[6]

About 1460, Yahya Shirvani moved from Shamakhi to Baku after a dispute with a rival Sufi. After settling at Baku, Shaykh Yahya soon created a significant religious and political movement. According to the Ottoman historian and hagiographer Ahmad Tashköprüzade, Yahya "attracted around him ten thousand people. He sent his *khalīfas* [Sufi delegates] to all parts of the region, and was the first person to do this. . . ."[7] Shaykh Yahya also had a number of disciples and men of charisma like Pir Ilyas of Amasya and Zakariya' al-Khalwati, who were instrumental in moving the headquarters of the Khalwati nucleus to Amasya in north central Anatolia after their *shaykh*'s death in 868 or 869/1463–65.[8] Their move from Baku to Amasya may have been connected with Pir Ilyas's personal origins: or it might have been undertaken if they had some dispute with the Shirvanshah at Shamakhi, or if they had been the allies of the Safavids in the last campaign of Shaykh Junayd in 1460, when he was defeated and killed by the Shirvanshah Sultan Khalil. The problem is to define the exact relation between the Safavids and Khalwatiya, which have a number of things in common, such as spiritual ancestors, similar practices, doctrines, and joint origins.[9]

With the transfer of the Khalwati nucleus to Amasya, the inner circle of the order gave it a decisive new direction. To follow the careers of these men, Dede 'Umar Aydini or Aydinli, Habib Qaramani, and Pir Ahmad al-Erzinjani (also known as Mulla Piri) is to see the next stage of the development of the Khalwatiya.[10] One important figure, however, remained behind in Azarbaijan. This was Dede 'Umar Aydini, known as Rawshani (from the Persian word for "illumination" or "brightness"). He had begun his education as a theological student at Bursa, according to Tashkö-

[6] *Ibid.*, pp. 114–115.

[7] Tashköprüzade, *Shaqā'iq*, I, 404.

[8] *Ibid.*, pp. 134–135.

[9] See Shaykh Ḥusayn b. Shaykh Abdal Pīrzāde-yi Zāhedi, *Silsilat al-nasab-i-Ṣafawīya* (Berlin, A.H. 1343), p. 40, where there is mention of the *khalvet,* the forty-day withdrawal (*arba'inī*) at the "famous *chilleh-khaneh* or *zawiya* of Ardabil," etc. Similar language appears in Faḍlallāh b. Ruzbihān Khunjī's *Ta'rīkh-i 'Alam-ārā-yi-Amīnī* (*Persia in A.D. 1478–90*, V. Minorsky, ed. [London, 1957], pp. 66–67), in connection with the career of Shaykh Ḥaydar Ṣafavī.

[10] Kissling, *Chalwetijje*, pp. 242 ff.

prüzade. Like his famous elder brother 'Ala al-Dīn 'Alī al-Khalwatī, mentioned below, 'Umar hailed from the town of Laranda, the capital of the Anatolian amirate of Karaman.[11] He went to Shamakhi to study under Yahya Shirvani, and after obtaining his *ijaza* or permission to teach, was called to Tabriz by Uzan Hasan of the White Sheep Turkoman dynasty. Dede 'Umar attached himself to the White Sheep, perhaps because he wished to stay away from Karaman, reincorporated into the Ottoman Empire in the 1470s. One of the wives of Uzan Hasan, Saljuq Khatun, the mother of his successor Ya'qub, gave Dede 'Umar a *zawiya* or convent in Tabriz, to which many pupils came.[12] Among them were two well-known Khalwatis who helped found the Egyptian Khalwatiya, Ibrahim Gulshani and Shaykh Taymurtash or Damirdash al-Muhammadi.

Dede 'Umar's fellow Khalwatis, Habib Qaramani and Pir Ahmad al-Erzinjani, led exemplary Sufi lives in Amasya and elsewhere in Anatolia as practitioners of the Khalwati way.[13] Although Amasya was on Ottoman territory, it had its traditions of Shi'ism and folk Islam, of heterodoxy and popular revolt. One of these revolts, that of the Baba'is, had taken place in and around Amasya in the thirteenth century. Such names as Baba Ishaq, leader of the Baba'is, Baraq Baba, Sari Saltuq, Yunus Emre and Hajji Bektash, Aq Shams al-Din, Hajji Bayram Veli, and Qadi Badr al-Din b. Qadi Samavna were important figures in this tradition. This popular tradition of resistance and revolt may be traced backward to Ahmad Yesevi, a Central Asian Turkish leader of the twelfth century. As Mazzaoui says, this "grassroots Islam" was an expression of "discontent and restlessness among the rural masses against the Sunni aristocracy of the Rum Saljuq state and the Ottoman ruling and religious institutions, which may be said to have found its culmination in the Shi'i revolts and terrible massacres" during the early years of Sultan Selim in Eastern Anatolia.[14]

Like Ardabil and Baku, Amasya was also an urban island in the sea of a Turkish nomad population. It was a provincial capital of some importance, and following the established Ottoman tradition, Mehmet II

[11] Tashköprüzade, I, 392–394.

[12] See V. Minorsky, *Ta'rīkh-i-Tabrīz*, 'Abd al-'Ala Karang, ed. (Tabriz, 1337 HS/1962), p. 40, for the Blue Mosque of Tabriz, and p. 85 n. 1, describing the *khaniqāh* or *zāwīya* formerly attached to it, which may well have been the building in question.

[13] See Tashköprüzade, I, 394–395, for Qaramani; and Kissling, *Chalwetijje*, p. 242, for Pir Ahmad.

[14] Mazzaoui, *Shi'ism*, pp. 139 ff. For further information on these subjects, see H. Sohrweide, "Der Sieg der Safaviden in Persien und seine Rückwirkungen auf die Schiiten Anatoliens im 16. Jahrhundert," *Der Islam*, XLI (1965), 95–223.

had sent his son Bayazid there as governor, to learn something of the practical side of government. Another son, Jem, had been sent to Konya for the same purpose. The princes were their father's representatives in their respective provinces. They were guided by the older members of a little court. Here, surrounded by his own following, each prince would make ready for the great test of his life, the day when his father would die and he would be called to the throne. By custom, the prince who reached Istanbul first and held it succeeded, killing his remaining brothers to prevent civil war.

If Prince Bayazid was a worldly person, he was inclined at intervals to mysticism and the company of mystics. Within his court at Amasya were a great number of *shaykhs* of brotherhoods who vied with each other for his attention and favor. One of them was a gifted pupil of Pir Ahmad al-Erzinjani, Muhammad Jamal al-Din al-Aqsara'i, better known as Chelebi Khalifa, who had also studied under 'Ala al-Din 'Ali al-Qaramani. This same Chelebi Khalifa eventually succeeded to the highest rank among the Khalwatis of Amasya, gaining the title of *shaykh al-sajjada.*[15]

Like the other courtiers of Amasya, the Khalwatis were aware of the increasing hostility being shown in the late 1470s by Mehmet the Conqueror to his son Bayazid. The Sultan frequently interfered in the provincial affairs of Amasya: in 1478 he condemned to death three men who were close to Bayazid. One was caught and executed, but two escaped, perhaps warned in time by the prince.[16]

Another affair of the same time which must have fueled the resentment of the ruler against Bayazid was the episode of Mulla 'Ala al-Din 'Ali, elder brother of Dede 'Umar Rawshani and one of the teachers of Chelebi Khalifa. From Karaman, like his brother, 'Ali al-Din 'Ali was a man of enormous charisma—according to Tashköprüzade he could "send people into ecstasy with a word or a glance." When this remarkable Khalwati *shaykh* turned up in Istanbul (some time between 1475 and 1480), the Sultan became very suspicious. With the exception of a few Qaramanlis, like his grand vazir Qaramanli Mehmet Pasha, persons from this region were suspect. It had just been reincorporated into the Ottoman Empire a few years before, having been an independent amirate. And Mehmet II's

[15] Kissling, *Chalwetijje*, pp. 243–245; Tashköprüzade, I, 398–401. British Museum Or. 12653, Section I, fols. 2*b*–18*a*, contains a short work probably by Chelebi Khalīfa, entitled *Te'vilāt-i-Ḥazret-i-Cemāl al-Dīn Khalvetī.*

[16] Kissling, *Chalwetijje*, pp. 244–245.

intelligence service had doubtless informed him that Dede 'Umar in Tabriz had been a friend of his old enemy Uzun Hasan, and an intimate of Sultan Ya'qub and Saljuq Khatun. As a Sufi, he might not necessarily favor the dynasty. As Tashköprüzade reports: "the *Shaykh* ['Ala al-Din] went to the city of Qustantiniya in the time of Sultan Mehmet Khan. The important and the influential gathered around him, and the rest of the people, too. Sultan Mehmet Khan feared him, that some misfortune might befall the state, and politely ordered him to go elsewhere. . . ."[17]

This episode seems to show that the Khalwatis leaders, or one of them, might have been harboring political ambitions, which might have led to some form of visible and violent action. All the same, the conqueror and his minister knew that it was best not to confront so powerful a Khalwati leader directly, but to suggest that he remove himself. It is quite possible that this incident cemented the ties between Bayazid and his Khalwati friends. If he came to power, they hoped to use him: to reach the throne, the prince was ready to use them.

In the spring of 1481, Bayazid and his court at Amasya were much disturbed by rumors from Istanbul that Qaramanli Mehmet Pasha had suggested to his master that the throne should pass to Jem. Bayazid was to be killed. As allies of Bayazid, the Khalwatiya and Chelebi Khalifa now deliberately entered the obscure world of high Ottoman politics, where intrigue, treachery, and murder were commonplace. Bayazid gave credence to the stories from Istanbul, and Tashköprüzade tells us that he repeatedly pleaded with Chelebi Khalifa to do something to assure his political future.[18]

The Sufi shaikh Chelebi Khalifa now emerges but in a new role, that of a magical practitioner of great skill, a master of black arts (*siḥr*), a specialist in the "science" of magic squares (*'ilm al-awfāq*). By his ability to peer into the future (*firāsa*), to see in a vision what the ruler, his vazir, and their magic man were doing, Chelebi Khalifa was able to anticipate and to frustrate their moves. Bayazid won in the end, and when the news reached Amasya of the unexpected deaths of Mehmet II and the minister, Bayazid took the road for Istanbul. There are differing versions of this story, but they may well mask a successful attempt by Bayazid and his friends (the Khalwatiya among them) to poison the ruler and liquidate the vazir before the same fate overtook them. If there is no conclusive

[17] Tashköprüzade, I, 392.

[18] *Ibid.*, pp. 398–401.

proof against Bayazid and his helpers, there is surely heavy circumstantial evidence, as Kissling suggests.[19]

The thirty-year reign of "Sufi Bayazid" (1481–1511), was the real heyday of the Khalwati order in Ottoman Turkey. The sultan himself attended Sufi exercises, and his presence doubtless attracted many persons to the order who thought that membership in it would be a useful handhold in the climb to a higher career. It may be that the tradition of Khalwati membership among certain urban classes of the Ottoman military, the upper ranks of the civil service, and aristocratic persons generally began in this era. Basking in royal favor, the Khalwatiya had no need to be anything but orthodox. Political activism was no longer a requirement of the moment. Chelebi Khalifa saw to it that the order consolidated its position. At royal request, the headquarters of the order were moved from Amasya to Istanbul, and when Chelebi Khalifa and his men reached the capital, they were presented with a former Byzantine church to remodel into a *tekke* or Sufi lodge. Royal favor for the Khalwatiya could not have been more marked: the rebuilding of the former church was entrusted by Bayazid to his vazir Khwaja Mustafa Pasha, and the *tekke,* to be the citadel of the Khalwatis in Istanbul for a very long time, was known by the minister's name. Bayazid turned over his son Ahmad to Chelebi Khalifa to be educated. Thus Bayazid repaid the huge political debt he owed to the order.[20]

About 1500, Chelebi Khalifa, who had served as the head of the order in its most crucial move and through an important period of establishment in the capital, died. There was no political contest within the order over the succession, as would sometimes happen in the future; in many *tariqa*s such disputes led to splits and schisms and new branches. The succession to the carpet of the *shaykh al-sajjada* passed affinally to Chelebi Khalifa's son-in-law, Sunbul Sinan. Sinan was a man of much spiritual power, and after the death of the order's royal patron in 1511, these qualities would be much in demand. The demise of Bayazid was clearly a watershed for the Khalwatiya. If the order was too well rooted, too powerful, and too well-liked by the population to be overturned, it would nevertheless be the target of serious attacks from both the new Sultan, Selim I, and the orthodox ulama, which would shake it, but not discredit it.[21]

Selim I was suspicious of his father's vazir, Khwaja Mustafa Pasha, and had had him killed. He knew that Khwaja Mustafa had helped his brother

[19] Kissling, *Chalwetijje,* pp. 250–251.
[20] *Ibid.,* pp. 251 and 256 ff.
[21] *Ibid.,* pp. 257 ff.

Ahmad in the succession contest, and believed that the vazir had been implicated in the unsolved mystery around the death of his uncle Jem.[22] The Khalwatiya was closely associated with the old regime: indeed their principal *tekke* had been built by the obnoxious minister. Selim now decided to have it torn down. According to a miracle of Sunbul Sinan reported by Enver Şapolyo, workmen sent for the task were confronted by a very angry Khalwati *shaykh* who turned them away. Hearing that the workmen could not or would not do the work of demolition, the Sultan jumped on his horse and went himself to the *zawiya*. Here he encountered Shaykh Sinan in his Sufi dress or *khirqa* and hundreds of silent dervishes. Selim was speechless. His anger left him, because of the spiritual power of Sunbul Sinan. The two men were reconciled and the order for the destruction of the Khalwati convent was canceled. Here again, the political power of the Shaykh and his order had been demonstrated to the ruler, who recoiled, which is the real point of the anecdote.[23]

In the long run, the attacks of the orthodox religious class, the ulama, were more serious. They attacked many orders, not only the Khalwatiya.[24] The criticisms of the ulama and their hostility had a more substantial basis to them than the criticism of the sultan. In these attacks, a number of elements may be discerned: a political one, which suggested that the Khalwatis were disloyal to the Ottoman state because of their vague Shi'i affinities; a doctrinal one—the Sufis were thought by the ulama to be too close to folk Islam and too far from the *shari'a*; and a kind of cultural hostility, which made the learned see the Sufis as the generators and enthusiastic spreaders of *bid'a*, undesirable innovation. This standpoint was derived by the ulama's view of themselves as the guardians of the "true" Islamic tradition. Then also, some of the ulama were very intolerant of the way of life, the clothing, the disorderly personalities, and other externals of some Sufis—including a number of Khalwatis. They disapproved of the extreme *ghulāt* or *malamātī* style in Sufism, which was as much a shock for them as the contemporary hippies and yippies are for some sections of the American middle classes.

Until the opening of the sixteenth century, there was little hostility

[22] See V. L. Ménage, "The Mission of an Ottoman Secret Agent in France in 1486," *JRAS* (1965), pp. 112–132.

[23] Şapolyo, *Mezhepler*, pp. 172–182, for the Sunbuliya and Sunbul Sinan.

[24] See H. J. Kissling, "The Role of the Dervish Orders in the Ottoman Empire," *American Anthropologist*, LVI, 2, ii (1954 [Memoir 76]), 25 ff., for the general background to the dispute between the dervishes and the orthodox. The German original of this article may be found in *ZDMG*, CIII (1953), 18 ff.

between the Ottomans and the rising Safavids of Persia. Under Selim I, these antagonisms sharpened, and the first Ottoman-Safavid war followed.[25] At the same time, the Sunni ulama gained new prominence and influence, and the relations between them and the brotherhoods became temporarily polarized. Neither the sultan nor the ulama had forgotten the rising of Shaykh Badr al-Din in 1416 which had nearly torn the Ottoman state apart, a bitter civil war in which Badr al-Din's allies had been the mysterious Burkluje Mustafa, described as the leader of a "communist underground movement," and Torlak Hu Kamal, a similar figure. All three had been inspired by undefined egalitarian ideas, yet they were determinedly hostile to a reestablishment of the authoritarian Ottoman regime. After Badr al-Din's execution, many of his followers had taken refuge with the Safavids at Ardabil.[26]

To many of the informed ulama, the beginnings of the Khalwatiya—and some other orders like the Badr al-Diniya, Baktashiya, and the Bayramiya—were suspect because they could be equated with the origins of the hostile Safavids. As the *silsilas* of these orders show, many of the forefathers of the Safavid order, like the Shaykhs Safi al-Din of Ardabil and Ibrahim Zahid of Gilan, reappear in the Khalwati and other chains of descent.[27] Further back, the Safawiya and the Khalwatiya have in common five out of twelve imams in the standard 'Ithna'ashari Shi'i series. The Khalwatis always remained Sunnis officially, the Safavids had done the same until late in the fifteenth century. In fact, these orders were twin brothers; had the Khalwatiya gone elsewhere but the Ottoman Empire, it might have turned Shi'i. That the leaders of the Khalwati order were very sensitive to suggestions of watered-down Shi'ism made against them, to criticism over their loyalties, is shown by the fact that the widely read, and Khalwati-inspired book of Nev'izade Ata'i, the *Hada'iq al-Haqa'iq*, written in the late sixteenth century (from materials supplied in part by Yusuf Sinan, another Khalwati author) simply strikes out the names of the five offending imams from the *silsila* without explanation.[28] Kissling, who first drew attention to this fact, notes that such suppression of the truth is quite in

25 H. R. Roemer, "Die Safawiden, ein orientalischer Bundesgenosse des Abendlandes im Türkenkampf," *Saeculum*, IV, 1 (1953), 34.

26 Mazzaoui, *Shi'ism*, p. 142; and Kissling, *Bajrâmijje*, p. 243.

27 Kissling, *Chalwetijje*, pp. 283–289, tables at end of article.

28 'Atā'ī, *Ḥadā'iq al-Ḥaqā'iq*, pp. 62–63. Other *silsilas* are found in Jabartī, *'Aja'ib*, I, 297, and in Shaykh 'Alī Ḥarāzim ibn al-'Arabī Barāda al-Maghribī al-Fāsī, *Jawāhir al-ma'anī wa bulūgh al-amānī fī fayd Abī'l-'Abbās al-Tijānī* (Cairo, 1382/1963), I, 179.

accord with the Shi'i doctrine of *kitman* or *taqiya,* deliberate concealment of the truth in a hostile environment.[29] A Shi'i doctrine thus finds its way into the Khalwati dogmatic structure. It is significant that the heads of the Khalwatiya thought it necessary to try to hide their real origins, in an effort to achieve a position of orthodoxy in the eyes of suspicious rulers or probing members of the learned classes.

As a part of the Ottoman establishment, the directors of the Khalwatiya felt they had to shake themselves free from their earlier close ties to the common people, which they had not minded cultivating in Baku or at Amasya. They believed that they had to come closer to the ulama, even if it meant sacrificing their earlier connections, and steering away from the "excesses" of folk Islam toward a fuller orthodoxy. In their own ranks, they were less tolerant of religious eccentrics or strange personalities who might erode their public image.[30] Assuming a rightist orientation also meant that the membership of the order would be increasingly a one-class affair, cutting horizontally across Ottoman society somewhere near the top, instead of a vertically organized order, which had been the essential structure of the Khalwatiya before its arrival in the Ottoman capital.

If the short but eventful reign of Selim I had not been a very favorable period for the Khalwatiya, the age of Sulayman the Magnificent (1520–1566) and that of his son Selim II (1566–1574) was an era of favor. But by the time of Sulayman, the leaders of the Khalwatiya had learned that they could not be too closely identified with one monarch, for if they did they risked a time of disfavor under the next one. In the case of Sulayman Qanuni, the sultan may have been guided to the Khalwatiya by his mother, the Crimean princess 'A'ishe Sultan, who had come into contact with the important Khalwati shaykh Muslih al-Din Merkez Efendi, later to be the successor of Sunbul Sinan at the convent of Mustafa Pasha. Although Sulayman had interests in other brotherhoods, he maintained his ties to the Khalwatiya.[31]

During the reigns of Sulayman and Selim II the Khalwatiya expanded both in the capital and in the provinces. It acquired or had built a number of new *tekkes* in Istanbul, and many more elsewhere. As new areas were

[29] Kissling, *Bajrâmijje,* pp. 245 ff.

[30] One of these eccentrics was a certain Divaneh Ahmet Dede who sat on an Istanbul street corner and made remarks about passersby, collected animal horns, and would dance for bystanders whenever he was given a new horn for his collection! See Kissling, *Chalwetijje,* p. 236, or Evliya Chelebi, *Siyâhatnâmeh,* Vol. I (Istanbul, 1314), pp. 384–385.

[31] Kissling, *Chalwetijje,* pp. 258 ff.

conquered by the Ottoman armies, new extensions and branches of the Khalwatiya appeared to keep pace with the additions to the *Dar al-Islam*.[32] Sometimes these new branches exhibited tendencies that must have upset the right wing of the Khalwatiya. One of them, the episode of a Khalwati *mahdi*, Davud Khalifa, in Damascus, must have provided a lot of ammunition for the foes of the order. Davud, who gathered around himself a crowd of malcontents and opponents of the regime, took over the provincial government for two days before he was killed by government troops. As this event took place not long before an Ottoman campaign against the Safavids, which led to the taking of Baghdad in 1534, Kissling suggests that this rising may have had a Safavid hand in it.[33] In the end, the episode did the order no real harm, and in other regions it forged ahead. In Egypt, the Gulshaniya branch of the order under Ibrahim Gulshani was making progress, and numbers of followers of Sunbul Sinan had settled in Albania. The surroundings of Istanbul itself, and Anatolia and Rumelia now supported an increasing number of Khalwati centers. The old branch at Amasya was still functioning, while at Kastamuni, the mushrooming suborder of the Sha'baniya, named for its founder Sha'ban Veli, enlisted many adherents. In Bulgaria the Khalwatis could be seen in the upper Maritsa Valley and the vicinity of Sofia. Edirne (Adrianople) Štip, Philoppopolis, and Tatar Pazarjiq were also among the important Ottoman provincial towns having settled groups of Khalwatis.[34]

As the order accommodated itself to its middle and upper class clientele, the hostile criticism that had come from the ulama was either muted, or deflected to branches of the order like the Uwaysiya, headed by Davud Khalifa, which had a Shi'i odor about it. Then too, by the beginning of the seventeenth century, the ulama seemed to be less disturbed by fundamental doctrinal questions than by a feeling that they had not yet overcome the *tariqas*, that they could not control them, and that the brotherhoods were promoting an improper kind of Islam. Having read their law books, they were convinced that they knew what Islam was all about and what it ought to be. The views of the ulama took no account of traditional popular religion, nor the variety and strength that it possessed. Hence they aimed a lot of noisy comment at the "excesses" of the *dhikr*, about the use of music at dervish gatherings (the *sama'*). In dervish practices they frequently found examples of *bid'a*, improper innovations, at which they rarely failed to take aim.[35]

32 *Ibid.*, pp. 260–261.

33 Kissling, *Bajrâmijje*, pp. 248–249.

34 Kissling, *Chalwetijje*, pp. 268 ff.

35 For example, a certain Ibrāhīm b.

During the third quarter of the seventeenth century, for instance, there was a prolonged public quarrel between Sivasi Efendi, a deputy of the Khalwati *shaykh al-sajjāda* in Istanbul, and the Imam Qadizade, a member of the ulama.[36] The fact that Qadizade was an apostate dervish and a clever and effective debater gave a sharp edge to his acrimony. Hajji Khalifa has a lot to say about the superfluous violence of their attacks on each other and the amount of partisan feeling that they were able to arouse. Each of them had his own group of outspoken followers who loved dispute and debate for its own sake. The pair argued over the merits of the *dhikr*, the vexed issue of the appropriateness of music at religious affairs, about the matter of reverence for saints dead or alive (also a favorite Wahhabi topic), and about justified or unjustified innovations in general. Although these displays of intolerance and enmity caused much ill-feeling, they nevertheless showed what questions contemporaries thought were of importance.

In his criticism of the Khalwatis over their *dhikr*, Hajji Khalifa comes very close to the orthodox position:

> Most of the Khalwati order have based their rites and observances on the community of aspirants. They have founded lodges and have made the *Hay*! and the *Hu*! which are the essentials of their vociferation into the instrument of their society, the pivot of their livelihood, and the prop of their stumbling. Their hypocrisy has turned their ordained music and their obligatory motions, which their ancient founders prescribed for a sound purpose and which ought to be freely permitted to those worthy, into bait for the trap of imposture and a snare for disreputable fools. This is the reason why the brutish common people flock to them and votive offerings and pious gifts pour into their lodges. Since their gyrations play an important part in this, they will not abandon their spinning. . . .[37]

Another controversy of the sixteenth and seventeenth centuries, in

---

Muḥammad al-Ḥalabī (d. 947/1547) wrote an attack on Sufi dancing called *al-Rahṣ wa'l-waqṣ li-mustahill al-raqṣ*, (British Museum Or. 12795, III, fols. 53*a*–59*b*) which was typical of these attacks, although it was written before the seventeenth century. Occasionally, the Sufis had their defenders amongst the ulama also. 'Alî Chelebî Qinâlîzâde, a *muftī* of Istanbul who died in 979/1572, wrote a short *Risāla fī dawarān al-Ṣūfiya* (see British Museum Or. 12933, III, fols. 28*b*–30*a*, in which he defended the practice of dancing). For another episode in 1105/1693–94, in which the Damirdashīya of Cairo were attacked by the local ulama for their dancing and other customs, see 'Abd al-Qādir b. Muḥyī al-Dīn al-Irbilī, *Hujjat al-dhākirīn wa radd al-munkarīn* (Baghdad [?], 1386/1966), pp. 52–59.

[36] Hajji Khalifa (Katib Chelebi, *The Balance of Truth*, trans. G. L. Lewis (London, 1957), pp. 132–134. The title of the Turkish original is *Mīzān al-ḥaqq fi ikhtiyār al-aḥaqq*.

[37] *Ibid.*, pp. 43–44.

some ways reminiscent of the contemporary argument over marijuana and other drugs, was the debate over coffee-drinking and tobacco-smoking. The Khalwatis were also involved in this controversy, which seems to have brought them a lot of popular support, perhaps even membership. Coffee, which had first come from the highlands of Abyssinian to Yemen and from there to Istanbul about 1540, was perhaps imported first into Sufi circles by members of the Shadhiliya order to keep themselves awake while they carried out their nightly devotions.[38] To hinder sleeping in the *khalwa*, the Khalwatis soon adopted coffee. Coffee-drinking was immediately attacked by the ulama as unlawful and dangerous. They claimed that when coffee was roasted, it became "carbonized," and so violated the provisions of Hanafi law. The *shaykh al-Islam*, Abu Su'ud, who was usually very tolerant, went so far as to sink ships loaded with coffee beans in Istanbul Harbor by having holes drilled in their hulls. But the real danger seen by the orthodox and the political right in coffee-drinking was the lively discussion in coffeehouses which had sprung up everywhere. They were frequented by poets, soldiers, storytellers, and "other idlers," and were said by the orthodox to be needless diversions that distracted the people from their religious duties. With time, the orthodox and the ulama became more mellow about coffee, and some of them even published rhyming *fatwas* in favor of it.[39]

In some quarters, tobacco was seen to be the more serious threat to public health, morals, and safety. It was known to cause fires; the orthodox, who disliked it on principle, were quick to attribute conflagrations in Istanbul to its use. The debater Qadizade Mehmet Efendi is said to have convinced Sultan Murad IV (ruling 1623–1640) that it was a "sinful innovation." If their enemy Qadizade was against tobacco, the Khalwatiya and the other orders were for it. The use of tobacco spread very rapidly in dervish circles, just as the drinking of coffee had done. The population was inclined to follow the dervish line, but not that of the higher clergy, whom they generally regarded as meddlesome killjoys. Like coffee, tobacco was a useful stimulant for the *khalwa*. Once its use had started, nothing could stop it. As Hajji Khalifa says,

> The late Sultan Murad IV, towards the end of his reign, closed down the coffee house in order to bar the gate of iniquity, and also banned smoking in consequence of certain outbreaks of fire. People being undeterred, the

[38] For the Shadhilis and their coffee, see 'Abd al-Qādir al-Anṣarī, *'Umdat al-safwa fi ḥall al-qahwa*, pp. 145–146, in Silvestre de Sacy, *Chrestomathie arabe*, vol. II (Paris, 1826), pp. 138–169 (Arabic text), also Kissling, *Chalwetijje*, pp. 276 ff.

[39] Kissling, *Chalwetijje*, p. 278.

imperial anger necessitated the chastisement of those who, by smoking, committed the sin of disobedience to the imperial command . . . many thousands of men were sent to the Abode of Nothingness . . . when the Sultan was going on the expedition against Baghdad . . . 15 or 20 of the leading men of the army were arrested on a charge of smoking and were put to death with the severest torture in the imperial presence. Some of the soldiers carried short pipes in their sleeves . . . they even found an opportunity to smoke during the executions. . . .[40]

In the 1650s another famous Khalwati *shaykh*, Niyazi al-Misri, aroused the Ottoman establishment with his public controversies with the Syrian Arab al-Ustuwani. Some of these arguments turned on tobacco and coffee, and in 1651 led to the fall of a *shaykh al-Islam*, Baha'ī Efendi, who was friendly to the Khalwatiya and other dervishes and had approved the use of both sorts of stimulants.[41]

Niyazi al-Misri (1617–1694) was doubtless the most famous of the Anatolian Khalwatis of the late seventeenth century. He was renowned for his poetry, his mystical achievements, and his outspoken opposition to the government. Most important, perhaps, he was a representative of the left wing of the Khalwatiya, having the sort of personality of its earlier leaders, in tune with the masses and their religious aspirations, many of which still had a strong Shi'i side to them. Some of his public statements could have been made by Shaykh Badr al-Din himself. He had connections with many brotherhoods, including the Sunni Naqshbandiya and Qadiriya, likewise the Bayramiya, which was considered by many Turks to be a barely camouflaged branch of the Safaviya in Turkey. He was closest, however, to the Khalwatiya branch of his first teacher, who had belonged to the Sha'baniya. About 1669, a trader who admired him built a *zawiya* for him in Kütahya. Three years later, he made some public remarks having political implications, based on a piece of divination (at which he was expert). For this he was banished to Rhodes. After a short time he returned, but was banished to Lemnos in 1676 for a similar offense. After fifteen years of exile, he was allowed to return home again in 1691. On a visit to Adrianople in 1693, during a war with Austria, Niyazi's unabashed public statements caused his second and final exile to Lemnos in 1693, where he died the following year.[42]

Niyazi's thinking, which was not very systematic, had a large Shi'i component in it; he also manifested a great admiration for Muhyi al-Din

[40] Hajji Khalifa, *Balance*, pp. 51–52.
[41] Kissling, *Chalwetijje*, p. 280.
[42] Abdülbaki Gölpinarli, art. "Niyazi," in *Islam Ansiklopedesi*, vol. IX (Istanbul, 1960), pp. 305–307.

ibn al-'Arabi, and for 'Ali. Niyazi also believed that Hasan and Husayn had been prophets. He was much taken up with astrology and divination, and at times claimed to be Jesus or the Mahdi. Even though he had had close ties at one time in his life with the Hamzavi group of the Bayramiya *tariqa*—he quarreled with them and accused them of not being Sufis at all, but heretics. Niyazi was even able to get away with accusing Sultan Murad IV of being a secret Hamzavi and suggesting that the time had come to replace him on the Ottoman throne with a member of the Crimean Tatar dynasty! His characteristics and actions made him most attractive to many of the common people, but as Kissling says, he gave the Ottoman Government "allerlei Kopfzerbrechen" in attempting to deal with him.[43] Perhaps Niyazi's Sufi poetry (for which he used the pen name Niyazi for poems written at night, and Misri for poems written in the daytime) will stand as his highest achievement.[44]

II

The Khalwatiya began to make its mark in the urban centers of Egypt just before 1500. In Egypt the Khalwatis had some of their support from the same classes as they had in Turkey, officials, soldiers, and civil servants. But generally, the Egyptian Khalwatiya seems to have had greater sympathies and affinities with the common man. Like the Anatolian branch, the Egyptian Khalwatis had their share of charismatic personalities and eccentrics. Yet the aura of naïve but sincere Sufism lasted longer in Egypt, and there was less deliberate identification of the *tariqa* with the Ottoman administration.

The first Khalwatis to reach Egypt were a trio of Turks, all of them students of Dede 'Umar Rawshani in Tabriz; Shams al-Din Muhammad Damirdash, or Damirdash al-Muhammadi, Shahin al-Khalwati, and Ibrahim b. Muhammad Gulshani. The first two were probably Azeri Turks from Azarbaijan, while Gulshani came from a village near Diyarbakr.[45] All three of them seem to have arrived in Egypt by the time of the Mamluk sultan Qansawh al-Ghawri, about 1500. The Arab writer Sha'rani says that

[43] Kissling, *Bajrâmijje*, p. 249.

[44] Gölpinarli, *op. cit.*, pp. 306–307, lists a number of Niyâzî's writings, as yet mostly unpublished. Some of his poems appear in German translation in H. Ritter, *Das Meer der Seele* (Leiden, 1955).

[45] Şapolyo, *Mezhepler*, p. 193, says that Damirdash came from a village of that name near Kütahya, and that his brotherhood was known as the "Mürdaşiyye" in Anatolia. No information is given as to the number of adherents —if any—which it had there.

Shahin al-Khalwati had been a mamluk in Sultan Qa'itbay's army (ca. 1465–1495). Shahin al-Khalwati had been one of the intimates of Qa'itbay, and had been released by him to go to Tabriz to study under Dede 'Umar Rawshani. He returned about 1500 from Persia and built a mausoleum and *ma'bad* ("place to worship") for himself under the Muqattam Ridge near Cairo.[46] Shahin al-Khalwati stood in the old tradition of Sufism: Sha'rani declares that in his old age, Shahin al-Khalwati was very well known. He was frequently visited by vazirs and great amirs, "and no one else had this reputation at this period in Egypt. He made many revelations, but was very silent; one could sit by him for an entire day without hearing a word from him. He went almost entirely without sleep, wore dirty clothing, and was very withdrawn from people. . . ."[47] All the same, Shahin al-Khalwati had had a number of students at one time, but was much concerned with "alchemical manipulations," which alienated them, according to al-Nabulusi.[48] The personality of the unworldly seer, the advanced mystic, is very tangible in the case of Shahin al-Khalwati. His reputation of remarkable spirituality was certainly well founded.

From Sha'rani also, something of the style and manner of Shaykh Damirdash al-Muhammadi can be seen. Damirdash was much less advanced a Sufi than Shahin al-Khalwati, but he was far better at organizational and institutional tasks. Like many Turks before him in the Mamluk era, he managed to integrate himself easily into Egyptian society and attract the support of native Egyptians. Generosity, as well as piety, makes him an attractive figure. He was famous for his orchard, which he and his wife cultivated. The produce of the orchard was not destined for Damirdash or his wife or children, "but for the unfortunate, wayfarers, and travellers." With a view toward permanence, the orchard was eventually made into a *waqf*, which was divided into thirds, a third of the gains earmarked for the upkeep of the orchard, a third for Damirdash's descendants, and a third for the poor who lived at Damirdash's *zawiya*. The sources do not give much information as to how Damirdash acquired the economic wherewithal to build his *zawiya*, but it can be assumed that it was by the

[46] 'Abd al-Wahhāb al-Sha'rānī, *Al-Tabaqāt al-kubra*, vol. II (Cairo, n.d.), p. 166, includes an account of Shahīn al-Khalwatī: 'Alī Pāshā Mubārak, *Khitat*, II, part 5, 30–31, gives a description of Shahīn's mosque drawn in part from al-Nabulūsī's *Riḥla*.

[47] Sha'rani, *Tabaqat*, II, 166–167.

[48] According to 'Abd al-Ghānī al-Nabulūsī's *Riḥla*, p. 139, quoted in Tawfīq al-Tawīl, *Al-Tasawwuf fi Miṣr ibbān al-'asr al-'Uthmānī* (Cairo, 1946), p. 78, Shahīn al-Khalwatī went to such lengths with his "alchemical activities" that his students abandoned him and joined Shaykh Damirdash.

usual routes of pious gifts from individuals and subsidies from the government, and from the pupils whom Damirdash attracted. In Damirdash's character, generosity and organizational skill were joined to extreme piety. Sha'rani says that Damirdash—a close friend of his—slept only a little, and that he got up and washed in the mornings long before dawn, and would then recite the whole of the Qur'an.[49]

Damirdash's mosque and *zawiya* can still be seen and are located in Cairo between the Husayniya quarter and the tomb of al-Ghawri. Although it was on the outskirts of the town when it was built, it is now in the center of the city. In his *Khitat al-Tawfiqiya al-jadida* ("New Tawfiqian Survey"), the nineteenth-century Egyptian writer 'Ali Pasha Mubarak describes it as it was about 1887.[50] Not only did the building include fifty *khalwa*s for Sufis, but had "a minaret, and the tomb of Ustadh Damirdash, situated on the north side of the *minbar* (pulpit), surrounded by a wooden enclosure, which is the objective of many pilgrims. His *mawlid* (birthday festival) takes place in the month of Sha'ban and lasts for three days. At this time the Sufis enter the *khalwa*s dressed for fasting and staying awake, and making their *wird*s (special prayers) in isolation. . . . They only come out for prayers with the congregation, but when the last night arrives they emerge to join in the sessions of the *dhikr* and to shake hands with the people. That is a custom which has continued until now. . . ."[51]

Like many other Khalwati figures and Sufis of other orders, Damirdash al-Muhammadi was buried in his own *zawiya*, probably at his own request. Even dead and buried, he was still an enormous asset to his order. In the minds of simple believers, *baraka* still radiated from him. The person who touched the tomb or its cloth covering himself obtained some of the unlimited magical virtue of the *shaykh* and took it away with him. As local places of pilgrimage and to reinforce the structure of belief, tombs and graves of *shaykh*s still have an important place. As Bannerth makes clear,

[49] Sha'rani, *Tabaqat*, II, 133: Yūsuf b. Ismā'il al-Nabhānī, *Jami' karamāt al-awliyā'*, vol. II (Cairo, n.d.), pp. 69–70, gives an account of his life. Among the details mentioned in that Damirdash also started life as a mamluk in Qā'itbay's army (?). Further and conflicting details may be found in Şapolyo, *Mezhepler*, p. 193. Damirdash was also a writer, and Jabartī, *'Aja'ib*, II, 147, lists a *Risāla fi'l-tawḥīd* by him. The full title of this *risāla* is *Risālat al-qawl al-farīd fī ma'rifat al-tawḥīd*, according to the British Museum copy (Or. 3199).

[50] 'Alī Pāshā Mubārak, *Khitat*, I, part 4, 112–113.

[51] Further details about the *khalwas* may be found in al-Nabulūsī, *Riḥla*, p. 139, some of which are quoted in Ṭawīl, *Tasawwuf*, p. 67. See also 'Alī Pāshā Mubārak, I, *op. cit.*, part 4, 109–110.

they may also serve as important backdrops for the unrolling of rituals, like the contemporary *dhikr* in the Damirdash mosque.[52]

After the death of Damirdash, *ca.* 930/1523–24, his descendants continued to maintain the family *zawiya*. They were successful in making it a going concern, and Jabarti records that two centuries later, the descendants of the humble but generous *shaykh* had become prominent members of the upper classes of the city, consorting with *walis* and *pashas*. Their lives of comfortable opulence offered the greatest possible contrast to the simple beginnings of the founder. Whether contemporaries thought that wealth and standing were compatible with the long-continued leadership of a going institution which might have been expected to serve the poor, is unfortunately not made clear by Jabarti.[53]

Shaykh Damirdash al-Muhammadi not only had the support of such unique personalities as Shahin al-Khalwati, but also of a remarkable Egyptian follower, Ibn Ahmad b. Muhammad Karim al-Din al-Khalwati (890–986/1485–1578). Karim al-Din was a man of *baraka*, singer, and a magician-astrologer. He came to the notice of Shaykh Damirdash by his fine singing at the *dhikr*. The Shaykh trained Karim al-Din in the *khalwa* and instructed him in the "science of magic squares" (*'ilm al-awfaq*) and the lore of the *za'iraja* (a technique of casting horoscopes using letters and concentric circles).[54] When Karim al-Din had mastered these techniques, which probably gave him a good income, he was chosen by Damirdash to succeed him. This he did not do immediately, as there was a political contest within the order. As a result, Damirdash's unworthy son gave away his father's *jubba* (overshirt) to an unqualified person, who had the temerity to wear it, but was killed while doing so. It was retrieved and given to the rightful successor, Karim al-Din. At a later time, however, the succession reverted to more meritorious descendants of Damirdash al-Muhammadi.

Al-Munawi declares that Karim al-Din had such a powerful personality and possessed such a concentration of charisma that "predatory animals fled from him." Karim al-Din was also a friend of Sha'rani, and when Sha'rani died, Karim al-Din went into seclusion. His prestige among the people of Cairo near the end of his life was so great that when he appeared on the street, there were scenes approaching mass hysteria. Throngs followed him, hoping to kiss his hands or feet. He died when he was nearly

[52] Bannerth, *Khalwatiyya*, pp. 5–7.

[53] Quoted in 'Alī Pāshā Mubārak *op. cit.*, I, part 4, 112–113.

[54] For these procedures, see Ibn Khaldun, *Muqaddima*, trans. F. Rosenthal, Vol. III (London, 1958), pp. 182–214.

ninety, "when the whole city went to his funeral and carried his body from his *zawiya* at the Aq Sunqur Bridge near the mosque of Husayn Pasha Abu Isba' to the Azhar, where he was prayed over and then brought back and buried in his *zawiya*."[55] Presumably this place, like the mosque of Damirdash, soon became a place of resort for believers.

As suggested by 'Ali Pasha Mubarak, the role of Karim al-Din which brought him the most credit was his function as a magician and astrologer, a role in many ways like that of Chelebi Khalifa. This was a common but essential function of the Khalwatiya and of other Sufi groups, and assured them of adherents and continued vitality. Karim al-Din was almost certainly serving as a "psychiatrist" for his following, probably listening to their troubles and attempting to help them. This role also comes close to that of the pastoral office. It was doubtless combined with medical assistance as well. The "science of magic squares" usually involves the writing of a charm, with verses from the Qur'an plus a square with letters or numbers on it. The individual for whom the charm is written soaks off the ink in a liquid and drinks it, or washes himself with it or carries it on his person. In the absence of effective medicine, the popularity of men like Karim al-Din is easy to understand. Speaking of a very similar situation in Ottoman Turkey in the late 1780s, Mouradgea d'Ohsson says:

Les vertus miraculeuses qu'on attribue a la plupart de leurs *scheikhs* leur attire une devotion particulière. Ils s'arrogent le pouvoir d'interpreter les songes et de guérir par des remedes spirituels les maladies de l'esprit et du corps . . . ils posent la main sur la tête, font des insufflations mysterieuses, touchent la partie souffrante et remettent au malade de petits rouleaux de papier sur lesquels sont ecrits des hymnes de leur composition ou des passages du *Cour'ann*. . . . Ils ordonnent aux uns de les jeter dans une tasse, et d'en avaler l'eau quelques minutes après; aux autres de les tenir sur eux, dans le poche ou sur le sein, pendant 15, 30 ou 60 jours, en recitant telle ou telle prière. . . .[56]

Not only were the little rolls of paper used for sick people, but also for those in good health as well, as a sort of preservative or preventive measure. D'Ohsson continues:

Ceux qui ont recours à ces talismans se persuadent qu'ils ont a vertu de les garantir de la peste, de la petite vérole et en general de tous les accidens

[55] 'Ali Pasha Mubarak, *op. cit.* I, part 4, pp. 109–110. Karīm al-Dīn al-Khalwatî is the author of a short polemical text (British Museum Or. 12703) on the right words for beginning the *dhikr*, *Radd al-mutawaqqif bi-lā maḥālla fī ibtidā' bi'l-dhikr bi'l-jalāla.*

[56] Mouradgea d'Ohsson, *Tableau général de l'empire Ottoman* (Paris, 1790), II, 313.

fâcheux, même des coups de l'ennemi. . . . Renfermés dans de petites châsses d'or ou d'argent, les uns se les attachent au bras, les autres dur le sommet de la calotte et sous le turban. . . . Tous ces rouleaux portent le nom de *yafta*, de *nousskha*, de *hamaïl*. . . . Les superstitieux de toutes les classes s'addressent à eux [shaikhs] avec zèle, et ne manquent jamais de leur donner des marques de generosité en argent, en effets, et même en comestibles de toute espèce. . . .[57]

The usefulness of magic squares, charms, and talismans in the spread of the Muslim brotherhoods, particularly in Subsaharan Africa, can hardly be underestimated. These techniques (and methods of divination as well) attracted many African non-Muslims, who saw them as a highly desirable addition to their own local techniques. From the use of them, to writing them, and making money by them was only a short step, and involved literacy in Arabic, and generally acceptance of Islam. In countries which were already partly or wholly Islamized, the successful magical expert, if he led a brotherhood, could count on the augmentation of its numbers.

Not long after the establishment of the Damirdashiya branch of the Khalwati order in Egypt, the activities of the order were reinforced by the arrival of the Rawshaniya or Gulshaniya, so called after its founder, Ibrahim b. Muhammad Gulshani.[58] Born at Diyarbakir, Gulshani left home at an early age to study in Transoxiana, but got only as far as Tabriz. Here he made a good impression on Mawlana Hasan, Qadi 'askar of Sultan Uzun Hasan. His intelligence and ability attracted both men's attention, and it was he who was sent to fetch Dede 'Umar Rawshani when Uzun Hasan invited him to Tabriz. This proved to be a turning point in Gulshani's life, and he became one of Rawshani's *khalifas*, like Damirdash and Shahin al-Khalwati. Gulshani taught for a time at Rawshani's *zawiya* in Tabriz, but with the political decline of the White Sheep Dynasty, he

[57] *Ibid.*, p. 314. At certain times certain Khalwatī *shaykhs* may have specialized in dream interpretation. At least this is suggested by the title of a MS in the British Museum (Or. 7555, Section II), entitled *Ta'bīrnāmeh-yi-mashayikh-i-sūfīye-yi-Khalvetīye*. This compilation is anonymous and without a date.

[58] For Gulshani or Gülşenî, see Kasim Kufrali, *Islam Ansiklopedesi*, IV, 835–836, which includes a bibliography of his writings: see also 'Atā'i, *Haqā'iq*, pp. 67–68, for a short biography. There also exists a hagiography of Gülşenî, *Menâqib-i-sherīf-i-Ḥazret-i-Sultān Gülşenī*, by Muḥammad Muḥyi al-Dīn, who died in 1026/1617. The British Museum copy was copied by Dervīsh Velī Gülşenī in 1072/1661–62, and is numbered Or. 12958. Another MS in the same collection (Or. 7578, copied in 1080/1669) includes Gülşenī's *Sa'dnāmeh, Mi'rājnāmeh, Maqālāt,* and others.

found himself under increasing pressure from the Safavids after his master's death, perhaps because he was too closely associated with the Aq Quyunlu. Rumors circulating in the town that he was guarding the jewels and other possessions of the family of Uzun Hasan subjected him to frequent molestation. With his son Ahmad Khayali, he finally fled to Diyarbakir, and then to Egypt via Jerusalem.

On reaching Egypt, Gulshani met Damirdash and Shahin al-Khalwati who asked him to stay. He was likewise invited to remain by the Chief Qadi, 'Abd al-Barr ibn Shihna. For a time, Gulshani stayed at Qubbat al-Mustafa not far from Birkat al-Hajj (about 11 miles northeast of Cairo), forming a circle of adherents and gaining the goodwill of the Mamluk ruler, Qansawh al-Ghawri. At length, Gulshani moved to Cairo and settled in the Mu'ayyadiya Quarter, where he started to build a *zawiya* opposite the Mosque of al-Mu'ayyadiya. This was to become the center of the Gulshaniya *tariqa*, its *dargah*. Within the structure, as Damirdash had done, Gulshani built himself a mausoleum, domed and tiled, and many *khalwa*s for his disciples.

In this establishment, there seems to have been more emphasis on public charity, at least on the feeding of the poor, than elsewhere. 'Ali Pasha Mubarak describes this building, which in his day still had resident dervishes, a weekly *dhikr* session, and an annual *mawlid* for the founder. Like the Damirdash foundation, it was a *waqf*: 'Ali Pasha reproduces the original *waqf* document that was preserved there. It shows that Gulshani's *dargah* was once an important and well-populated structure. Not only did it have an *imam* and a *mu'adhdhin*, but also two doorkeepers, a prayer reader, a supervisor of the *waqf* (*mubashir*), a baker and a cook, and a "tablesetter for the poor," a revenue collector—probably because the *dargah* owned extensive properties—servants for the *khalwas*, a water carrier, and some other personnel.[59]

After the Ottoman conquest of Egypt in 1517, Gulshani continued to teach at his *zawiya* as he had under the Mamluks. In fact, his son Ahmad married the widow of the last Mamluk sultan, Tuman Bay. Through his tangible charisma, Gulshani attracted to his institution many Ottoman cavalrymen and Janissaries. They had such total belief in Gulshani, al-Munawi says, that they were ready to fight one another in order to drink what remained of his washing water![60] It is possible that Gulshani went

[59] 'Alī Pāshā Mubārak, *op. cit.*, I, part 3, 50, and II, part 6, 54–55.

[60] Quoted by Ṭawīl, *Tasawwuf*, p. 163, from an unpublished MS of al-Munāwī's *Al-Kawākib al-durrīya.*

himself, or sent representatives along with the Ottoman forces, to encourage them and to build up their morale by encouraging them to "do their duty" as Muslims. D'Ohsson mentions that in his time there were still solitary dervishes, or groups who followed the armies on campaign, praying for the success of Ottoman arms. These were not restricted to the Khalwatiya and its branches, but included men from all orders.[61] Here the role of an attendant dervish may have been similar to the function of the Baktashi order, encapsulated in the ranks of the Janissaries.

By the age of Sulayman the Magnificent, Gulshani was important enough to have attracted the attention, and the dislike, of the Ibrahim Pasha, the Ottoman viceroy in Egypt. The viceroy obtained an order compelling Gulshani to leave for Istanbul. In spite of his advanced age, Gulshani was forced to go. In the end, he was less damaged than enhanced by the pasha's intrigue, and won the support of Kamalpashazade, the *Shaykh al-Islam,* and of other influential officials. While in Istanbul, Gulshani regained his eyesight through treatment. He also won a following in Istanbul because of his preaching, and the favorable attention of the Sultan himself, and the Gulshaniya formed a branch in Turkey as a result. Eventually, he was permitted to go back to Egypt, where he continued to supervise the construction of his *zawiya.* He died in Shawwal 940/April–May 1534, aged about 104, and was succeeded by his son Ahmad Khayali, who died in 977/1569–70.[62] According to Sha'rani, who made it his business to meet all important mystics, Gulshani was "illiterate, very taciturn, and barely articulate."[63] Nevertheless, a number of literary works in Persian and Turkish are attributed to him, likewise a *diwan* in Arabic; these are still unpublished. After the death of Ahmad Khayali, the Gulshaniya must have lost momentum in Egypt, although it languished until the 1880s, in the time of 'Ali Pasha Mubarak. D'Ohsson (*Tableau Général,* Vol. II, plates 119 and 120) includes illustrations of costumes worn by Anatolian Gulshani dervishes at the end of the eighteenth century.

The final phase in the development of the Egyptian Khalwatiya opened during the middle of the eighteenth century. In this period, it was probably the most important and influential order in Egypt. The final phase of the order's development is associated with the name and career of a Damascene *shaykh,* Mustafa ibn Kamal al-Din al-Bakri.[64] Al-Bakri was a

61 D'Ohsson, *Tableau,* II, 313.

62 Kufrali, "Gulşenī," p. 836.

63 Sha'rānī, *Tabaqāt,* II, 133, where Gulshani is listed as "Ibrāhīm, [Demirdash's] brother in the *ṭarīqa.*"

64 For the life of al-Bakrī, see Murādī, *Silk,* IV, 190–200; Jabartī, *'Aja'ib,* I, 165–166; and Muḥammad Tawfīq al-Bakrī, *Bayt al-Siddīq* (Cairo, 1323/1905–06), pp. 156–65.

prolific author, an innovator of Sufi techniques, and personally of much charisma. He was also a frequent traveler in Palestine in Egypt and the Hejaz, accompanied on some of these journeys by Raghib Pasha, a rising Ottoman politician. Al-Bakri had had two important masters himself; one was the famous intellectual and writer 'Abd al-Ghani al-Nabulusi, a member of the Naqshbandi order; the other was a Khalwati *shaykh* from Aleppo. Before the middle of the eighteenth century, al-Bakri had launched his own branch of the Khalwatiya, the Bakriya.

The Bakriya was a huge success, and in the mid-1730s, its founder was visited in Jerusalem by the man who was to amplify and promote his ideas and schemes from Egypt at the end of the century: Muhammad b. Salim al-Hifni (or al-Hifnawi), who soon emerged as a leading member of the Bakriya. On a number of occasions, al-Bakri visited al-Hifnawi in Cairo: as with Karim al-Din al-Khalwati, these were the occasions of mob scenes, the crowds attempting to touch al-Bakri or obtain his blessing. On the last of these visits, in April 1749, al-Bakri died in Cairo and is buried in the great Qarafa cemetery, where his tomb is still visited regularly by many Muslims.[65]

The revival of the Khalwatiya in Egypt, inspired by al-Bakri and sustained by his friend and pupil al-Hifnawi (d. 1768), coincided with stirrings of reform and change, not only in Egypt, but elsewhere in the Islamic world. Some of these changes were accelerated by European encroachments and pressures, others by the visible decay of the Ottoman Empire. After 1517, despite the Ottoman turning from Persian to Arab culture, Egypt and its capital lost much prestige. Istanbul was now the capital of the Islamic world: Cairo was merely an appendage. Already bleak, the Egyptian situation had been made worse by unfortunate political developments.[66] By the eighteenth century, Egypt had entered an era of confusion and helplessness, which Gaston Wiet has rightly called "the agony of Ottoman rule."[67]

If political power in Egypt was theoretically divided among the Ottoman viceroy, his *diwan*, and the Mamluk beys, the beys were becoming ever bolder and less responsible. The mutually hostile factions among the Mamluks grouped and regrouped constantly, often taking the local Otto-

65 Bannerth, *Khalwatīya*, p. 12.

66 For Islamic reform and the breakdown of the Ottoman Empire at this time, see Jamal al-Din al-Shayyal, *Muhadarāt fi'l-harākāt al'-islāhīya wa marākiz al-thaqāfa fi'l-sharq al-Islāmī* (Cairo, 1958), II, chap. 1.

67 G. Wiet, "L'agonie de la domination ottomane en Egypte," *Cahiers d'histoire egyptienne*, Vol. II (Cairo, 1950), pp. 496–497.

man troops as allies. To provide themselves with cash, these undisciplined soldiers now specialized in extortion, irregular tax levies, and brigandage. As time went on, the Egyptian religious classes found themselves more and more playing the role of mediators between a tyrannized and frightened population and the military gangsters. As the rate of troubles and exactions accelerated, the people looked increasingly to the lower ranks of the ulama and to the *shaykhs* of brotherhoods for redress against acts of oppression and plundering. The people did not trust the higher ulama, as they were dependent for their salaries and advancement on the Mamluks, and could be expected to act as their silent partners.[68]

This was not the case with the *shaykhs* of brotherhoods, many of whom became very outspoken over the worst abuses of Mamluk misrule. Jabarti and Heyworth-Dunne both cite many examples in which the *shaykhs* were so involved.[69] The Egyptian Khalwatiya joined in: Ahmad al-Dardir was one participant, and Shaykh Hifnawi another. The *shaykhs* were able to take on this role because they were financially independent. Many of their *zawiyas* were supported by *waqfs* which were hard to plunder, and the *shaykhs* continually received gifts and presents from the population, and sometimes from foreign rulers. Thus their standing was unassailable and they were immune to pressures. They were closer to the people, and as part of their "pastoral" function, listened to their complaints and advised them whenever they could. Egyptians in the majority, they obtained and kept the confidence of their fellow citizens as the "Ghuzz," Ottomans, or Mamluks never did.

Like many of the ulama, a large number of the leaders of brotherhoods (like the Khalwatiya) had connections with the Azhar Mosque in Cairo. Some had been entirely trained there: others had come from provincial madrasas to complete their studies at the richest and best equipped institution at the capital.[70] The Azhar's sixty to seventy professors, hundreds of itinerant intellectuals and students formed a community that was the best and most advanced of its kind during the Ottoman period. The Azhar also had a small population of students from other Islamic countries, including the Muslim areas of Africa.[71]

[68] Shayyal, *Muhādarāt*, II, 8, 9, 24.

[69] J. Heyworth-Dunne, *An Introduction to the History of Education in Modern Egypt* (London, 1939), pp. 31–36, with many references to passages in Jabarti in the footnotes.

[70] Shayyal, *Muhādarāt*, II, 8–9.

[71] See Heyworth-Dunne, p. 25 n. 4, for the dormitories of foreign students: for the career of a student from Dārfūr at the Azhar, see Muḥammad b. 'Umar al-Tūnisī, *Tashhīdh al-adhhān bī-sīrat bilād al-'Arab wa'l Sūdān* (Cairo, 1965), pp. 393, 411.

For these reasons, even more perhaps than the pilgrims or merchants who traveled to foreign lands, the Egyptian ulama and *shaykh*s of *tariqa*s were always well informed of developments in the Islamic world, no matter how remote they were. From their personal contacts and sources of information they knew of the anti-Sufi activities of Muhammad ibn 'Abd al-Wahhab and the Wahhabis, of the reforms of Shah Waliallah of Delhi, and others.[72] Their sources might well have included such men as Shaykh Murtaḍa al-Zabidi, a Yemeni intellectual, author of the *Taj al-'Arus,* and a pupil of Shah Waliallah, who made his way successfully in Egypt, or the equally famous learned man 'Abd al-Rahman al-'Aydarus from Tarim in the Hadramawt.[73] At the same time that they learned of these new currents and changes, the ulama were just as much aware of the increasing tempo of European activities in the Middle East and countries adjoining.

In the collapse of the Moghul Empire and the advance of the British in in India, in the appearance of a Russian fleet in the Mediterranean in 1770, and in the unbroken defeats of Ottoman armies at the hands of the Austrians and Russians, the Egyptian learned classes would have been blind indeed not to discern a serious threat to Islam from Europeans. This conviction was compounded by domestic developments in Egypt, the dislocation of daily life, and the violence from the Mamluks. Thus it is not surprising that they saw challenges to Islam from two sources. And, as if further proof of Muslim weakness were needed, it was supplied by the French invasion of Egypt in 1799.

The Egyptian ulama and *shaykh*s had neither battalions to strike back at the unwanted foreigners, nor any effective force to protect their own people from the ravaging Mamluks. But at least they could take a leaf from the book of Shah Waliallah by attempting reforms, recruiting more students, and spreading the activities of their brotherhoods. In this way they hoped to man the defenses of Islam.

In the light of these developments, it is possible to understand some of the main lines of the Islamic revival of this time. The revival was centered on the Azhar, and was inspired primarily by foreign and domestic events, and then by Shaykhs al-Bakri and al-Hifnawi. The Khalwatiya served as the organizational framework for the revival and one of its most important channels of action. Other brotherhoods, such as the cluster of

[72] For an interesting short study of Shah Walīallāh, see Shayyal, *Muhādarat,* I, 34–51.

[73] See *ibid.,* II, 45–79, for the life of al-Zabīdī, and for 'Aydarūs, see Murādī, *Silk,* II, 328–329 and Shayyal, *Muhādarāt,* II, 50–51.

them around the Ahmadiya of Ahmad b. Idris al-Fasi (d. 1837), took their motive force from the Khalwatiya. Even by the end of the eighteenth century, the outpourings of the new energy of the revival would not only filter into the Khalwatiya in Arabia, but would also flood into the Sudan and Ethiopia, into Algeria, into parts of the Maghrib, and into West Africa.

After al-Bakri himself, the first of the standard-bearers of the new style Khalwatiya-Bakriya was Muhammad b. Salim al-Hifnawi (1690–1768) *shaykh* of the Azhar (1758–1767).[74] Himself an energetic teacher and organizer, al-Hifnawi was clearly the most effective promoter of the ideas of al-Bakri after his master's death. A man of good education, a prolific writer and commentator, al-Hifnawi had a long list of students of whom Jabarti mentions only the more important. It is also worth noticing that many of al-Hifnawi's students were also members of the Qarabashiya (or Qarabashiliya), which al-Hifnawi had accepted before he joined the Bakriya. Can the Qarabashiya have become a special nucleus within the Khalwati movement reserved for the pupils and proteges of al-Hifnawi?[75]

Like al-Bakri, al-Hifnawi had an impressive and charismatic personality, and was concerned with the woes and hardships of the people of Egypt. In turn, they regarded him as one of their best supports against the Egyptian government of the day. Jabarti quotes an anecdote attributed to Raghib Pasha about al-Hifnawi being "Egypt's roof against disaster" and the many stories about him show just how much he was loved and admired by his contemporaries.[76] In him, the Khalwatiya had reverted to something like the naïve but sincere Sufism of an 'Umar al-Khalwati, coupled with the political skill of a Sunbul Sinan. Among the better known of his dis-

[74] See Jabartī, *'Aja'ib*, I, 289–304, and Murādī, *Silk*, IV, 49–50.

[75] For the career of 'Alī 'Alā' al-Dīn Qarābāsh Velī, see H. J. Kissling, "Sa'ban Veli und die Sa'banijje," in *Serta Monacensia*, Festschrift Babinger, (Munich, 1952), pp. 86–109, and Şapolyo, *Mezhepler*, pp. 188–89. This important Khalwati came from Arapgir, and studied at the Fātih Madrasa in Istanbul. He then lived at Kastamonu and at Çankiri near Ankara. By 1670 he had established his branch of the Sha'bānīya, and was called "Velî" in reference to his ability to work miracles. At this time, his headquarters was the Meḥmet Pasa Mosque at Üsküdar, and he acquired the nickname "Qarābāsh" because he wore the tall black turban typical of the Sha'bānīya. He also stayed for some time at the *zāwīya* of Mihrumāh Sultān in Istanbul. As "gossip" arose about him, he was banished like Niyāzī to Lemnos, but was released after some time and went on the pilgrimage. He died near Cairo in 1686 as he was returning to Turkey. He had a son named Mustafa Ma'nevi Efendī, also a Sufi. Kissling lists further sources for his life and career (p. 109).

[76] Jabarti, *'Aja'ib*, I, 295.

ciples who helped propagate the Khalwatiya-Bakriya, or their own slightly modified versions of it, were Muhammad b. 'Abd al-Karim al-Samman, Mahmud al-Kurdi, Ahmad al-Dardir, Muhammad ibn 'Abd al-Rahman al-Azhari, and Ahmad al-Sawi. The careers of these five *shaykhs* show how and where the energies of the revival were diffused and what form they assumed.

According to Le Chatelier, Shaykh Samman (1717–1775) got his name one day when he and his followers were without food. Samman let down a pail into a well, which came up filled with butter. With this, he managed to feed himself and his disciples, who gave him the name of Samman ("butter merchant").[77] In Egypt, he had been a student of al-Hifnawi and of al-Kurdi, and had also taken the tie of the Bakriya from al-Bakri during one of his visits to the Hejaz. Samman founded a number of *zawiyas* there and in Yemen and attracted a great number of followers. One of them, Shaykh Ahmad al-Tayyib ibn al-Bashir (d. 1823) spread the Sammaniya in the Sudan, along the banks of the Blue and White Niles, and in the vicinity of Umm Durman. Other *shaykhs* like Adam al-Kinani carried the message of Samman to Eritrea and southwestern Abyssinia. The Sammaniya also had branches in Sinnar and elsewhere. At one time the Sudanese *mahdi* Muhammad Ahmad was an adherent of one of these branches.[78]

Like Samman, Mahmud al-Kurdi (1715–1780) had been a pupil of both al-Bakri and al-Hifnawi.[79] Jabarti declared that al-Kurdi had a personal magnetism "in which high and low believed." He was able to see the Prophet at will in dreams and had reached the highest stage of mysticism (*kamāl*), and "had obtained many strange revelations."[80] Jabarti also says that al-Kurdi was the direct heir of al-Hifnawi, for it was he who "carried on spiritual guidance and the opening of the mystical path after the death of his *shaykh*. By his guidance, many traveled over it . . . and those who came later followed him."[81] One of al-Kurdi's followers was 'Abdallah al-Sharqawi, *Shaykh* of the Azhar from 1793 to 1812. Another famous pupil was the Algerian Ahmad al-Tijani, who founded his own order, the Tijaniya. Tijani's biographer reports that al-Kurdi granted Tijani a full

77 Le Chatelier, *Confréries*, p. 51; see also Murādī, *Silk*, IV, 60–61. Sammān was also the author of *Al-Nafahāt al-Ilahīya fī kayfīyat sulūk al-ṭarīqat al-Muḥammadīya*, of which there is a MS in the British Museum (Or. 12694).

78 'Abd al-Raḥmān Zakī, *Al-Islām wa'l-Muslimūn fī sharq Ifrīqīya* (Cairo, 1965), p. 25.

79 Jabarti, *'Aja'ib*, I, 298, and II, 61–68.

80 *Ibid.*, I, 298.

81 *Ibid.*

ijaza to teach the Khalwati way of Sufism.[82] This order has perhaps been the most successful ever seen in West Africa in recent times. Al-Hajj 'Umar Tall, a Senegalese adherent of al-Tijani, spread the order far and wide, in Nigeria, Guinea, Mali, Ivory Coast, and the adjoining regions until he was killed in 1864. It is probably true to say that the *jihād* and the conversions to Islam made by al-Hajj 'Umar gave more currency to a somewhat modified Khalwati brand of Sufism than the actions of any other individual in Africa during the nineteenth century.[83]

Another near disciple of al-Hifnawi was the Algerian mystic and founder of the Rahmaniya branch of the Khalwatiya, Muhammad ibn 'Abd al-Rahman al-Azhari (1720–1784).[84] Al-Tijani, incidentally, had his first contacts with the Khalwatiya at the hands of al-Azhari. Without specifying his sources, the French writer Rinn claims that al-Azhari was dispatched by Shaykh al-Hifnawi "on a number of missions for religious propaganda to the Sudan and to India . . . at least this is what he says in his own writings. . . ."[85] Rinn also claims that al-Hifnawi then sent him to Algeria to teach "the pure doctrines of the Khalwatiya," which al-Azhari did with great success. Al-Azhari was able to work posthumous miracles: for reasons of *baraka*, the mountaineers of his native Kabylia disputed his burial place with the local Algerian Turks. The body of the saint was moved from place to place, and two tombs were erected for him, one under Turkish control, the other on Kabyle territory. Eventually the saint managed to give himself two bodies, one of which was interred in each of the tombs. In this way, al-Azhari acquired the nickname of Abu Qabrayn, "the man of two tombs."[86]

Shaykh Ahmad al-Dardir was equally a pupil of al-Hifnawi. Doctrinally, Dardir (1715–1786) attempted to reconcile the differences between the Khalwati and Naqshbandi orders, and saw his own brotherhood

[82] 'Alī Ḥarāzim, *Jawāhir*, I, 50.

[83] See B. G. Martin, "Notes sur l'origine de la ṭarīqa des Tiǧanīyya et sur les débuts d'al-Haǧǧ 'Umar, *Revue des Études Islamiques*, II (1969), 267–290.

[84] For a study of the *dhikr* of the Rahmānīya, see W. S. Haas, "The Zikr of the Rahmanija-Order in Algeria: A Psycho-Physiological Analysis," *Muslim World*, XXXIII (1943), 16–28. In this important paper, Haas discusses the psychological mechanisms for achieving a *hāl*, such as hyperventilation. There is more on this subject in J. H. Gibbon, *Surgery of the Chest* (Philadelphia, 1962), pp. 4–6.

[85] L. Rinn, *Marabouts et khouan* (Algiers, 1884), pp. 452–456. Rinn unfortunately does not say what al-Azhari's writings are. There is more information about al-Azhari in O. Depont and X. Coppolani, *Les Confréries religieuses musulmanes* (Algiers, 1897), pp. 382 ff.

[86] Rinn, *op. cit.*, p. 453.

very much as a bridge between the two. Jabarti includes a long list of his writings, one of which was a commentary on Shaykh Damirdash al-Muhammadi's *Risala fi'l-tawhid.* Dardir was a Maliki from Upper Egypt, and at one time was the chief of the students from that area in the Azhar and the director of their *waqf*. He was also famous in other Maliki regions, and sometimes received gifts from the Sharifian ruler of Morocco. He inspired many disciples by his kindness and generosity, and frequently defended many of the common people of Cairo against oppressors and plunderers, which enhanced his popularity. Even now, he is remembered by the people of the city. Bannerth includes three stories about Dardir which bring out the traits of his character: one of them is an anecdote about a woman who tries to seduce him but is then converted herself.[87]

Dardir founded a *zawiya* in Cairo on his return from the pilgrimage in 1199/1784–85. In the conventional manner, he is buried there, with a disciple, Sidi Ahmad al-Siba'i 'Ayyan. The *zawiya,* according to 'Ali Pasha Mubarak, contained two libraries of "precious books."[88] The *zawiya* still exists and is situated in the Ka'kiyyin Quarter, not far from the Mosque of Sidi Yahya al-'Uqab. Dardir had many followers, some of whom started suborders of their own. One was founded by al-Siba'i, another by al-Shubrawi, and another by al-Hajj Ahmad Khālid al-'Imrani some time before 1850 and is called the Khālidiya after him. A constellation of further subgroupings also existed inspired by the teaching of Dardir: the Lassiya, the Dayfiya, the Musallamiya, and the Sawiya. Of these smaller orders, the most important was the Sawiya, named for Ahmad al-Sawi (1764–1825). Sawi was more successful than his rivals in Egypt, Yemen, and the Hejaz.[89] In his *Jami' karamat al-awliya'*, al-Nabhani gives an account of one of al-Sawi's miracles.[90]

Since its inception in the fifteenth century, the Khalwatiya has adapted many times over to the social mosaic, to the varied demands of time and place, and to the personalities who have molded it. Reaching its peaks of influence and vitality in the Ottoman Empire in the sixteenth and seven-

[87] Jabartī, *'Aja'ib*, II, 147–148; Bannerth, *Khalwatiya*, pp. 14–74, has a great deal of information about Ahmad al-Dardīr, including a French translation of one of his pamphlets, the *Tuhfat al-ikhwān fī adab al-tarīq*.

[88] 'Alī Pāshā Mubārak, *Khitat*, II, part 6, 27.

[89] For al-Shubrawī, see Bannerth, *Khalwatiya*, pp. 63–64. For the Khālidīya, see 'Abd al-'Azim b. Ibrāhīm Muḥammad, known as Abū Sawwāda, *Al-Sa'adat al-'Azalīya fī awrād al-ṭarīqa al-Khalwatīya al-Khālidīya* (Cairo, 1371/1952. For the other small groups, see Le Chatelier, *Confréries*, p. 55.

[90] Yūsuf al-Nabhānī, *op. cit.*, I, 565–566.

teenth centuries, then in the Egypt of the eighteenth century, and in some parts of Africa in the nineteenth century, the Khalwatiya at the present time seems to have outrun its resources. Yet in Turkey, West Africa (Nigeria and Senegal), and also in Indonesia, the Tijaniya branch continues to be a religious movement of importance, with inspiring leaders and many devout adherents. Elsewhere it seems to be moribund. Given its history, however, it would be premature to think that the Khalwatiya is dead. Its future resurgence cannot be ruled out.

12 | Doctor and Saint*

ERNEST GELLNER

ACCOUNTS OF SOCIETIES in terms of the beliefs and values of their members often assume that each member has *one* set of beliefs about the world, and *one* set of values. This seems to me a major mistake. Any professional sports team invariably has more than one reserve in addition to the set normally presented to the public, ever ready to replace the first lot, either one by one or, if necessary, as a whole. The same is generally true about our cosmological picture or about our moral values. There is, of course, an interesting difference. When the cosmological picture or the moral values claim unique and exclusive validity, the overt possession and display of rival alternatives would be shameful, heretical, and scandalous. Apart from anything else, it would undermine confidence in that unique cosmological picture or set of moral values. One of the points of having the picture and the values is, of course, to reassure both oneself and others, and to proclaim that certain ideas and certain attitudes are simply not negotiable. A person who made it plain that his confidence in his own supposedly unnegotiable basic positions is less than total, and that he is keeping an alternative ready and available, would thereby undermine the credibility of his own stance and encourage intransigence in others. This would never do.

Thus the alternatives are decently hidden away. There is nothing unusual about this, and there are many parallels in social and political fields. For instance, a government recognizes the legal and legitimate authorities in a neighboring country, and it would be a hostile and provocative act to recognize at the same time some "government in exile," heading a revolutionary movement which hopes to dislodge the present rulers of the neighboring state. But, of course, it would be most unwise to have no relationships at all with that revolutionary movement: after all, they might win. So, while the department of state charged with diplomacy entertains cor-

*The material used in this paper is presented in greater detail in *Saints of the Atlas* (London and Chicago, 1969).

dial and exclusive relationships with the official government, the covert intelligence services are at liberty to maintain just as significant relationships with the revolutionaries.

The importance of the ulama is that they are the openly displayed, official first eleven of Islam. They are the norm-givers of the community of the faithful; they are the repositories and arbiters of legitimacy. So much for theory. There is one well-known manner in which reality diverges from theory: the verdict of the ulama regarding legitimacy, like the flight of that much overrated bird the Owl of Minerva, takes place only after the event, and hence in effect ratifies the actual power situation, rather than sitting in judgment on it. From the viewpoint of understanding the general social structure of Islam, this particular limitation does not matter too much, perhaps: it does mean that in general the ulama cannot do very much about determining the identity of the ruler, but are constrained to ratify whichever ruler prevails by force of arms. This is indeed so. But while they cannot determine the specific identity of the ruler, and must bow to superior strength, whether they like it or not, it does not preclude them from being extremely influential on the general *kind* of society over which the ruler presides. A group of men may be powerless with respect to filling individual roles in a society and yet extremely influential with respect to what kind of system of roles there is to be filled. This, I suspect, is indeed the role of the ulama in Islamic society: not very powerful in deciding between one ruler or dynasty and another, they were most influential in determining the general nature of the society.

But there is another limitation on their influence of quite a different kind: the limitation not on their choice of personnel, but on their influence on the general social structure. This limitation is notoriously well attested by the fact that such large segments of Muslim populations look not only, and not so much, toward the ulama for spiritual guidance, as they do toward other types of religiously significant groups, whom there is a tendency to lump together under the heading of Sufism.

It should be said that this kind of indiscriminate lumping together of what is in effect a residual category is probably a mistake. Under the general category of Sufism, people tend, for instance, to group together genuine mystics and tribal holy men whose connection with mysticism is minimal. Both may be classified by the same kind of terminology, not only by scholars but also by the local populations, but this does not mean that the two phenomena are homogeneous and deserve to be classed together, either from the viewpoint of social significance or from that of religious phenomenology. Roughly speaking: urban Sufi mysticism is an *alternative* to the legalistic, restrained, arid (as it seems to its critics)-Islam of the ulama. Rural and tribal "Sufism" is a *substitute* for it. In the one case, an alternative is sought for the Islam of the ulama because it does not fully satisfy. In the other case, a substitute for it is required because, though its endorsement is desired, it is, in its proper and urban form, locally unavailable, or is unusable in the tribal context.

There are within Islam three major types of legitimation: the Book (including its extension by Tradition), the consensus of the community, and the line of succession.

The Book is a repository of the divine word, publicly available, not incarnated in any one person, group, institution, or policy, and hence capable of sitting in judgment on any one of them. This transethnic and transsocial quality of the Book is, of course, of the utmost importance in understanding the political life both of Muslim societies and of the expansion of Islam. Even if the sociologists were right in supposing that the divine is merely the social in camouflage, it is a fact of the greatest importance that the camouflage (if such it be) is so rigorously maintained, and hence emphatically ensures the nonidentification of the divine with any *one* concrete human or social representative of it.

Another important form of legitimation, in Islam and elsewhere, is, of course, the consensus of the community. In Islam, this approach has complemented rather than opposed the Book. Islamic societies have never been what might be called "pure" democratic societies; they have not maintained that the *only* sort of legitimacy is the consent of the community. That consent was invoked only for the supplementing of divine truth by interpretation where interpretation was required, rather than as an independent and equally powerful source. In practice, the Book required scholars to read it and consensus to interpret it, and hence, concretely speaking, the authority of the ulama as religious scholars, and that of the community as interpreters of the Words, were in harmony.

But there is a third type of legitimation within Islam, that of Succession. Succession can be either physical or spiritual, and sometimes one genealogical line may employ both physical and spiritual links. The physical links, of course, arise from the fact that there is no requirement of celibacy on religious leaders. The spiritual links are made possible by mystical doctrine: mystical illumination can be passed on from teacher to disciple in a legitimacy-preserving way, analogous to the manner in which paternity maintains legitimacy of authority from father to son.

This third principle of legitimation is, of course, not always in harmony with the other two. In Shi'i Islam, it becomes, of course, the main principle bringing with it the possibility of overruling the other two. But even within Sunni Islam, which does not have the same stress on locating religious legitimacy in a lineage, succession can become extremely important, and particularly so in social conditions that display a particularly strong requirement that the Word should become Flesh. There are such milieus. The most obvious examples are, of course, tribal societies, cut off from the Book by the fact that their members are illiterate (and, one should add, that they do not possess the means for sustaining or protecting a class of literate scholars), and in some measure cut off from the wider Islamic consensus by a relationship of hostility (and yet of economic interdependence) with those urban centers which are somehow the visible incarnation and center of gravity of the Muslim civilization. In such tribal milieus, there is a shift of stress in legitimation from the Book or the abstract consensus, toward the lineage. The stress is, of course, exemplified in practice rather than expressed in any kind of theory.

This, then, is the general setting: the significance of the tribal holy lineages is that they satisfy a need for the incarnation of the Word in a milieu that through lack of literacy and of towns cannot use the ulama. Thus the lineages of holy men are an alternative to the ulama, an alternative that at the same time, within the wider spiritual economy of Islam, is parasitical on them. It provides an alternative and in effect serves and represents values other than those of the ulama, and yet at the same time indirectly endorses the values and views of the ulama. Tribal society has its values and attitudes, and these are served and symbolized by the tribal holy men. The tribesmen do not wish to be any different from what they are. But they are, in the eyes of their more learned urban folk, sinful and/or heretical. They know that this is how they are seen, and they do not really repudiate the judgment. They accept it, and yet wish to persist in their attitudes. At the same time, they do not in any way desire to opt out of the wider community of Islam. Their attitude really is that of Saint Augustine: Lord, make me pure, but not yet. They recognize standards of purity in terms of which their own tribal society fails, yet at the same time wish to remain as they are, indefinitely. They are quite aware of the conflict and contradiction, yet at the same time the contradiction is not articulated clearly or stressed. It is there, yet is clouded in decent obscurity.

The significance of the tribal holy men lies in the manner in which they help to perpetuate this situation.

The Berbers of the central high Atlas are an outstandingly fine example of the manner in which the Word must become Flesh when incarnated in a tribal society. In addition to factors frequently found elsewhere in Islam, there are here some additional ones, which perhaps once operated throughout the Maghreb, but which in any case are most clearly preserved here. These local factors are a most remarkable case of tribal separation of powers, inspired not by either modern or any political theory, but tied in beautifully with the requirements of religious representation.

The political and social system of these tribes is segmentary, which is to say, each tribe divides and subdivides again and so forth until family units are reached. At each level of size, all segments are equal and there is no division of labor between them, either of an economic or of a political nature. Neither within segments nor between them are there any specialized political institutions or groups. Thus, from the viewpoint of the tribe as a whole, the tribe possesses a treelike structure, dividing and subdividing in the manner of the branches of a tree—though there is no central and preeminent trunk, all branches being equal. From the viewpoint of any one individual or family, this means that he or it are at the center of a number of concentric circles—the intravillage clan, the village, the group of villages forming a local clan, the larger clan, the tribe, and so forth. None of these superimposed groupings, from the individual's viewpoint, ever cuts across another and thus ideally they give no rise to conflicting obligations. Conflict at a lower level in no way precludes cohesion and cooperation at a higher level: in other words, two clans may be hostile to each other yet cooperate jointly as members of the tribe against another tribe. Everything is symmetrical and egalitarian: although, of course, some men and some groups manage temporarily to be richer or more influential than others, this gives no rise either to a permanent, or a symbolically ratified, stratification. Only complete outsiders to the tribe can be located, socially speaking, above or below: negroid or Jewish artisans and holy men are the only significant exceptions, in the traditional system, to the pervasive symmetry and equality.

The general features of such segmentary societies, with their diffusion of power and the maintenance of order by the opposition of groups to one another at all levels, are well known. The only remarkable thing about the Berbers of the central high Atlas is the degree of perfection to which they have brought the system. They approximate more closely an ideal type of segmentary society than do most other socities of this kind, including those most frequently cited when the principles of segmentation are expounded.

A crucial feature of the society, which conveys its general nature, is chieftaincy. Chieftaincy among these tribes is elective and annual. Moreover, the manner of election is remarkable: it observes the principles of what I call "rotation and complementarity." These work as follows: suppose a tribe to be subdivided into three clans, A, B, and C. Any given year it will be the turn of one clan only to supply the chief. But the clan that supplies the chief does not elect him. Suppose Clan A supplies the chief: then it is the turn of the men of clans B and C to be the electors. In other words, any given year, a clan can supply either candidates or voters, but not both.

This system of rotation and complementarity operates at a number of levels of segmentation at once, so that the political system as a whole could be compared to a number of rotating wheels-within-wheels. The system is somewhat modified at the top and at the bottom ends of the scale, in terms of size. At the top, the wheel may turn only if there is need of it: in concrete terms, a topmost chief may be elected only if there is need of him, if there is some issue of concern to the topmost unit. There will be no filling of chieftaincy posts for the sake of continuity alone. At the very bottom, rotation and complementarity may not be observed. If it is a matter of choosing heads of tiny segments, say, of the three subclans within a village, the total population of which is in the neighborhood of two or three hundred people, then the chief of these miniscule subsegments will be chosen from the segment as a whole and not from a restricted area of candidacy, so to speak. At that level, the number of people available with suitable talents may be so small that such restriction would prove too cumbersome. But for the village of about two or three hundred inhabitants, rotation and implementing will be observed.

The relationship of lower level chiefs to higher level chiefs is obscure and eludes the categories of neat political or administrative theory. The lower level chiefs are at once elective heads of their units, and representatives within their units of the higher level chiefs.

A particularly bewildering feature of the system is what I call leapfrogging in the hierarchy. It works as follows. Suppose there are four levels of size of segmentary units. It may happen that top chiefs of units at the level of size 1 will have their agents and representatives chiefs at level 3, whereas chiefs at level 2 will act through representatives at level 4. In other words, there will be two hierarchies which, as it were, pass through each other without affecting each other, articulated as they are in two different media. In an ordinary, centralized, nonsegmentary society, where the maintenance of order is the concern of some specialized agencies in the society, this would be madness. It would be inconceivable for the government, or for the courts, or for the police to be concerned with conflicts and violence only selectively, according to the level of size at which they occur, with one police force concerned with conflicts at one set of levels and another police force concerned with conflicts at another set, the two sets being related to each other like alternate layers in a cake. In a segmentary society, where violence and aggression is a tort and not a crime, and where conflicts of units of different size are kept apart and do not implicate one another, this kind of arrangement makes perfectly good sense.

The political system of the lay tribes of the central Atlas does not concern us directly, but only for its implications for the holy lineages. What are the relevant features of this political system? Its most obvious features are weak chieftaincy and lack of continuity. All chiefs are lame ducks. As soon as elected they are within a year of the termination of their office (even if, rather exceptionally, their tenure may be prolonged). Moreover, they depend on the votes of the members of the rival clans, in a society built upon the rivalry of clans. They have no agents or sanctions, other than minor chieftains elected in a manner similar to their own: they have no secretariat and no police force. The only backing they have are the moral pressures of public opinion and the normal mechanisms of segmented societies—the anger of the offended subgroup in the case of an offense against it.

All these factors militate against the emergence of permanent and tyrannical chieftains and privileged political lineages, and indeed, their political system did enable the Berbers of the central High Atlas to escape the kind of ephemeral but harsh tyranny which characterized, for instance, the western High Atlas in this century.

But if the merit of the system is to provide checks and balances against tyranny and political ambition, its corresponding weakness is, as indicated, a lack of continuity and of order-maintaining agency. Yet these tribes do need a measure of order. They are not made up of small, inward-turned communities. They are ecologically most diversified and complementary. The natural environment is highly diversified, with extremes of climate and season between the Sahara edge and the high pastures of the Atlas mountains, whose highest point rises above 4,000 meters. The shepherds and their flocks can survive thanks only to a complex pattern of transhumance, involving movement over large distances and the drawing up of complex pasture rights, synchronized use, and deferment of use, of the better pastures, and the drawing of boundaries in time (seasonally) as well as in space. Many tribes must trade if they are to survive, being grossly deficient in their production of staple cereals, and all of them trade if they are to procure salt, and what might be called the essential luxuries of sugar and tea, and, in the olden days, firearms and ammunition. At the same time, order is not maintained, in the traditional situation, by the central government: on the contrary, the tribes ensure that central government does not interfere in their affairs. In brief, we have a situation of great ecological and economic interdependence, combined with only very weak and, in themselves, inadequate political institutions for the maintenance of the order required by economic life and for purposes of communication. How is this paradox resolved?

This is, of course, the point at which the holy lineages enter the argument.

It might be best first of all to describe them briefly. The holy men (*igurramen,* in the local Berber dialect) live in settlements generally centered on the shrine of the founding saintly ancestor. They possess a genealogy linking them to this ancestor. In the central High Atlas, the genealogy generally stretches back beyond the founding ancestor and leading, finally, to the Prophet through his daughter and his son-in-law, Our Lord Ali.

The settlements around the shrine may be quite large and have up to something like three hundred inhabitants. In some cases, virtually all the members of the settlement may be descendants of the founding saint (in the sense of believing themselves to be such and having the claim generally recognized). Nevertheless, even in these cases in which this genealogical qualification is widely diffused, by no means all of them will actually perform the function ascribed to igurramen. This function will only be performed by a small number among them, and in a limiting case, by only one of them. The others may be described as laicized or latent saints. Presumably their ancestors once were effective saints, but the offspring were pushed out into a lay condition by demographic pressure and by the crucial fact that it is of the very nature of this kind of sanctity, that it is concentrated in a small number of people. Excessive diffusion is incompatible with its very nature.

What is the role of the effective saints? They provide the continuity and the stable framework that the political system of the lay tribes so conspicuously lacks. For instance: the lay chiefs are elective. But elections are procedures that require some kind of institutional background, and this society, needless to say, has no civil service or secretariat or anything of the kind that could look after these matters. So the elections take place at the settlement and near the shrine of the hereditary holy men, which is, of course, also a sanctuary within which one must not feud. Thus the saints provide the physical locale and the moral guarantee that make it possible for rival clans to assemble and carry out their elections. They also provide the means of moral persuasion and the mediation that help ensure that the elections, in the end, arrive at a unanimous conclusion.

Or again: the saints provide the cornerstone for the legal system (or perhaps one should say, arbitration system) of the lay tribes. The legal decision procedure is trial by collective oath, with the number of cojurors dependent on the gravity of the offense. A theft might require two cojurors; a rape, four; a murder of a woman, twenty; a murder of a man, forty. The rule is that issues requiring less than ten cojurors are settled on the spot, among the lay tribes, but issues requiring ten or more cojurors are taken up to the shrine of the founding saint of the holy lineage, and settled with the moral assistance of the saints who are the progeny of the enshrined founder.

The saints and their settlements are thus arbitrators between tribes, and between their clans, and they are physically located on important boundaries. This indicates a further important function performed by them: their physical location at important boundaries indicates and guarantees those boundaries. Their moral authority also helps to guarantee the complex seasonal arrangements connected with transhumancy between the high mountain pastures and the desert edge. Their location on the frontier also greatly assists trade. Tribesmen visiting markets in neighboring tribes can pass through the settlement of the saints, deposit their arms there, and be accompanied on their way to the market by a saint from the settlement or a representative of an important saint. This holy fellow traveler then provides simultaneously a guarantee of their safety from their hosts and a guarantee of their good conduct toward their hosts.

The political life of the saints is quite different from that of the lay tribes. There is a neat contrast in almost every respect. Lay chiefs are chosen by the people: saints are chosen only by God. Lay chiefs are, in principle, annual: saints are permanent, and in principle permanent over generations. Lay tribesmen are addicted to feuding and litigation: saints are obligatorily pacific and must not litigate. (In the tribal mind, litigation and violence are very close to each other. The collective oath is the continuation of the feud by other means.)

The basic contradition in the life of the saints arises from the fact that there must not be too many of them: their role and influence hinges on the one-many relationship between them and the tribes, for one saint must arbitrate among many tribes or tribal segments. At the same time, saints proliferate, and yet they have no rule of succession to decide the inheritance of saintly role. The rule of inheritance among the saints is the same as among the lay tribes, and is symmetrical as between brothers. There is only a very slight predisposition in favor of primogeniture, a predisposition that is certainly not decisive.

How then is the succession decided? In the local mind, it is only God who decides. It would be presumptuous indeed for men to decide where grace, *baraka,* is to flow. God makes his choice manifest through the possession by the elect of the crucial attributes of pacifism, uncalculating generosity and hospitality, and prosperity.

In reality it is, of course, a kind of unconscious choice by the tribesmen which decides the succession. By using this rather than that son, by using this rather than that rival saintly lineage, the tribesmen in effect choose and elect the given son or lineage as the "real" saint. But the fact that the voice of God is really the voice of the people is not made manifest and explicit. The voice of the people manifests itself through making feasible the possession or attribution of characteristics which are then seen as signs of divine election. A man who is used by the tribesmen as a saint and revered as such can afford to be pacific, to turn the other cheek, with impunity. A man who is not respected as a saint would, if he behaved in this kind of way, only attract aggression. A man who is revered by the tribesmen as a saint will receive plentiful donations and can afford to act with what appears to be uncalculating generosity, and yet also retain that other attribute of election, namely, prosperity. A man, on the other hand, who did not receive adequate donations from the tribe but who behaved as if he were in effect a saint would impoverish himself and thereby make most manifest his lack of divine grace.

Thus the choice of the tribesmen externalizes itself and comes to appear as a divine choice. The mediating factor is, of course, the stress of the specifically saintly virtues of pacifism and of uncalculating generosity. The possession of these virtues is the test: one can acquire them only with the cooperation of the lay tribesmen. Pacifism and a consider-the-lilies attitude among the saints cannot be explained as some kind of diffusion or survival of values derived from the Sermon on the Mount. They are much too inherently and visibly a necessary corollary of the local social structure, of the role performed by saints within it and the manner of attributing sanctity within it. They are in no way generalized beyond the role that requires them.

Thus both the conceptualization and the rhythm of political life are quite different among the saints from those that are found among lay tribes. The political life of the saints is a game of very slow musical chairs, played out over generations not by the removal of chairs but by the addition to the number of contestants. Success and failure in it are in principle for keeps and are seen as the consequences of supernatural, divine favor. By contrast, election to chieftaincy among the lay tribes is in the hands of men, not of God, and is for a limited period only. There is a belief among nonanthropologists that tribesmen generally see their tribal arrangements as supernaturally sanctioned. Berbers of the central High Atlas do not: they know their own tribal arrangements to be secular and based on the will of men, and they have the conceptual equipment that enables them to be clear about it. This equipment is, of course, derived not from secularist philosophers, but simply from the fact that within their own society, they need to distinguish between the divine factor in political life, represented by the saints, and the secular factor, complementing it and represented by themselves. What the saints decide is, in local belief, a reflection of divine will: but what the tribal assembly decides, though deserving of respect as perpetuation of ancestral custom, springs from a human source and can on occasion be consciously and deliberately changed by consent.

There is, however, one further function performed by the saints, over and above the invaluable role they visibly fulfill in the local socio-political structure. This additional role is to anchor the local society in the wider system of Islam. The saints are not merely saints: they are also, in local belief, the descendants of the Prophet. The tribesmen know that in the eyes of inhabitants of the urban centers of literate Islam, they are held to be at worst heretical and sinful, and at best sadly ignorant of religion. They know that only Muslims may own land, and that a tribe convicted of not being Muslim would provide a most enviable justification for all its neighbors to dispossess it. Admittedly, the city dwellers would not have the means to deprive a mountain or desert tribe of its land, but they could encourage other tribes to combine in a joint act of aggression against it. So every tribe needs, and in any case wishes, to display its Muslim status. They can hardly do this through Koranic scholarship. They are illiterate. But they *can* do it by showing due reverence to those supposed descendants of the Prophet who are so conveniently settled among them, helping to guarantee tribal frontiers and in other ways assisting the tribes to manage their affairs.

This, then, is one further function of the holy lineages. Though the holy lineages are often assimilated to Sufism, their real life and function has little to do with mysticism and the diffusion of mystical ideas. (On the contrary, some supposedly Sufi practices may in fact derive from tribal customs, tribal styles of dancing, and so forth.)

The political system in which permanent and pacific saints divide the political role with elective, secular, and feud-addicted tribal chieftains is elegant and, *structurally*, sufficient unto itself. But it is not *conceptually* sufficient unto itself. Conceptually, it is other-directed and looks toward the wider world of Islam. Spiritually speaking, the holy lineages are lords of the marches. They represent the religion of the central tradition of the wider society for the tribesmen, and guarantee the tribesmen's incorporation in it. As described, they also help the tribesmen to avoid being saddled with physical, military lords of the marches, by giving continuity and stability to a system otherwise possessing only minimal political leadership.

How is this local other-directedness concretely manifested?

The manifestations vary in kind. They are found both among the lay tribes and the holy lineages. Take, as a simple example, some legends circulating both about and among one of the most backward, savage, and religiously ignorant among the Atlas tribes, the Ait Abdi of the Ait Sochman. When I say that this tribe is particularly backward, savage, and ignorant of religion, I refer to a stereotype held of it not just by outsiders to the region, urban folk and such, but by other tribes *within* the region itself, and, most significantly, by the tribe itself. Though all mountain tribes without distinction may seem to be licentious, violent, heterodox savages to the bourgeoisie of Fez, once you get in among the tribes you find, as so often, that further subtle distinctions and nuances can be made by anyone with local knowledge. All tribesmen may seem savages from Fez, but for the connoisseur, some are much more so than others, even, or especially, in their own estimation.

The Ait Abdi are at the end of the road, literally and figuratively speaking. Or rather, literally speaking they are a good way beyond the end of the road, for no road at all makes its way to their desolate and stony plateau. Even nowadays, you can get there only on foot or on the back of a mule, and the plateau is held to be almost inaccessible in winter. Figuratively speaking, they are at the end of the road, for almost anyone can look down on them as savages, and as far as I know there is no one more savage on whom they can look down, though there are some who are perhaps their equals in this respect.

The interesting thing is that the Ait Abdi themselves share this view. There is one legend that circulates among and about them which is particularly suggestive. This legend is something utterly familiar to every child among the Ait Abdi, as Father Christmas is to a child in Western society.

The legend runs as follows: a false teacher of Islam, in fact a Jew, appeared among the Ait Abdi, and was received by them and recognized as a true religious teacher. He made a good living among them as a *fqih*, that is to say, scribe and Koranic teacher. He was in fact quite devoid of the religious knowledge he was supposed to teach, but he did not allow this to dismay him: instead of reciting the Koran, he simply rattled off various well-known local place names, ending this recitation with the words—I show you your land, O heads of asses—*ichfau n'ighiel*. Despite this blatant effrontery, it took the Ait Abdi quite some time to unmask him—and the rest of the legend does not concern us.

Note the point of the story: it illustrates, of course, the perfidy, cunning, and effrontery of the infidel-foreigner, but it also illustrates, indeed highlights, the stupidity, gullibility, and total religious ignorance of the Ait Abdi themselves. Yet they themselves tell the story!

This is not the only legend in which the Ait Abdi display a kind of joking relationship to their own image and history. Another story, as popular and familiar among them and their neighbors as is the story of the scurrilous religious teacher, concerns a man, Ohmish, and his wife, Tuda Lahcen, whose intransigence and pugnacity triggered a murderous chain reaction of feud and killing, all started by a trivial quarrel on a pasture. It is actually *forbidden* among the Ait Abdi to tell this story, on the assumption that its recounting will bring bad luck and perhaps a repetition of such episodes, yet at the same time the story is utterly familiar to all of them. The moral of the situation is—we know we ought not to be so quarrelsome and feud-addicted, and we know at the same time perfectly well that this is just how we are.

Another legend—this one told about rather than among them—explains why it is that they find themselves on their particularly bare and stony plateau: the reason is that they fought so ferociously against their rightful Sultan, Mulay Hassan (referring to the nineteenth-century monarch of this name, and not to the present king). It is a curious explanation, insofar as they were by no means the only tribe, or even the most important one, which joined in resisting the attempts of that ruler to penetrate the mountains. But, as so often in these legends, the explanation is, so to speak, differential: what counts as an explanation in one case would not count as such in another. Explanations are not universalized.

What concerns us of course is that the legend underscores once again the recognition of a value—submission to the central state—which is in fact not practiced by the very tribes who repeat the story (or rather, was not practiced till the modern world forced them to practice it, and of course the legend antedates the centralization imposed under modern conditions).

So much by way of illustration of the kind of self-ironizing attitude, the joking relationship with one's own image, as manifested in legends circulating among the lay tribes. The situation becomes even clearer and more conspicuous among the holy lineages.

Here nature has arranged a nice experimental situation. All other factors being held constant, one factor alone is varied, as if for our benefit. This independent variable is: the proximity to the plain and hence to the urban centers from which scripturalist, puritanical, and reformist Islam emanates.

In the central High Atlas, there are a number of centers of sanctity, of holy settlements that act as sanctuaries, centers of arbitration, and pilgrimage, for the surrounding tribes. In many ways, these centers are very similar to one another (though of course they differ in size, influence, and one or two other associated features). On their own account, of course, they ought indeed to resemble one another, insofar as they all have the same ancestor: within quite a wide area of the mountainous terrain where the

Middle Atlas fuses with the High Atlas, most holy men, and virtually all holy men of influence, are descended from one founding saint, Sidi Said Ahansal. They are, or believe themselves to be, of one flesh and blood, though this of course does not preclude bitter rivalry among them.

But as stated, they are geographically separated, living as generally they do on important frontiers *between* lay tribes. Some of them are in the very heart of the mountains while others are not far from the edge of the plain. For purposes of comparison, we shall take the dramatic contrast between the founding and central lodge, Zawiya Ahansal, and another lodge, somewhat to the north and much closer to the plain, named Temga.

The holy men of both lodges agree on one important point of faith and morals—namely that dancing (*ahaidus*) is immoral and un-Islamic. This point is widely accepted in Morocco and has received much support and endorsement from the Muslim Reform movement. At the same time, of course, this form of dancing is a well-established and extremely popular part of the folklore of the Berber tribes. The issue of the dance has all the potent emotive coloring that the theater had for seventeenth-century puritans. What urban Muslims and those under their influence find particularly shocking is that in the course of this kind of tribal dance, men and women mingle and it can even happen that they dance shoulder to shoulder! This reaction was shared by the great leftist leader Mehdi Ben Barka, later kidnapped and presumably murdered, who was a great champion of the equality of women. For instance, he rejected with scorn the argument that Muslim polygamy was acceptable because it was merely a legalized version of the informal polygamy current among Europeans, with their habit of having mistresses. As he put it, polygamy, whether legalized or informal, was wrong. In consequence of his nationalist activity, Mehdi Ben Barka had at one time been imprisoned by the French and placed for safe custody among one of the central High Atlas tribes, the Ait Haddidu. In the course of his imprisonment in the mountain fastness, he had opportunity to witness this form of dancing. Yet even he, left-wing modernist, was shocked, as he later told me, by these dances and the possibility of women, even married women, being involved!

This perhaps illustrates the deep feeling that is involved in this rejection of tribal dancing. Anyway, to return to our saintly lineages: the two centers, both the founding lodge and Temga, agreed that dancing is highly improper. Some time probably before the turn of the century, the two saintly settlements held a joint meeting to discuss such theological and no doubt other outstanding issues, and in the course of it decided that henceforth, as good Muslims and descendants of the Prophet, they would refrain from dancing. As a matter of fact, Temga and its group of lodges have kept to this self-denying ordinance to this day, at least to the extent of imposing and enforcing fines on any of their own number who are caught dancing. The meeting at which this was agreed, and the subsequent events can be roughly dated; they occurred when a man named Ahmad u Ahmad was leader in the main lodge, and his "reign" overlapped with the passage of Father de Foucauld through the area of Ahansal influence—though he was unable to visit the lodges in question. Father de Foucauld's passage through the area took place in 1883 and 1884.

As stated, the saints of Temga and their group stuck to the agreed principles. Not so the saints of the main or founding lodge. Soon after the agreement, a male infant was born in one of the leading families. The overjoyed family and their kinsmen simply could not restrain themselves, and in no time, as anyone who is familiar with the habits of the main lodge would indeed expect, they were off, dancing like nobody's business.

This blatant transgression of holy law *and* violation of solemn agreement did not, of course, pass unnoticed. Such a combination of religious transgression and violation of solemn agreement was too much for the men of Temga, and they took up arms against their lax, irreligious, and self-indulgent cousins. The conflict and feud are said to have lasted seven years (a suspect figure, which with some other evidence suggests that the whole episode is now on the borderline of history and legend). In the end, the conflict was brought to a close by the intervention and arbitration of the surrounding lay, feud-addicted tribes. The irony of this part of the story of course in no way escapes the attention of either the lay tribes or the saints. The ferocious, savage, feud-addicted lay tribes had to exercise strong moral pressure and arbitration to bring to an end murderous violence between holy, obligatorily and essentially pacific saints.

One should add that another feature of the situation is quite obvious to all the locals: they are not at all taken in by the theological occasion of the conflict between the two saintly centers. "Everyone knows" that, however emotively septic the issue of dancing may be, the real underlying cause of the conflict was a rivalry between the two lodges for influence—a rivalry that normally is kept within the bounds imposed by the obligation of pacifism on saints, but which on this occasion transcended those bounds.

The whole story is highly instructive from a number of viewpoints. It illustrates our general argument in the following way: everyone concerned endorses and formally accepts the values that are believed to be those of urban, central Islam, exemplified above all by Fez. In particular, those values prohibit dancing. There is no disagreement at the level of theoretical endorsement.

But some are under greater pressure to conform to these values than others. The Temga group of lodges is close to the edge of the plain, and some of its client tribes are right on the edge of the plain. In other words, they have to satisfy a tribal clientele who are also close to urban centers of religious propaganda, and they have to compete for the favors of this clientele with other religious leaders, some of them actually urban, who can exemplify values and ideals closer to the scriptural and puritanical ideals of the ulama. To meet this competition and answer its arguments, the holy men of Temga and its groups have no choice but to try to emulate those standards.

The main lodge is in quite a different position. It is much older established than Temga and thus, not being on the make, does not have to extend itself to establish its own holiness. More important, it is located right in the depth of the mountains, within half a day's march of the main Sahara-Atlantic watershed. The tribes that form its clientele are likewise overwhelmingly drawn from the heart of the mountains, and from the area between the mountains and the Sahara. Though these saints also need to compete for their followership with other saints, they do not need to compete with any urban-based religious centers. In other words, the urban puritanical ideals are far away and have no local anchorage or sanction. No wonder that there was so little countervailing power available in the hearts of the men of the main lodge, to help them to resist the temptation of the dance!

In the purely tribal context, exemplified by the main lodge, the "central" values are endorsed but not practiced. The local tribesmen require the holy lineages, the incarnation of Islam, mainly for purposes such as arbitration, mediation, social continuity, facilitation of trade, and so forth, and are not at all interested in purity. On the contrary, they are interested in a kind of cover for impurity. If they can have their own, very own, local saints, who like themselves dance but at the same time, being descendants of the Prophet, can claim to be as close to the source of Islam as the learned men of the city, so much the better. That way, one can legitimate one's Muslim status and persist in the ancient practices, and no very serious tension need be felt by anyone.

Things become a bit different as one comes closer to the plain, or when for one reason or another the urban world exercises stronger pressures.

The hereditary holy men of Temga still perform the same functions as do their cousins of the main lodge, but they have to do so in a context that in part is open to the influence from the plain.

Thus the same ideals are proclaimed throughout, but the way in which a compromise is reached with the exigencies of tribal life differs according to circumstance.

Or take another illustration. In the area of Ahansal influence there is one legend that is particularly popular and which with some variation in detail is often recounted. I shall call it the Kingmaker story.

Its hero is Sidi Mohamed n'ut Baba, an ancestor of the effectively saintly sublineage within the main lodge. If this legend is true, he would have had to have been alive toward the end of the seventeenth century. The story begins during the reign of the Sultan Mulay Rashid. This sultan apparently sent a messenger to the saint, to inquire how he managed to acquire so much holiness. The saint impressed the messenger by additional displays of saintly powers, such as making a mule give birth to a young mule. In return he asked the monarch to liberate some tribesmen from among his client tribes, whom the monarch had imprisoned. The monarch refused, and the incensed saint decided to punish the monarch by magical means. He hammered a magical *tagust* into the ground. A *tagust* is a metal peg used for attaching animals, and as it is hammered into the ground it is extremely phallic in appearance and function. The word is in fact also used to mean "penis." But I shall not dwell on the obvious and suggestive Freudian aspects of the story.

As a result of hammering the *tagust* into the ground the monarchy came upon a troubled period and in the end Mulay Rashid died. This was not the worst: his death was followed by one of those anarchic interregna which are not infrequent in Moroccan history.

The next sultan-to-be, Mulay Ismail, failing to overcome these difficulties, came to the saint for advice. He stayed at the main lodge for a few days, presenting his case. The saint, evidently convinced by the strength of this pretender's claims, in the end gave him advice. The details of this advice and Mulay Ismail's adventures in carrying it out do not concern us, but they involved his finding the magical *tagust*, pulling it out of the ground as prearranged by the saint, and finding himself at that moment back in Fez, acclaimed by the populace as King!

Given the Freudian undertones of the liberated *tagust*, the legend is a fine specimen of a "Waste Land" story, in which the peace and prosperity of the kingdom depends on the virility of the monarch. But this is not the aspect I wish to dwell on.

The aspect that is interesting from the viewpoint of our theme is a certain ideological naïveté of the story. The manifest purpose and moral of the story is obvious: it is meant to heighten the prestige of the local holy lineage by turning it and its ancestor, contrary to all historical probability, into a kingmaker and arbitrator of the political fortunes in the distant capital of Fez. (The legend is unhistorical to the extent that the striking feature of this particular holy lineage is its stability and continuity in its mountain homeland, and its abstention, in the main, from interference in or impact on politics at the urban centers of the country. The two things may well be connected.)

This is the only too obvious purpose of anyone telling the story: the story wears its heart on its sleeve, and it would be almost impossible to retell the story without empathizing its moral. Yet unwittingly, in its simplemindedness, the story also endorses the ultimate legitimacy of that central monarchy, which had no effective power locally and which the local tribesmen defied, and from whose power they had collectively seceded. The local tribesmen paid no taxes to Fez and received no officials from it: if the peripatetic court and army attempted to enter their territory, they fought to stop it. In order to raise the prestige of their own little local holy men and their link with Islam, they retell the story showing how influential and crucial those holy men are. Yet in telling the story, they unwittingly recognize the ultimate authority of the center. The story does not even hint that its hero, the saint, should have himself become a sultan: it only hints that by magical means it was he who enabled the sultan to rule effectively.

These various legends and situations illustrate, though of course they do not by themselves prove, the main contention of this argument: Islam embraces various types of social structure, and while the ulama are its ultimate and most important expression, its constitutional court so to speak, yet many of those social structures, notably tribal ones, cannot accommodate or use these learned scribes, and need other anchorages for religion. A typical specimen of these anchorages are the holy lineages, so highly developed among the Berbers, but by no means unparalleled elsewhere. These holy lineages are tied by links of terminology and even organization to mystical urban clubs, but despite the similarity of terminology, and sometimes organizational relations, the two phenomena are quite distinct in nature and function. Thus very little is explained by any simple reference to the diffusion of Sufi ideas. It is important to understand just what the saints do and what they mean in their context. In the case of the holy lineages of the recesses of the mountains, their acquaintance with or interest in Sufi ideas is negligible. What they do and what thy mean can only be understood by reference to the tribes whom they serve.

But while these lineages are very unlike urban ulama, and sadly deficient when the standards proclaimed or even practiced by urban ulama are applied to them, they should not be seen as unambiguously hostile to them. Their role is inherently ambiguous. They must serve tribal, non-urban ends, but they must also link the tribes with a wider and urban-oriented ideal of Islam. They serve both local tribal needs and universal Islamic identification. They hamper the diffusion of good and proper Islam, in a way, by giving the tribesmen an excuse for pretending that they are *already* good Muslims, that they already possess the institutional framework of faith: and yet at the same time, they keep the door open for the propagation of "purer" Islam by endorsing it in the course of those very practices in which they deviate from it.

13 The Hamadsha

VINCENT CRAPANZANO

THE RELIGIOUS BROTHERHOOD, or *tariqa,* has been related by both Western and Eastern Orientalists to an idealized picture of Sufism and has suffered, thereby, from too rigid a definition. Although many of the beliefs and practices of the members of the various brotherhoods find their origin in the teachings of the Sufis, there are many others that appear to have scant relation to either the teachings of Islam in general or Sufism in particular. These beliefs and practices have been conceived as peripheral to what scholars arbitrarily maintain is the central aim of the orders, the mystical[1] union with God. They are summarily dismissed as vestiges of pre-Islamic religion, which have a strong appeal for the illiterate masses, rather than interpreted as constituent elements within a comprehensive system of ritual and belief.

Sufism itself is no one thing. It has been reified, romanticized, and understood in terms that may be appropriate to the Christian mystical tradition but not necessarily to non-Western "mysticisms." To generalize about Sufism is like generalizing about Western European philosophy, or at least Scholasticism. Not only is all the subtlety of the individual thinkers lost in such an approach but the depth and variety of their emotional and mystical experiences are flattened. Sufism is better conceived, as Clifford Geertz has recently put it, as "a series of different and even contradictory experiments." It has been, he maintains, "less a definite standpoint in Islam, a distinct conception of religiousness like Methodism or Swedenborgianism than a diffuse expression of that necessity . . . for a world religion to come to terms with the variety of mentalities, the multiplicity of local forms of faith, and yet maintain the essence of its own identity."[2] This approach appears to shed Sufism of the distinctly idealized interpreta-

[1] Throughout this paper I use "mystical" in a restricted sense: of, resulting from, or manifesting an individual's direct communion with God (Allah).

[2] Clifford Geertz, *Islam Observed: Religious Development in Morocco and Indonesia* (New Haven and London, 1968), p. 48.

tion it has received in at least the writings of some Orientalists and to have opened its study to a more dynamic approach which can incorporate some of the more heterodox beliefs. A similar approach must be taken to the tariqa, both in its own right and as an offshoot of Sufism.

In this paper, I examine, in both its urban and shantytown settings, a Moroccan brotherhood, the Hamadsha, whose ostensible purpose is not a mystical union with God but the curing of the devil struck and the devil possessed. The Hamadsha belong to a category of brotherhoods, the *confréries populaires*, as the French have called them, which appeal primarily to the lowest strata of Islamic society. The members of such orders often engage in extreme practices, such as drinking boiling water, licking red-hot steel blades, or stabbing themselves with long knives, practices that have been vigorously condemned by the Orthodox. Their beliefs often appear unsophisticated and heterodox to the scholar, and they make little attempt to integrate them with the orthodox tenets of Islam. The adepts are indirectly dedicated to God. The object of their devotion is often a saint or a demon whom they must placate. Such amalgamations of beliefs and practices do form systems, however, which meet, with varying degrees of success, the social and psychological needs of their adepts and followers. In the case of the Hamadsha, these needs vary from the shantytown which has not yet developed structured institutions or even a communal spirit of its own to the old quarter (*madina*) with its established institutions and neighborhoods, and, in as rapidly a changing society as Morocco, these needs are changing. The Hamadsha of the shantytowns appear to have been more successful in adapting to the demands imposed by their new social setting than those of the medina, who have been more conservative. While the former are thriving, at least in the city of Meknes, the latter are rapidly dying out. By presenting the order in two of its settings, I hope to underline not only the differences that can occur within a single brotherhood but also its adaptability (or lack of adaptability) to differing social conditions.

Despite a certain notoriety that the Hamadsha have attained in the literature on Maghrebian brotherhoods as a result of their practices of self-mutilation—usually by slashing at their heads with knives and axes—they have never been the subject of a detailed investigation. Their fame rests primarily on a few eyewitness accounts in French and Moroccan newspapers, occasional observations in monographs devoted to other subjects, and on two longer articles, one of which, by the archaeologist

J. Herber, is of some merit.[3] The founders of the order and their followers have left no writings, and although the descendants of one of the two founders have in their possession a handwritten history of the Hamadsha, recently prepared by a scholar from Fez, it appears to be little more than a genealogical justification for their use of the title *sharif*. The material presented in this paper is largely the result of a year of fieldwork with the Hamadsha in the city of Meknes and on the nearby Jebel Zerhoun.[4]

The Hamadsha in fact are members of two distinct brotherhoods that are frequently confused: The 'Allaliyyin (or rarely but perhaps more appropriately 'Aliwiyyin) who are followers of the saint Sidi 'Ali ben Hamdush, and the Dghughiyyin, who follow Sidi 'Ali's servant or slave Sidi Ahmad Dghughi.[5] Both saints are buried some sixteen miles northwest of the city of Meknes on the south face of the Zerhoun massif. Sidi 'Ali, whose tomb is one of the largest in Morocco, is buried in the comparatively wealthy village of Beni Rachid, and Sidi Ahmad is buried about a mile up the mountain from Beni Rachid, in the much poorer village of Beni Ouarad. Sixty percent of the population of Beni Rachid and forty percent of that of Beni Ouarad claim descent from their respective saints. Although the "children" of each saint are divided into lineages, they are all subject to the rule of a single leader, the *mezwar*, at least in matters concerning the saint's tomb and property and the associated brotherhoods. There are no defined rules of succession for the "mezwarship" in either village—a situation that has led to considerable intravillage bickering and jealousy—and in both villages the present mezwars belong to the richest and politically most influential families. The tombs of each saint are visited daily by individual pilgrims anxious to obtain some of the blessing, or *baraka*, of the saints and are the site of a collective pilgrimage, or

[3] J. Herber, "Les Hamadsha et les Dghoughiyyin," *Hesperis*, III (1923), 217–236. See also: Charles-Tristan Pehau, *Cahiers du Sud* (1931), title, volume number, and pagination unknown; Anon., "A Safi, fête traditionalle 'du sang' (Hamatcha) marquée par des violences contre les juifs," *Le Petit-Marocain*, Oct. 12, 1924; R. Le Tourneau, *La Ville de Fèz avant le Protectorat* (Casablanca, 1949), pp. 303, 366, 391, 594, 609; René Brunel, *Le Monachisme errant dans l'Islam: Sidi Heddi et les Heddawa* (Paris, 1955); Eugene Aubin, *Le Maroc d'aujourd 'hui* (Paris, 1904).

[4] The fieldwork upon which this paper is based was sponsored by a training grant from the National Institute of Mental Health. Special thanks are given to my field assistant and to my wife Jane Kramer.

[5] In this paper I use the word Hamadsha when referring to both orders or to practices and beliefs common to both.

musem, a week after the Prophet's birthday. In the village of Beni Rachid the pilgrims also visit a small grotto, or hollow, under an enormous fig tree. It is here that the camel-footed she-demon 'A'isha Qandisha is believed to live.[6]

Historically little is known of the two saints. Sidi 'Ali is said to have come from the Wulad Mulai 'Abdeslem ben Meshish ('Abd al-Salam ben Mashish al-Hasani), the teacher of Shadhili, who was the founder of the *tariqa shadhiliyya* from which many of the Maghrebian brotherhoods claim spiritual descent. He obtained his baraka from Bu'abid Sharqi (Muhammad ben Abi 'l-Kasim al-Sharqi al-Sumairi al-Za'ri al-Ojabiri), the patron of the horsemen, who is buried in Boujad; Sharqi himself was a disciple of Shadhili's most important student Jazuli, who died in the Valley of the Sous and was exhumed by one of the Saadian sultans and brought to Marrakech as a sort of political rallying point at the time of the Portugese invasions of Morocco in the beginning of the sixteenth century.[7] We have here not only the typical confusion of the spiritual genealogy of a saint, the *silsila*, with his socio-biological one but also an example of an almost visceral conception of the actual passage of baraka from saint to saint. It is claimed that Sidi 'Ali obtained Sharqi's baraka, or bread, as it is sometimes called, by drinking down a pail of Sharqi's vomit. This theme of oral incorporation of baraka occurs again and again in the Moroccan hagiographies.[8]

Sidi 'Ali spent years praying in the courtyard of the Qariwiyyin University of Fez before moving to the 'Ain Kebir, or Big Spring, on the Jebel Zerhoun, where he was visited by countless pilgrims—among them Sidi Ahmad Dghughi, who became his servant—and where he performed the ecstatic dance, or *hadra*, whenever he heard the words: *Allah! Allah! Daim Allah! El Ma'bud Allah!* (God! God! God the Eternal! God the Adorable!) The Hamadsha still chant these words as they perform the hadra. Sidi 'Ali died in 1131/1718–19. Legend has it that Sidi Ahmad, who had been away in the Sudan, began to slash open his own head in despair the day he returned to the Zerhoun and learned of his master's death, and that from that day on the followers of Sidi Ahmad have slashed at their heads during the *hadra*. Although some of the early accounts of the Hamadsha suggest

[6] There is also a hole in the courtyard of Sidi Ahmad Dghughi's mausoleum which is dedicated to 'A'isha Qandisha.

[7] Edouard Michaux-Bellaire, "Essai sur l'Histoire des Confréries Marocaines," *Hesperis*, I (1921), 117–148.

[8] Jacques Berque, *Al-Yousi: Problèmes de la Culture Marocaine au XVII ième Siecle* (Paris and The Hague, 1958), for another example of oral incorporation of baraka.

that the Dghughiyyin alone mutilate themselves, today followers of both saints do.[9]

Even less is known about the life of Sidi Ahmad, who died a few years after his master. Although it has been claimed that he came from the Beni Dghugh of the Dukkala tribe, the present mezwar assures me that he came from the Beni Hsen and left family and property there. The single most important legend associated with him concerns his mission to the Sudan, where he was sent by Sidi 'Ali to bring back the *hal,* or ecstasy. This he did by stealing from the king of the Sudan a flute, a drum, and 'A'isha Qandisha herself.

This legend, which suggests a sub-Saharan origin for some of the beliefs and practices of the Hamadsha, points to the central importance of 'A'isha Qandisha in their rite. 'A'isha Qandisha is a vaguely defined "being" whom Westermarck identifies with Astarte[10] but whose exact status in the Moroccan Arab pantheon of supernaturals has never been specifically determined.[11] Some say that she is a female jinn, a *jinniyya,* like Lalla Mira, Lalla Malika, and Lalla Mimuna, who are often companions to women—especially to women of the Gharb and of the Beni Hsen—and who occasionally visit men as succubi at night. Others claim that she is an *'afrita,* a giant, jinn-like creature who often practices cannibalism or vampirism. Some of the Hamadsha believe that she was once a woman, Sidi 'Ali's slave, who was converted into an "invisible" when she died. To the coastal Arabs, she is a siren, and to those of the interior she is a sort of chthonian mother associated with earth, mud, water, and rivers. Like Kali-Parvati, she may appear to her believers as either a beauty or a hag with long pendant breasts, and she is both venerated and feared by the Hamadsha and, in fact, by a good many other northern Moroccan Arabs. Throughout the north, there are places sacred to her. These are usually

[9] Edouard Michaux-Bellaire and George Salmon, "Les Tribus Arabes de la Vallée du Lekhous," *Archives Marocaines,* IV (1905), 334.

[10] Edward Westermarck, *Ritual and Belief in Morocco,* Vol. I (London, 1926), pp. 395–396.

[11] Interesting parallels can be drawn between the Ḥamadsha's belief in 'A'isha Qandisha and other devils (jnūn) and the beliefs in the Zar worshipers of southern Egypt and northern Ethiopia, of the Bori worshipers among the Hausa, and of the devotees of other religions found immediately south of the Sahara. There is reason to believe that some of these beliefs were brought north to Morocco by black African slaves. For the Zar cult, see Michel Leiris, "Le Culte des *Zars* à Gondar" (Etiopie Septentrionale), *Aethiopica,* II (1933), 96–103, 125–136. For the Bori, see A. J. N. Tremearne, *The Ban of the Bori: Demon and Demon Dancing in West and North Africa* (London, 1914), *passim.*

mudholes, grottoes, springs and fountains, as well as other spots where someone is said to have seen her or where something especially uncanny has taken place. The Hamadsha say that her principal residence is in the grotto at Beni Rachid, but that she is capable of appearing at many places at once.

When 'A'isha Qandisha presents herself to a man as a beautiful woman, a seductress, that man is believed to have no defense against her power unless he immediately plunges a steel knife into the earth. He is then privileged to reject her entirely or to make a "marriage contract" with her which is to his own advantage. (This is infrequent, since 'A'isha usually masks her identity by hiding her camel's feet under a flowing caftan.) If a man is unfortunate enough to sleep with her before discovering her identity, he becomes her slave forever and must follow her commands explicitly or she will strangle him to death. Often 'A'isha will demand that the man wear old, dirty clothes and never cut his hair and fingernails. She usually will restrict his sexual activities as well. Such men are said to be married to 'A'isha Qandisha and are treated circumspectly. Their special relationship to 'A'isha seems to bear no relation to membership in the Hamadsha brotherhoods. In fact only a few of 'A'isha's husbands are Hamadsha. In general her husbands are found to be either completely or selectively impotent. Their marriage to her protects them from encounters with women which would be especially humiliating in a country that puts as much stock in a man's virility as Morocco.

Marriage is by no means the only possible relationship with Lalla 'A'isha, as she is sometimes called. One may also rest on (*mwali*) her. Such a person is said to be her *taba'*, or follower. The nature of *this* relationship, which is the one characteristic of many of the Hamadsha, is not precise. A man or a woman who rests on 'A'isha has usually been struck by her, and thereby paralyzed or made sick, and has had to appease her in one way or another. Appeasing 'A'isha may involve the sacrifice of a black or a red chicken at one of the places to which she is said to gravitate. In some cases, it will involve an invitation to the Hamadsha to perform the hadra. The person whom she has struck will then either see 'A'isha as she "emerges" from the ground on which the dance takes place, or he will become possessed by 'A'isha and manifest all the classical symptoms of the "possession state" so often described by anthropologists. Once having danced, he may then be compelled, psychologically, to dance whenever he hears one of her favorite rhythms. Often, he will have to invite the Hamadsha to perform for him again, at least once every year, or risk a relapse of the same precipitating symptoms. Women and men who follow her are required to wear one of her favorite colors, red, black, or sometimes bright green, to burn a special incense (black *jawi*), and to visit her grotto and other areas sacred to her. They may have to adhere to certain food taboos and even construct a private shrine to her in a corner of their houses. Men who rest on her, like men married to her, are often forbidden to have sexual relations with any women whatsoever, or with anyone but their wives and other women who are her followers. Should one of 'A'isha's followers disobey her, he is immediately struck and suffers grave misfortune or bodily harm. The Hamadsha, as her special devotees, are said to be favored by 'A'isha and are very proud of the intimacy of their relations with her.

Little is known of the development and spread of the Hamadsha. At the time of the French occupation in 1912, their cult seems to have been widespread in the cities of northern Morocco among the lowest strata of urban society—the porters, tanners, shoemakers, employees at baths and ovens[12]—and also in rural areas, especially in the Gharb or Western Plain and on the Jebel Zerhoun itself. Draque lists the membership, presumably of both the 'Allaliyyin and Dghughiyyin, at 3,399 in 1939, with roughly one-third of that number living in the region of Meknes.[13] His figure is probably much too low. Not only does the author of *Esquisse d'Histoire Religieuse du Maroc* himself consider these figures to be very approximate but, as we shall see, it is almost impossible to obtain an accurate census for the Hamadsha because of the very fluid boundaries of their organization. Today, both brotherhoods have *zawiyas*, or lodges, in most of the larger cities of northern Morocco but these, for the most part, are moribund if not already defunct. The Hamadsha appear to be most active in the madinas and shantytowns of Meknes and Kenitra, in the Gharb, especially around Sidi Sliman, Sidi Kacem, Sidi Yahya du Gharb, and Dar bel Amri, and in the region of the Zerhoun. They are not inactive in Fez.

The city of Meknes, like Kenitra and the other major cities of Morocco, has experienced something of a population explosion as more and more immigrants arrive from the countryside. There were about thirty thousand inhabitants in 1926, and by the time of the last census in 1960, the population was nearly five times as great. Many of the rural immigrants have moved into shantytowns like Bordj Moulay Omar, which was first settled in 1930 and by 1960 had reached a population of nearly nineteen

[12] Le Tourneau, *op. cit.*, p. 366.
[13] George Draque, *Esquisse d'Histoire Religieuse du Maroc* (Paris, n.d.), p. 122.

thousand.[14] Beside such geographically definable quarters, a number of the immigrants have moved into the old town, often living in shelters propped against the thick city walls which were built by the city's founder, Mulai Isma'il. They too have retained their old country ways. Both groups live from hand to mouth, surviving largely on odd jobs in the city itself and on gifts from employed relatives. Not an insignificant number, especially in the shantytown of Sidi Baba, receive pensions from the French as veterans of World War II and the Indochinese wars. At harvest time, many of the men leave for the country to earn enough money to pay their debts at the local grocers, who are primarily Berbers from the Valley of the Sous, and to meet the expenses of marriages and circumcisions, which occur with almost epidemic frequency just after the harvest. The shantytown dwellers have brought with them the hadra of the countryside and have made little contact with the Hamadsha of the madina.

There is considerable difference between the organization and ritual of the Hamadsha in the zawiyas of the old quarter and the shantytowns. This difference reflects the even deeper cleavage between the madina people, who are proud of their urban background, and the shantytown dwellers, who still have strong ties with their rural homeland and look down, not without a touch of envy, at the "soft" madina inhabitants. They often joke about their own rough, country accents and ridicule the marriage and circumcision practices of the city. They are proud of the violence of their hadra and their endurance during it.

At first one has the impression that these shantytown Hamadsha are increasing, but closer analysis suggests that it is more a question of displacement from countryside to shantytown than of an actual increase in the number of initiates. Whatever new recruits there are appear to be suffering from some sort of mental disturbance. In any event, the relation that membership in the Hamadsha brotherhoods might once have had to the social structure of the village or tribe has been lost in the shantytown setting, with its looser social organization, its population of diverse origins, and its orientation in terms of job and market to the city of Meknes itself. Like many other institutions that were once closely articulated to the social structure of a village or tribe, Hamadsha recruitment in its new shantytown setting appears to be less closely allied to social structural factors than to psychological disposition.

There are two zawiyas today in the madina of Meknes, one for the

[14] Jean Franchi, "Urbanization d'un bidonville: Bordj Moulay Omar," *Bulletin Economique et Social du Maroc,* XXIII (1959), 257–259.

'Allaliyyin and the other for the Dghughiyyin. They are located close to each other in a poor section of the city, not too far from the smiths' quarter, and they consist of enclosed courtyards in which grave plots have been sold to wealthy Arabs anxious to facilitate their entry into heaven by partaking of some of the baraka of the zawiya. Originally the orders were able to obtain the zawiyas by promising the revenue from the sale of these plots to their previous owners.[15] Members of the brotherhood itself are usually too poor to buy the plots which are very expensive. In the center of the *zawiya dghughiyya,* there is a fig tree dedicated to 'A'isha Qandisha; women have tied rags to the tree as signs of their various promises to the she-demon, most often promises to sacrifice a chicken to 'A'isha if a child is born.

The organization of both lodges is much simpler than that of many of the other brotherhoods. These lodges come under the direct charge of their particular mezwar, who not only receives all the money they collect for a supposed distribution among his saint's children but also acts as an arbiter in cases of dispute among the lodge members, or *foqra,* or between the lodges of his brotherhood. He approves the choice of a local leader, or *moqaddam,* who is selected by the foqra themselves, and provides the moqaddam with both a letter of authority and a flag. The moqaddam is then charged with administering the lodge, collecting alms, organizing and directing ceremonies, caring for the ill during the ceremonies and at other times, and acting as an arbiter himself in minor disputes between lodge members. "He must be intelligent, a good judge of people, and not overly powerful and must have the ability to speak to people at all levels." He is assisted by a *khalifa,* and, among the 'Allaliyyin, the two of them are responsible for guarding the alms and gifts. Among the Dghughiyyin, there is a treasurer (*khzana*) who keeps the money; the moqaddam and the khalifa also keep separate records of the funds, as a check on the treasurer and on each other. There are usually two women caretakers as well, who clean the zawiya and care for the female participants during the ceremonies. All the above receive, in one way or another, remuneration for their duties from the mezwar.

The foqra themselves—today there are about fifteen in each zawiya—are not organized into any hierarchy. Neither do they go through any form of initiation or receive any secret instruction. They are simply men who attend the meetings at the zawiya and assist at ceremonies regularly. Al-

[15] This is a common practice in Morocco.

though they usually dance the hadra, this is by no means a qualification for membership, nor is any detailed knowledge of the litanies (*hizb* and *dhikr*). Most of the foqra will have invited their fellow lodge brothers to their homes for a *sadaqa*—a seance at which litanies are recited, the hadra performed, and a meal served—shortly after beginning to attend the zawiya with any regularity. The sadaqa will usually have been accompanied by the sacrifice of a he-goat or a ram.

Adepts of the zawiyas are nearly all employed in some menial occupation—they are weavers and menders, dealers in secondhand clothes and shoes, gardeners, butchers, barbers, blacksmiths, and tanners—which brings them in a minimal income. There appears to be no relationship between membership in either order and in a professional guild. With one exception, none of the foqra are descended from either Sidi 'Ali or Sidi Ahmad, although several claim to be children of other saints. The fathers of two-thirds of the regular Dghughiyyin were also Dghughiyyin, but less than half the fathers of the regular 'Allaliyyin were members of the order. A few of the adepts have switched from one zawiya to the other, usually because of a dispute with the moqaddam. There are no rules preventing membership in other fraternities, but none of the present adepts belongs to any other. Nearly all of them were born in Meknes, but few of their grandfathers were. Between a third and a half of them trace their origin to the Tafilelt (Sahara). The majority appear to be over fifty, although there are a few younger members.

Besides the regular adepts, who often play the drums at a sadaqa, there are, attached to the order, *ghita*, or oboe, players who are professional musicians. The ghita, as we shall see, is the most important instrument of the hadra and playing it requires considerable skill and endurance. Although the ghita players have been affiliated with the zawiyas for years, they are treated as distinct from the foqra, both because they receive remuneration for each performance and because they ply their trade at other ceremonies.

The last and largest group associated with the zawiyas are *muhibbin*, or devotees, of the order. This group is the most difficult to define. It consists of all the men, women, and children who are in some manner attracted to the hadra of the Hamadsha and who attend the performances—usually of one or the other of the two brotherhoods—whenever they can. They may simply enjoy watching the spectacle; they may be compelled psychologically to listen to the music or to dance the hadra; they may fall into trance and even mutilate themselves; or they may just give a sadaqa from time to time to obtain some of the baraka of the saints. They come from the great mass of madina inhabitants who are either completely or quasi-illiterate and who fall within the lowest economic strata of the city. They do not belong to any one profession or occupational group, nor do they come from a single tribe or region of Morocco. They are, like the foqra, almost invariably of Arab descent. Many of them, particularly those who trance, trace their devotion to the Hamadsha to an illness, usually conceived in terms of being struck (*madrub*) or possessed (*maskun*) by 'A'isha Qandisha or some other jinn, which was cured either by the Hamadsha themselves or by a pilgrimage to the tombs of the founding saints. When asked, they will always admit to being muhibbin, and they are recognized as such by friends, neighbors, and relatives. There appear to be more women than men in this category. In fact, with the exception of the two caretakers, who are already past menopause, women can only be muhibbin in the order. Their status, as such, is similar to that of women in other popular Moroccan orders.

The doors of the zawiyas are open every Friday afternoon to both the foqra and the muhibbin. The regular members of the lodge gather then to drink tea, gossip, and chant a few of their litanies—whichever litanies they know best and like the most. They do not perform the hadra there "because the entire floor [of both zawiyas] is covered with tombstones." There are usually some male visitors who stop by to leave a few francs, a candle or so, or even occasionally a chicken, but the majority of the visitors are women who come to glean some of the baraka of the place, to have a *fatiha*[16] said over them by the moqaddam or another brother, and to listen to the litanies. Aside from acting out of a general devotion to the saints and to 'A'isha Qandisha, who often obliges them to leave something at the zawiya each week, the women usually come to ask for something—a child, relief from stomach pains or "pinching bones," the preservation of a marriage, or simply good luck. They too leave candles, money, bread, sugar, or couscous. The food is distributed among the poorer lodge mem-

[16] Fatiha refers to the first verse of the Koran, but it is used among the Hamadsha and other Arabs of their class for a prayer or invocation to God and the saints. It often includes the appropriate Koranic verse. The following is a typical fātiḥa: "O, my brothers, pray for me. I shall be cured thanks to your invocation. Cover me with your wings. O Children of Mustafa, the chosen, the elected. There is only one God. O, Prophet, cure me." All the lines but the last are repeated three times.

bers. The candles and money are kept for the children of the saint, although at times a portion of the money may be given or lent to a brother who has had the expense of an illness, a death, a marriage, or a circumcision in the family. The zawiya is, in part, a society for mutual protection.

The majority of the brotherhoods' income is derived not from the Friday afternoon meetings but from name-day ceremonies, in which the foqra are asked to name a child who was born after a pilgrimage to the founding saint, and invitations to perform the hadra. The invitations, which is often called a *lila*, or night, because it begins in the evening, is usually performed in private homes. The host lets the moqaddam know that he wants to sponsor a lila, a date is set, and a deposit is left.

On the appointed evening, the foqra and ghita players parade in front of the host's house to attract attention. They play a few of the popular hadra tunes and dance a little. There is seldom any trancing at this stage. The performers are surrounded by excited men, women, and children who often follow them into the sponsor's house. Once in the house the moqaddam repeats a fatiha for the host and his family, and then all the brothers sit down in a corner of the courtyard as the host tends to them and his other guests. All the guests are served milk and dates—a sign of welcome and early return—or mint tea. After the women, who are usually seated in a side room or on the roof, have been served, the moqaddam leads the brothers in a responsive recitation of the hizb.

A. In the name of Allah, the compassionate and
 the merciful—
B. May eternal happiness rest with our lord
 Muhammad, his family, and his companions.
A. Let us praise Allah the benevolent.
B. Him, the adored Allah,
A. May he hear my wishes,
B. May he pardon me and grant me his mercy.
A. I am a sinful slave,
B. And I implore my lord
A. Because it is my duty
B. To ask Him to guide me.
A. O, the compassionate one, the merciful one,
B. Protect us from hell.
A. You are the only one, the unique.
B. You are the unique and the omnipotent one. . . .

The moqaddam does not take a special place when he leads the recitation but remains seated with the brothers who are pressed close together and who may sway slightly from side to side. They do not engage in any of the gymnastics reported for other brotherhoods but they often close their eyes during the recitation of the hizb.

Sometimes, in place of the hizb, short moralistic tales and prayers called *lunasa* are recited. A pilgrim, for example, makes no provision for his journey to Mecca but is aided by another "pilgrim" and makes a successful journey.

> I made a pilgrimage with faith and conviction.
> I came back happy and with changed name.
> All listeners called me *hajj*.
> My heart was filled with joy.
> Allah satisfied my wishes.
> I came back surrounded by friends and brothers. . . .

When the hizb or lunasa is completed—it lasts from about five minutes to over an hour—there may be a pause for more tea before the recitation of the dhikr is begun. The dhikr phrases are shorter than those of the hizb or lunasa and are said more rapidly. The foqra who are still seated may accompany the recitation with drumming or handclapping. The guitar (*genbri*) may be played.

> A.B. In the name of Allah the compassionate, the merciful—
> A. I begin with the name of Allah.
> B. To him I dedicate the following words:
> A. Muhammad, O Perfect Creature,
> B. You are as soft as beeswax.
> A. You, who have brought the light,
> B. You, who have come as an envoy,
> A. You are the enlightened man.
> B. You are the savior at the last judgment. . . .

Although the foqra still remain seated, they do sway back and forth more rapidly and hyperventilate as they recite the short dhikr phrases. I have been told that they have the fear of God at this time. As the dhikr is repeated faster and faster and louder and louder both the adepts and the spectators become excited. A wave of heat passes through the court. The women in their separate room, or on the roof, begin to ululate (*zeghret*) with excitement. Children become more belligerent and are treated roughly by adults and the curious teenage boys who inevitably show up at these nights. Finally when the excitement has reached a very high pitch —this may have taken from five to forty-five minutes or more—the foqra stand and begin to dance the hadra as the ghita players blare out their whining tunes and the drummers beat their monotonous rhythms.

The hadra[17] is divided into three principal parts: the hot part (*es-skun*), in which the ghita is played along with the snare drum (*tbel*) and with an hourglass shaped drum called the *gwal*; the cold part (*l-berd*), in which the ghita is replaced by a recorder (*nira*) or sometimes a guitar; and the *hadra gnawiyya*, which uses the same instruments as the cold part but which is derived from the ceremonies (*derdbas*) of the black fraternity called the Gnawa.

The hot part of the hadra comes first and is the loudest and most violent. The foqra and any male guests who want to line up, shoulder to shoulder, pound up and down on their heels, raise and lower their shoulders in a sort of continual shrug, and hiss out their breath as they seek the hal, or ecstatic trance. Standing opposite the musicians, they form an outer boundary to the dance area in which the moqaddam leaps, turns in midair, lands on his knees, leaps again, stabs at his chest with his hands, and generally encourages the others to breathe faster and pound down harder on their heels. A few women are usually drawn by the music of the ghita from their separate quarters to the center. They bob up and down, entranced, or pitch from side to side. Their feet remain in place, and at this stage of the hadra they are usually ignored.

For the Hamadsha, "hal" is both a generic and a specific term. Generically, it refers to any trance that occurs during the hadra; specifically, it seems to refer to a nonviolent trance—not dissimilar to the light-to-medium trance of hypnosis—which may be preliminary to the more violent trance, or *jidba*. Its semantic field probably varies slightly in reference to men and women; for it seems to encompass a deeper trance and more frenetic behavior when used for women. This may result from the fact that the women fall into trance with more ease and dance with more abandon than the men. Generally, the dancer in hal is able to follow the rhythm and dance steps of the hadra; his movement may be simplified and appear graceful or even dreamy. His eyes appear fixed and exhibit a slight exophthalmos. His limbs may quiver slightly or become stiff. His speech is slurred, and he seems disoriented. He is able to fall out of trance with ease, especially if the situation demands conscious behavior, as, for exam-

[17] There are striking resemblances between the practices of the Hamadsha during the ḥaḍra and those of the worshipers of Baal, the Syrian Mother Goddess, and the *castrati* of the late Roman Empire, although there is no evidence to support a diffusionist view. All of these cults involved masochistic and emasculating practices. It should be pointed out that in Moroccan Arabic the word for head *ras* may also be used to refer to the glans of the penis. Cf. J. G. Frazier, *Adonis, Attis, Osiris* (New York, 1961), pp. 266 ff.

ple, attending to his guests if he should happen to be the host. Subjectively, informants report a loss of temporal and spatial orientation and consciousness of the body, except for the head, which feels swollen and warm and may itch slightly. They hear nothing but the music of the ghita and see shadows (*khail*) before their eyes. Often, they remember nothing of the experience.

Occasionally, when a dancer's special tune, or *rih*[18]—each person is said to have a special rih that sends him into trance—is played, he will fall into the center in a cataleptic state that is sometimes followed by epileptoid movements and violent tremors of the limbs. Gradually, as the musicians continue to play the particular tune to which he is responsive, his body will relax, and he will stand and charge frenetically around the dance area, screaming and scaring the women and children in the audience. He exhibits marked exophthalmos and appears to be hallucinating. He is unable to follow the dance rhythms, although he may become obsessed with the ghita and charge at it or beckon it seductively. Sometimes, he stimulates his genitals with his hands or by rubbing himself against another dancer of the same sex. He may scratch his head and will occasionally ask for a pocketknife with which he will slash at his head until his face and shoulders are drenched in blood. Traditionally—and still today at the musem—the Hamadsha bashed their heads with axes (*shaqria*) that resembled halberds. Certain dancers in this state are compelled to imitate pigs and camels.

This frenzy is known as jidba, a word derived from the Arabic for attraction and used by the Sufis for the mystical attraction to God. Subjectively, the dancer in jidba reports the same symptoms as for hal but in more extreme form. He hears nothing but the sound of the ghita and the blood throbbing in his head, which feels as if it will explode and which itches intensely. This itching (*msuwwek*) sensation has been likened to that of a wasp under the skin. When it occurs, the dancer may see 'A'isha Qandisha before him, slashing at her own head with a piece of iron and compelling him to do the same. Most of my informants who had experienced jidba recalled nothing of the experience. It is said that the itching is what makes the dancers slash and that the flow of blood calms 'A'isha. There is no consciousness of pain during the jidba or immediately after-

[18] The plural of rih is *l-ariāh* which is used to refer to the jnun that cause diseases. The music of the ḥaḍra comes from several tribal areas—from the Gharbawa, the Beni Hsen, the Zrahna, the Bukhara, and the Wulad Khalifa of the Gharb.

ward, when the dancer has "cooled down" and is again in hal, or after the dance itself. Often the dancers do not know that they have wounded themselves until they discover bloodstains on their clothes. They do nothing to cause the wounds to heal. If the hadra has been "a good one", the dancers will sleep well and will awake with renewed energy the next morning. (Most male informants report an inability to have sexual intercourse after the hadra.) If the hadra has not been good, the dancer will spend a restless night, hearing the music of the hadra over and over again, will awake tired and depressed. If he does not perform the hadra, it is claimed that he will fall sick. In fact, he usually does.

The hot part of the hadra may last from five or ten minutes to over an hour, depending on the mood of the musicians and the state of the dancers. The music cannot be stopped if any of the dancers are in jidba, for then the dancer will fall into a cataleptic paralysis and will later suffer from general malaise, depression, and aching bones if, in fact, he does not remain paralyzed. Once the hot part is over, the moqaddam leads the brothers and other members of the audience in the recitation of the fatiha, which is said for any one who offers the moqaddam a few coins. The fatiha is the main source of income for the brotherhood. The host is obliged only to pay the ghita players and provide food for all the guests—fifty or sixty relatives, neighbors, and muhibbin may show up for a lila—but he usually gives generously whenever fatihas are said.

When the recitation of the fatihas has been completed, the cold part of the hadra begins. This part is quieter and is danced individually rather than in line. When an individual hears his particular tune, he dances in front of the musicians and may fall into jidba. There appear to be many more women and children who dance at this time, especially when 'A'isha's special rih is played and the lights are turned out. 'A'isha Qandisha is said then to emerge from the earth and dance before the participants as they chant:

> O 'A'isha! Rise and place yourself in the service of the
>   cause of Allah and the Prophet.
> O Sire! Greetings to the Prophet. Welcome, O Lalla 'A'isha.
> The altar is prepared. O Lalla 'A'isha! Welcome!
> Welcome, O Daughter of the Sudan. Welcome, O Gnawiyya.
> Welcome, O Daughter of the river. Allah! Allah! Lalla 'A'isha!
> She has come. She has come. She has come. Lalla 'A'isha.

("Daughter of the Sudan" and "Gnawiyya" remind us of 'A'isha Qandisha's alleged sub-Saharan origin.) 'A'isha's rih is usually accompanied by screams of terror, and when the music stops and the lights go on, there are often several children on the floor, whimpering, in a state of semiconsciousness. They must be danced through trance until they have "had enough" or they too will fall sick.

The cold part of the hadra, which may be interrupted from time to time for the recitation of the fatiha, flows directly into the hadra gnawiyya which is "played for the women." Usually, in the course of the cold part, certain tunes are played which throw women in particular into trance but which do not appear to satisfy them. A special repertory of musical tunes is then played, until the tune that will satisfy each particular woman has been found. These tunes, which are all associated with certain devils and with special colors and incenses, are often accompanied by chants like the one dedicated to Lalla 'A'isha. Rags of the color that happens to please the woman's particular devil are tied to her if she has not come to the night wearing the appropriate color, and the correct incense is burned. The hadra gnawiyya resembles not only the dance of the Gnawa but also the last part of the ceremonies of several other popular brotherhoods: the 'Isawiyya, the Jilala, and the followers of Sidi Rahal.

When all the participants have been satisfied, the hadra ends, more fatihas are said, and dinner is served. The ceremony seldom takes less than four hours. Dinner includes couscous and a stew that has been made from an animal sacrificed before the ceremony. Such sacrifices are not compulsory and do not play an important part in the formal ritual of the lila. They do entail considerable expense on the part of the host and are taken as a sign of generosity by all concerned.

Although a few of these lilas are given in order to obtain the blessing of the saint in general, the majority are given to cure an individual who has been struck by the devil or is possessed by one. In either case the hadra is not specifically conceived as a means of attaining some sort of mystical union with the Supreme Reality (*fana' fi-l-haqq*) but as a means of obtaining *something* through the saint as an intermediary to God. This "something" may be conceived of, in its most abstract fashion, as baraka, which has been translated as "blessing" but which incorporates within it notions of well-being, good fortune, and plenitude, or in more concrete terms like the cure of an illness or the establishment and maintenance of a good relationship with a jinn, usually 'A'isha Qandisha. The extent to which 'A'isha Qandisha dominates the ceremony is demonstrated by the fact that the average Hamdushi, when asked, will explain that the word hadra, which is derived from the Arabic meaning "presence" and which is used by the Sufi mystics to refer to the presence of God (*hadra Allah*) means that 'A'isha Qandisha herself is present. In effect, the hadra is not the hadra Allah but the hadra 'A'isha Qandisha.

This, obviously is an oversimplification of an essentially more complex phenomenon. The foqra do not attempt to reduce their ceremony to a single theme but accept it as it has developed over the years and has been handed down to them. The ceremony is an aggregate, which has been borrowed not only from the high tradition of orthodoxy and Islamic mysticism but also from local custom and belief. The order of events, with the variegated sentiments and feelings it inspires, is not to be questioned or analyzed but is to be accepted straightforwardly and understood, if necessary, as a manifestation of 'A'isha Qandisha's whims and the saint's blessing.

In the shantytowns, where the Hamadsha are primarily curers, the adepts are more explicit in their devotion to 'A'isha Qandisha and the other *jnun*, or demons. They perform both in public and in private. The public performances, which take place on Friday afternoons and on religious and national holidays, are a major source of income. They fall midway between a religious ceremonial and a secular spectacle and consist simply of the hot part of the hadra. The audience is made up of devotees, who feel the need to listen to or join in the hadra, and the curious, who are seeking diversion. Occasionally, some one who is ill will participate in the hope of a cure. The private ceremonies consist of little more than the hadra—a few lines of the dhikr may be recited but this is very rare—and the communal meal at the termination of the ceremony. The dances tend to be more violent and longer than those of the madina. They are financed in much the same way as in the old town, although many more fatihas are said to extract as much money as possible from the guests. Patterns of trance are the same as in the urban ceremonies, but women participate in the dances much more freely. It is not unusual to dance a single woman through trance for several hours. Occasionally, they mutilate themselves. Aside from the muhibbin invited by both the host and the Hamadsha, anyone who happens to hear the music may enter the house and expect to participate and be fed. Often there are more than seventy-five people in attendance.

The adepts of the shantytowns are not associated with a lodge but are organized into teams, or *ta'ifa*, of musician-curers which have a following of devotees. Each team is dedicated to one of the two saints, although in reality the allegiance of the members in one ta'ifa is often mixed. The teams are headed by a moqaddam, who has been given a letter of authority and a flag by the mezwar. The ta'ifas have no permanent meeting place but work throughout the city and in the nearby countryside and often accept invitations from as far off as Fez and Rabat. They usually consist of the moqaddam, who acts as dance leader and cares for the sick during the hadra, and six musicians: two ghita players, who also play the recorder and guitar, a snare drummer, and three gwal players. Each team makes its own arrangement with the ghita players, who are considered part of the team itself. They receive greater compensation than the other musicians because their work is considered the hardest and because they know all the rihs that will "please the jnun"—drive the dancers into trance—and thereby control the progress of the ceremony. Their importance often undermines the position of the moqaddam whose authority, aside from what personal charisma and esoteric knowledge he may have, lies solely in his possession of the mezwar's letter. The ta'ifas tend, therefore, to be very fragile. The members of the seven teams operative in the shantytowns of Meknes in 1968 were constantly shifting allegiance from one moqaddam to another. Whatever stability there was resulted from the economic success of a particular team, since the team members share among themselves all the proceeds from their public and private performances and only once a year, at the time of the musem, give their mezwar a token payment for the flag and the letter of authority. The latter is the mezwar's only hold over the team members—they do not accord them the same esteem as do their confreres in the madina—since they must present it to the municipal authorities to obtain permission to perform the lucrative public dance.

The fact that the teams do not give all the money they collect to their respective mezwars has led to considerable resentment on the part of the faqra of the madina, who are not unaware of the moribund condition of their organization and of the unequal sharing among the children of the saints of their gifts. Idealogically their justification for giving the money they collect to the descendants of the saints—an extension of the saints themselves—is an exchange for the baraka they receive from their saint. The baraka is understood not just in terms of well-being and good fortune but also in terms of their ability to trance, cure the devil struck and the possessed, and come to some sort of working relationship with Lalla 'A'isha. Failure to give money to the descendants of the saints entails ill-fortune, business failure, illness, and even insanity. Since most of these disasters have not befallen the Hamadsha of the shantytowns, a dissonant situation has been created and only partially resolved by the foqra.[19] They argue that the Hamadsha of the shantytowns are not true Hamadsha and that their failure to give to the children of the saints accounts for their abject poverty. The mezwars themselves let it be known publicly that their letters and flags are given in charity. In fact, the mezwars do their best to extract as much money as possible from the renegade Hamadsha of the shantytowns, who are, economically speaking, the most successful Hamadsha, and vie with one another for their allegiance.[20]

With one or two exceptions, the team members have no other occupations, although the ghita players do perform at circumcisions and marriages and even occasionally at the ceremonies of other popular brotherhoods like the 'Isawiyya. The team members, the majority of whom come from the Gharb, are illiterate and have only a fragmentary knowledge of the litanies, if they have any knowledge of them at all; they are not as familiar with the hagiographic legends as are the foqra of the madina. Their work, as they conceive of it, has to do with the jnun, and their success is the result of Sidi 'Ali's and Sidi Ahmad's blessing. They recognize no explicitly mystical purpose to it and would consider the suggestion of a union with God, through their work, to be extremely blasphemous.

The vast majority of the Hamadsha in the shantytowns are the devotees, or muhibbin, and like the devotees of the city, they are difficult to trace socially. Most of them have immigrated to the city in their own lifetime. They have menial jobs, if any, and tend to follow a single team. Given the fragility of the teams, this usually means that they follow a particular ghita player who happens to please them and often comes from their tribal area. Like the muhibbin of the madina, they frequently trace their devotion back to some illness, although many of them come from

[19] For a more detailed examination of the reactions to cognitive dissonance, cf. Leon Festinger, Henry W. Riecken, and Stanley Schachter, *When Prophecy Fails* (New York, 1964).

[20] This competition is dramatically portrayed during the annual musem. Toward sundown on the third day of the musem—the seventh day after the Prophet's birthday—the mezwar of Sidi Ahmad leaves the village of Beni Ouarad on horseback trailed by thousands of his followers, for Beni Rachid. As he approaches the village, he is traditionally greeted by the mezwar of Sidi 'Ali, whom, dismounting, he follows on foot to Sidi 'Ali's tomb. The mezwar of Sidi Aḥmed has recently refused to dismount and enter Beni Rachid. He simply approaches the mezwar of Sidi 'Ali near two palm trees on the outskirts of the village, and then, without a word, turns back toward his own village.

families in the countryside in which there were many Hamadsha. Like the team members, they are less reticent in talking about the devils that possess them than the devotees of the madina and are often proud of their relationship with them. They see the team members as essentially curers, and their invitations are responses either to illness, usually paralysis or rheumatoid or paresthetic pains in the joints, described as "pinching bones," or the commemoration of a cure. The illnesses, like those of the madina, often appear to be of a hysterical nature, although there are often depressive and schizophrenic reactions as well. Very occasionally, organic illnesses with symptoms similar to the psychogenic ones are treated. That many of these illnesses are of a hysterical nature (conversion reactions) is demonstrated by the fact that if, a year after the cure, there is no commemorative invitation, the patient will develop the same symptoms that had necessitated his original invitation.

The belief in jnun serves not only as a satisfactory explanation for the Hamadsha and their followers of their illnesses but is also a convenient idiom through which psychic conflict can be symbolized.[21] Material collected by free association suggests that the breaking of arbitrary command of a jinn one follows is in fact symbolic, at one level, of a breach in public or private morality and, at another level, of the "guilt" that this breach has caused in the individual. A woman, for example, who had been attached to 'A'isha Qandisha for several years tried to prevent her husband, a Hamdushi, from sponsoring his annual ceremony to commemorate a cure he had once had, and shortly thereafter she developed a paralysis of the left leg. This, she explained, was the result of 'A'isha's rage.

In analyzing life histories of typical Hamadsha, I have frequently found that the circumstances surrounding an initial illness interpreted as an attack by a jinn were such that a Westerner, given the Moroccan Arab moral code, would describe as having "caused a guilty conscience." Having once defined their "feelings" in terms of the jinn, the Hamadsha will interpret every subsequent "guilt reaction" of similar magnitude with reference to the jinn. Extreme reactions are often somatized in the form of paralysis or other conversion reactions. The jinn to whom one has become attached is, as it were, an externalized superego, and the Hamadsha's interpretation of their illnesses bears an uncanny resemblance to the interpretations of hysteria proferred by psychoanalysis.

[21] The relationship between an individual and his jinn or the jnun in general is considerably more complicated than can be indicated in this paper.

Thus, the Hamadsha appear to have incorporated their heterodox beliefs and practices into what are, superficially, the ideological and organizational forms of "high tradition Sufism." In so doing, they have created a system of ritual and belief which not only provides their adepts with an apparently satisfactory world view (including a theory of illness) but also with a means of symbolizing and dealing with psychic conflict. Their system is, if you will, a system of folk psychiatry, and they are its practitioners. A small brotherhood of limited appeal, even within the lowest strata of society, they were never a political threat either to French or Moroccan rule. In fact, despite a certain distaste that both Europeans and the majority of Muslims had for their practices, they were left to their own adaptive devices and have suffered a fate not dissimilar to that of many other popular orders in Morocco and the rest of the Islamic world. In the madina of Meknes the two zawiyas, which have maintained a closer resemblance to the "classical tariqa," are moribund. The Hamadsha of the shantytowns, although more active, are not growing at any appreciable rate and cannot be classified with the many ecstatic cults that have sprung up recently in economically depressed areas throughout the world. They appear to have taken on fully the more specialized role of curers without any mystical aim whatsoever. So long as their idiom serves as a satisfactory means for dealing with hysterical illness and other mental disturbances, their survival seems assured.

14 | Religious Symbolism and Social Change: The Drama of Husain*

GUSTAV THAISS

GUSTAVE VON GRUNEBAUM has remarked that "Few culture areas have been subjected to so much and so violent change as that of Islam; [and] none perhaps has so consistently refused to accept the ontological reality of change."[1] The crux of the problem involving modernization and Islam seems to be humanistic; for while an anthropocentric conception is the starting point for the Western view of the universe, it is an attitude unknown in classical Islam. In Islam, God and not man remains the key figure of the universe dominating man's political, social, economic, and cultural life.[2] The onslaught of Westernization and modernization continues and in the encounter with a theocentric world view intense social discontinuities and psychological strains are created and existing ones exacerbated. From anthropological studies of religion it is well known that all societies have the problem of providing an outlet for the conflicts, antagonisms, and frustrations of social living. These socio-psychological strains are often expressed in symbolic form in myth and ritual, and it is not unusual to find under conditions of social change that the meanings and interpretations of myths tend to be modified as each generation reinterprets the past in terms of its own current premises and values. It is in such circumstances that occasionally we encounter a symbol that seems to enshrine the major hopes and aspirations of an entire society.[3] In Iran and among the Muslim Shi'a the figure of Husain is such

* This paper is based on eighteen months of anthropological fieldwork in the bazaar of Tehran sponsored by a research grant from the National Institute of Mental Health. I would like to thank my field assistant Behruz Jahanshahi and my wife Nahid for their invaluable assistance.

1 *Modern Islam: The Search for Cultural Identity* (Berkeley and Los Angeles, 1962), p. 209.

2 Aziz Ahmad, "Problems of Islamic Modernism with special reference to Indo-Pakistan Sub-Continent," *Archives de Sociologie des Religions*, 23 (1967), 115.

3 Eric Wolf, "The Virgin of Guadalupe: A Mexican National Symbol," reprinted in W. Lessa and E. Vogt, eds., *Reader in Comparative Religion* (New York, 1965), p. 226.

a symbol. In this paper then I should like to discuss the place of Husain in Shi'a thought and to specifically note the relationship between symbolic forms and social change. Before getting into a discussion of the problem it is necessary to provide some background information on the Shi'a and of Husain's martyrdom at Karbala.

Theology of the Shi'a

Theologically, the Shi'a believe that God is essentially good and that he cannot do evil. He has created man with free will and desires man's welfare and salvation. It follows, then, that He would not leave man without guidance and for this reason the books of the prophets have been sent down through the ages culminating in the revelation of Muhammad. On the basis of knowledge and reason and through the exercise of free will man is given the opportunity to choose the right path. Even so, confusion arises and because of this God has given man in addition to the Prophet an infallible guide in religious matters. This guide is the Imam. It is also clear that the selection of the Imams is a matter that could not be left to human error; they were divinely appointed from birth. The true Imams are the direct line from Ali and his wife, the Prophet's daughter, Fatima who bears the *baraka* (spiritual power) of the Prophet. Eric Wolf notes that the symbolism associated with the concept of Fatima is ordered by agnatic thinking since it is through her that the spiritual line of the Prophet continues into the future, for Muhammad had no male heir.[4]

The descent line of Ali is considered by the Shi'a to be pure (*ma'sūm*) and without sin. Following the creed of Ibn Babawayhi, one of the greatest Shi'a theologians, it is also believed that the Prophet and all the Imams were murdered and suffered martyrdom.

The Iranian Shi'a belong to the group known as the Ithnā'āshariyya or the Twelvers since they recognize twelve Imams, the last of whom, al-Mahdi, the awaited messianic figure, is believed to be alive and in a state of occultation (the *ghaybat-i kubrā*) and will return to usher in the ideal state. In his absence, the "pupils of the Imams" are to guide the people. These "pupils" are the Shi'a ulama who, as one of my ulama informants told me, "have found the orders of God in themselves, that is, are just (*'ādel*) and who do not commit any sin. They rule because the Imam is not here and because they don't think about worldly and material things."

[4] Eric Wolf, "Society and Symbols in Latin Europe and in the Islamic Near East: Some Comparisons," *Anthropological Quarterly*, 42 (July, 1969), 299.

We shall see later in this paper some of the implications this brief presentation has for understanding the dynamics of religion and social change in Iran today.

The Martyrdom of Imam Husain

The following is my own, somewhat literal translation of the tragedy at Karbala as found in Persian elementary school readers for the fifth and sixth classes.

Imam Husain, who is also called Sayyid al-Shahadā, that means Lord of Martyrs, is the esteemed son of Amir al-mo'menīn and brother of Imam Hasan.

Imam Husain, when his brother was martyred, became Imam. Mo'āvieh had previously made an agreement with Imam Husain that he [Mo'āvieh] would not choose anyone to become caliph after himself. But, despite his promises, he desired that his son Yazid succeed him as leader of the Muslims. To achieve this purpose he used to spend large sums of money and he destroyed anyone who was against this plan.

Yazid, who introduced himself as the successor of the Prophet after Mo'āvieh, was a profligate pleasure-seeker and wine-drinker who was disrespectful of religious laws. Imam Husain felt that if he keeps quiet and lets Yazid do whatever he wants to do, the laws of Islam may disappear and all the tribulations of the Prophet and past Imams would be ineffective. So he refused to accept Yazid as caliph.

Meanwhile the people of Kufa who were not satisfied with the caliphate of Yazid wrote many letters to Husain and asked him to come to Iraq. They promised him all kinds of help and cooperation. Imam Husain found himself in a situation where he realized on the one hand that Yazid and his followers were planning to kill him and on the other that the people of Kufa had invited him to go there and with their help, to resist Yazid.

So, during the period of the Haj, when large numbers of people were coming from different cities to Mecca, he gave a speech and informed the people that he is not going to perform the Haj that year in order to fulfill his duty and go to Kufa. Yazid, on his part, sent an army from Damascus to Kufa.

Imam Husain, with his brothers, children, wives, and friends and a small number of people of Kufa fought, in the desert of Karbala, thousands of soldiers who were either ignorant or in the hope of acquiring wealth and position. On the Tenth of Muharram, which we call *'āshurā,* in the year 61[680], Imam Husain suffered an honorable martyrdom. The enemy captured the women and smaller children and took them to Kufa and Damascus by the order of Yazid.

Imam Husain did not accept oppression (*satamgarān*) and injustice (*ẓolm*) and he didn't pay attention to those who wanted him to accept Yazid or keep quiet. Sayyid al-shahadā with this brave insurrection (*qiyām-i mardāneh*) gave a new spirit to Muslims. His martyrdom at Karbala served as an example of resistance against tyranny (satamgarān). Imam Husain often said, "I see life under a tyrannic government (*hokumat-i satamgarān*) to be tiring (*khasteh konandeh*) and unacceptable (*nārvā*) and I consider it happiness and pleasure to leave this world." At the battlefield also, when he had lost all his friends and he alone was facing all of the enemy, he often said, "we will never accept the shame of colluding with tyrants."

All Muslims have a special attachment to this Imam. For this reason in the month of Muharram, which is the month of his martyrdom, many gatherings are organized for the purpose of the remembrance of that Imam's self-sacrifice (*fedākāri*), and in those gatherings the story of the self-sacrifice of Imam Husain and his friends is told [in order] to protect the bases of Islam. The story is also told of that great one's devotion and resistance to those who were ruling over people and who were not suitable for that position.

Structure and Organization of Religious Gatherings

The gatherings that are mentioned here to commemorate the martyrdom of Husain and his followers take several forms in Iran at the present time. It should be mentioned that commemorative gatherings are also held, ostensibly to honor the death or martyrdom of *other* holy personages in Shi'a Islam, especially the twelve Imams, but which, in almost all cases I have participated in, have ended as a narration of the events at Karbala. These are named speech events,[5] the most important of which are the *ta'ziyā* (passion plays), *hei'at-i mazhabi* (religious gatherings), *dasteh-yi 'azadāri* (ritual funeral processions), and the *sofreh hazrat-i abbas* (religious gatherings to fulfill a vow). For the purposes of this paper I concentrate on the hei'at-i mazhabi.

There are two basic types of religious gatherings (hei'at-i mazhabi). One type, known as *hei'at-i mahalleh*, is usually organized by pious individuals in their own homes and is open freely to neighbors, friends, and other people from the particular district of the city. Hei'ats are usually named groups such as *hei'at-i husaini* (the gathering for Husain) and the *hei'at-i zā'erīn-i karbala* (the gathering of the pilgrims to Karbala).

[5] Dell Hymes, "The Ethnography of Speaking," in T. Gladwin and W. Sturtevant, eds., *Anthropology and Human Behavior* (Washington, D.C., 1962).

The other type, also named groups, with which we concern ourselves here is the *hai'at-i senfi* (the gatherings associated with the guilds). This group is generally not organized by the guild as a formal organization, but rather by individuals who share a common occupation or craft in the bazaar and who are, of course, Muslim. The non-Muslim members of the guild do not participate in Islamic rituals and interact only in business matters in the bazaar or through the formal structure of the guild.

The meetings may be arranged on either a fixed or an itinerant schedule. The former indicates that the place is always known as is the day of the week and the time. It is usually held weekly, often on Wednesday, and begins about sundown at which time most bazaaris are closing up their shops and preparing to say their evening prayers.

The itinerant meetings are similar but more common and move weekly from one home to another. They are always held on a particular day of the week. The members try to have it at least once a year in the home of each participant and allotments are made on a yearly basis to the individuals who participate. Individuals often request that they be assigned the hei'at on or near a particular holy day that is of special significance for them. For example, one of my informants arranged it so the hei'at he would host would correspond with the birthday of the Prophet. This was the result of a vow (*nazr*) he had made earlier that if a certain wish came true he would give a special hei'at at that time each year. The making of vows is most common among women where the resultant gathering is known as sofreh hazrat-i abbas.

The structure and organization of a hei'at-i senfi is as follows. Circulars announcing the date and place of the hei'at are printed and paid for by individual bazaaris who regularly make up the group. One man from among the group is requested by the others to act as a representative or delegate of the group (*ma'mūr*) in order to set dates, arrange meetings and speakers, collect money and have the announcements distributed. He also acts as master of ceremonies at the gathering, introducing speakers and maintaining order. He may lead discussions of business, personal and social problems, and other "nonreligious" matters that often come up at a hei'at after the ritual performance. Marriage arrangements may be informally discussed here; or an announcement may be made that one of their colleagues is in financial difficulty and needs help. A suggestion may be made to finance the construction of a school or mosque and individuals usually pledge money or building materials and the like for this purpose.

At one hei'at I attended the equivalent of about sixty thousand dollars was pledged in money and materials for a private, religiously oriented school being planned.

A particular hei'at is generally held once a week, although individuals usually participate in at least two different groups each week—one associated with the occupation and the other based on friendship ties or neighborhood groups. These relationships are in addition to interaction with people at the mosque, in the bazaar, and possibly in a Sufi brotherhood as well. In other words, a given individual has an extensive network of ties and affiliations with formal groups such as the guild and with informal associations of people based on a variety of common interests. It is these and similar groups that have been the backbone of urban Muslim society and which have provided the interstitial framework for group consolidation between the kin group and the state. Generally the hei'at lasts for three to four hours beginning just after sundown. Those who arrive at this time perform their ritual ablutions (*vuzū'*) and follow the *pishnamāz* in performing the evening prayer. About 7:00 P.M. or so the actual ritual performances begin.

After the prayers, a *vā'ez* or preacher speaks for half an hour to an hour usually praising the Prophet and his descendants. At each mention of the Prophet's name the audience responds in unison with a *salavāt* (a special praise to God, Muhammad, and his descendants). Often the vā'ez himself will call for a salavāt response from the audience, perhaps just in order to give him a brief moment of rest from his continual speaking. Such action has a rhetorical purpose as well, in that it enables the vā'ez to get the audience to chant in unison at frequent points in order to gain their emotional participation and build up a group feeling of emotional tension for consummation at a later point.

The role of the vā'ez and specifically the introductory remarks of praise are essentially to set the stage for the *rauzeh-khān* or narrator who is to follow. It often happens that the rauzeh-khān takes on the duties of the vā'ez as well, so that he first recites the prologue and then delivers the rauzeh.

The rauzeh-khān often begins by reciting a surah (verse) from the Koran or recites a hadith in Arabic. This use of Arabic in a religious context concentrates the attention of the audience to the minbar and carries them away from the material world into a somewhat spiritual one. A particular rauzeh-khān (or vā'ez, for that matter) is chosen by the group largely on the basis of his ability to speak well (*bayān-i khub*.) This includes a good knowledge of spoken classical Arabic and specifically the ability to involve the audience emotionally in the dramatic presentation. The words and expressions used are metaphysically symbolic as well as symbolic at a much more mundane level. The words and expressions are generally simple enough to appeal directly to the emotions of the audience. Complex terms are not used. But it is not the words alone that give meaning and affectivity to the utterances; a word is in a sense neutral until it is placed in a context and related to other words.

Izutsu, for example, speaks of the "basic meaning" of a word such as *yaum* or "day" which holds that meaning even when taken out of the Koranic context. But, put into a context with other words it assumes wider meanings. The "relational meaning" is something connotative that comes to be attached and added to the basic meaning by that word's having taken a particular position in a particular semantic field, standing in diverse relations to all other words in that system. Izutsu notes that within the total Koranic context there are numerous "semantic fields," one of which is that composed of words relating to Resurrection and Last Judgment. This field or conceptual network that is constituted by these words can be called the "eschatological field." "As is natural, an intense atmosphere of a very unusual nature pervades the whole field and reigns over it. Right into this atmosphere you put the word *yaum* with its proper, neutral meaning of a 'day', which it has in normal situations; at once you see a variety of conceptual associations formed around it, and the concept of 'day' becomes tinged with a marked eschatological coloring. In short, *al-yaum*—'the day' means in this particular field not an ordinary day, but the Last Day, i.e., the Day of Judgement."[6] The sum total of all the semantic fields and their component words make up, then, a vast and intricate network of multiple relationships which, in the present context, can be seen to make up the ethos or *Weltanschauung* of the Shi'a.

This is clearly seen in the rauzeh. During the narration of the drama at Karbala the rauzeh-khān discusses in the minutest detail certain aspects of the events that occurred. The long march to Kufa by Husain, his family, and small band of followers is described in glowing adjectives as a trek of six days over scorching desert sands. Once at Karbala, "Ibn Ziyad [commander of the opposing army] cuts off the small party from the only possible source of water with the hope of forcing them into submission with an unquenchable thirst for water in a blazing desert. The children and women begin to wither away as the burning breath of the desert en-

[6] T. Izutsu, *God and Man in the Koran* (Tokyo, 1964), pp. 20–21.

velops them." Each day one of the men goes out to get some water and is subsequently killed fighting against Yazid's army. The prolonged agonies of each individual death are recounted in great detail.

With his six month old son Ali Asghar in his arms, the Imam cried out to the enemy that as this innocent babe had defiled none, at least he should be spared and a little water given to him to allay his thirst. But the reply was an arrow shot at the child's neck which pinned it to his father's arm. After returning the cruelly murdered child to its sorrowing mother's arms (who then sang a mournful mother's lament over her dead child) the Imam returned to pay the last of the sacrifice with his own blood. Arrow after arrow followed piercing his body into a sieve until, when the aged Imam fell from his horse his body did not touch the ground but was held off the ground by the arrows which were sticking out of his body. Shemr, who has earned everlasting shame for himself, after deriding the fallen hero, cut off his head. Ruqaiyeh, Husain's young daughter, weeps over the death of her father whose head is then brought into her presence whereupon she falls upon it moaning and sobbing until she, too, dies of sorrow, prostrate over the severed head.[7]

At each narration of the details noted here the audience bursts into loud, unrestrained sobbing, moaning and slapping of the forehead and beating of chests. The words, as we have seen, are carefully chosen by the narrator to maximize the sentiments and emotions associated with filial and parental love which are strongly felt by each of the participants. Certainly, the problem of death and suffering is the most difficult and serious of the personality tensions with which religions attempt to deal. Talcott Parsons, following Malinowski, sees religious beliefs as symbolic resolutions of these frustrations.[8] Men face the fact that the highest earthly rewards obviously do not always go to those who most closely follow the codes of society; the just and the righteous may suffer and fail while "the ungodly" may prosper. Why do men suffer; why is there evil in the world? These are basic religious problems. It should be clear that these problems not only threaten the integration of the individual personality but are also disruptive of social order.

Culturally constituted defense mechanisms must be developed to deal with them. Geertz has noted that "As a religious problem, the problem of suffering is, paradoxically, not how to avoid suffering but how to suffer, how to make of physical pain, personal loss, worldly defeat or the helpless contemplation of others' agony something bearable, supportable—some-

[7] Based on field data gathered at a rauzeh and taped. Translation mine.

[8] Talcott Parsons, *Essays in Sociological Theory Pure and Applied* (New York, 1949), pp. 58–59.

thing, as we say, sufferable. The problem of suffering passes easily into the problem of evil, for if suffering is severe enough it usually, though not always, seems morally undeserved as well. . . ."[9] The problem of evil and suffering "raise[s] the uncomfortable suspicion that perhaps the world and hence man's life in the world, has no genuine order at all. . . . And the religious response to this suspicion is in each case the same: the formulation, by means of symbols, of an image of such a genuine order of the world which will account for, and even celebrate, the perceived ambiguities, puzzles and paradoxes in human experience."[10]

The Shi'a look to the Imams, whom they consider sinless, for intercession and mediation between man and God. The martyrs at Karbala took it upon themselves to focus in their personal lives the war between good and evil in which goodness and sanity are redeemed through the sacrifice of the physical self. Von Grunebaum briefly discusses the Shi'a Passion plays (ta'ziyā) and also gives a translation of a conversation between the angel Gabriel and the Prophet Muhammad.

> Gabriel delivers [to Muhammad] this message from the Lord: "None has suffered the pain and afflictions which Husain has undergone. None has, like him, been obedient in my service. As he has taken no steps save in sincerity in all that he has done, thou must put the key of Paradise in his hand. The privilege of making intercession is exclusively his. Hussain is by My peculiar grace, the mediator for all."
>
> The Prophet, handing over the key [to Husain] remarks, "Go thou and deliver from the flames everyone who has in his lifetime shed but a single tear for thee, everyone who has in any way helped thee, everyone who has performed a pilgrimage to thy shrine, or mourned for thee, and everyone who has written tragic verse for thee. Bear each and all with thee to Paradise."[11]

Such a statement makes it abundantly clear that Husain's death is seen as a vicarious sacrifice and that his people may benefit from taking part in the mourning over his sufferings. In this way they merit his intercession. But the participants in a rauzeh by crying for Husain not only gain intercession but also are protesting, in their way, the existence of injustice and evil in the world, while at the same time reaffirming their belief in the triumph of good over evil, justice over tyranny, and belief (*imān*) over disbelief (*kufr*).

[9] C. Geertz, "Religion as a Cultural System", reprinted in Lessa and Vogt, eds., *op. cit.*, p. 211.

[10] *Ibid.*

[11] G. Von Grunebaum, *Muhammadan Festivals* (New York, 1951), pp. 91–94.

The Quranic outlook divides all human qualities into two radically opposed categories, which—in view of the fact that they are too concrete and semantically too pregnant to be called "good" and "bad", or "right" and "wrong"—we might simply call the class of positive moral properties and the class of negative moral properties, respectively. The final yardstick by which this division is carried out, is the belief in the one and only God, the creator of all beings. In fact, throughout the Quran there runs the keynote of dualism regarding the moral values of man: the basic dualism of believer and unbeliever.[12]

As we have seen, basic to the Shi'a world view is a sense of persecution—*unjust* persecution. Much as the underlying assumptions of Freudian psychoanalysis focus on certain negative attributes of the personality, so the Shi'a are preconditioned to see the negative, the sad, the tragic and those who are persecuted. The Shi'a see themselves in a *passive* situation as people who are and have been *acted upon.* There is no doubt that historically, from the time of the Ummayads to the persecution by the Sunni Ottoman Turks of the Shi'a minority in eastern Anatolia, there is ample justification for such a view. While at a high level of generalization it might be correct to say, with Sayyid Husain Nasr, that the Twelver Shi'a have been content with being *observers* of the political scene rather than the originators of political movements, it is no longer fair to make this assumption.[13]

Religion and Social Change

The Shi'a are continually seeking a better world. With their eschatological doctrines, the whole of history becomes restructured. Historical events become mythologized as the past is reinterpreted, while contemporary daily events are seen in the light of a perfect world. The entire process of Islamic history is viewed as a continuous decline from the perfection of the golden age of the Prophet. The Shi'a await the advent of the Mahdi but meanwhile strive to achieve the goals inherent in Shi'a theological doctrines. If everything were satisfactory and perfect it would indicate the presence of the Mahdi and the end of the ghaybat-i kubrā and hence no further need for striving or change. But this is not the case. One participates in the world and realizes it is not perfect. The fundamentalist religious explanation of this decline from a pristine past is a continuous

[12] T. Izutsu, *Ethico-Religious Concepts in the Qur'ān* (Montreal, 1966), p. 105.

[13] S. H. Nasr, *Ideals and Realities of Islam* (London, 1966), p. 167.

drifting away from the early simplicity of Islam through centuries of innovations, especially the incorporation of extra-Islamic elements in Muslim canon law.[14] This is seen to be the result of a conscious, premeditated policy of Islamic rulers who no longer follow the policy to "enjoin the good and prohibit the bad." One informant told me, "If we had good leaders, Islam would have progressed. We have examples from history; for example, Salmān was the governor of some cities and he governed wisely. All people were perfect, there was no stealing, there was no complaining from others, all were brothers. When there had been stealing the thief had always been from other cities; he had been a foreigner."

What then can be done to alleviate this situation in which evil and justice are perceived to flourish? One answer to this question can be found in the rauzeh of one of the Shi'a ulema in the bazaar of Tehran.

"If we cry for Imam Husain, it is because he is the one who was sent by God to rise up and bring justice for human beings. So *right now*, if we want to have justice among human beings we should bring Imam Husain back to life. . . . Imam Husain still asks for help. He says 'Come to the battlefield and help me.' What should I do? I have to follow him. How? By rising against tyranny (*ẓolm*) and oppression (*setam*). That is, I don't consider it more important to obey created beings to the creator."

The following excerpt, taken from the rauzeh sermon given by Sayyid Mahmud Taleghani during the month of Muharram in 1963 just a few days prior to the riots and demonstrations against the Shah and the government which resulted in a considerable loss of life, demonstrates the additional meanings that are given to the drama of Husain.

> This is one of Imam Husain's speeches and its aim was to make his goal clear to everybody. . . . "People, God's prophet has said that if there is an oppressive sultan breaking God's promises, committing sin among the people, disregarding God's orders and acting against God's messenger, it is the *duty* of everyone who is aware of these to stand against him to try to change him either with advice, or if this is not possible, with *power*. If one keeps quiet, then God will give him the same punishment as he gives to the Sultan. Because by being quiet, he has acted as his partner in crime."

Then, in a loud emotional voice, Taleghani turned to the audience and still quoting Husain said, "You have written letters to me and promised to help me and stay beside me [referring to the people of Kufa]. If you are still willing to keep your promise, I am Husain, the son of Ali and the

[14] Ahmad, *op. cit.*, p. 108.

son of Fatima who is the daughter of God's prophet."[15] From the phrasing and particularly the direct quote from Husain in the *present tense*, there is little doubt in the mind of the audience what is being asked for . . . namely support of the ulama (Husain's spiritual heirs) against an oppressive government.

At still another rauzeh during this troubled period in 1963 the narrator, again *quoting Husain*, says:

Husain said, "This is not a type of revolt that you can cooperate with by giving wealth or giving speeches or giving religious magazines or newspapers to people, the only way you can cooperate with this revolt (*qiyām*) is with martyrdom and with self-sacrifice." Husain, in his last sentence said, "I am not asking help from merchants or from powerful writers. The only help I can get is from those sincere devotees, and heroes, who are willing to sacrifice themselves, who are truly willing to sacrifice their blood." We, the prophet's descendants, deserve more to be your ruler, to be the leader of your religion and your world.

It is interesting to note the use of anachronisms in Husain's purported speech. The references to newspapers and magazines obviously do not apply to the tribal situation in seventh-century Arabia. Often, the words of Husain are stated first in Arabic and then discussed in Persian. By doing so, the narrator not only gives the scene a realistic hush but also adds to the variety of tone and affectivity in the presentation.

The ulama are protesting against a government that they do not consider legitimate. The perfect government is that of the Imam. In his absence every form of government is of necessity imperfect, for the imperfection of men is reflected in their political institutions. The distrust of all worldly government after the disappearance of the Mahdi and the early experiences of the Shi'a community made Twelve-Imam Shi'ism apathetic toward political life until the establishment of the Persian Shi'a Safavid dynasty. During the Constitutional Revolution in Iran from 1905 to 1911 the ulama were again extremely active in agitating for political reform. Secret societies were formed by modernist intellectuals as well as religious leaders in order to combat the abuses of the government and to prevent the encroachment of foreign influence. At this time it was claimed that Imam Husain was the prototype of all founders of secret societies and it was further declared that at the end of each clandestine meeting, a rauzeh

[15] S. M. Taleghani, text of rauzeh sermon entitled "Jihād va Shahādat" given during Muharram 1382/June 1963 printed in *Goftar-i 'Āshurā* (Tehran, 1341/1964–64), pp. 93–119. Translation and italics mine.

would be presented.[16] One of my bazaar informants who personally remembers the activities during the Constitutional Revolution, in answer to a question about the origins of the rauzehkhāni, stated:

Since Shah-Abbas's time or maybe before, they had this, but it was rauzehkhāni-ye mahalleh [those associated with the districts in the city] but not for the senf [guild]. I think that during the Constitutional period they wanted to make people used to the revolution. The secret societies started among the guilds. All the workers got together and put a flag up [announcing the rauzeh] and it was held weekly. They would go for religious reasons but they had another motive. They would get together and talk about the government situation; they were political.

Nikki Keddie notes that during the nineteenth century the power and influence of the ulama was increasing rapidly and cites "the call for a jihad against Russia in 1826, the demand for the repeal of the all-embracing Reuter concession in 1873, the struggle for the repeal of the British tobacco monopoly concession in 1891–92, and the Constitutional Revolution itself" as evidence for this trend.[17] The Constitutional Revolution was brought about largely by an alliance between the bazaar merchants and the ulama—an affinity that had been growing in strength since the increasing popularity of the Mujtahids in the sixteenth century.

There are numerous reasons for this alliance among which are patterns of intermarriage; the need for ulama support in the resolution and adjudication of conflict in the market; the need for a believer to choose and follow a particular religious guide (*marja' al-taqlid*) in religious matters and interpretation of doctrine. Another important reason is that one's religious guide or his representative can allow a portion (the *sahm-i imām*) of one's alms to be used to help a fellow merchant who is in financial difficulties. A bazaar merchant needs to keep on the good side of the ulama and also needs to maintain at least the outward appearance of proper religious performance in order to benefit from this and similar forms of aid and cooperation. The religious leaders are also very influential and their "connections" are continually sought by individuals. Finally, each Muslim and particularly each Muslim family needs a religious leader to officiate at rituals during the life and developmental cycles.[18]

[16] A. K. S. Lambton, "Secret Societies and the Persian Revolution of 1905–1906," *St. Anthony's Papers*, 4 (London, 1958), 55.

[17] N. Keddie, "The Roots of the Ulama's Power in Modern Iran," *Studia Islamica*, 29 (1969), 34, esp. n. 1.

[18] See Clifford Geertz, "Ritual and Social Change: A Javanese Example," *American Anthropologist*, 59 (1957), 32–54, for a discussion of the performance of Islamic rituals under conditions of social change.

The pattern of transactions between the ulama and the bazaar merchant is not one-sided. In return for the mediating role of the religious leader in bazaar affairs and also his mediating role between the spiritual world and the mundane world, the ulama receive material gifts usually in the form of alms. A portion of these alms is kept by the alim for the maintenance of himself and his family while the remainder is redistributed throughout the community for various purposes including the upkeep of theology students and contributions to the marja' al-taqlid of that particular alim. The religious stature and piety of a particular marja' al-taqlid is intimately associated with his political views. This was clearly brought out in my interviews. While trying to determine rough percentages of followers for certain mujtahids I asked many bazaar merchants whom they consider to be their marja' al-taqlid. The answer, almost invariably, was, "If you are interested in religion, why do you ask political questions?" The personal following that is built up by the ulama on the basis of their piety and learning, as well as by their distribution of money, food, and favors, is used by them not only in political matters vis-à-vis the state, but also within the religious institution itself.[19] Since the government has assumed control of religious endowments the ulama have become even more directly dependent on the support that they derive from the people and which they resent.[20] The ulama generally have a low opinion of the people upon whom they are dependent for support. A religious bazaar merchant, whose relatives include members of the ulama, told me "the rohāniyūn [ulama] look down on the bazaaris. They will never waste their time for them although they *use* the bazaaris. Because they are strong they don't care about other people. They only want them to pull a load for them" (faqat mikhāhand bāri az ash bekeshand [the word *bāri* is used in Persian only in reference to draught animals, especially donkeys, pulling loads]).

Despite these differences both the bazaar merchants and the ulama are concerned with the prevention of the undue and unjust exercise of governmental power. During the Constitutional period in the late nineteenth and early twentieth centuries, the merchants saw themselves hurt by Western economic competition and the extortionate demands and threat to the national credit, entailed in the foreign loans to the Shahs to finance their pleasure trips to Europe. Opposition to the British tobacco monopoly, the reasonably successful movement in Isfahan to boycott Western-made

[19] A. K. S. Lambton, "A Reconsideration of the Position of the Marja' al-Taqlid and the Religious Institution," *Studia Islamica*, 20 (1964), 134.

[20] *Ibid.*, pp. 132–134.

goods, and hostility to Belgian control over Iranian customs can all be cited as largely government-inspired moves that threatened the economic well-being of the merchant community in the early years of this century. The ulama, for their part, saw growing foreign (equated with Christian) influence as a threat to Islam and their privileged social position.

During recent years, especially since the reign of Reza Shah in the 1930s, there have been extensive changes in Iranian society. There has been a continued strengthening of the central government, including the growth and relative efficiency of the bureaucracy. The merchants especially have been feeling the increasing effectiveness of the tax office. To the merchant the tax office is, not without some justification, a prime example of governmental corruption. The rest of the governmental bureaucracy is hardly better in terms of excessive red tape and corruption. The central government has entered new fields, particularly agriculture, and land reform has brought government agents into contact with rural Iran more than ever before. The government-sponsored literary corps and the development of secular village schools have also meant a new prominence for government representatives in the villages.

The government's encroachment into spheres formerly the province of the ulama has also been reinforced in recent years. The recent growth of secular elementary education, the beginnings of government regulations of *vaqf* land leased to tenants, and the introduction of voting for women despite clerical objections are all signs of the trend to lessening clerical power.[21]

The frustrations felt by the ulama as a result of their declining power and influence in social life owing to increased secularization and government autonomy is reflected in the drama of Husain. Kluckhohn, in his seminal article on myth and ritual, has stated that "Ritual is . . . often a symbolic dramatization of the fundamental 'needs' of a society, whether 'economic,' 'biological,' 'social' or 'sexual.' Mythology is the rationalization of these same needs, whether they are expressed in overt ceremonial or not. . . . Ceremonies tend to portray a symbolic resolvement of the conflicts which external environment, historical experience and selective distribution of personality types have caused to be characteristic in the society."[22]

[21] N. Keddie, "The Iranian Power Structure and Social Change 1800–1969: An Overview," paper presented at Conference on the Structure of Power in Islamic Iran, University of California, Los Angeles, June 1969.

[22] C. Kluckhohn, "Myths and Rituals: A General Theory," in Lessa and Vogt, eds., *op. cit.*, p. 158.

But myth does not reflect all aspects of the social structure. Rather it is always selective. In the case of Shi'a myth and ritual the Husain drama is associated with conflict and conflict resolution.

The historical conflict between Husain and Yazid was a political event in that it was concerned with the question of who should make and carry out decisions regarding public policy and the common good. It was a struggle for the power to command. Although, as we have noted, there is an intense spiritual message in this drama this aspect is not singled out for discussion or elaboration in the rauzeh by the ulama. In the mythologizing of the tragedy of Husain and the Imams and the reenactment of these events in ritual in Iran today, the political dimension is stressed. The persistence of this ritual over time is attributable to the reflective nature of that ritual vis-à-vis the contemporary society—whether it be Ummayad, Abbasid, Safavid, Qajar, or Pahlavi.

The form did not persist merely because it was "traditional" nor has it been reenacted yearly because one's ancestors performed it thus and so. The performance and ritual remembrance of the myth are the result of the desire to express certain sentiments associated with basic problems confronting man as Being and man as Iranian.

In presenting this form the ulama (and specifically the rauzeh-khān) make many decisions that affect their rhetorical perspective. The linguistic variations that are available to the speaker are bounded by the historical events at Karbala and are also constrained by the socio-political situation of the moment as perceived by the speaker and his audience. The existence of secret police and the threat of imprisonment prevent the speaker from voicing his grievances directly.[23] They are phrased in a religious idiom,

[23] Sayyid Mahmud Taleghani commented further in the same rauzeh discussed in the text: "Gentlemen, today the Zionist is like the imperialist. In our country it is in the form of Bahaism. They have penetrated in all our government. Oh, you gentlemen who are the representatives of the government—those who are here secretly or not secretly, this is the request of Islam. It doesn't matter if you are the head of the government or beneath him you get angry and ask why I say these things. Well, don't let me say it, prevent me then it won't be my duty anymore to talk about these things. But when I come here I have to talk about the Islamic laws and boundaries." [Taleghani goes on to explain why he is angry over the persecution of certain individuals]: "I tell you my nerves are shattered. Whatever I say I am responsible for it. Don't go to the host (*sahib-i khāneh*) tomorrow and question him and ruin his life. He is not responsible. Come to me and tell me that I have lied or I have talked against religion or I have colluded with embassies, say anything you want, even make a file for me. Mr. Minister of Agriculture, isn't there any Muslim advisor in this country? If we don't have

in the form of elaborations on a myth whose content is extremely well known. The political meaning that is communicated is "decoded" by the audience on the basis of a common understanding of the meanings of certain symbols based on their use in a particular context; and on subtle qualities of speech such as tone, pitch, melody, and use of dramatic formulas in order to raise the passionate emotions of the audience, and various poetic meters common to Persian and Arabic verse. Certain melodic patterns connote, for example, "sincerity," others "irony," "sarcasm," or even "hostility." Certain tones, ways of accenting, abbreviating, or elongating words convey similar meanings.[24]

Conclusion

In conclusion, I quote part of an interview I had with one of the leading Shi'a ulama of the bazaar of Tehran.

> If you see we are mourning, it is because we want to show our sincerity toward Imām Husain because we know him as an Imām who fought against tyranny (ẓolm) and oppression (satamgarān) by God's order. We cry today because we don't want to give up to tyranny. We beat our heads and our chests because we don't want to go under the pressure of dictatorship or accept coercion. . . . We have been crying for 1,000 years, it doesn't matter if we cry for another 10 million in order to bring justice against tyranny. I cannot laugh as long as tyranny *is* ruling. I cry in order to resist. . . . The reason I say "Husain brought his little child in front of the crowd and asked for a drop of water" is because I want to tell the people what a low character they had. We [ulama] are trying to make justice popular among society, and to prevent cruelty and tyranny. To make people close to Husain and those like him and far from Yazid and his kind. We are crying because justice is gone.

Despite the attempts of the ulama to start a revitalization movement that would bring back an idealized way of life based on Islamic principles, there is no evidence that their political activities are having the effect they wish. There is evidence, however, that the ulama are undergoing a period of change and reevaluation not only along the lines that Lambton notes[25]

---

an engineer bring one from Switzerland, or India or Germany. Does it have to be a Zionist Jew as an advisor for land reform?" (in *Goftar-i 'Āshurā*, pp. 106–108). Lambton notes that Taleghani was arrested at this time (Muharram 1382/June 1963) and sentenced to ten years imprisonment (*op. cit.*, p. 120).

[24] See J. B. Adams, "Culture and Conflict in an Egyptian Village," *American Anthropologist*, 59 (1957), 226, for a similar analysis of the expressive functions of speech patterns in the Middle East.

[25] *Op. cit.*, pp. 134–135.

but also in terms of education. The rohāniyūn [ulama] have finally begun to realize, at least many of them, that they are not reaching the youth of the country. They are therefore making a concerted attempt, within their present capacities, to communicate their views to a new generation of Iranians. The younger generation, even the religiously oriented, rarely participate in the type of hei'ats we have been discussing in this paper. The reason usually given is that the rauzeh-khan and other speakers usually have set themes that they repeat over and over again. There is rarely anything new. "If I feel that the subject they are going to discuss is new and interesting for me, and I will learn something from it, I will go there, otherwise I can read something on my own and benefit."

Although it is difficult to be certain, the trend seems to be away from physical resistance movements such as those during Muharram of 1963 and more toward ideological resistance through involvement and participation in the decision-making apparatus of the government. Religiously oriented individuals who may oppose the government nevertheless join its ranks in the hope that they will have the opportunity to implement policies that will be more in accord with their view that Islam is an all-encompassing system of beliefs.[26]

[26] For a further development of these ideas see my paper "Religion and Social Change in Iran: The Bazaar as a Case Study," in E. Yarshater, ed., *Iran Faces the Seventies* (New York, 1971).

15 | Mahdis, Walis, and New Men in the Sudan*

JOHN VOLL

ISLAMIC ORGANIZATIONS and Muslim religious notables have had a vital role in the development of the modern Sudan. It has often been noted that Sudanese politics in much of the twentieth century have been dominated by two prominent religious leaders, Sayyid 'Ali al-Mirghani and Sayyid 'Abd al-Rahman al-Mahdi, but the involvement of Muslim notables is more than this. The major religious families have provided personnel for party executive committees, parliaments and cabinets, constitutional commissions, and Supreme Councils.[1]

These prominent leaders with religious prestige come from established families in the Sudan. The prestige and influence of these families are based on their leadership of Islamic popular organizations. The families are widely recognized in the Sudan as possessors of special sanctity and the heirs of special traditions of religious leadership. They lead a variety of types of organizations; some are decentralized and of limited geographic influence, others have a broader regional influence, and two have centralized organizations with power and influence throughout most of the northern Sudan.

The common feature of all these organizations is that they are based on modes of operation justified by traditional Islam in the Sudan. The decentralized groups are the heirs of the tradition of Sufi orders (*tariqas*)

* In this discussion, "the Sudan" refers to the Republic of the Sudan whose capital is Khartoum, rather than to the broad geographic region stretching across Africa just south of the Sahara. It should also be noted that this discussion focuses on the experience of the Islamic northern Sudan and does not deal with the problems posed by the non-Muslim southern part of the Sudan.

[1] For example, in 1968, prominent religious families provided the presidents of both major parties (Umma Party, Sayyid Sadiq, a great-grandson of the nineteenth-century Mahdi; Democratic Unionist Party, Ismail al-Azhari of the family of a nineteenth-century religious notable, Ismail-al-Wali), three of the five members of the Supreme Council which functioned as head of state, four cabinet members in the coalition government, and at least four members of the Constitution Commission.

introduced into the Sudan before the nineteenth century, especially the Qadiriyya and the Shadhiliyya. These early groups were responsible for the firm establishment of Islam in the northern Sudan and the early leaders were both respected teachers and revered saints. It was as miracle-working saints with reputations for sanctity and closeness to God, in other words, as *walis*, that they won the loyalty of the majority of the Sudanese.

The nineteenth century saw the introduction of centralized, area-wide religious organizations, the most important of which were the Khatmiyya Tariqa and the Mahdist movement. The Khatmiyya was the earlier of the two and, as in the pre-nineteenth-century orders, the leaders won popular support on the basis of being recognized as walis. The difference was that the Mirghani family, in leading the Khatmiyya, established a centralized organization with many followers in most of the regions of the northern Sudan, rather than following the earlier pattern of small, locally autonomous units. The leader of this large organization in the twentieth century, until his death in 1968, was Sayyid 'Ali al-Mirghani. As the head of an important religious family and leader of a major religious organization, Sayyid 'Ali was one of the most prominent and influential men on the Sudanese scene.

Sayyid 'Abd al-Rahman al-Mahdi was the leader, during the first half of the twentieth century, of the other large-scale religious organization in the northern Sudan, the Mahdist movement. This movement represents a tradition somewhat different from that of the wali-led tariqa. In Islam, eschatological traditions had developed which described the Last Days in terms of the coming of a leader who would be rightly guided by God to establish justice and righteousness on earth. This expected leader was called "the Mahdi." In contrast with the wali, the Mahdi was seen as a political and military leader as well as a religious guide.

In the second half of the nineteenth century, popular discontent with social and political conditions in the Sudan resulted in a growing feeling that the coming of the Mahdi was near. When a Sudanese religious teacher, Muhammad Ahmad, declared himself to be the Mahdi in 1881 and won a series of spectacular military victories, he was able to win significant support throughout the northern Sudan. Despite the defeat of the movement by Anglo-Egyptian forces in 1898, Sayyid 'Abd al-Rahman al-Mahdi, a son of the Mahdi, was able to reorganize the Mahdist followers into an effective and influential group in the twentieth-century Sudan.

It is the leaders of these various Islamic organizations who are prominent in the Sudanese scene. The Islamic scholar class, or ulama, has never assumed, as ulama, a position of comparable importance, and modernist Islamic organizations or groups like the reformers of the Manar School in Egypt or the Algerian Association of Ulama have made little headway in the Sudan.[2] More militantly activist Islamic movements like the Muslim Brotherhood have had some importance since World War II, but their influence and power have been much less widespread than that of the religious families.

In the past, leaders of tariqas have had power and influence in many areas of the Islamic world. One of the significant features of modern Islamic history, however, has been the relatively rapid decline in the importance of these leaders in most areas.[3] It is, then, of interest to investigate the apparent continued importance of such leaders in the Sudan.

Perhaps the simplest explanation would be to state that the process of modernization in the Sudan has been relatively gradual with the result that traditional attitudes have maintained greater strength. A glance at some of the statistics often used in discussing modernization would help confirm this. The per capita domestic product in the Sudan around 1955–1960 was substantially lower than in other Middle Eastern countries (less than half the per capita domestic product in Algeria, Morocco, or Tunisia, and less than two-thirds that of Egypt). At the same time, the position of agricultural production in relation to total production in the Sudan is greater than in other Middle Eastern countries.[4] In general, traditional styles of personal identification have remained strong, with most Sudanese maintaining a tribal identification and relatively strong family ties.[5] In this context, it would appear natural that ties of loyalty and personal identification with the traditional Sudanese religious organizations would also

[2] One such movement in the Sudan was the Azmiyya which stirred some enthusiasm in the first quarter of the twentieth century but had little influence. See, for further details, J. Spencer Trimingham, *Islam in the Sudan* (London, 1965), pp. 239–240.

[3] For the situation in North Africa, see Leon Carl Brown, "The Role of Islam in Modern North Africa," *State and Society in Independent North Africa*, Leon Carl Brown, ed. (Washington, 1966), pp. 97–122. A discussion of the situation in Egypt can be found in M. D. Gilsenan, "Some Factors in the Decline of the Sufi Orders in Modern Egypt," *Muslim World*, LVII, no. 1 (Jan., 1967), 11–18.

[4] For example, see the statistics used in Frederic C. Shorter, "The Application of Development Hypotheses in Middle Eastern Studies," *Economic Development and Cultural Change*, XIV, no. 3 (April, 1966), 353–354.

[5] A good summary of this continuing style of identification can be found in Alan W. Horton, "The Social Dimension of Sudanese Politics," *American Universities Field Staff Reports*, Northeast Africa Series, Vol. XI, no. 4 (June, 1964).

remain strong, and the leaders of these organizations would continue to have power and influence.

The problem, however, is not so simply explained. The Sudan, although underdeveloped, has made significant steps in modernization. An important class of Sudanese with a modern-style education and modern experience has developed, and most political activity is in the hands of these people who can be called the "new men."[6] Of importance to the question of the position of the religious leaders is the fact that they have a continuing influence, not only among the "traditional" Sudanese, but also among Sudanese with modern outlooks, and they have influence in associations of modern style. In new associations like the trade unions, for example, religious affiliation was sufficiently strong in 1953 for union members to vote for religiously backed candidates, whereas one of the most prominent officers of the Sudan Workers Trade Union Federation received negligible support in the area of his own headquarters.[7] In the early organizations of secondary school and college graduates like the Gordon College Old Boys Club (established in 1919) and its broader successor, the General Graduates Congress, religious affiliation and loyalty to different religious leaders provided a major means of identification for the factions within these associations. Similarly in the post-World War II era, the major political parties have represented a continuing alliance between the new men and religious leaders, with a significant number of new men maintaining true personal loyalty to one of the major religious leaders or groups.

The continuing influence of the older religious leadership thus has a broader base than the simple explanation of gradual modernization in the Sudan. This influence has extended to the modern sectors of Sudanese society as they have developed. It is this feature that seems to be noteworthy in the continued vitality of mahdi- and wali-led groups in the Sudan.

There are two important features in the history of the modern Sudan which have influenced the relationships among mahdis, walis, and new men in the Sudan. The first of these is the unusual imperial experience of the Sudan, and the second is the initial success and subsequent history of the Mahdist movement in the Sudan.

[6] For a more complete discussion of the meaning of the term "new men," as used here, see William R. Polk, *The United States and the Arab World* (Cambridge, Mass., 1965), Chapter XIV, "The Accelerating Social Revolution: The New Men."

[7] Saad ed-Din Fawzi, *The Labour Movement in the Sudan, 1946–1955* (London, 1957), p. 101.

The unusual character of the Sudan's imperial experience begins in the nineteenth century. The medieval Islamic sultanate of the Funj had controlled most of the northern Sudan, at least nominally, since the early sixteenth century. This sultanate was brought to an end by an invasion of a modernized army in 1820–1821, but the conquering power was the Ottoman governor of Egypt, not a European power. The Turko-Egyptian government that was established in the Sudan under the control of the rulers of Egypt was brought to an end by the Sudanese Mahdi in the 1880s. Thus the first modern imperial experience of the Sudan was not with a European power and the first effective act of Sudanese national self-assertion was against a Turko-Egyptian government.

The Mahdist state was destroyed and non-Sudanese control was reestablished by 1898 through a "Reconquest" in which Egypt and Great Britain participated jointly. The dual nature of the new government was established legally in the Condominium Agreement of 1899 and was symbolized by the fact that the Egyptian and British flags were flown side by side in the Sudan. As Lord Cromer, the British representative in Egypt, explained to a gathering of Sudanese notables in Omdurman in 1899, this meant that the Sudan would "be governed by the Queen of England and by the Khedive of Egypt."[8] Thus the Sudan was legally ruled jointly by two different powers. Great Britain was the senior partner in this arrangement and, for most purposes, had complete control over the operation of the government of the Sudan until the period of self-government beginning at the end of 1953. The Sudan, however, was neither a British colony nor a British mandate territory, and could not be classed as a British protectorate. It was a special area under the guidance of the Foreign Office rather than the Colonial Office.

Although the British dominated the Sudan Government of the Condominium era, Egypt had a recognized position as "co-ruler" of the Sudan. Thus, decisions about the future of the Sudan were subject to Anglo-Egyptian negotiation, and the question of the Sudan became an important issue in the development of Egyptian nationalism. Despite the fact that Egypt's direct political role in the imperial governing of the Sudan was limited, Egyptian journalism and the development of Egyptian nationalism played important roles in the development of nationalism in the Sudan.

The unusual imperial experience of the Sudan helped to shape its modern political development and the way that its nationalism emerged.

[8] Earl of Cromer, *Modern Egypt* (New York, 1909), II, 116.

The Sudanese had to relate and react not to one but to two powers, and the result was the development of two modes of nationalist expression. Some Sudanese saw their primary goal as the end of British control and viewed Egypt as an ally in this effort. In this way they became supporters of the idea of "unity of the Nile Valley." Other Sudanese worked directly for an independent Sudan and, fearing Egyptian dominance, tended to cooperate with the British in an effort to create a "Sudan for the Sudanese."

The second feature of modern Sudanese history to influence the relationship between religious leaders and the new men in the Sudan was the history of the Mahdist movement.

The nineteenth-century Sudanese Mahdi had met, and defeated, "modern" armies. His success made possible the establishment of a state that represented both an Islamically inspired state structure and an independent Sudan. Although Muhammad Ahmad the Mahdi died in 1885 at the peak of his success, the state did not collapse. His successor, the Khalifa Abdallah, was able to consolidate the gains made by his leader and teacher and, for more than a decade, the Sudan remained an independent state. The success of the Mahdi, and the continued existence of the state he founded, confirmed the belief in the Sudan that the Mahdi had in fact come. The subsequent defeat of the Mahdist state by the Anglo-Egyptian forces did not destroy this faith.

This relatively widespread Mahdist sentiment, in the twentieth century, was focused by the leadership of a son of the Mahdi, Sayyid 'Abd al-Rahman. The Mahdist experience had created a new prominent religious family in the Sudan, the descendants of the Mahdi, and this family carried on the Mahdist tradition. The family of the Khalifa Abdallah also remained respected and provided leadership.[9] As a result of the leadership of Sayyid 'Abd al-Rahman, a new area-wide mass organization of Mahdist followers, known as the Ansar, was formed.

The Ansar were a "traditional" Islamic group in that the foundations of the group were built on a long-standing Islamic tradition. Yet the roots were in the particular forms of revivalism and militancy associated with the concept of the Mahdi. It was not a Sufi order, but rather, it rejected various mystical interpretations and forms. The regular meetings of local Ansar groups did not adopt the Sufi style of the dhikr, or organized recitation of mystic poetry. At the same time, although Mahdism initially rep-

[9] For example, a grandson of the Khalifa was appointed to a cabinet post in 1968 and a son of the Khalifa became a member of the Supreme Council elected in 1968.

resented a rigorous puritanism, it had the flexibility allowed to a leader believed to be directly guided by God. Hence its revivalism was not forced into as strict and limited a framework as were ulama reformers or Wahhabi-type revivalists in other Islamic areas.

The modern Mahdist movement was thus a movement that had potential ideological flexibility and an accepted mode of action of direct political involvement. The movement was reinforced by the fact that it was the bearer of a tradition of pious activism with success within the living memory of many of its members. Unlike other revivalist movements, the Ansar did not have to look into the distant medieval history for their inspiration.

The Mahdist tradition had two important parts: a theocratic tradition and a memory of a Mahdist-led independent Sudan. These two aspects were gradually merged in the twentieth century. The theocratic tradition was one of direct political action. The eschatological expectations associated with it were gradually transformed by Ansar leadership and became increasingly applied to the goal of a Mahdist-led independent Sudan. In this way the Ansar became the strongest supporters of a nationalist program of "Sudan for the Sudanese." The Mahdist tradition thus formed the basis for a Sudanese nationalist movement which, at the same time, had firm foundations in traditional Sudanese Islam.

The development of the Mahdist tradition gives a distinctive tone to modern Sudanese history. As a widespread and powerful movement, the Ansar could not be ignored by anyone, and the Ansar actions influenced the actions of most northern Sudanese, whether anti-Mahdist or pro-Mahdist, wali or new men.

The Mahdist tradition had not arisen nor did it act in a vacuum. In the pre-Mahdist Sudan a firm foundation for religious leadership had existed in the hands of the leaders of the tariqas. The families leading the older tariqas had relatively limited power and influence, but the Khatmiyya Tariqa under the leadership of the Mirghani family had assumed area-wide importance. Although the Khatmiyya had real political influence, members of the Mirghani family had not taken political offices. Rather, the order had accommodated itself to the political circumstances of the Turko-Egyptian rule and the leaders remained men of religious prestige, respected for piety and spiritual power. In short, the Mirghani family leaders were regarded as walis, and were not mahdis.

The wali leaders of the Khatmiyya firmly opposed the Mahdist movement and consistently allied themselves with anti-Mahdist forces. Thus, they were associated with the Anglo-Egyptian Reconquest and gained prominent positions of prestige and influence in the early years of the Condominium. In the twentieth century the Khatmiyya-Ansar rivalry became an important factor in Sudanese development.

Thus the special imperial experience of the Sudan and the development of the Mahdist tradition formed the basis for two dualities that shaped Sudanese history in the twentieth century: Great Britain–Egypt and Mahdist–anti-Mahdist. These features also provide an important key to the relationship between the religious leaders and the new men because these dualities provided the framework for the structure of personal and political loyalties of most northern Sudanese.

In the rivalry between the two large religious organizations, the leaders of both recognized quite early in the twentieth century the importance of the new educated classes. They took an interest in the organizations of the modern educated Sudanese; they gave advice and financial support to young men in the new schools, and, from time to time, they exerted their influence on behalf of these new groups. As early as the 1920s it was possible to identify groups of the new men who were closely associated with either Sayyid 'Abd al-Rahman al-Mahdi or Sayyid 'Ali al-Mirghani. For example, when factions developed in the Gordon College Old Boys Club in the 1920s, one of the important identifying features of the factions was association with one or the other Sayyid.

When political parties were being formed at the end of World War II, the two Sayyids again gave their encouragement and popular support to competing parties. In addition, both the Ansar and the Khatmiyya organized youth groups. The youth, or *shabab*, organizations were active in organizing demonstrations and were important in bringing popular and active support to the new political parties. At the same time they created a special kind of tie for many young men to the traditional religious leaders.

In general, then, a special cooperative relationship was built up between the politically active new men and the religious leaders. The religious rivalry had given impetus to the creation of this relationship. It is also important to note that the religious leaders were sufficiently flexible and aware of the nature of the newly developing society to recognize the importance of the creation of this relationship. It was felt by these leaders, as Sayyid 'Abd al-Rahman noted, that the educated class without the support of the religious leaders would be branches without roots, while the religious leaders without the educated classes would be roots without branches.[10]

At the same time many educated Sudanese recognized the importance of this cooperation. The activities of organizations of new men could use the resources of the Sayyids. When, for example, the General Graduates Congress, formed in 1938, began a program of building nongovernmental schools, the encouragement and financial support of religious leaders were most welcome. In the development of nationalism and of political action groups, the educated Sudanese soon became convinced of the need for broad popular support. The British, for example, rejected a memorandum from the General Graduates Congress in 1942 demanding self-government, on the grounds that the Congress could speak for only a small minority of the Sudanese people. Thus when political parties were formed, the patronage of the prominent religious leaders was welcomed because it brought with it a well-organized mass following for the parties. In this way the major parties became associated with the major religious groups. A firm and practical basis of cooperation was built and the maintenance of "traditional" religious identification was given a modern significance.

Within this context it is useful to examine in more detail three potential crises for the continuation of the influence of Sudanese religious leaders: the potential crisis through identification with an imperial power in days of growing nationalism; the crisis posed by the context of independence; and the broader potential crisis of an open "traditional"-modern split.

Leaders of traditional Islamic organizations in many parts of the Muslim world found it convenient and relatively easy to come to an agreement with imperial powers who ruled their areas. Frequently the imperial power was not consciously concerned with changing attitudes or social structures of their subject peoples. At the same time they were very concerned with the problem of maintaining public order and political stability, and they usually wanted to do this as inexpensively as possible. As a result, imperial powers worked to win the support of leaders of the subject peoples who had mass followings and were not actively working for radical social and political change. Although wali-style leaders sometimes led movements of opposition to non-Muslim control, as was the case with 'Abd al-Qadir in Algeria in the first half of the nineteenth century, leaders of tariqas quite soon learned that their organizations would not be destroyed by

[10] al-Sādiq al-Mahdī, ed., *Jihād fī sabīl al-istiqlāl* (Khartoum, n.d.), p. 177.

foreign rule. Even more, it soon became apparent that the importance of the leadership and the power of the orders could be increased by cooperation with the imperial powers.

The development of nationalism in Islamic countries during the twentieth century began to undermine the gains made by religious leaders through imperial cooperation. Reformers and nationalists charged traditional leaders with having betrayed their nation and faith as well as with being the major obstacle to necessary reforms. With this kind of indictment, many traditional religious groups rapidly lost influence in the changing societies of which they were a part, as appears to have been especially true in the countries of French North Africa. The result of the imperial experience of the walis in places like the Maghreb was that most of the groundwork for a constructive wali–new man relationship was destroyed.

The unusual imperial experience of the Sudan meant that the possible crisis for traditional religious leaders of association with an imperial power was less serious. The major religious leaders in the Sudan did in fact have close and relatively good relations with imperial powers, but the peculiar Condominium arrangement and the distinctive history of the Ansar did much to offset the potential dangers of these relations.

The Ansar and Sayyid 'Abd al-Rahman, after a few years of mutual distrust, came to work closely with the British. Sayyid 'Abd al-Rahman aided the British in calming the potential explosiveness of the Mahdist excitement and by his example helped to win the submission to the Condominium government of tribes who might have been involved in Mahdist revolts.[11] During World War II and in the postwar era, the Ansar under Sayyid 'Abd al-Rahman cooperated with the moderate British program of introducing self-government rather than joining forces with the more radical nationalist groups calling for more rapid progress toward independence.

Despite this kind of cooperation with Great Britain, the Ansar leadership built and maintained the confidence of many Sudanese nationalists. An important contributing factor was that Great Britain was not the only imperial power in the Sudan. Despite the fact of strong linguistic, cultural, and religious ties, many Sudanese mistrusted the Egyptians. There were memories of the nineteenth-century Egyptian rule of the Sudan

[11] A discussion of this with specific reference to some tribes in southern Darfur can be found in *Sudan Monthly Intelligence Report*, no. 331 (Feb., 1922).

which caused some of the distrust. In addition, many Sudanese new men were convinced that the Egyptians had often disregarded Sudanese interests and Sudanese popular opinion. For example, the Egyptians had negotiated an agreement with England on usage of Nile waters in 1929 which even pro-Egyptian Sudanese felt was detrimental to Sudanese interests.[12] In 1936 Egypt negotiated a treaty with England that discussed, among other matters, the future of the Sudan. Educated Sudanese were concerned that neither Britain nor Egypt had made any attempt to consult Sudanese opinion on the matter. This concern was part of the impetus that brought about the creation of the General Graduates Congress in 1938. In this situation, although Ansar had cooperated with one imperial power, they could also act as the staunch opponent of the other "co-ruler." Thus they were able to win the cooperation of many of the anti-Egyptian nationalists among the new men.

In a positive sense the Ansar could also appeal to this group of new men. The Mahdist tradition was the strongest aspect of the growing sentiment of "Sudan for the Sudanese," with the Mahdist state representing a firm foundation for the claim for the independent Sudan. Ansar leadership encouraged the view of the Mahdi as being the "first Sudanese nationalist." In this way even non-Ansar who supported the idea of an independent Sudan were attracted to the leadership of Sayyid 'Abd al-Rahman. The broad popular base of the Ansar made an Ansar–new man alliance a powerful force in Sudanese politics working toward the independence of the Sudan.

The peculiar imperial circumstances of the Sudan and Mahdist history thus made it possible for Ansar leadership to build a firm relationship with many new men.

These same factors operated, although in different ways, to help the Khatmiyya build and maintain the loyalty of many new men. At the beginning of the Condominium the Khatmiyya was closely associated with the British. As the British began to show favor to Sayyid 'Abd al-Rahman, however, the friendship between Sayyid 'Ali al-Mirghani and the British cooled. The rise to prominence of Sayyid 'Abd al-Rahman and the Ansar did not mean that the Khatmiyya was forced out of the political arena,

[12] A rather complete discussion of the Nile waters issue, from an Egyptian point of view, is in Abd El-Fattah I. S. Baddour, *Sudanese Egyptian Relations* (The Hague, 1960). A summary of editorial comments of pro-Egyptian Sudanese who objected to the Egyptian position on Nile water usage can be found in *Sudan Herald*, no. 5518, Sept. 12, 1950.

though, because the Condominium context had created an alternative source of outside support, Egypt.

In the twentieth century Egyptian support and encouragement were given to the more radical nationalists in the Sudan. These Sudanese mistrusted or did not believe British promises of eventual Sudanese self-determination. Given support by the Egyptians, the rallying cry of this brand of Sudanese nationalism became "the Unity of the Nile Valley." Many Sudanese who believed in and worked for the goal of an independent Sudan but who were strongly anti-Mahdist, joined the various "unity" parties rather than back the Ansar-supported parties.[13]

In his opposition to a Mahdist-dominated Sudan, Sayyid 'Ali al-Mirghani became increasingly associated with the Egyptians and pro-unity groups. This cooperation was mutually advantageous because the patronage of Sayyid 'Ali brought a broad base of mass support to the pro-unity parties. The result was that Sayyid 'Ali and the Khatmiyya under his leadership came to represent opposition to the British, and the Khatmiyya became the largest group supporting radical nationalism. Consequently, although Sayyid 'Ali and the Khatmiyya had cooperated closely with an imperial power, the unusual imperial situation and the development of the Ansar had created the conditions for a very strong relationship between the leadership of a traditional tariqa and a substantial number of new men in the Sudan.

The imperial experience of the Sudanese religious leaders was thus an opportunity, not a crisis. The major religious leaders became identified with and provided popular support for the two most potent political themes of the new men, creating bonds of personal loyalty and close cooperation between mahdis, walis, and new men.

The attainment of Sudanese independence in 1956 marked the beginning of a new era of Sudanese history and set the foundations for the second potential crisis in the relations between religious leaders and new men. The momentum of loyalties created during the years preceding independence would certainly continue into the period of independence. If the ties between new men and religious leaders represented simply a "marriage of convenience," then relations between these two groups could be expected to break down. In discussing this crisis, it must be

[13] Ismail al-Azhari, who led the major pro-unity party, recognized that his party received support from people who desired Sudanese independence but did not want to support the Mahdists. Interview with Ismail al-Azhari by the author, Feb. 18, 1964.

remembered that the period of independence has been short, and long-term patterns of interaction are difficult to determine. It is equally difficult to distinguish between features that represent a simple continuity of patterns set before independence and patterns that are based on the new political reality. In any event, in the period since independence, the political influence of religious leaders has remained strong and close ties between these leaders and a significant portion of the new men have been maintained.

In the period of "self-government" leading to independence (1953–1955) and during the first years of independence, the wali–new man alliance appeared to be breaking down, although the Mahdist-supported groups remained quite closely united. In the political activity after World War II, a number of parties calling for some kind of unity with Egypt had been formed. The most active of these had been the Ashiqqa party led by Ismail al-Azhari. In 1952 the various pro-unity parties united to form the National Unionist Party (NUP) under the presidency of Ismail al-Azhari and the patronage of Sayyid 'Ali al-Mirghani. The NUP won control of the first self-governing parliament, elected in 1953. (The events leading up to the proclamation of an independent Sudan by a parliament controlled by the prounity party are of interest but beyond the scope of this chapter.) In the period from 1953 to 1956 a conflict developed within the National Unionist Party which has been viewed as a clash between those closely associated with Sayyid 'Ali al-Mirghani and those who opposed the idea of the intimate involvement of the Sayyid in party affairs. The conflict came into the open as a struggle between Ismail al-Azhari and the close associates of Sayyid 'Ali for control of the party.

The result of this conflict was the creation in 1956 of a new party, the People's Democratic Party (PDP), led by the elements of the NUP who had been the closest to Sayyid 'Ali. With the creation of the PDP, the Khatmiyya became more directly associated with a political party than it had been previously, although it should be noted that some Khatmiyya elements remained in the NUP. In the public clash between the NUP and the PDP, the NUP led by al-Azhari argued vigorously against the involvement of religious leaders in politics. This was an attack not only on the PDP but also against the Ansar-supported Umma Party, whose president was a son of Sayyid 'Abd al-Rahman.

In 1956 a political action that was virtually unprecedented in the Sudan took place when the Ansar and the Khatmiyya openly joined forces to create an Umma-PDP coalition government. "On every vital point of policy, the two parties had different and opposed objectives."[14] What united them was their opposition to Ismail al-Azhari.

In this situation it would simplify the discussion if it were possible to say that the dispute between the NUP and the PDP-Umma coalition represented the beginnings of an open political struggle between the new men and the Sayyid-backed groups. To some extent this is true since the NUP maintained strong support largely in the urban areas, and the issue of religious leaders in politics was openly debated. The potential, long-term implications of this issue, however, were not worked out in the open political arena. Party activities were brought to an end in November 1958, when military officers led by Ibrahim Abbud took control of the government.

All political parties found themselves out of power and legally no longer in existence. Leaders of these parties joined together from time to time to demand the return of parliamentary government. The military government of Abbud lasted until 1964 and at least some of the political ground rules were changed by the experience of this period. After the downfall of the first military government, the Azhari-led NUP was willing and able to form an effective political alliance with the Umma Party and, in December 1967, the NUP and the PDP joined forces again in the Democratic Unionist Party (DUP). Even in 1958 before the military take-over, there were apparently well-founded rumors of an Umma-NUP alliance. With these facts in mind, it is difficult to maintain either that the religious leaders had lost a significant amount of political influence following independence or that, in terms of any of the major parties, the new men–religious leader clash could be considered a fundamental issue.

A further consideration is that even during the 1956–1958 period a significant proportion of the new men maintained loyalty to and political connections with the major religious leaders. Some of the most radical nationalists—measured in terms of support for positive neutrality, support for revolutionary governments in the rest of the world, and statements about future social reforms in the Sudan—were in the leadership of the Khatmiyya-supported PDP.

One is drawn to the conclusion that, at least so far, in the era of independence the influence of the religious leaders and their ties with the new men have remained strong and viable. This continuing strength and the view of the future are related to the third potential crisis.

The basic issue and potential crisis in relations between new men and

[14] Peter M. Holt, *A Modern History of the Sudan* (New York, 1961), p. 174.

traditional leaders is whether or not there is a sufficient common ground of goals and basic understandings to create genuine ties of loyalty and respect between the two groups. Where this common ground is insufficient, brief alliances of convenience may be possible but permanent cooperation and productive interaction are impossible. Without this common ground a real division is created which puts "modern" in conflict with "traditional." It is the actions for resolution of the crisis of a modern-traditional split which have formed the basic foundations for the new men–religious leaders relations in the twentieth-century Sudan and it is this potential crisis which holds the key to the future of the relationship.

The leaders of the major Islamic organizations in the Sudan have been remarkably adaptable and have shown an awareness of the nature of the developing society in the Sudan. Although this discussion of religious leadership in the Sudan has spoken of this leadership as though it were a group different from the men with modern education, this distinction is not in reality clear nor totally valid. The education of the religious leadership itself has, to a large extent, been more modern than traditional in style and content. The son and grandson of Sayyid 'Abd al-Rahman al-Mahdi, who were the successive presidents of the Umma Party, were graduates of Gordon Memorial College and Oxford University, respectively. Members of the Mirghani family, although frequently taught by private tutors, were taught in "modern" as well as traditional subjects and some have received an education in England. The two older Sayyids themselves were not men of limited vision or experience. Educated Sudanese and foreign observers alike had real respect for the learning and political sagacity of these two prominent leaders. Thus, in general, the new men and the religious leaders shared not only common political goals but also a common understanding of things in modern terms.

The Ansar leaders have been, as befits the Mahdist tradition, more directly active in political affairs. The Ansar leaders directly involved in political affairs have been men with modern educations.[15] The development of Ansar leadership was such that when a conservative-modern split appeared to be developing within the Ansar political organizations after the fall of the first military government, there was a descendant of the Mahdi to lead each faction.

[15] For example, Kamal Abdallahi Fadl al-Mahdi, Minister of Animal Resources in 1968, was an Oxford graduate, and Fadl Bushra al-Mahdi, Member of Parliament, 1954–1958, and member of the Supreme Council in 1968, graduated from Kitchener Medical School.

The wali leaders have been less directly involved in political action, although the Mirghani family encouraged and worked closely with many new men. For example, the newspaper that was the organ of the Khatmiyya, *Sawt al-Sudan*, was a training ground in journalism for a number of Sudanese who later became prominent journalists in their own right.[16] In general the fact that Sayyid 'Ali was not directly involved in political leadership gave the Khatmiyya political activities a relative flexibility. At the same time, his guidance and political sagacity made it possible to combine into one party tribal notables and radical nationalists.

The leadership of the Khatmiyya entered a new era in 1968 with the death of Sayyid 'Ali. The core of new men who directed the activities of Khatmiyya-supported political organizations continue to work with Sayyid Muhammad 'Uthman, the son and successor of Sayyid 'Ali. The sons of Sayyid 'Ali, however, appear to be more directly involved in political activities than their father was. Sayyid Muhammad 'Uthman, for example, was on the Constitution Commission appointed in 1968, and both the Sayyid and his brother, Sayyid Ahmad, were included in the executive committee of the Democratic Unionist Party when it was formed as a result of the merger of the NUP and the PDP in December 1967. Whatever the mode of operation, the Khatmiyya leadership continues to be provided by men with a breadth of experience and modern views that make a common understanding with the new men possible.

In general the situation in the Sudan has been that most prominent "new men politicians" have found a basis of common action and understanding with the major religious leaders. These men remain tied to a religious style of indentification through ties of affection, respect, and mutual interests. Even new men politicians, who tend to consider themselves "secularized" at least in political terms, frequently maintain an older style religious identification. Ismail al-Azhari, for example, was proud of his family heritage with its leadership in the Ismailiyya Tariqa.

The major question for the future is whether or not this common basis of understanding will continue. The current generations of students at the University of Khartoum tend not to be associated directly with the major political parties. Most of the activist students belong to the Muslim Brotherhood, the Communist Party, or a group supporting some form of Arab socialism. Although these groups represent only a small minority of the Sudanese as a whole, they are very strong among the younger gen-

[16] For example, Ismail Atabani, Muhammad Ahmad al-Sulamabi, and Muhammad Mirghani.

erations of new men in the Sudan. Religious leadership faces the crisis of finding some way to create an effective relationship with these new generations who call for radical changes in the Sudan.

To maintain perspective, it should be remembered that the Muslim Brotherhood and other radical groups were strongly represented among the students in the 1940s and 1950s and yet, those generations of new men later came to work quite well with the religious leaders. This was not only a result of the conservative influences of graduation and getting a job, but also a result of the flexibility of the religious leaders and the continuing strength of their mass support.

At present, however, the potential "traditional"-"modern" gap appears to be wider than in the early years of the nationalist movement and the potential crisis for the religious leaders is greater. For the first dozen years of independence, the continuing influence of the religious leaders depended on maintaining with new men close ties that had already been established before independence. Political leadership was in the hands of established politicians who had gained prominence in the nationalist movements. Even the military government of 1958–1964 was led by a man who had had an established position as commander in chief before taking over the government, and most of the other officers involved were senior officers. A new generation of Sudanese new men has been emerging into political prominence, with this trend being dramatized by the new military government that took control of the Sudan in May 1969. It is with this new generation that the religious leaders must now deal.

The relations of the Sayyids with the new younger leaders of the Sudan will show how deep the crisis of the "traditional"-"modern" split is in the Sudan. If a new cooperation does not emerge, then the apparent influence of the religious leaders in the first twelve years of independence will be shown to be the result of momentum built up during the period leading to independence.

Sudanese religious leadership is not without resources or potential in this new period of Sudanese history. It is the religious leaders who have been the teachers of modern politics to the majority of the Sudanese. Even with an increasing number of Sudanese receiving a modern education, there will continue to be a tendency to work with religious leaders. These leaders will continue for some time to become able to mobilize substantial popular support. In this position they will remain desirable allies for new men politicians, but the position is stronger when the Sudan is governed by political parties for whom mass support is necessary. The relative inability of government by popular political parties to solve some of the pressing problems facing the Sudan, such as the war in the southern Sudan, may have weakened the ability of the religious leaders to influence those in control of the government of the Sudan. The influence of the Sayyids will depend on the extent to which those in control of the government must rely on active popular support rather than on passive popular acceptance.

In a more positive sense, the religious leader–new man alliance will also continue if the religious leadership can "stay as modern" as their allies. The tradition of Sayyid ʻAbd al-Rahman al-Mahdi and Sayyid ʻAli al-Mirghani is one of flexible leadership able to recognize the new social and political forces as they emerge in the Sudan. If the present religious leadership can avoid attitudes and policies that would appear reactionary to the new generation of Sudanese, they will continue to have a fruitful alliance with the new men. The dangers in this situation became obvious in March 1970, when the new military government became convinced that the Ansar were preparing for a "counterrevolutionary" rebellion. In the fighting that resulted, most of the Mahdist leadership fled from the country or were killed.

Perhaps the religious leaders have a more general source of strength as well. Part of the whole process of modernization and the development of nationalism is the search for a satisfactory means of self and national identification. In the Sudan the relationship between the religious leaders and the new men, and the style of religious leadership, have made it possible to create a national identity for most northern Sudanese which is at the same time both modern and solidly rooted in the traditions of Sudanese Islamic society. As tutors of the masses and mediators between the traditional and the modern, the Sudanese religious leaders have played an important role in the past.

This leadership survived the crises of association with imperial powers and the attainment of independence. They now face the broader crisis of being able to continue to bridge the gap between "traditional" and "modern." If the religious leaders can continue to be "modern" enough to understand and work with the new generation of modern Sudanese, the importance of their position in Sudanese society will continue.

16 | Variation in Religious Observance among Islamic Women*

ROBERT A. FERNEA *and*
ELIZABETH W. FERNEA

THE MALE WORLD is so predominant and conspicuous in the Middle East that it has held the attention of even the comparatively few female scholars who have interested themselves in Middle Eastern culture. Yet probably nowhere in the world has the sexual distinction had more far-reaching social consequences, consequences that have only barely begun to be studied and analyzed. Until now, Western scholars have generally been guilty of assigning Middle Eastern women to a residual category when, in fact, they are an equal but different half of the Islamic universe.

Although Muhammad was quite explicit in outlining the religious rights and duties of Muslim women, both Islamic theologians and Western scholars have continued to define and redefine the place of women in the religious practices of the faithful. Women are expected to fulfill the basic obligations of the believer: profession of faith (*shahada*); prayer (*salat*); fasting (*saum*); the giving of alms (*zaka'at*); the pilgrimage (*hajj*). The questions that have interested the theologians are largely concerned with accommodating the formal duties of the Muslim to the physical nature of the woman and to her roles as wife and mother. A further complication has arisen in trying to reconcile the egalitarianism of Islam with beliefs concerning woman's temporal nature which is considered to be both different from and in several ways inferior to that of men. This partial discrepancy between creed and tradition has furnished a great deal of material for formal religious discussion and controversy throughout the centuries.

Still, the rules for participation of Islamic women in worship represent only slight modifications of the behavior prescribed for men, a slight tailoring of practice to suit the special circumstances of womanhood. Women have generally been encouraged or obliged to pray at home rather than

* We wish to express our appreciation to Professor and Mrs. Najm Bezirgan for information and for criticism of this article, though they are of course not responsible for the authors' views.

in the mosques; their pilgrimage to Mecca is essentially the same as for men, but they are cautioned to take special care not to distract men from their religious goals and to avoid certain religious rituals while they are menstruating. Nowhere in the Koran or hadith can a basis be found for prescribing special rules for female worship, nor do the formal histories of Islam reveal women-oriented or -initiated movements or institutions.

Historically, however, the religious activities of Muslim women have varied considerably from place to place. This is in large part because the segregation of the sexes and the sequestration of women does not accord well with public acts of worship. While Muhammad is believed to have permitted women to pray in his company and to have declared they could go to the mosque regularly with their husband's permission, fear of loss of family honor through exposure of the harem to the view of strangers seems to have discouraged this practice during the centuries after the Prophet.[1] Today, local custom with regard to women's attendance at the mosque differs from country to country (it is more common in Tunis and Damascus in recent years than in Cairo, for instance), from city to village and provincial town, and may differ with the social position of the women's families. Any general statement is impossible because so much variation does exist and so little research has been completed on this subject, but it may prove interesting to examine briefly the range of expression about which we have some limited data. Information is scarce about the most public aspects of women's practice of Islam, and our material is even more scanty with respect to those religious activities of women which take place out of public view.

Published anthropological studies of the Muslim world which include specific sections on the life of women reflect this. From Anne Fuller's study of Buarij, a Lebanese Muslim village, we learn only that as far as their religious life is concerned "women, through child-bearing and child-rearing, feel greater exposure to the capricious agencies of life, and since they do not attend the mosque, they must look elsewhere for support."[2] Granquist, in her study of a Palestinian Muslim village, states:

> An evening scene in a Muhammadan home *has been described to me:* the little daughter of the house hands her father the Koran because the mother is unclean and may not touch it. A ritually unclean man is also forbidden to touch the Holy Book but a woman is so much oftener ritually

[1] Reuben Levy, *The Social Structure of Islam* (Cambridge, 1962), pp. 130–131.

[2] Anne H. Fuller, *Buarij: Portrait of a Lebanese Muslim Village* (Cambridge, Mass., 1961), p. 83.

unclean. It may be for this reason or because the women cannot read, but on the whole it seems that both the men and the women think that the Koran is something which does not concern the women and this may account for their holding fast to the ancient customs.[3]

Clara Colliver Rice, not a scholar, but a long-time resident of Iran, states the case as follows in *Persian Women and Their Ways,* a book of experiences (highly colored, one might add, by her own preconceptions):

When we come to the actual practice of religion, what do we find that Islam gives to women? Those who can read the Qur'an for themselves are few in number. Mosques are numerous, and here, as we have seen, the women sit behind a screen or curtain. Many mosques exist which women may enter only from a side street and by a back entrance; others they are not allowed to enter at all. According to the Qur'an, women are not forbidden to go to the mosque, but are told that it is better for them to pray in their own houses. Upper class women seldom go to a mosque. The majority learn all they know from the public readings which are given in the bazaars or private houses, during the sacred months.[4]

The impression one receives from these accounts is certainly that the women are somehow less devout, less regular, less concerned, less knowledgeable, in their religious duties, than are men, partly because of the restrictions surrounding their participation in the regular prayers in the mosques and in the home, partly also perhaps because their activities, being mostly in the home, are less accessible to visiting Western scholars.

In Iraq, Egypt, and Syria, as in Iran and in other Muslim countries, women pray regularly in their houses, and often are more careful and devout in their observance of the five daily prayers and of the other pillars of Islam than their husbands, brothers, sons, and fathers. Henny Harald Hansen has documented this among the Kurds of northern Iraq:

The characteristic features of the women's recital of the five daily prayers were: the women acted individually, never in concert and not always at the same time (though, as the law prescribes, within the several prayer periods, which do not end until the next begins). Prayers were said in the home with the life of the family going on around the person praying. Children might be fighting for a knife in dangerous proximity to a samovar filled with glowing charcoal and boiling water, the son might be shaving himself, with the only pressure lamp in the room placed on one of the octagonal smoking tables, the room could be full of talking, tea-drinking people, nothing disturbed the deep concentration that is necessary if the

[3] Hilma Granquist, *Birth and Childhood Among the Arabs* (Helsingfors, 1947), p. 154. Italics ours.

[4] C. Colliver Rice, *Persian Women and Their Ways* (London, 1923), p. 103.

prayer is not to lose its value and be repeated. Nor did anyone present make any direct attempt to commit the unforgivable sin of interrupting the worshipper.[5]

When respected, as is the case among uneducated women in the villages and towns, the five daily prayers interrupt the daily work and constitute a form of intellectual life. These pious exercises cause one to concentrate on things other than the purely material; they give content and a feeling of relaxation to daily life. One is five times reminded in the course of the day that one is a member of a Muslim community totalling more than 350 million people, and takes part in ceremonies that one knows in common with them. This great feeling of religious affinity dissipates any sense of loneliness and desolation. Five times a day it is the duty of a woman to wash herself and arrange her dress, and to concentrate on something other than her monotonous labours, a right and a duty to withdraw into herself, and to demand this respect by all in the vicinity. It bolsters up a person's self-esteem to know that five times a day one can demand a square metre's space and 3–4 minutes, during which no disturbance is allowed, even from the naughtiest child; that in this space a person's spiritual side is isolated from its surroundings, yet as one with millions of others praising God, a unity that transcends race and frontiers.[6]

Dr. Hansen's account is a good statement of the importance of Islam in a woman's life, yet her study also points up once more the limitations of her material and the difficulty of generalization. She further states "the women in the educated urban milieus of Sulaimani [*sic,* Sulaimaniya] did not pray."[7] Other informants insist this is not true of Sulaimaniya; it is certainly not true of Baghdad or Cairo.

Personal experience attests to the veracity of Dr. Hansen's first statement, for the withdrawal of women into prayer in the midst of a busy household has been observed in Hilla, Diwaniyah, and the villages of southern Iraq, and we are told that it is true of all milieus in Baghdad, at least until the past decade.[8] Women pray in their houses in Cairo and as far east as the villages of western Afghanistan, although in the rural areas of the Egyptian Delta, they are not all inclined to observe the formal cycle of five daily prayers.

. . . some old women prayed regularly; younger ones did not. Women are not knowledgeable about Islam; they do not go to the kuttab as children

[5] Henny Harald Hansen, *The Kurdish Woman's Life* (Copenhagen, 1961), p. 147.

[6] *Ibid.*, p. 152.

[7] *Ibid.*, p. 148.

[8] Unless otherwise attributed, all comments and evidence are based on the authors' own fieldwork in Iraq, Egypt, and Afghanistan.

and do not attend the mosque; they hear the Koran only during Ramadan when it is read in their own houses, and that happens only in houses of women of higher socio-economic position, or when they listen from outside guest houses during funeral recitations or when they go to tombs on days of special observance. On the other hand, women are well informed about magical practices; they go to the shaikh in a nearby village for cures, preventives of harm, divining, and also for magically harmful objects. Men also employ such means, but women are more open about it while men are more likely to conceal it, especially if they are somewhat more sophisticated.[9]

Women's attendance at the mosque also varies greatly. In some countries regular mosques may not be visited by women, but shrine-mosques are not subject to this restriction.[10] A daughter of a prominent Shi'a upper-class Baghdad family remembers going often with her mother to pray at Khadhimain, the Shi'a shrine in Baghdad. This was twenty years ago, and at that time, pious Shi'a Muslim families commonly made the *ziyara* or pilgrimage to Khadhimain together. The husband, wife, and children would enter the shrine as a group, to pay their respects and pray; afterward, in the courtyard of the mosque, men and women would divide into separate groups for the more public prayers.

In Damascus, men and women are frequently seen together, praying in the Umayyad mosque; in Cairo, it is common only on special feast days and *maulids* (celebrations marking the death or birth of a saint, shaikh, or holy man). During the maulid of Sayyid al-Badawi in Tanta, men and women mix freely in the mosque, and in their obeisances at the shrine-tomb of the shaikh.[11]

Women are expected to observe the third pillar, saum or the fast, though they are exempted during pregnancy and nursing, and are not allowed to fast during menstruation. During pregnancy and nursing, however, women frequently fast for one or several days, to fulfill a vow, or simply to participate in the general atmosphere of piety sustained in the house and the community during Ramadan.

Hansen states that women also "fast on their own for a day as a result

[9] Lucy Wood Saunders, personal communication.

[10] A shrine-mosque usually contains a tomb or cenotaph of some holy person with whom *baraka,* or charismatic religious grace, is associated. Thus it is believed that special blessings may be obtained by visits to such shrines.

[11] Maulids range from elaborate feasts involving hundreds of thousands of people (as at Tanta) to more simple prayer observances at small shaikhs' tombs. The maulid most widely celebrated throughout the Muslim world is Maulid al-Nabi, the birthday of the Prophet Muhammad.

of a promise to do so,"[12] and Mrs. Colliver Rice notes that in Persia the fast during Ramadan was "generally observed by all women in health, though many are said not to keep the fast very strictly."[13]

The fourth pillar of Islam is zaka'at, or the regular tax that Muhammad instituted, and stated was incumbent upon all members of his community. Zaka'at, frequently translated as alms-giving, is usually a family matter; the husband calculates the amount to be given, stipulated as one-tenth of the common property of the family, including the wife's jewelry if it is not in use. The man may let his wife distribute it, or more likely he may himself give the money or goods to the mosque, to a needy family of recognized piety, to the muezzin or some other functionary of the mosque, if he be in need. Before many traditional houses in Muslim cities, beggars regularly line up on Fridays for the distribution of alms by the lady of the house, or her husband; this is not zaka'at but *sadaqa* (charity), which is recommended but not required of the believer like the tax. Zaka'at might be more aptly translated as the tithe, and the practice is similar to tithing in the Judeo-Christian tradition.

The fifth pillar is the hajj or pilgrimage, and is the outstanding religious occasion during which men and women from all Muslim countries mix freely and perform exactly the same rites and ceremonies. Since it is one of the few socially-sanctioned reasons for a woman to travel, and provides the excitement of a journey as well as an opportunity for gaining religious merit, social status and honor, it is not surprising that the hajj is embraced by many Muslim women. Women make pilgrimages regularly, not only to Mecca (in most cases a long and costly journey which can be undertaken only by the rich, or by the poor after a lifetime of saving), but to the various shrines throughout the Muslim world. Shi'a women try to make the ziyara or visit to the tombs of the twelve Shi'a Imams; those living close to Najaf or Karbala will visit these shrines many times during their lives.[14] Before their resettlement in Kom Ombo in 1964, Nubian women regularly used to travel long distances by steamship or sailboat in order to participate in the maulids or saints' day celebrations held before the shaikhs' tombs in the northern Kenuzi villages.

One may infer that insofar as the society of men and women is more

[12] Hansen, *op. cit.*, p. 149.

[13] Rice, *op. cit.*, p. 104.

[14] Women are not allowed to make the ziyara if they are menstruating, but during the hajj special provisions are made in case menstruation takes place while the hajj is in progress. Women may offer extra sacrifices in Mecca, for example, to take care of this exigency.

segregated, the likelihood is greater that women will develop separate religious ceremonies and leaders. Folk tales and travelers' accounts, as well as some literature, suggest that this is true, that since the time of the Prophet women have at many times and in many different parts of the Middle East developed their own religious rituals and observances as expressions of popular Islamic religion. Unfortunately, popular or "folk" religion has only very recently become a proper subject of scholarly attention and no systematic surveys, no comparative studies have been made of this important social and religious phenomenon. We know very little about popular rituals even in their most obvious, male-oriented and -dominated expressions in villages, towns, and cities. Perhaps Western Orientalists have considered Sufism in its myriad forms to be the exhaustive popular response to the formalities of orthodox Islam. Yet as anyone knows who has been attentive to the patterns of behavior and belief in Middle Eastern villages (or towns, or cities), these worlds are full of holy men and women, shrines, incarnate forces of good and evil, evil eyes, incantations, and ceremonies, all of which help to make up a cosmological outlook in which formal Islam plays an important but by no means exclusive role. Thus, our ignorance of the special religious worlds of Middle Eastern women is only a subcategory in our general lack of knowledge of popular belief systems.

In southern Iraq, among Shi'as, the religious *qraya* or popular reading is common to both men and women during the holy months of Ramadan and Muharram. The men we observed at qrayas were rather passive and reserved, confining themselves to ritualized weeping during the recitations of stories of martyrdom, sitting quietly rather than moving about. Women in the same locality tended to take a more active part in the proceedings, as can be seen in the following description of a women's qraya in a small southern Iraqi town.

Ramadan had been under way for a week when Mohammed asked me if I would like to go to an evening qraya with his sister Sherifa. . . . Bob had already been to several qrayas for men, and I was eager to go, for the women talked about the qrayas as great social as well as religious events. . . .

The qraya, Sherifa said, would begin about half past eight. It was still only seven-thirty, but fifteen or twenty women and numerous children were already present. I had never seen any of the women of *ahl-es-suq* [the market people] before, the shopkeepers' and artisans' wives, and I watched them as they filed in, greeted friends, and kissed with deference the older women present.

For the occasion, young and old, carrying babies, leading toddlers, had donned their best black. There were some beautiful *abayah*s [all-enveloping cloaks] of heavy silk crepe, and a few of the black head scarves were heavily fringed. Many wore a wide-sleeved full net or sheer black dress, which Sherifa identified as the *hashmi,* the ceremonial gown worn for qrayas and similar religious services. Underneath was a hint of color; as the women seated themselves cross-legged and arranged their hashmis over their knees, bright satin petticoats shimmered through the smokey net; green, blue, red. They wore black stockings, and the rows of clogs left at the door were almost all black.

There was a stir; the mullah had arrived, a tall woman with a hard, strong face, carrying worn copies of the Koran and her own Book of Qrayas. Everyone made way for her as she strode across the court and seated herself ceremoniously in the chair near us, the only chair in the room. Sherifa and Fadhila rose to kiss her hand, and then she spied me and looked again, narrowing her eyes. I nodded politely, not feeling that it was appropriate for me to indulge in the customary hand kissing since I was an unbeliever. She addressed a couple of questions to me in a loud, shrill voice which I did not understand, but the hostess stepped in and explained that I was the guest of the El Eshadda; Sherifa added that I wanted to see a qraya and they had invited me. The mullah nodded, said *"Ahlan wusahlan"* [Welcome] perfunctorily and looked away. More women and children were pouring into the court; we were forced to move over and make room for others.

Finally, when it seemed that not a single person more could be jammed into the court, the mullah stood up and clapped her hands to quiet the crowd. The two young women who sat near us took their places on each side of her (they were novices, I later found out, in training to be mullahs themselves) and the qraya began.

The mullah sat down and the two young girls stood to lead the congregation in a long, involved song with many responses. Gradually the women began to beat their breasts rhythmically, nodding their heads and beating in time to the pulse of the song, and occasionally joining in the choruses, or supplying spontaneous responses such as "A-hoo-ha!" or a long-drawn-out "Oooooh!" This phase lasted perhaps ten minutes, the girls sank down into their places, and the mullah arose to deliver a short sermon. She began retelling the story of the killing and betrayal of the martyr Hussein, which is told every night during Ramadan and is the beginning of the important part of the qraya. At first two or three sobs could be heard, then perhaps twenty women had covered their heads with their abayahs and were weeping. In a few minutes the whole crowd was crying and sobbing loudly. When the mullah reached the most tragic parts of the story, she would stop and lead the congregation in a group chant, which started low and increased in volume until it reached the pitch of a full-fledged wail. Then she would stop dead again, and the result would be, by this time, a sincere sobbing and weeping as the women broke down after the tension of the wail.

I sat silently, frozen by the intensity of it all, and hoping that none of the women, and especially the mullah, would notice that I was sitting without beating my breast, without chanting or weeping—in fact without participating at all. I contemplated throwing my abayah over my head, as all the other women had done, so the hawk-eyed mullah would not be able to tell whether I was crying or not, but by this time I thought she was sufficiently carried away by the force of her own words so that she wouldn't have cared. I was right. Real tears were coursing down that hard, shrewd face as she told, for the hundred thousandth time probably, the story of the death of the martyr.

Abruptly the weeping stopped, the women were drying their eyes and everyone stood up. I nearly tripped and fell as I tried to rise, for my abayah was caught under me and one leg had fallen asleep in the cramped position in which I had been sitting for the past hour. Sherifa caught my shoulder as I stumbled, fortunately, for the mullah was beginning the third stage of the qraya. Flanked by her two novices, she stood in the center of the court rocking forward with her whole body at each beat, slowly but regularly, until the crowds of women formed concentric circles around her, and they too rocked in unison, singing and beating their breasts. Three older women joined the mullah in the center, throwing aside their chin veils so they might slap their bared chests.

"A-hoo-ha!" sounded the responses.

All her veils flying as she rocked, the mullah struck her book with her right hand to indicate a faster tempo, and the novices clapped and watched to make sure that all were following correctly. I shrank back out as the circles of women began to move counterclockwise in a near-ceremonial dance: a step to the left, accompanied by head-nodding, breast-beating, the clapping of the novices, the slap of the mullah's hard hand against the book, and the responses of "A-hoo-ha!" "Ya Hussein," they cried. The mullah increased the tempo again, the cries mounted in volume and intensity, the old women in the center bobbed in time to the beat, there was a loud slap against the Koran, a high long-drawn-out chant from the mullah, and everyone stopped in her tracks. The three old ladies who had bared their chests readjusted their veils, and many of the women stood silently for a moment, their eyes raised, their open hands held upward in an attitude of prayer and supplication. But the mullah was already conferring with her novices. The qraya was over.[15]

Qrayas were held almost every evening during Ramadan, in the different houses of the village. The personality of the *mullah* who officiated determined the tone of each ceremony, but the basic ritual was always the same. First came the *latmyya* invocation with preliminary chant and breast-beating; then a sermon, different for each day of Ramadan, but always

[15] Elizabeth Warnock Fernea, *Guests of the Sheik* (New York, 1965), pp. 107–112.

followed by the telling of Husain's betrayal. Then came the *latmyya* again, at a faster pace, with the circles of women moving together in strict tempo, the spontaneous cries and wails, the profession of inspired penitence by the few women who join the mullah in the inner circle. Finally comes the *du'a*, or moment of silence and prayer. This concluding moment is considered the climax of the qraya, we were told, for then, in a state of purification, the women may ask great favors from Allah and expect to have them granted. Often these favors are requested conditionally. A woman may pray for a son, and vow that if her prayer is granted, she will hold qrayas in her house during Ramadan for a stipulated number of years. Such vows are sacred, and if for some reason the woman cannot fulfill them, she may be released only by a gift to the mullah.

Informants, both men and women, explained the qrayas as comparatively recent innovations into Shi'ite ritual, dating from the sixteenth century when they began as a form of protest after the Ottoman Turks conquered Mesopotamia. Although the Turks were Muslims, they were Sunni Muslims; and thus hated doubly by the Shi'ites, as conquerors and as representatives of a rival sect. The qrayas, as they gained in popularity and acceptance throughout the Shi'ite world, became the means by which the Shi'ites asserted their religious differences from the Turks and, by implication, their dissatisfaction with the Ottoman regime.

Qrayas still are held today in Shi'a communities. They obviously provide religious fulfillment for both men and women; in the lives of the women, they also seem important as social occasions.

Women pay for the qrayas held in their houses, for it is considered a great honor to "hostess" a qraya. The money for the cigarettes and for a gift to the officiating mullah comes out of the woman's own savings or is granted to her by her husband. One informant stated that her family always gave two chickens and a gallon can of clarified butter to the mullah on the two great feasts, and in return the mullah would officiate at several qrayas, either during Ramadan or Muharram. Sayyids, however, might ask the mullah to come for nothing, as it is considered an honor for the mullah to hold a qraya in the house of a Sayyid.

The qrayas in El Nahra were not often followed by Koranic readings, simply because most of the women could not read. Only at Laila's house, where the two middle girls, Laila and Basima, were in the sixth class of the girls' primary school, did this take place. The women of the settlement told me that the qrayas at Laila's house were always good, because of the Koranic readings at the end. It was considered a great treat: Basima would read, and Laila, and finally their mother, Um Fatima, would take the Koran and read a few of the most important suras. As a girl in her father's house, Um Fatima had been taught the rudiments of reading by a woman mullah, and she still retained this limited ability. Laila was competent, but Basima was better than either. More intelligent than Laila and better educated than her mother, Basima seemed to sense the power of the words she was reading. They were not just groups of characters to her, and as she sat on the mat and read sura after sura in a slow, expressive voice, women would shake their heads, murmur to themselves, or raise their open hands to heaven in the traditional gestures of supplication. When she had finished, there would be a pause, a sort of hush before the women sighed, gathered their abayahs around them, and prepared to leave.[16]

For the women, the qraya in the village was one of the few community-sanctioned opportunities for meeting socially in each other's homes, in groups that cut across the ordinary kin groupings and which included representatives from all segments of the community, tribal as well as townsfolk. For the men, not subject to the same restrictions of social intercourse as the women, the qraya tended to draw together the same men who daily met in tribal guesthouse or village coffeeshop. The shaikh and the wealthy merchant, already community leaders, were the natural sponsors of the men's qraya, but among the women, who had little opportunity for other such inclusive patterns of interaction, qraya sponsorship was not so clear a responsibility and the question of who would hold qrayas and who would attend them was not so obviously resolved.

The sexual exclusiveness of the qraya in southern Iraq parallels local social attitudes which preclude social relations between men and women, except for closely related kinsmen. Where such restrictions are not so pronounced, a different set of responses to Islamic ceremonialism may be observed.

In Egyptian Nubia, for example, where some sexual exclusiveness is maintained, but not to the degree found in Iraq, separate women's religious rituals are involved in the maintenance of shrines, the making of *nithr* or vows and in the creation of children's religious rituals paralleling the adult ones.

The exception to the pattern of constructing a sheikh's shrine after an *isha'ra* (or signal in a dream) is found in the case of the children's shrines, which are built by the children with the help of their mothers or female relatives in imitation of adult shrines. . . . there seems to be no pattern for the choice of a children's sheikh; they may select the sheikh of

[16] *Ibid.*, p. 115.

the tribe, a relative as mentioned above, or another sheikh which they have only heard about . . . the mulids are supported and financed by a group of them with the help of their mothers, who will usually supply the children with dates, bread and tea. Guests at the children's mulid are usually girls and boys of the local school rather than children of the particular tribe or naga; all are between four and 12 years of age. . . .[17]

The staff of the shrines usually consists of a *nakib*, or male functionary, who is assisted by a female functionary, *nakiba*. The nakib's position is more or less honorary, but the nakiba has specific duties: to keep the shrine clean, and the candles lighted. The nakiba also is present when women come to pray and declare solemn vows. During the maulid or saint's day ceremony of the shrine, the nakib and nakiba are temporarily assisted by others, usually the butcher, the dancing master, and the drumbeater.

Thus, in the maulid, both sexes actively participate; they not only cooperate in preparing and serving the food which is a feature of such occasions, but they join together in the processions to the shaikh's tomb, and most dramatically in the dancing. The dancing provides both sexes with an opportunity for statement and response even though there is no actual physical contact between male and female participants, and the women, when they dance, are often veiled.

From Morocco to the Indus Valley, throughout the Islamic world in fact, millions of village shrines exist, dedicated to men and women whose saintly lives are believed to offer baraka or blessings to the living. The shrines, if one is looking for them, are as familiar a sight as the traditional village bazaar; they are one of the most stable ingredients of local culture. Sometimes religious devotions to the holy men and women are elaborated into formal ceremonies, sometimes not. Sometimes, in the histories of Islamic religious movements, revered women are noted, such as Rabi'ah al-'Adawwiyah, one of the greatest of the Sufic saints. Other holy persons are remembered only by a pile of stones, decorated with tall irregular sticks from which flutter bits of rags, multicolored mementos left by generations of village women who have come to vow and to pray. For in all parts of the Middle East, women visit shrines and make vows from time to time, seeking supernatural assistance in matters over which they have little or no control: conception, childbirth, the loss of childhood friends, the choice of husbands, the health of their families.

Formal religious practice and ancient appeal to the supernatural may

[17] Nawal El Messiri Nadim, "The Sheikh Cult in Dahmit Life," in *Contemporary Egyptian Nubia*, Vol. II, Robert A. Fernea, ed. (New Haven, 1966), pp. 219–237.

merge in different ways; in Egypt, especially in Nubia, the holy persons to whom shrines are dedicated are not the only source of appeal in distress. Supernatural inhabitants of the river Nile are often placated with food, prayers, vows, and seances.[18] The seances, called *zars*, or possession performances, take place on Thursday and Sunday evenings, preferably; why? "Because," it is said, "the Prophet favored those two days." The practitioners of zars in Nubia are women or *shaikhas*; in Ethiopia, Sudan, and Lower Egypt, the zar tends to be led by a man, whose performance bears remarkable similarities to some formal Sufi rituals.

The zar is found among many social classes in Egypt, and in the Delta, the zar flourishes, not only as an exorcising ceremony for women, but for men as well. *Weekly* zars are held in Daqhaliya province, and the ceremonies are separate for the sexes. Male shaikhs who conduct the women's ceremonies, however, are often assisted by their wives, a practice which conforms to the fact that in this community and area, women are less segregated, own land, and even belong to the Agricultural Cooperative as voting members.[19] Northern Iraq's *takiya* ceremony has been compared to the zar; men conduct the ceremony, a seance involving hypnotic activity, with Sufic overtones. Women watch, but often end up participating themselves.

Mourning ceremonies or *azzas* form another category of religious ritual which may differ markedly for men and women. Any visitor to Cairo has observed the great, colorful appliqued tent (*sura'dig*) that is set up, sometimes occupying a whole street, after a death. Here men mourners come to sit formally and drink tea or coffee, while expressing condolences to the male members of the family of the deceased. The Fatiha from the Koran is recited. Women receive mourners in the home, where a different ceremony is observed. Iraqi women also mourn separately from their men, and the women's wake, though formally patterned, is much more emotional than the men's.[20] The Fatiha is not recited but the Koran may be read by a mullah. In Egyptian Nubia, a special temporary enclosure is erected at the side of the house for the male mourners to gather and pay their respects to the male members of the deceased's family. The occasion is subdued and formal, the greetings stylized. Tea or bitter coffee is served. The Fatiha is recited. Nubian women gather separately in the courtyard of the family of the deceased.

[18] Fadwa El Guindi, "Ritual and the River in Dahmit," in *Contemporary Egyptian Nubia*, II, 239–256.

[19] Lucy Wood Saunders, personal communication.

[20] E. W. Fernea, *op. cit.*, pp. 291–292.

We had been walking nearly three kilometers through the sand, in the hot sun, talking naturally of every-day matters, but suddenly as we got closer to the house, the women accompanying us took off their *tarhas* (or head scarves) and tied them around their waists, thus uncovering their heads. Each woman took a handful of dust and sand from the ground near the deceased's house and put it on her head, at the same time beginning to weep and wail loudly. From inside the house, a strange monotonous chanting reached us. It was not very high pitched, like the ululation usually heard at the keening after death in other parts of Egypt. It was not piercing, or penetrating, like an ululation, but more like a regular, low-pitched chant such as is heard in the Coptic churches in Cairo or some of the Coptic monasteries during the high Masses. It was very sad, very regular, very monotonous and very moving. Afaf said there was nothing Moslem about it, there was no chanting of the Koran involved, it was something quite different, yet did not vary in pitch like the usual wailing—ululation.

When we entered the court, it was so full of women, hardly a corner was left for another person to stand, or think of sitting. At least 250 women stood there close together, crying and chanting. In the center of the court stood a thin, yet strong-looking elderly woman who interrupted the monotony and regularity of the chanting by stretching her arms wide, as in a benediction, and then folding them upon her chest, while repeating a kind of prayer in the Nubian language.

This was translated to us later as a eulogy of the dead woman:

"What a great loss! She was in the prime of life! She was so good to me! She never uttered an ugly word! She was more than a daughter to me!" And so on. This woman was the dead woman's mother-in-law, who had really, it seemed, loved the younger woman dearly. She was a kind of focal point of the whole scene, for the women as they changed partners, wept for a moment on each other's shoulders, and then moved on, tried all the time to shift around the court, so as to greet the mother-in-law and stay close to her as long as possible.

As soon as we entered, we tried to make our way to her, but it was very difficult in the crowd. Finally we came up to her, each of us shook her hands, and each of us put our hands on her shoulders, as we had seen the other women do. She cried and sobbed loudly, and we cried too, although we had never met her before. After about three quarters of an hour of ritually weeping with each woman present, we managed to make our way to Seyida, sister of the dead woman, who looked exhausted but who continued to weep and chant, although her voice was barely audible. After expressing some formal condolences, we passed on out into the center of the court again, and were pushed along from one woman to another, putting our heads together for a minute and then parting. All this time the strange, continuous chanting did not stop for a second. When it seemed about to fade or die out in one corner of the court, another group would pick up the dying tune and continue much louder.

The entire scene and the experience affected us both very strongly; the formalized weeping, one woman with another, in pairs, like bereaved sisters or mothers and daughters; the court crowded with women, clad in black but with their heads uncovered, an unheard-of thing in this part of the world. The hot sun beat down upon us, on the mud floor of the court, on the black garments of the women, and on their smudged hair and sweating tear-stained faces, while the strange chanting kept on like a song, a humming, a song of sorrow and anguish, of defeat and of loss. No Koranic readings took place, the *Fatiha* was not recited, yet the women themselves told us later that they felt this to be a truly religious ceremony.[21]

We know little about women's religious ceremonies, and less about the mullahs, the shaikhas, the nakibas, and the many other women religious functionaries who officiate at these ceremonies. A category of religious women certainly seems to have developed side by side (separately but equally perhaps?) with their male counterparts.

In southern Iraq, among women, the vocation of mullah is usually handed down within a family. Widows, or young girls who do not expect to marry, often choose to become mullahs. It is a highly esteemed profession, and profitable as well—a gifted woman can support an entire family.

An Iraqi woman mullah is trained by older mullahs in the same village and she goes regularly for lessons from the time of puberty. She learns to read and write and recite the Koran, and is instructed in the ritual of the qrayas; she also begins to memorize the Koranic suras, the stories, and history that will be incorporated eventually into her own Book of Qrayas. An experienced, educated Shi'ite mullah compiles a sophisticated and well-documented source book which she uses to conduct her qrayas; tribal and village mullahs depend on legend and oral tradition to supplement the standard material of the sermons, hadiths, and rituals.

Religious women leaders have also been identified by Nancy Tapper among the Shahsavan tribes of the Meshkin region of Azerbaijan, Iran. In the women's subsociety, she states, women establish among themselves a range of relationships "based on achieved and ascribed statuses, rules of social behaviour, and leaders."[22]

Miss Tapper classifies categories of women who may gain achieved status in the community as midwives, ceremonial cooks, and washers of the body after death, and religious leaders.

21 Afaf El Deeb and Elizabeth Warnock Fernea, unpublished field notes from Nubia, 1962.

22 Nancy Tapper, "The Women's Sub Society in the Shahsavan" (unpublished manuscript), p. 1.

In each *tira* (clan or family group) . . . were one or two women held to be knowledgeable on religious matters. Commonly, they are women who, with a male relative, have made the pilgrimage to the shrine of Imam Reza at Mashhad and are thereafter referred to by the title of *Mashadi*. In fact the position of Mashadi among women is comparable to that of a Hajji among men. The Mashadis are among the few women who pray regularly; their position is a highly conservative one and they firmly support traditional Shahsavan customs and moral attitudes, sometimes by reference to imaginary Koranic injunctions. The opinions of such a woman in matters of family law and custom are sought by both men and women and her advice is given equal weight with that of men. In one case, a question of fosterage as a permanent bar to marriage was raised; a betrothed girl was said to have been suckled by her fiance's mother, but no one could remember or would admit the extent to which this took place. It was therefore uncertain whether the engaged couple were foster-siblings according to Islamic law and hence forbidden to marry. A Mashadi gave her opinion—that there was no bar to marriage, and there was general agreement that her decision must be right. The marriage ceremonies were completed two years later in the usual manner. . . . Ceremonial cooks and mashadis . . . are essentially public figures and it is through such specializations that a woman achieves a position of leadership.[23]

In Daghghara, southern Iraq, somewhat equal weight was given to the words and advice of the one elderly woman who had made the pilgrimage to Mecca and was given the honorific title Hajjiya. Alwiyahs (female descendants of Imam Ali), were also respected. An old woman, even though she had not been to Mecca, but only to Najaf, Karbala, and Khadhimain, was referred to as Hajjiya; we were told that this title is often given to pious elderly women, in the hope that the title itself might be fulfilled in a real pilgrimage to Mecca. Hajjiya is a term of great respect in the community and these women's counsel was often sought by younger women, and even occasionally by men. Similar respect is accorded women religious leaders in the Egyptian Delta, where women shaikhas are recognized and pointed out at maulids by both men and women villagers.

What are we to make of this wealth of ritual, this diversity in forms of worship? Presumably, beneath the surface of such ceremonies as the zar, the qraya, the maulid, and the azza, a common core of belief is present, a belief shared across sexual and regional differences. This common core of belief is not enforced by an ecclesiastical hierarchy, for such is lacking in Islam, but rather by the pressures and consensus of community tradition,

[23] *Ibid.*, p. 17.

which allows diversity of response while condemning behavior that goes beyond that commonly held belief.

However sexually segregated Middle Eastern communities have been, religion has normally provided women with a legitimate arena of activity outside the home; in many instances women have utilized this freedom to develop meaningful rituals that reflect their own needs and concerns. Their freedom to do this has perhaps been enhanced by a greater distance from the influence of the ulama, the learned men of Islam who have defined and protected orthodoxy. In this regard, the position of women may differ slightly from that of men.

Yet if the variety of expressions of popular Islam is obviously constrained by both orthodoxy and local custom, then to understand the constraints that mold the rich variation we have sampled, much more systematic research is required. The traditions and rituals are changing rapidly and in many cases already disappearing. If we wish to understand the Community of the Faithful, as it was in the past and continues to be in some areas in the present, we might do well to direct more of our scholarly attention to popular Islam, not neglecting religious practices among women.

We must also consider that all men pass through the world of women, and as they wait to take their places as young men in a man's world, they cannot help but be influenced by the example of their mothers, sisters, aunts, and grandmothers. Thus the opportunity for women to influence the shared conception of Islam has never been lacking, despite the conspicuous absence of most forms of joint ceremonialism. To be properly understood, Islam as lived today must be viewed through the contributions of both men and women among the faithful.